Jim Crow New York

Jim Crow New York

A Documentary History of Race and Citizenship, 1777–1877

EDITED BY

David N. Gellman and David Quigley

New York University Press

NEW YORK AND LONDON

NEW YORK UNIVERSITY PRESS
New York and London

Library of Congress Cataloging-in-Publication Data
Jim Crow New York : a documentary history of
race and citizenship, 1777-1877 /
edited by David N. Gellman and David Quigley.
p. cm.
Includes bibliographical references (p.) and index.
ISBN 0-8147-3149-X (cloth : alk. paper) —
ISBN 0-8147-3150-3 (pbk. : alk. paper)
1. African Americans—Segregation—New York (State)—
History—Sources.   2. African Americans—Civil rights—
New York (State)—History—Sources.   3. African Americans—
Suffrage—New York (State)—History—Sources.
4. Slavery—New York (State)—History—18th century—Sources.
5. Slavery—New York (State)—History—19th century—Sources.
6. New York (State)—Race relations.
7. New York (State)—History—1775-1865.
8. New York (State)—Politics and government—1775-1865.
I. Gellman, David Nathaniel.   II. Quigley, David, 1966-
E185.93.N56J56   2003
323.1'1960730747'09034—dc21   2002155242

Manufactured in the United States of America
10 9 8 7 6 5 4 3 2 1

To Our Teachers

Contents

Acknowledgments   xi

Introduction   1

PART I Slavery, Abolition, and Citizenship,
1777–1817   13

Context   13

Chronology   19

Map   24

Documents   25

A. Franchise Provision, New York State Constitution, 1777   25

B. Veto Message, 1785   30

C. Anti-Abolition Article, 1785   33

D. "Mungo Speaks," 1788   36

E. Antislavery Orations, 1797 and 1798   39

F. Gradual Abolition Act, 1799   52

G. African American Political Oration, 1809   56

H. An Act Regulating Black Suffrage, 1811   64

I. Act Declaring 1827 as the End of Slavery
in New York, 1817   67

PART II   The Convention of 1821
          and the Politics of Disfranchisement   73

          Context   73

          Chronology   79

          Map   80

          Documents   81

    J.   Connecticut Constitution
            Confirms Disfranchisement, 1818   81

    K.   Resolution Opposing the Missouri Constitution, 1820 84

    L.   Antiblack Article, *National Advocate*, 1821   87

    M.   Extended Excerpts from the Convention of 1821   90

PART III   The Long Reconstruction, 1821–1877   201

          Context   201

          Chronology   207

          Map   211

          Documents   212

    N.   First African American Newspaper, 1827   212

    O.   Emancipation Addresses, 1827   218

    P.   Address, African American State Convention, 1840   236

    Q.   Excerpts from the Debate on Suffrage,
            New York State Constitutional Convention, 1846   249

    R.   Land Reform Proposal, 1846   260

    S.   Declaration of Sentiments, Seneca Falls, 1848   265

    T.   Anti–Property Qualification Pamphlet, 1860   271

    U.   Report on Suffrage, New York State
            Constitutional Convention, 1867–1868   278

    V.   Letter to the Editor:
            Elizabeth Cady Stanton on Sojourner Truth, 1867 286

    W.   "Appeal to Christians," 1869   292

    X.   Fifteenth Amendment to the U.S. Constitution, 1870 295

Y. Newspaper Coverage of First Equal Manhood
         Suffrage Election, 1870   300
Z. Excerpts from Tilden Commission Report, 1877   307

     Bibliographic Essay   319

     Notes   331

     Index   343

     About the Editors   353

Acknowledgments

Fortuitous circumstances launched this book toward publication. Nearly two decades ago, the authors were placed on opposite ends of the hall in a freshman college dormitory. Several years later, both of us undertook doctoral dissertations about race in New York: Gellman on the abolition of slavery, Quigley on the Reconstruction Era. As we wrote those dissertations, both of us kept an eye on history in between our two eras, especially the fateful New York Constitutional Convention of 1821. To satisfy our curiosity, we organized a conference panel for which we presented two separate papers examining the 1821 disfranchisement of African Americans and its legacy. The papers meshed far better than either of us could have anticipated. Almost immediately, we began plans for a joint publication. This book is the result.

We have drafted many friends and colleagues, some unwittingly, into the process that produced this work. We express our deep gratitude to all of them. Eric Zinner, Despina Papazoglou Gimbel, and Emily Park at NYU Press have guided the project with enthusiasm and confidence. Fellow scholars have made themselves available as sounding boards and advisers at every step of the process. We incurred our first scholarly debts at the 1999 annual meeting of the Society for Historians of the Early American Republic in Lexington, Kentucky. Commentators Graham Russell Hodges and Michael Vorenberg offered penetrating insights that helped stitch together the papers further, while members of the audience pushed us to think more clearly. Alison Waldenberg, now at NYU Press, attended the session and encouraged us to think that a book might be the appropriate result. NYU Press provided superb anonymous readers who helped us imagine how the volume could best serve students and teachers. Joanna Mullins copyedited and improved the manuscript. The Office of the Dean of Boston College's Graduate School of Arts and Sciences provided support for the acquisition of maps and illustrations.

As closely as we have worked together on the project, burning a well-worn electronic path between Boston, Massachusetts, and Greencastle, Indiana, we also have incurred individual debts.

David Gellman: I thank research assistant and former student John Leffler for cheerfully taking on a variety of onerous tasks associated with compiling a document collection. My colleagues in the Department of History at DePauw University have made the basement of East College a delightful home away from home. In particular, thanks are due to my chair, John Schlotterbeck, who provided departmental work-study funds for a research assistant and who generously shared his expertise on early American history. I also thank John Dittmer for giving the project a valuable push. Linda Elman in Modern Languages, Pedar Foss in Classical Studies, Andrea Sununu in English, and Dan Wachter in Economics answered questions beyond my ken as I worked on the footnotes and headnotes. My greatest debts and deepest gratitude are reserved for my family. My children, Hannah and Ben, renewed my energy even when they shortened my sleep. My wife Monica's love and friendship made imaginable this project and everything else.

David Quigley: Colleagues in the Boston College History Department have been generous with both ideas and friendship. In particular, Peter Weiler and Jim O'Toole have helped this project along. I thank Michael Swanson and the staff at the Center for Media and Instructional Technology for their helpfulness and patience in preparing the maps of New York. Justin Pariseau, my undergraduate research assistant, merits particular credit for his heroic work scanning documents. Ben DeMott offered astute readings of the contextualizing essays. Closer to home, Nathaniel and Tyrone put up with a father often lost in a haze of documents and daily called me back to the twenty-first century. Once more, Megan carried me through.

Introduction

This book demonstrates that America's highest ideals and its most objectionable practices collide at the intersection of politics and culture. In 1821, New York's political leaders met from late August to early November to rewrite the state's constitution. The new document produced by the delegates sitting in Albany secured the right to vote for the great mass of white men while denying all but the wealthiest African American men access to the polls. Placing racial exclusion in constitutional bedrock, white New Yorkers simultaneously repudiated and echoed the state's complex racial history. In the process, they helped usher in an era of hardening segregation, separating blacks from whites in many aspects of public life.

As a result of decisions made in the convention of 1821, New York defined democracy in explicitly racial terms at the dawn of an era of unprecedented popular political participation. Subsequently labeled Jacksonian Democracy, popular politics had already begun to acquire distinctive outlines in New York several years before Andrew Jackson became the seventh president of the United States. The growing free black population of New York protested that this new form of white "self-rule" came at their expense. Heard by some whites, ignored or shouted down by more, those black voices insistently demanded that freedom and the freedom to exclude were not the same thing. Nonetheless, the disfranchisement of African American New Yorkers in 1821 crystallized for generations the paradoxes of free black life. African Americans living in New York would no longer be slaves. But would they be citizens?

Throughout the Jacksonian period and into the era of the Civil War, the ideas and language of the New York constitution resonated in national debates over race and democracy. The state was rapidly becoming the central place of American capitalism and American democracy, pivotal to the economic life of the nation and to national politics alike. New York State also stood as a central site in the making of racialized citizenship, helping to set the terms of recurrent debates over such issues as racial caste and the content of American freedom. New York's paradoxical role in the United States as a hothouse of cultural racism, haven for runaway slaves from the South, and home for dynamic antislavery organizations comes into particularly sharp focus through the lens of the 1821 convention. New York's history is thus America's history.

A historical turning point such as the New York constitutional convention of 1821 did not occur in a vacuum. Neither the causes nor the results were predetermined or inevitable. Rather, this turning point was the product of and response to constellations of events and experiences shaped by human beings making choices. White New Yorkers did not have to deny blacks the vote and push them to the margins of official political life any more than did black and white New Yorkers have to work to abolish slavery during the half-century after independence from Great Britain. And once black citizenship became so severely restricted, neither blacks nor whites had to accept those limits as permanent.

In other words, the struggle for equal rights is a story—a story with many voices and many actors. Although that story stretched back beyond the beginning of the American Revolution and continued well beyond the end of Reconstruction, the one hundred years covered by the documents in this book constitute a long and painful chapter in the history of American race relations. The pivotal century spanning 1777 to 1877 illustrated a central fact of American life, overlooked by historians and students at their own peril. Racial justice and democratic freedom do not always move together in an upward slope toward greater enlightenment, their stories one of slow but steady movement from oppression to liberty. "Progress" and "prejudice" cannot simply be determined by proximity to or distance from the present day. A careful examination of the century extending from the Revolution through Reconstruction instead demonstrates that breakthroughs and breakdowns punctuated the struggle over African American citizenship. The convention of 1821, six years shy of the midpoint of this story, is only the most dramatic instance of a recurring pattern by which the rationale for racial exclusion—and the tools for enforcing it—overwhelmed and sometimes reversed earlier gains. In short, even though it is often easy to distinguish right from wrong in this story, the story of the struggle for black citizenship is rarely simple.

I. *"Jim Crow New York"*

The book's title, *Jim Crow New York*, serves as a historical reminder of racism's pervasiveness in the United States. The term *jim crow* is not customarily used to describe the nineteenth-century North. Rather, "jim crow" usually describes the system of legalized racial subjugation and the culture of segregation that gradually took hold in the South in the generation after Reconstruction ended. From the 1890s until the victories of the modern Civil Rights movement in the 1950s and 1960s, the reign of jim crow in former Southern slave states meant the exclusion of African Americans from political power, educational opportunity, and even the basic human dignities of equal access to water fountains, lunch counters, and bathrooms.

The origins of the term *jim crow* are both obscure and revealing. The practice of imitating on stage the foibles and speech patterns of certain regional groups, if not the term *jim crow* itself, seems to have been imported to America from the English stage. New York's eighteenth-century newspapers employed a print version of this practice, frequently including humorous anecdotes of various minority groups, including African Americans, in part by having them speak in broken English dialects. In the late 1820s, a new form of popular theater was invented—the minstrel show—that extended and transformed these traditions with tremendous commercial success. On the New York City minstrel stage, "Jim Crow" and other racially stereotyped African Americans were played by white actors, faces and hands blackened for their roles. These performances, especially popular with New York City's white, often immigrant working class, played black characters for laughs, as well as for melodramatic tears. Pretend black minstrels also sang songs written for the stage in alleged imitation of real songs sung by real black slaves in the South and in certain districts of New York City. Some of these lyrics would become popular with Americans for generations, such as "Oh! Susannah" and "Old Folks at Home [Swanee River]." New York thus helped launch into the mainstream of American culture a popular form of entertainment and long-living racial stereotypes, including the unsophisticated black country bumpkin Jim Crow. The term later took on a second life, ultimately migrating southward to describe racist laws, rather than inspiring racially derisive laughter.

Given the New York origins of the term and the history of black life in the state, the concept of *Jim Crow New York* is as appropriate as it is provocative. Racism in New York was about something far more virulent than working-class laughter. First, it was about slavery. Slavery came to New York with the original Dutch administrators of New Netherland, as the Dutch called their colony along the Hudson River. Slavery officially lasted in the state until 1827 and, due to various loopholes and legal provisions, as well as New York's extensive economic and political connections to the slave South, shaped the experience of black New Yorkers far beyond that year.

In New York State's countryside, the legacy of slavery often meant isolation in white households and labor on white-owned farms. Although free black communities did form in rural New York, access to resources, land, power, and fellow African Americans was limited. Particularly in the early nineteenth century, newly free African Americans continued to live in households separate from their immediate family members.

Many rural New York blacks migrated to New York City, where racism confined African Americans to the worst jobs, the roughest neighborhoods, and the least healthy conditions of urban life. Racism encouraged the creation of distinct black and white churches, segregated transportation, and separate schools. Racism also meant violence, including the threat of being kidnapped or sold into Southern slavery. Violence also took the form of assaults by white mobs on black institutions and black individuals. And, as this book repeatedly illustrates, racism was very much about politics: political harassment, political exclusion, denial of political access, and antiblack political organization. In the nineteenth century, jim crow was a deep, abiding, and often brutal fact of New York life.

II. The Meaning of Citizenship

Race and citizenship lay at the center of American political culture during the nation's first century. Thus, at the very heart of the black struggle for equality from 1777 to 1877, especially after the gradual abolition of slavery commenced in 1799, was a contest over the meaning of citizenship. "Citizenship" refers to the variety of rights and obligations that connect a person to a place and its government. A citizen, for example, is eligible to hold a passport, which entitles that person to enter and exit the country. Citizens can also be called upon to defend their country from a foreign foe. Like all laws, laws surrounding citizenship have generated a large number of technicalities and exceptions. Historically in this country, moreover, the complete rights of citizens—full citizenship—have been extended to certain groups far more readily than to others: men more than women, whites more than blacks. Technically, a person might not have the same rights, privileges, and obligations as every other person and yet still be an American citizen in some basic sense. That remains true, for example, of children under eighteen to this day. But citizenship has deeper meanings that include but go beyond a checklist of minimal attachments to state or nation. Thus, historians and political scientists often refer to "citizenship" in a broader, nontechnical sense to describe who has enjoyed a full stake in the rights and obligations of American life and who has not.

Central to the concept of citizenship, in the formulation of the late eminent political scientist Judith Shklar, are the right to vote and to sustain economic autonomy through work—literally, to earn a living. To this definition we might add the right to be a full participant in public debate and the obligation to protect the nation and the rights of one's fellow citizens. Because possessing citizenship is central to sharing in the many benefits of American life and to protecting access to those benefits from threats from other citizens and even the government itself, debates over the meaning of citizenship have been far more than intellectual exercises.

Until the very end of the period under consideration, state citizenship was particularly important because U.S. citizenship, prior to the enactment of the Fourteenth Amendment in 1868, had no clear, unified, national definition. All the participants in the struggle over black voting rights between 1777 and 1877 understood that suffrage was absolutely central to defining a person's "standing" as a citizen of New York. All the voices present in this documentary reader acknowledged in one way or another that voting was linked, through citizenship, to the kind of work a person might expect to do, the right to represent oneself in public debate, and the obligation to support the government through paying of taxes and, in emergencies, bearing arms. That is why New Yorkers, black and white, fought so hard and so long over this issue. Even as the African American proportion of New York's exploding population dwindled, opponents of black suffrage understood that granting African Americans the rights they demanded would mark a fundamental alteration in the meaning of citizenship for everyone in New York.

III. Freedom's Fortunes: New York and the Nation

The politics of race during the nation's first century in large part hinged on the question: If African Americans were no longer to be slaves, who would they be, and what place would they occupy in America's democracy? New York was a central site, but far from the only site, of the struggle over this question. Indeed, as the nation lurched from crisis to crisis in the 1840s and 1850s and then into bloody Civil War, the sites of struggle multiplied by the dozens: Congress, the Supreme Court, Texas, Mexico, "bleeding" Kansas, Harper's Ferry, Fort Sumter, Bull Run, Antietam, Vicksburg, Gettysburg, Richmond, Atlanta, Ford's Theater. And as these sites multiplied, it may have seemed that Americans were fighting over something more elemental, more existential than segregated citizenship. But they were not.

The difference between slavery and citizenship, the relationship between freedom and self-government, had marked the path of U.S. history all along. As Abraham Lincoln acknowledged in 1865, "All knew" that slavery "was, somehow the cause of the Civil War"; and at Gettysburg in 1863, Lincoln proclaimed that "a new birth of freedom," with "government of the people, by the people, for the people," was at stake in that war. The denial of equality to African Americans, in law and in practice, had fanned the flames of sectional tensions in one way or another, from the Missouri Crisis to the conflict in the 1850s between Northern personal liberty laws protecting African Americans accused of being runaway slaves and the federal fugitive slave law meant to summarily reenslave the accused. During the Civil War, equality and its absence created defining moments, such as the decisions to issue the Emancipation Proclamation and to put black men in uniform as soldiers in the Union army.

In 1865, war subsided into peace, acute crisis into relative calm, but the problem of unequal citizenship remained. Questions solved by force of arms again were to be arbitrated by ballots, by voters, by citizens. To reconstruct the torn nation, Congress virtually rewrote the U.S. Constitution, first by banning slavery, then by federalizing the rights of citizens, and finally by enshrining the right to vote. Yet the defeat and victory of America's democratic ideals were as hard to untangle in New York as any place in America—a house divided, half free, half slave, transformed into a house united in freedom. Indeed, after an amendment to the U.S. Constitution forced New York, like its Southern sister states, to open the polls to African American citizens, New York's elites began to mount a new offensive against meaningful mass-participation democracy itself.

Race and citizenship again would assert themselves at the center of American political culture in the nation's second century—and beyond. New York would continue to be a central site for working out the meaning of democracy in a multiracial society. In the late nineteenth century, and throughout the twentieth century, the groups and the struggles multiplied. The meaning of citizenship has not remained any more static than New York's and America's population has. The reformer Jacob Riis, in his famous investigation of New York City's slums, which he wrote about in *How the Other Half Lives*, ranked African Americans as the most American of New York's shockingly poor tenement dwellers. Still, the problems of urban poverty and rural isolation, of segregation and exclusion from meaningful political participation, continued to plague New York's African American population, whose struggles sometimes were mirrored, but never duplicated, among the dozens of other marginalized groups who came to New York.

In the mid–twentieth century, the central battle over race and citizenship in American life was led by the descendants of former slaves far to the South, in the states of the old Confederacy. Yet all the questions left over from the nineteenth century that America as a whole would struggle to resolve in the twentieth had been debated in some form or another in New York State between 1777 and 1877. What is the legacy of slavery? What is the content of freedom? Is there more than one kind of citizenship? What is the difference between a citizen and a voter? What does a citizen look like? Does democratic citizenship permit certain kinds of exclusions and not others? Who speaks for African Americans? What forms of African American protest are most effective? The struggle over these questions in the Empire State, during New York's long reconstruction, shaped American life during the nation's first century. Similar struggles will continue to shape the nation's identity in its third century.

IV. The Approach: Attending to the Voices of New York's History

Given the high stakes of the debate over citizenship, and given New York's central role in nineteenth-century U.S. history, a book focusing on the struggle for black voting rights in New York is long overdue. The New York constitutional convention of 1821 has seldom received the historical attention that it merits. Extended published excerpts of the convention proceedings were last published in 1966, in Merrill D. Peterson's *Democracy, Liberty, and Property: The State Constitutional Conventions of the 1820s*, a volume focused on three different states and a wide variety of issues.

There has been a revolution, perhaps several revolutions, in the study of American history since Peterson's book. That revolution has profoundly transformed how we study politics, law, and society. That revolution has brought African Americans to the center of how we look at the past and has emphasized not only the victimization of African Americans, free or slave, but also the many ways in which African Americans shaped their own lives and fought battles on their own behalf. Historians also have learned to ask a host of new, more precise questions about the relationships between culture and politics, language and power. Moreover, the explosion of historical scholarship in the last thirty-five years has encouraged historians to redouble their efforts to do what their profession has always done: ask questions about cause and effect, change over time, and context, all while telling a story with a beginning, middle, and end.

The documents assembled in this reader reflect many of the developments that have influenced investigations in political history and the study of African American life. The New York Constitutional Convention of 1821, in which race became directly tied to citizenship, was a culmination and a departure. Thus, we have surrounded the extensive excerpts of convention debates, in which both opponents and proponents of stripping from black men the right to vote laid out their arguments quite openly, with twenty-five documentary selections, drawn almost equally from before and after the convention. These documents present many different kinds of voices, heard in many different kinds of forums, for many different purposes. Laws and lawmakers share the spotlight with ordinary citizens. African American community leaders share space with newspaper editors, orators with artists. Every action taken or advocated in this struggle was contested, from plans gradually to abolish slavery in the wake of the American Revolution, to the disfranchisement of African Americans at the dawn of the Age of Jackson, to the restoration of voting rights in the aftermath of the Civil War. The documents assembled here attempt to capture the diversity of the debate in all its aspects.

Although politics and the right to participate in politics lie at the core of this study, we urge readers to pay close attention to language—not just what was said but also how it was said. The writers and speakers presented here chose their words and the form in which those words were delivered carefully. They made claims for and against black citizenship by what they wrote and the way in which they wrote it. They asserted and demanded power. Moreover, present to a greater or lesser degree in many of these documents are assertions about culture—about white as well as black culture, about how blacks actually lived, or how they should live, or how they could live. Many of the voices present here made connections between race and citizenship, based on what they alleged to be intrinsic to white or to black people because of skin color. Others insisted that the link that really mattered was that between humanity and citizenship— that personhood, at least for adult males, was the crucial prerequisite for citizenship, not race. In tackling such issues from the past, we wish readers to appreciate that politics is not just a culture unto itself, with certain norms and assumptions, but also reflects and shapes culture.

V. A Documentary in Three Parts

The documents themselves are the principal feature of this book. *Jim Crow New York* provides ready access not only to the proceedings of the 1821 Constitutional Convention, but also to a variety of documents usually confined to rare-book rooms and esoteric microfilm collections. By including entire documents where possible and lengthy excerpts in other instances, we hope to provide students and researchers of all kinds with the materials out of which they can write their own histories. By juxtaposing documents that range widely across time and cultural perspective, we hope to uncover the origins and impact of the 1821 convention, as well as to expose the multiple ways in which history is made. Thus, this book is organized with three overlapping audiences in mind—students, teachers, and scholars.

Jim Crow New York divides these documents into three distinct chronological parts. This organization reflects the three-part nature of the story: (1) the struggle to end slavery and to replace it with interracial citizenship (2) disfranchisement and (3) the variety of attempts to reconstruct Northern democracy according to more egalitarian political principles.

The first part, "Slavery, Abolition, and Citizenship, 1777–1817," tells the story of the abolition of slavery in New York from the writing of the newly independent state's first constitution through the decision to set a terminal date after which all New York's slaves would be free. Efforts to promote abolition legislation were shadowed by debates over whether former slaves could become equal participants in New York's expanding republican political culture. New Yorkers debated whether African Americans possessed, or could ever possess, the characteristics of citizens. Once gradual abolition became law and New York's free black population began to participate in political life, these questions resurfaced in more concrete form, with African Americans asserting their right to the public arena and some white antagonists seeking ways to push blacks out of that same arena.

The second part, "The Convention of 1821," focuses on disfranchisement—the decisive stripping away of voting rights from black people, even as more and more white men came to enjoy those same rights. This section first explores the complex regional and racial politics that immediately preceded the New York Constitutional Convention of 1821. Then it presents extended excerpts from the convention debates, drawn from the massive transcript published just after the close of the convention. Here, in remarkably explicit terms, New York's leading politicians, including future U.S. president Martin Van Buren, offered explanations for state-sponsored racism, not *despite* but *because of* the emergence of democracy. These excerpts also include voices of protest against this fateful decision, voices that present an alternate version of America's core principles, drowned out then but resonating still.

The third part, "The Long Reconstruction, 1821–1877," documents persistent attempts by some to establish equal citizenship as a governing principle of New York life and by others to secure a segregated political regime. The disfranchisement and the end of slavery in New York, both occurring in the 1820s, remained touchstones—seminal, if contradictory, events. Early African American publicists, antebellum politicians, Gilded Age proponents of suffrage restriction—all invoked the constitution of 1821 for their disparate purposes. And all operated in the wake of slavery's gradual abolition in the North, its tenacious growth in the South, and its abrupt end at the close of the Civil War. The unit and the book close with New York's ambiguous version of reconstruction—as blacks in New York regained the franchise and white politicians launched plans to undermine government by democratically elected officials.

We have included a variety of additional features to assist readers who approach this material with varying levels of knowledge and background. Each part includes a brief contextual essay, placing its documents in perspective by describing the historical events that mark the period and link the documents together. Here readers will find essential details about the process of emancipation, the reasons why New York called a constitutional convention in 1821, and how the echoes of 1821 shaped racial politics for the next half-century. These introductions also explain the relationship between events inside and outside New York State, in terms of both slavery and broader political developments during this century of upheaval. To emphasize further the resonance of events in New York with events elsewhere, and to provide readers with essential historical background, each unit provides a chronology that highlights significant developments in the state, the nation, and the world. Readers are thus reminded that the struggles over slavery and racial hierarchy were occurring throughout the Atlantic world—in the Americas, Africa, and Europe—during this pivotal century. Moreover, because not all readers come to the work with the same level of familiarity with New York geography—and because that geography changed dramatically between the American Revolution and the beginning of the Civil War—each part contains a map. We also have included illustrations to give readers a sense of what New Yorkers read and saw as they debated critical questions of race and citizenship, as well as a bibliographic essay highlighting the sources of our interpretations and helping readers embark on their own investigations.

An extended headnote introduces each document, identifying not only the source and author of the passage but also its historical context. Here the reader will find information regarding issues such as community politics, organizational sponsorship, and the legal landscape essential to interpreting the document. Each introductory note concludes with focusing questions, designed to encourage the reader to connect the document to previous selections. The documents themselves contain editorial notes to ensure an understanding of the significant individuals and events referred to by the various authors. So that readers can concentrate their energies as much as possible on the documents themselves, the number and lengths of these notes have been limited to the minimum consistent with providing vital information. In the interest of readability, excessively long paragraphs in a few documents have been divided into shorter sections. Original spelling has been maintained throughout.

Part I

Slavery, Abolition, and Citizenship, 1777–1817

Context

Little about New York's future was fixed or stable in 1777. As the year dawned, it was not even clear how radical the revolutionary break from Great Britain would be. Everyone who had joined the patriot camp by July 1776 had renounced loyalty to the mother country and its monarch, King George III. They no longer wished to be subjects of an empire. But what new form of government would take the place of colonial rule? And, perhaps more important, who would participate in this experiment in self-government, and to what degree?

New Yorkers, like other Americans, had to begin the challenging process of defining the nature and content of citizenship. A critical first step was the writing of a state constitution, a task assigned to New York's revolutionary congress in the summer of 1776 and not completed until the following spring. The compromise reached in Kingston, New York, between conservative and radical patriots at the Provincial Convention created a political order that mixed old and new. A man still had to own property to vote in New York, but for some elections, less of it than in colonial times. Elections were to be more frequent than in the colonial period, and were to include higher offices, such as governor and state senator. Independence had not brought democracy but had set in motion profound changes and given wing to new hopes.

Yet there was a good chance the new constitution that New York's political leaders approved in April might not be worth the parchment it was printed on by summer's end. British forces already occupied Manhattan, where they would remain for another six years. To the north, British forces massed in Canada for a two-pronged offensive through New York's western wilderness and the Hudson Valley, hoping to slice the infant United States of America in two. New hopes jostled uncomfortably with gloomy possibilities.

The almost twenty thousand black slaves who lived in the new state also looked to the future while coping with the disruptions of the war. With many of their masters, patriot and loyalist alike, preoccupied with the military conflict, and with New York City under British control, new ways of pursuing old strategies of resistance to slavery presented themselves. Many slaves took up British commander-in-chief Sir Henry Clinton's promise to free slaves who abandoned their patriot masters for Tory-held territory. Some of these former slaves gladly took up arms against their former masters in skirmishes in the "neutral zone" that surrounded Manhattan. Liberty acquired more than one meaning in this war for American freedom from Britain's "enslavement" of the colonies.[1]

In 1777, "enslavement" was something New Yorkers had been familiar with for 150 years. People of African descent caught up in the Atlantic swirl of trade and conquest had first come as slaves to the Dutch colony of New Netherland in 1626. Their numbers swelled in the English colony of New York during the early eighteenth century, their status as permanent bondspeople fixed by the same sorts of laws that ensnared African peoples in every English colony from Massachusetts to the West Indies. White New Yorkers benefited both directly and indirectly from slavery. The colony's economic prosperity owed to the provisioning trade with the sugar colonies of the Caribbean, where labor was performed almost exclusively by enslaved Africans. The white residents of Manhattan employed some of the people caught in the vortex of the Atlantic slave trade along the docks, as well as in artisan shops and merchant homes. White farmers in the Hudson Valley and on Long Island also found work for slaves; owned individually or in small groups, slaves contributed to the livelihood of many Dutch and English families throughout the province. At the time of the Declaration of Independence, slaves comprised just short of 12 percent of the colony's population.[2]

As the American Revolution itself indicated, the Atlantic world was changing dramatically during the late eighteenth century. These changes went well beyond the effort of English settlers to fashion a new American national identity for themselves. The talk of liberty, equality, and natural rights that American patriots borrowed freely from their British cousins had potentially profound implications for the future of slavery as well. So, too, did the spirit of religious awakening and revival that rocked much of the English-speaking world during the second half of the eighteenth century. For the first time in human history, people began to organize themselves around the emerging conviction that buying, selling, and owning other human beings was philosophically wrong or sinful. Quakers on both the British and American sides of the Atlantic led the way in renouncing slaveholding in their communities and encouraging others to do the same. Politicians and writers, including some directly involved in the American Revolution, began to denounce slavery as well, with particular focus on the inhumanity of the international slave trade. As they considered the shape of their new political order, some of New York's leaders even sought—unsuccessfully—to include plans for gradually abolishing slavery itself in the state constitution.

Abolishing slavery in New York, let alone granting full citizenship to African Americans, would prove a difficult challenge in the wake of the American Revolution. Slavery survived the war in New York almost entirely intact. Even though more than four hundred former New York slaves, part of a group of three thousand African Americans, joined the British evacuation of New York City rather than remain in American bondage, the number of slaves held in the state would begin to grow again.[3] But also surviving the war were calls for the gradual abolition of slavery. Neighboring Vermont and Pennsylvania had already taken such action during the war, and several New England states would do so in its aftermath. New York itself had promised manumission to slaves fighting for American independence, while confiscating slaves owned by British loyalists. Soon a mix of prominent New York politicians and Quakers would found a Manumission Society to encourage slavery's demise. Still, overcoming resistance to any formal program of emancipation in the state with the most slaves north of Maryland would prove extremely difficult.

Racial fears over what might replace slavery combined with slaveholder self-interest to block attempts to secure passage of a gradual abolition. Opponents of abolition raised the specter of free blacks voting and holding political office to undermine the initial push for gradual emancipation. During the 1780s, antislavery advocates had to satisfy themselves with legislation banning the sale of slaves into or out of New York State. At the same time, slavery's future in the nation as a whole was secured in the new U.S. Constitution through concessions to the Southern states

such as the three-fifths clause, the domestic insurrection clause, and protection of the slave trade until 1808. In the 1790s, a renewed effort to
pass abolition legislation had to overcome calls from owners for compensation and fears that newly freed blacks would be improvident and
would become a public burden.

Nevertheless, attitudes regarding slavery, race, and citizenship continued to shift in ways that ultimately benefited the abolitionist cause in
New York. Slaves themselves ran away in increasing numbers during the
1790s, while the Manumission Society won the freedom of a small number of blacks by detailing owner violations of the postwar slave code.
New York's newspapers printed a variety of items exposing the cruelty of
the institution and giving some credence to the concept of racial equality.
Even the slave insurrection in the French sugar colony of Saint Domingue
was cast in a relatively positive light. The expansion of the state into non-
slaveholding regions and ambitious plans for economic growth, as well as
a tendency to identify slavery with the South, all undermined the ability
of New York's slaveholders to protect their institution.

When the New York legislature finally passed a gradual abolition law,
it did not deny African Americans the rights of citizenship on the same
terms as whites. To be sure, the law freed blacks on a strikingly elongated
schedule, offering freedom to the children born of slave mothers after July
4, 1799, and requiring those children to serve their masters well into
adulthood. But given the strident opposition to the notion of black citizenship when gradual abolition almost became law fourteen years earlier,
the law was a major accomplishment, undermining the strength and the
legitimacy of the institution. Indeed, in the early 1800s free black communities grew much faster than the pace set by the law, in part due to increased numbers of private manumissions, negotiations between masters
and their slaves, and running away. Thus, while in the expanding Southern regions of the United States slavery underwent a period of dramatic
growth, and Southerners increasingly stopped paying lip service to the
Revolutionary Era goal of emancipation, in New York slavery was unde-
niably dying. With slavery already banned in the old Northwest Territory,
the stage was set for an entire region of the country to become a slaveless
democracy.

As the process of gradual abolition went into effect, New York's growing free black community seized the twin reins of citizenship and com-
munity-building during the early 1800s. This transitional period was one
of opportunity and danger. Black voters gravitated toward the Federalist

Party in its increasingly unsuccessful rivalry with the Jeffersonian Republicans. More important, African Americans in New York City, like other working-class New Yorkers, asserted their right to the street, publicly celebrating the official U.S. withdrawal from the international slave trade.

The thousands of free blacks who lived in New York City also built a range of institutions to shelter this marginalized community from the worst hardships of city life. Benevolent societies, along with an emerging network of black churches, harnessed the communal energies of a population grouped throughout the city's working-class neighborhoods, as well as living in the private white homes where individual African Americans worked. Some of the city's black children also attended the Manumission Society's African Free School, which over the years produced many black community leaders. John Teasman, an African American, served as the school's principal from 1799 to 1809. In the early years of the nineteenth century, free blacks held a variety of occupations. Many free black men worked as laborers and sailors on the city's waterfront. A significant number of free blacks worked as artisans, plying as freemen the trades they learned as slaves. Black men and women also worked as domestic servants and street vendors. The urban black community as a whole was poor; the unsanitary conditions of the city fell hard on African Americans. Nonetheless, as a community, free blacks showed a remarkable degree of ingenuity, diversity, and ambition.

Many rural blacks made their way to New York City, but for the thousands more who remained in the countryside as slaves, indentured servants, or freedpersons, life could be characterized by isolation and uncertainty, as well as efforts to draw together black families and small black communities. Children technically free under the terms of the gradual emancipation law often toiled as servants in white homes. The difficulty of acquiring land compelled many free adults to work as agricultural laborers on white-owned farms. Rural life was still joyfully punctuated by the celebration of Pinkster, a Dutch holiday that over the course of the eighteenth century had been adapted by black slaves as a major public festival. Meanwhile, the stirrings of Christian revival reached out into the nineteenth-century countryside, as did the desire to found black churches.

The threat of being illegally sold or kidnapped into Southern bondage plagued African American New Yorkers, a painful legacy of slavery as well as a bitter fruit of gradual emancipation. Meanwhile, the alliance forged with the Federalist Party in the state's intensely partisan political environment provoked the enmity of the ascendant Republican Party. In 1811, the state's Republican legislature passed a law requiring black voters to prove that they were not slaves. That same year, in Albany, local authorities banned the celebration of Pinkster. As long as New York—and, for that matter, the nation—recognized slavery as a legitimate institution, black personal safety, black cultural freedom, and black citizenship would not be secure.

In summary, the second decade of the nineteenth century brought further hope of freedom and ominous signs of increased racial hostility. During the War of 1812, New York governor Daniel Tompkins called on President James Monroe to allow him to enlist black troops from New York in defense of the nation. And in 1817, the legislature finally acceded to the Manumission Society's and Governor Tompkins's requests that a final date be set for the freedom of all slaves in the state. The new law, which also affirmed the existing laws governing both slavery and private manumission, slated slavery to end in 1827, almost exactly two centuries after black bondage first began in New Amsterdam. The legislature chose July 4, 1827, as the final day of slavery in New York. As the clock wound down on slavery, a new threat to black American citizenship had begun to secure the support of many prominent white Americans, even some who saw themselves as allies to African Americans in the struggle against slavery. The American Colonization Society, founded in 1816, proposed to solve the young nation's race problem by removing free blacks to the coast of Africa. Intimately connected for some, abolition and citizenship were sharply at odds for others.

Chronology

1777 New York: State adopts new state constitution.

The Nation: Vermont, which does not become a U.S. state until 1791, adopts constitution that bans slavery.

Continental Congress approves Articles of Confederation for U.S. national government; the Articles not ratified by the states until 1781.

1778 The Nation: Rhode Island passes law allowing slaves to serve in its regiment of the Continental army; slaves granted freedom in exchange for service, with former masters receiving monetary compensation for the loss of enlisted former slaves; act rescinded after only three months.

Virginia bans slave importation.

1780 The Nation: Pennsylvania enacts first gradual abolition law in the United States; the law frees slaves born after March 1, 1780, with required service to mothers' masters until age twenty-eight.

1781 New York: New York passes law offering payment to slaveholders who volunteer their slaves for service, with slaves to receive their freedom at the end of the war.

New York Friends (Quakers) Yearly Meeting, having committed itself during the 1770s to eliminating slaveholding among its membership, further resolves to require Quakers to make "a Settlement between" former slaves and their former Quaker masters and to educate black children.

The World: British surrender to General George Washington in Yorktown, Virginia, securing U.S. victory in the war for independence.

1783   New York: British evacuate New York City, the final British out-post in the thirteen newly independent former colonies, in No-vember; three thousand African Americans who had crowded into Manhattan from throughout the United States join British ships headed for Nova Scotia, Canada.

The Nation: William Cushing, chief justice of the Massachusetts Supreme Judicial Court, grants freedom to runaway slave Quok Walker and finds slavery not compatible with Massachusetts state constitution.

Maryland bans importation of slaves from Africa.

The World: The United States and Britain conclude the Peace of Paris, officially recognizing U.S. independence.

British Quakers submit anti–slave trade petition to Parliament.

1784   The Nation: Rhode Island slaves born after March 1, 1784, de-clared free; males obligated to serve their mothers' masters until age twenty-one, females until age eighteen.

Connecticut revision of laws includes gradual abolition of slavery, with the children born after March 1, 1784, obligated to serve their mothers' masters until age twenty-five.

Pennsylvania Abolition Society, originally founded in 1775, re-sumes operations.

1785   New York: First meeting (January 25) of the New-York Manu-mission Society.

Council of Revision vetoes gradual abolition law; state enacts lan-guage banning the importation of slaves into New York and eas-ing the voluntary manumission of slaves.

1786   New York: New-York Manumission Society publicly announces plans to open a school for free black children in the city; the African Free School opens the next year.

The World: Thomas Clarkson's antislavery treatise *An Essay on the Slavery and Commerce of the Human Species* published in Britain.

1787   New York: Long Island black poet Jupiter Hammon publishes "Address to the Negroes in the State of New-York."

The Nation: Congress enacts Northwest Ordinance, banning

slavery in territories that would become the states of Ohio, Michigan, Illinois, Indiana, and Wisconsin.

U.S. Constitutional Convention meets in Philadelphia; approves Constitution with several provisions protecting the future of slavery.

Rhode Island prohibits citizens from taking part in international slave trade.

The World: British establish Sierra Leone colony on west coast of Africa for former British American slaves.

1788   New York: New York passes revised comprehensive slave law, confirming the continuance of slavery in the state; the law makes it illegal to sell New York slaves out of the state.

The Nation: New York becomes the ninth state to ratify the U.S. Constitution, helping ensure national ratification.

Connecticut, Massachusetts, and Pennsylvania prohibit citizens from taking part in the international slave trade.

The World: French antislavery society founded.

1789   The Nation: New York City becomes temporary home of U.S. federal government; George Washington inaugurated as first president of the United States.

Providence Society for Abolishing the Slave Trade founded in Rhode Island.

The World: French Revolution begins.

Anti–slave trade resolutions debated in British Parliament.

1790   The Nation: U.S. Congress, during its final year in New York City, witnesses bitter debate over attempts to regulate role of U.S. ships in the international slave trade.

1791   New York: First American edition of *The Interesting Narrative of the Life of Olaudah Equiano, or Gustavas Vassa, The African. Written by Himself* published in New York City two years after the path-breaking memoir of a former slave was published in England.

The Nation: Addition of the Bill of Rights to the U.S. Constitution ratified.

U.S. Congress passes law governing the composition of U.S.

militias that bars blacks and Indians from service during times of peace.

The World: Slaves of Saint Domingue, the French Caribbean sugar colony, revolt in midst of civil war.

1792 New York: Candidate for governor John Jay criticized for anti-slavery views during unsuccessful challenge to incumbent George Clinton.

The Nation: Kentucky admitted to United States as a slave state.

The World: France grants equal rights to free blacks and mulattoes in its colonies.

1793 The Nation: Cotton gin invented by Eli Whitney.

The World: Gradual abolition enacted in British Canada.

1794 The Nation: American Convention for Promoting the Abolition of Slavery and Improving the Condition of the African Race holds first annual meeting in Philadelphia.

The World: France abolishes slavery in its colonies, grants full citizenship to all men.

1795 New York: John Jay elected governor of New York.

1796 New York: Gradual abolition bill proposed in state assembly.

The Nation: Controversial treaty negotiated in 1794 by John Jay with Great Britain accepted by U.S. Congress; critics decried lack of compensation to U.S. slave owners for former slaves who escaped with the British at the conclusion of the Revolutionary War.

Massachusetts Federalist John Adams wins narrow victory over Virginia Democratic-Republican Thomas Jefferson in first contested U.S. presidential election.

Tennessee enters the Union as a slave state.

1799 New York: "Act for the gradual abolition of Slavery" becomes law.

1800 The Nation: Gabriel's Rebellion, an uprising planned by Virginia slave Gabriel Prosser, is thwarted just before its intended launch.

1801 The Nation: Thomas Jefferson becomes third president of the United States after Congress resolves deadlocked election.

The World: Former slave Toussaint L'ouverture holds control of both French and Spanish portions of Saint Domingue/Santo Domingo.

1803 The Nation: Purchase from France of vast Louisiana Territory adds millions of acres to U.S. territory.

The World: France retracts abolition of slavery and black citizenship in its colonies in the midst of war for control of Saint Domingue.

1804 The Nation: New Jersey enacts gradual abolition law.

The World: Former French colony Saint Domingue becomes the independent nation of Haiti, joining the United States as the only other independent nation in the Americas.

1806 The Nation: Virginia law enacted that demands any slave receiving freedom exit the state within a year of receiving freedom.

President Jefferson cuts off all U.S. trade with Haiti.

1807 The World: Britain abolishes its participation in the slave trade.

1808 The Nation: Law goes into effect banning U.S. participation in the international slave trade.

1812 The World: War of 1812, between the United States and Britain, begins.

The Nation: Louisiana enters the Union as a slave state.

1814 The Nation: The United States and Britain negotiate treaty to end War of 1812.

1816 The Nation: American Colonization Society founded.

The World: Latin American leaders Simón Bolívar and José de San Martín offer freedom to slaves willing to join the wars for independence against Spain.

1817 New York: Law to end slavery in state as of 1827 enacted.

DeWitt Clinton becomes governor of New York.

The Nation: Philadelphia blacks protest American Colonization Society.

New York's Republican governor, Daniel Tompkins, becomes vice president of the United States under Virginian James Monroe.

Mississippi enters the Union as a slave state.

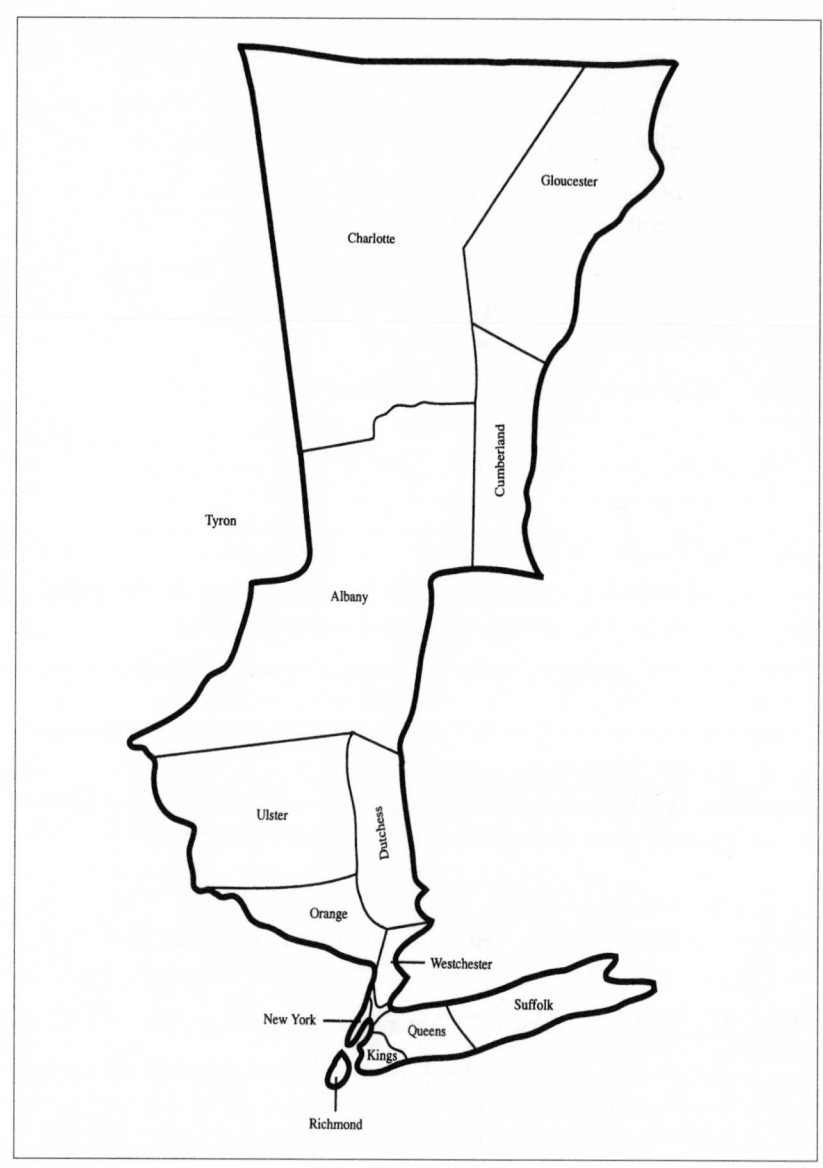

Figure 1 Map of New York State in 1779
At the time of the American Revolution, the organized counties of New York
hewed to the Hudson River Valley and the Atlantic Ocean. Gloucester and Cum-
berland Counties were soon conceded to Vermont. By 1800, New York had created twenty new counties, primarily to the west of the original counties. [Map of
New York State in 1779, based on Claude Joseph Sauthier, *A Chorological Map
of the Province of New York* . . . (London, 1779).] *Courtesy of the Boston College
Center for Media and Instructional Technology.*

A. Franchise Provision,
New York State Constitution, 1777

On July 2, 1776, the Continental Congress, meeting in Philadelphia, voted to separate from Great Britain. On July 4, the Congress approved the Declaration of Independence. Five days later, New York's congress endorsed independence and officially joined the new nation.

Independence from Great Britain required Americans to craft new political identities. They were no longer living in colonies subject to a distant king. Americans, including New Yorkers, were now citizens. With the old colonial charters obsolete, each new state had to write a constitution, laying down the fundamental principles and laws to define and guide it through the new political order. One of the most important tasks facing constitution writers was to decide who would get to vote to elect which governing officials. However they were to be chosen, elected officials would have responsibility for governing their states, not in the name of the king but on behalf of the people of each state.

In the midst of war with Great Britain, and after much debate and disagreement in the drafting committee, the state's provisional congress finally reached agreement in April 1777 on New York's first constitution. The 1777 constitution approved in Kingston, New York, combined the revolutionary rhetoric of the Declaration of Independence with a modified version of preindependence government overseen by a legislature, a governor, and a judiciary. In a nod toward greater democracy, the royal council was replaced by an elected senate, and the governor, no longer a royal appointment, would be chosen through election every three years. The constitution made assembly elections a yearly event and more than doubled the number of legislators in the lower house.

The 1777 constitution retained the principle that a freehold (owner-ship of land or a lease for life of land) be the basic standard for deter-mining the right to vote. Yet the partially liberalized provisions for elect-ing the members of the state assembly, the state senate, and governor var-ied dramatically. In elections to the lower house of the state legislature, the amount of land a potential voter had to own was lowered from colo-nial times, thus expanding the electorate. But elections for state senator and governor actually became more restricted, as the constitution in-creased the amount of property one had to own to vote for these higher offices. New York kept in place the broader principle that the ownership of property was a proper standard for defining which adult males could vote. The Constitution did not include any language defining voter eligi-bility by race or skin color.

The 1777 constitution left the institution of slavery intact. Some prominent participants in the constitution-writing process, most notably John Jay, future U.S. Supreme Court chief justice and future New York governor, favored incorporating antislavery principles in the state's fun-damental law. A provision introduced by Gouverneur Morris that "future Legislatures of the State . . . take the most effectual measures consistent with the public safety, and the private property of individuals, for abol-ishing domestic slavery" won temporary support from the constitutional convention but did not survive in the final version of the document.[4]

What the New York constitution of 1777 said and did not say raises several questions important for understanding subsequent events: Were the political institutions and voting laws consistent with the broad prin-ciples expressed in the Declaration of Independence, such as the assertion that "all men are created equal"? What standards did the New York con-stitution use to define voter eligibility? Why did the constitution establish different requirements for voting in different sorts of elections? Why did the legislature restrict voting on the basis of sex but not color? What prompted New Yorkers in 1777 even to consider abolishing slavery as a goal of their new political system?

*   *   *

I. This Convention . . . in the name and by the authority of the good people of this State, doth ORDAIN, DETERMINE and DECLARE, that no authority shall, on any pretence whatever, be exercised over the people or members of this State, but such as shall be derived from and granted by them. . . .

VI. AND WHEREAS, an opinion hath long prevailed among divers of the good people of this State, that voting at elections by Ballot, would tend more to preserve the liberty and equal freedom of the people, than voting *viva voce:*[5] To the end therefore, that a fair experiment be made, which of those two methods of voting is to be preferred:

BE IT ORDAINED, that as soon as may be, after the termination of the present war, between the United States of America and Great-Britain, an act, or acts be passed by the legislature of this State, for causing all elections thereafter to be held in this State, for Senators and Representatives in assembly, to be by Ballot, and directing the manner in which the same shall be conducted. AND WHEREAS, it is possible, that after all the care of the legislature, in framing the said act or acts, certain inconveniencies and mischiefs, unforeseen at this day, may be found to attend the said mode of electing by Ballot:

IT IS FURTHER ORDAINED, that if after a full and fair experiment shall be made of voting by Ballot aforesaid, the same shall be found less conducive to the safety or interest of the State, than the method of voting *viva voce*, it shall be lawful and constitutional for the legislature to abolish the same; provided two thirds of the members present in each House, respectively shall concur therein: And further, that, during the continuance of the present war, and until the legislature of this State shall provide for the election of Senators and Representatives in assembly by Ballot, the said election shall be made *viva voce*.

VII. That every male inhabitant of full age, who shall have personally resided within one of the counties of this State, for six months immediately preceding the day of election, shall, at such election, be entitled to vote for representatives of the said county in assembly; if during the time aforesaid, he shall have been a Freeholder, possessing a Freehold of the value of twenty pounds, within the said county, or have rented a tenement therein of the yearly value of forty shillings,[6] and been rated and actually paid taxes to this State: Provided always, that every person who is now a freeman of the city of Albany, or who was made a freeman of the city of New-York, on or before the fourteenth day of October, in the year of our Lord one thousand seven hundred and seventy-five, and shall be actually and usually resident in the said cities respectively, shall be entitled to vote for Representatives in assembly within his said place of residence.[7]

VIII. That every elector, before he is admitted to vote, shall, if required by the returning officer or either of the inspectors, take an oath, or if of the people called Quakers, an affirmation, of allegiance to the State.[8] . . .

X. And this Convention doth further, in the name and by the author-ity of the good people of this State, ORDAIN, DETERMINE and DECLARE, that the Senate of the State of New-York shall consist of twenty-four free-holders, to be chosen out of the body of the freeholders, and that they be chosen by the freeholders of this State, possessed of freeholds of the value of one hundred pounds, over and above all debts charged thereon.[9]. . . .

XIII. And this Convention doth further, in the name and by the au-thority of the good people of this State, ORDAIN, DETERMINE and DE-CLARE, that no member of this State shall be disfranchised, or deprived of any of the rights or privileges secured to the subjects of this State, by this constitution, unless by law of the land, or the judgment of his peers. . . .

XVII. And this Convention doth further, in the name and by the au-thority of the good people of this State, ORDAIN, DETERMINE and DE-CLARE, that the supreme executive power and authority of this State shall be vested in a Governor; and that statedly once in every three years, and as often as the seat of government shall become vacant, a wise and dis-creet freeholder of this State shall be by ballot elected Governor, by the freeholders of this State, qualified as before described to elect Senators; which elections shall be always held at the times and places of chusing representatives in assembly for each respective county; and that the per-son who hath the greatest number of votes within the said State, shall be Governor thereof. . . .

XXXVIII. AND WHEREAS we are required by the benevolent princi-ples of rational liberty, not only to expel civil tyranny, but also to guard against that spiritual oppression and intolerance, wherewith the bigotry and ambition of weak and wicked priests and princes, have scourged mankind: This Convention doth further, in the name and by the author-ity of the good people of this State, ORDAIN, DETERMINE and DECLARE, that the free exercise and enjoyment of religious profession and worship, without discrimination or preference, shall for ever hereafter be allowed within this State to all mankind. Provided that the liberty of conscience hereby granted, shall not be so construed, as to excuse acts of licentious-ness, or justify practices inconsistent with the peace or safety of this State.

XXXIX. AND WHEREAS the ministers of the gospel are, by their pro-fession, dedicated to the service of God and the cure of souls, and ought not be diverted from the great duties of their function; therefore, no min-ister of the gospel, or priest of any denomination whatsoever, shall, at any time hereafter, under any pretence or description whatever, be eligible to, or capable of holding, any civil or military office or place, within this State. . . .

XL. AND WHEREAS it is of the utmost importance to the safety of every State, that it should always be in a condition of defence; and it is the duty of every man, who enjoys the protection of society, to be prepared and willing to defend it; this Convention therefore, in the name and by the authority of the good people of this State, doth ORDAIN, DETERMINE and DECLARE, that the militia of this State, at all times hereafter, as well in peace as in war, shall be armed and disciplined, and in readiness for service. That all such of the inhabitants of this State, being of the people called Quakers, as from scruples of conscience, may be averse to the bearing of arms, be therefrom excused by the legislature; and do pay to the State such sums of money, in lieu of their personal service, as the same may, in the judgment of the legislature, be worth: And that a proper magazine of warlike stores, proportioned to the number of inhabitants, be, for ever hereafter, at the expence of this State, and by acts of the legislature, established, maintained, and continued in every county in this State.

XLI. And this convention doth further ORDAIN, DETERMINE and DECLARE, in the name and by the authority of the good people of this State, that trial by jury, in all cases in which it hath heretofore been used in the colony of New-York, shall be established, and remain inviolate forever. And that no acts of attainder shall be passed by the legislature of this State, for crimes other than those committed before the termination of the present war; and that such acts shall not work a corruption of blood. And further, that the legislature of this State shall, at no time hereafter, institute any new court or courts, but such as shall proceed according to the course of the common law.

XLII. And this Convention doth further, in the name and by the authority of the good people of this State, ORDAIN, DETERMINE and DECLARE, that it shall be in the discretion of the legislature to naturalize all such persons, and in such manner as they shall think proper; provided all such of the persons, so to be by them naturalized, as being born in parts beyond sea, and out of the United States of America, shall come to settle in, and become subjects of this State, shall take an oath of allegiance to this State, and abjure and renounce all allegiance and subjection to all and every foreign King, Prince, Potentate and State, in all matters ecclesiastical as well as civil.

Source: *The Constitution of the State of New-York* (Philadelphia, 1777).

B. Veto Message, 1785

Plans to commence the gradual abolition of slavery in New York State almost went into effect in 1785, less than two years after the controversial British evacuation of New York City, which included three thousand African Americans who chose not to gamble on freedom by remaining in the United States. Gradual abolition legislation followed a model first established by Pennsylvania in 1780. No persons actually enslaved received their freedom under such plans. Rather, the children born after a date established by law technically would be born free but could claim their freedom only in their twenties. In other words, such children would serve their mothers' masters until well into adulthood. By the strict provisions of such a plan, it would take many years for slavery truly to end. Even such a gradual emancipation scheme met strong opposition, particularly in those regions of the state with relatively high concentrations of slave ownership, such as Staten Island, King's County on Long Island, and Ulster County in the Hudson River valley.

Concerns about the status of free African Americans prompted the state assembly to propose amendments that significantly curtailed the meaning of freedom for former slaves and their descendants. Amendments to the gradual abolition bill proposed: (1) imposing a significant fine on whites and persons of African descent who married one another; (2) forbidding people defined as black or partially black from holding office and serving on juries or testifying in cases involving whites; (3) barring any "negro, mulatto or mustee"[10] from voting "in any case whatsoever." The state senate successfully persuaded the lower house to retract the first two provisions. The provision making it illegal for people of color to vote, however, remained in place.

The attempt to define voting eligibility through race ultimately led to the defeat of the entire gradual abolition bill. As the document that follows indicates, New York's Council of Revision vetoed the proposed gradual abolition bill. The council left little doubt as to the nature of its objection, emphatically denouncing color and descent as means for restricting the right to vote.[11] The state assembly failed to muster the necessary two-thirds majority to override the council's veto. The opponents of abolition had effectively outmaneuvered the majority of state legislators, who at least nominally supported the concept of abolition. Moreover, opponents of gradual abolition had effectively exposed the shallowness of political support for black freedom. Many white legislators were enticed by the prospect of using racist legal provisions to blunt the projected impact of emancipation. The resulting controversy ultimately killed the gradual abolition bill.[12] Gradual abolition would not receive such serious legislative consideration again until the mid-1790s.

This episode raises a number of questions: On what principles did the Council of Revision reject the gradual abolition bill? What views on citizenship did the Council of Revision express? What views on race did the council advocate? What vision of the future did the Council of Revision project, and why? Were people of African American descent voting already in 1785? Would a deeply flawed law have been better than none at all?

* * *

The Council object against the bill, entitled, "An Act for the gradual abolition of slavery within this State," becoming a law of this State.

1st. Because the last clause of the bill enacts, that no negro, mulatto or mustee, shall have a legal vote in any case whatsoever. Which implicatively excludes persons of this description from all share in the Legislature, and from those offices, in which a vote may be necessary, as well as from the important privilege of electing those by whom they are to be governed; the bill having in other instances, placed the children that shall be born of slaves in the rank of citizens, agreeable both to the spirit and letter of the constitution, they are as such, entitled to all the privileges of citizens; nor can they be deprived of these essential rights, without shocking those principles of equal liberty, which every page in that constitution labours to enforce.

2dly. Because it holds up a doctrine, which is repugnant to the principle on which the United States justify their separation from Great-Britain, and either enacts what is wrong, or supposes that those may rightfully be charged with the burdens of government, who have no representative share in imposing them.

3dly. Because this class of disfranchised and discontented citizens, who at some future period, may be both numerous and wealthy, may, under the direction of ambitious and factious leaders become dangerous to the State, and effect the ruin of a constitution whose benefits they are not permitted to enjoy.

4thly. Because the creation of an order of citizens, who are to have no legislative or representative share in the government, necessarily lays the foundation of an aristocracy of the most dangerous and malignant kind, rending power permanent and hereditary in the hands of those person who deduce their origin through white ancestors only, tho' these at some future period should not amount to a fiftieth part of the people. That this is not a chimerical supposition, will be apparent to those who reflect, that the term *Mustee,* is indefinite; that the desire of power will induce those who possess it, to exclude competitors, by extending it as far as possible; that supposing it to extend to the seventeenth generation, every man will have the blood of many more than 200,000 ancestors running in his veins, and that if any of these should have been coloured, his posterity will by the operation of this law be disfranchised. So that if only one thousandth part of the black inhabitants now in the State, should intermarry with the white, their posterity will amount to so many millions, that it will be difficult to suppose a fiftieth part of the people born within this State two hundred years hence, who may be entitled to share in the benefits which our excellent constitution intended to secure to every free inhabitant of the State.

5thly. Because the last clause of the bill being general, deprives those black, mulatto and mustee citizens, who have heretofore been entitled to vote, of this essential privilege, and under the idea of political expediency, without their having been charged with any offence, disfranchises them in direct violation of the established rules of justice, and against the letter and spirit of the constitution, and tends to support a doctrine which is inconsistent with the most obvious principles of government, that the Legislature may arbitrarily dispose of the dearest rights of their constituents.

Source: *Journal of the Assembly of the State of New-York* 8, pt. 2 (New York, 1785), 119–120.

C. Anti-Abolition Article, 1785

In post-Revolution America, newspapers provided readers with access to a broad range of information and opinion. Articles did not follow the standard journalistic format familiar to twenty-first-century readers, with the author listed just below a large-type headline. Opinion and news mixed promiscuously in the jam-packed columns of newsprint, with authors often either unidentified or identified only by a pseudonym. Writers often were literally correspondents, people who wrote to the newspaper of their own volition. Thus, newspapers provided readers with access to the vigorous political debates of the day, competing, of course, with discussions in pubs and on street corners as a means of conveying information and ideas.

In the following piece, an unidentified writer challenged the Council of Revision's logic (document B), not in order to defend gradual abolition but rather in an attempt to further discredit the desirability of black freedom. Indeed, the prospect of gradual abolition inspired racist taunts and exposed unhealed political wounds from the Revolutionary War. During the fight for U.S. independence, New Yorkers were not all united behind the patriot banner. Loyalty to the British Crown was widespread. The British held Manhattan for most of the war, making New York City a center of loyalist activity. Hundreds of African Americans fled to freedom behind British lines. Many of these former slaves joined British forces in fighting against the patriots, some of whom were their former masters, in the surrounding countryside of New York and New Jersey. Although New York patriots also attempted to enlist black soldiers, the decision to fight rested with a slave's owner, not with the slave himself. Thus, for many African Americans, the unconditional British promise of freedom for those who abandoned their owners was more attractive.

With the restoration of peace and the withdrawal of the British, many New Yorkers sought to punish those who had identified themselves with the British. New York passed various laws limiting the rights of former loyalists and stripping them of their property. The charge of pro-British leanings was hurled against political rivals, particularly by radicals competing with conservatives for office.

Quakers, as members of the religious Society of Friends are called, faced charges of disloyalty throughout the war. The Friends's creed renounces war. Thus, Quakers practiced and preached pacifism, which precluded active participation in the patriot cause. Moreover, Quakers, in America and in Britain, were the first organized religious group to denounce slavery. Friends Meetings required their members to free their own slaves. Many Quakers went a step further, participating actively in the first American antislavery societies, including those in New York and Pennsylvania. Thus, this newspaper essayist found ample targets in the brief printed below against abolition and black citizenship.

How did this writer reconcile the principles of freedom and representation with the desire to exclude black people from politics? What images of African Americans did the writer urge upon readers? How did the writer connect political concerns with a rejection of emancipation? What feelings about the past and fears about the future did the author attempt to stimulate?

*   *   *

To deny that all men are born free, is contrary to the principles of our independence without doubt, or to disfranchise citizens and not allow them a representation; the latter has been done not long since, in denying citizens a vote at an election, but with a motive very different from that of perverting the subject's right, on the contrary it was done to preserve the liberty of the state; upon this principle, it is better that an individual should suffer an inconvenience, than a community at large. Therefore notwithstanding "every man is born free," I conceive on the same principle as above, it would be greatly injurious to this state if all the negroes should be allowed the privileges of white men, unless there could be derived some possible means consistent with liberty, to separate them from white people, and prevent them from having any connection or intercourse with them; if they are emancipated on any other terms, it must be evident to the most common understanding, what will be the consequence in a short time; besides the shame we should most inevitably incur from a mixture of complexions, and their participating in government, seated in our Senate and Assembly, General Quacco here, Col. Mingo[13] there, &c. &c. A still greater consequence is to be dreaded, which is a total subversion of our liberties; they, in combination with their friends the Quakers, would give every assistance to our enemies, as we have already experienced their fidelity in the late contest, when they fought against us by whole regiments, and the Quakers at the same time supported every measure of Great-Britain to enslave us. Those pretended supporters of liberty now preach up, let us emancipate the slaves, conceiving it more for the benefit of their souls to have the negroes *now* set at liberty, than they thought it just that white people should have had it in the year 1776 and 1777. Their motives are obvious; for the moment the period of the emancipation of negroes arrives, it will cause them, with others who wish to join them, to have a greater influence in the government, which the Quakers as well as some others, fervently wish for. If they were free and on equal footing with us, God knows what use they would make of their power; a very bad one I fear.

Source: *New-York Packet*, April 4, 1785.

D. "Mungo Speaks," 1788

Newspapers in late eighteenth-century New York published many items besides news and commentary. Advertisements, including those for runaway slaves, comprised a large proportion of each edition. Poetry was also a regular newspaper feature, usually on the back page in a special "poet's corner." These poems did not aim merely to entertain readers. Like the following example, poems often spoke in verse form to the same public issues that filled the news columns. Indeed, antislavery poetry was a common means of expression for slavery's critics in England and America.

American newspapers, moreover, connected readers to conversations taking place not just across the state and nation but around the world. New York publishers borrowed liberally from one another and from the English press. New York's intensified interest in race and slavery took place at the same time that the former mother country experienced an unprecedented organized agitation to end the British slave trade. News of English debates over the transportation of Africans to England's West Indian island colonies proved irresistible to American printers. On both sides of the Atlantic, criticism of slavery involved attempts to consider the humanity of the enslaved. Basic human equality was perhaps the ultimate argument against the slave trade and slavery itself.

The poem "Mungo Speaks" has thought-provoking origins. An Albany, New York, newspaper reprinted this poetic soliloquy from the London publication *Gentleman's Magazine*. The poem itself was composed as a response to the play *The Padlock*, by Isaac Bickerstaff (1735–1812), first performed in 1768 for the London stage. Bickerstaff based his play on a novel by the great seventeenth-century Spanish writer Miguel de Cervantes. Among the characters in Bickerstaff's romantic comedy is a black servant named Mungo (adapted from Cervantes's black eunuch character Luis), who speaks in broken English throughout the play. Although Mungo bemoans the cruelty of his master at one point in the play, his character is primarily that of a comic fool, fond of music, drink, and small bribes. The soliloquy does not appear in the original version of the play.[14] Rather, the poet makes ironic use of Bickerstaff's Mungo character for the purpose of social commentary.

The name Mungo is one of many African-sounding names used in newspapers to represent fictional black speakers. But the imagined Mungo in this poem explicitly rejects the role of the buffoon to which blacks were often relegated in printed jokes and letters. Although the audience addressed was clearly British, the poet's observations on race and equality resonated well beyond their British context.

Modern readers of poems such as "Mungo Speaks" may wish to ask whether poetry might be a particularly effective form of making an argument about racial equality. What features of this poem contributed to its persuasiveness? Is the argument made in this particular poem applicable to the abolition of American slavery or just of the slave trade? What particular features of slavery did the speaker criticize? Did this poem in any way respond to the kinds of concerns raised in documents B and C?

*   *   *

"Tank you my Massas! have you laugh your fill?"—
Then let me speak, nor take the freedom ill.
E'en from my tongue some heartfelt truths may fall,
And outrag'd nature claims the care of all.
My tale, in any place, would force a tear,
But calls for stronger, deeper feelings here.
For whilst I tread the free-born British land;
Whilst now before me crouded Britons stand;
Vain, vain that glorious privilege to me,
I am a slave, where all things else are free.
    Yet was I born, as you are, no man's slave,
An heir to all that liberal Nature gave;
My thoughts can reason, and my limbs can move,
The same as yours; like yours my heart can love;
Alike my body food and sleep sustains;
Alike our wants, our pleasures, and our pains.
One sun rolls o'er us, common skies around;
One globe supports us, and one grave must bound.
    Why then am I devoid of all to live,

That manly comforts to a man can give?
To live untaught Religion's soothing balm,
Or life's choice arts; to live, unknown the calm
Of soft domestic ease; those sweets of life,
The duteous offspring, and th' obedient wife,
To live, to property and rights unknown;
Not ev'n the common benefits my own.
No arm to guard me from opression's rod,
My will subservient to a tyrants nod.
No gentle hand, when life in decay,
To smooth my pains, and charm my cares away;
But, helpless, left to quit the horrid stage;
Harrass'd in youth, and desolate in age.
　　　But I was born on Afric's tawny strand,
And you in fair Britannia's fairer land.
Comes freedom then from colour? Blush with . . . me,
And let strong Nature's crimson mark your blame.
I speak to Britons,—Britons, then, behold
A man by Britons snar'd, and seiz'd, and sold.
And yet no British statute damns the deed,
Nor do they more than murderous villains bleed.
O sons of Freedom! equalise your laws;
Be all consistent—plead the Negroe's cause:
That all the nations in your code may see
The British Negro, like the Briton, free.
But, should he supplicate your laws in vain,
To break for ever this disgraceful chain,
At least, let gentle use so abate
The galling errors of its passing state,
That he may share the Great Creator's social plan;
For though no Briton, Mungo is a man.

Source: *Albany Journal*, March 17, 1788.

E. Antislavery Orations, 1797 and 1798

Organized white opposition to slavery began in 1785 with the founding of the New-York Manumission Society (NYMS). This New York City group advocated the gradual abolition of slavery, encouraged voluntary private grants of freedom, and worked to enforce laws restricting the sale of slaves in and out of New York State. The NYMS also founded a school for free black children, hoping to use the school to supervise the behavior of free blacks and to counter white prejudices. The group's first president was John Jay (1745–1829). Jay, a leading figure in national and state politics, was himself a slaveholder. Another prominent founding member of the society was Alexander Hamilton (1755–1804), who would become the secretary of the treasury and architect of George Washington's financial and foreign policy programs in the 1790s. Many of the organization's members were Quakers.

The organization's activities and influence were largely confined to New York City, although the NYMS also regularly petitioned the state legislature on behalf of the society's causes. White philanthropists and former black slaves did not always see the needs of African American New Yorkers in the same light. Nonetheless, blacks and whites cooperated successfully in a number of cases to win the freedom of individuals who claimed they were being held in slavery in violation of various New York statutes.

The NYMS and other opponents of slavery stepped up their campaign for gradual abolition legislation in the mid-1790s. Prospects for success had revived. A national organization had been established to coordinate antislavery efforts, and John Jay became governor of New York in 1795. Support for gradual abolition in the state legislature was widespread and growing. Nonetheless, opponents of gradual abolition delayed its passage as long as they could, demanding that slaveholders be compensated by the state for the loss of future labor.

In the midst of the renewed initiative for gradual abolition legislation, the NYMS sponsored and published addresses that articulated at length the case for abolition. In 1797, Samuel Miller (1769–1850), a Presbyterian minister in New York City, vigorously critiqued slavery and racial prejudice. Just twenty-seven years old, Rev. Miller would publish books and pamphlets on a variety of religious, historical, and scientific subjects during his long career. In 1798, New York City physician Elihu Hubbard Smith (1771–1798) attacked the legislature for its foot-dragging on the matter of gradual abolition. In addition to practicing medicine, the twenty-six-year-old Smith was a trustee of the African Free School in New York City, as well as a published poet and dramatist. He died in a yellow fever epidemic only months after giving this speech. In the view of both speakers, the time had come for New York to commit itself to a program of emancipation. They urged supporters to remain steadfast in their principles.

Compare Miller and Smith to each other and to the previous documents. Why do you think that these young white professionals participated in the antislavery cause? For each speaker, what was the principal argument against slavery? What was the attitude of these men toward those who would defend slavery or who would seek compensation for financial losses incurred through abolition? Why did the speakers favor gradual rather than immediate abolition? What role did Miller and Smith think the slaves themselves should play in the effort to end slavery? What opinions did they express about race? What status did they anticipate for African Americans once freedom was achieved?

*   *   *

Samuel Miller, April 12, 1797

. . . That, in the close of the eighteenth century, it should be esteemed proper and necessary, in any civilized country, to institute discourses to oppose the slavery and commerce of the human species, is a wonderful fact in the annals of society! But that this country should be America, is a solecism only to be accounted for by the general inconsistency of the human character. . . . [T]he humiliating tale must be told—that in this free country—in this country, the plains of which are still stained with blood shed in the cause of liberty,—in this country, from which has been proclaimed to distant lands, as the basis of our political existence, the noble principle, that "ALL MEN ARE BORN FREE AND EQUAL," in this country there are slaves!—men are bought and sold! Strange, indeed! that the bosom which glows at the name of liberty in general, and the arm which has been so vigorously exerted in vindication of human rights, should yet be found leagued on the side of oppression, and opposing their avowed principles!

Much, indeed, has been done by many benevolent individuals and societies, to abolish this disgraceful practice, and to improve the condition of those unhappy people, whom the ignorance or the avarice of our ancestors has bequeathed to us as slaves. Still, however, notwithstanding all the labours and eloquence which have been directed against it, the evil continues; still laws and practices exist, which loudly call for reform; still MORE THAN HALF A MILLION of our fellow creatures are deprived of that which, next to life, is the dearest birth-right of man. . . .

That enslaving, or continuing to hold in slavery, those who have forfeited their liberty by no crime, is contrary to the dictates both of justice and humanity, I trust few who hear me will be disposed to deny. . . . And what can be a more plain and indisputable principle of republican government, than that all the right which society possess over individuals, or one man over another, must be founded either upon contract, express or implied, or upon forfeiture by crime? But, are the Africans and their descendants enslaved upon either of these principles? Have they voluntarily surrendered their liberty to their whiter brethren? or have they forfeited their natural rights to it by the violation of any law? . . .

Pride, indeed, may contend, that these unhappy subjects of our oppression are an *inferior race of beings*; and are therefore assigned by the strictest justice to a depressed and servile station in society. But in what does this inferiority consist? In a difference of *complexion* and *figure*? Let the narrow and illiberal mind, who can advance such an argument, recollect whither it will carry him. In traversing the various regions of the earth, from the Equator to the Pole, we find an infinite diversity of shades in the complexion of men, from the darkest to the fairest hues. If, then, the proper station of Africa is that of servitude and depression, we must also contend, that every Portuguese and Spaniard is, though in a less degree, inferior to us, and should be subject to a measure of the same degradation. Nay, if the tints of colour be considered the test of human dignity, we may justly assume a haughty superiority over our southern brethren of this continent, and devise their subjugation. In short, upon this principle, where shall liberty end? or where shall slavery begin? . . .

But, perhaps, it will be suggested, that the Africans and their descendants are inferior to their whiter brethren in *intellectual capacity*, if not in complexion and figure. This is strongly asserted, but upon what ground? Because we do not see men who labour under every disadvantage, and who have every opening faculty blasted and destroyed by their depressed condition, signalize themselves as philosophers? Because we do not find men who are almost entirely cut off from every source of mental improvement, rising to literary honours? To suppose the Africans of an inferior radical character, because they have not thus distinguished themselves, is just as rational as to suppose every private citizen of an inferior species, who has not raised himself to the condition of royalty. But, the truth is, many of the negroes discover great ingenuity, notwithstanding their circumstances are so depressed, and so unfavourable to all cultivation. They become excellent mechanics and practical musicians, and, indeed, learn every thing their masters take the pains to teach them. And how far they might improve in this respect, were the same advantages conferred on them that freemen enjoy, is impossible for us to decide until the experiment be made. . . .

Again—Avarice may clamorously contend, that the *laws of property* justify slavery; and that every one has an undoubted right to whatever has been obtained by *fair purchase* or *regular descent*. To this demand the answer is plain. The right which every man has to his personal liberty is paramount to all the laws of property. The right which every one has to *himself* infinitely transcends all other human tenures. Of consequence, the latter can never be set in opposition to the former. I do not mean, at present, to decide the question, whether the possessors of slaves, when called upon by public authority to manumit them, should be indemnified for the loss they sustain. This is a separate question, and must be decided by a different tribunal from that before which I bring the general subject. All I contend for at present is, that no claims of property can ever justly interfere with, or be suffered to impede the operation of that noble and eternal principle, that "all men are endowed by their Creator with certain unalienable rights—and that among these are life, liberty, and the pursuit of happiness."[15]

These principles and remarks would doubtless appear self-evident to all, were the case of the unhappy Africans for a moment made our own.

Were it made a question, whether justice permitted the sable race of Guinea to carry us away captive from our own country, and from all its tender attachments, to their own land, and there enslave us and our posterity for ever;—were it made a question, I say, whether all this would be consistent with justice and humanity, one universal and clamourous negative would show how abhorrent the principle is from our minds, when not blinded by prejudice. Tell us, ye who were lately pining in AL-GERINE BONDAGE![16] tell us whether all the wretched sophistry of pride, or of avarice, could ever reconcile you to the chains of barbarians, or convince you that man had a right to oppress and injure man? . . .

Let none say, that, notwithstanding all these reasonings, the slaves are *happier* in a state of servitude, than they would be if set at liberty, especially when they are treated with lenity, and provided for in a comfortable manner. That there are different degrees of wretchedness among them, in different circumstances, no one can doubt: and when they fall into the hands of the humane and kind, their depression is less—far less miserable, than when the torture of whips, the pains of hunger and nakedness, and the unreasonable impositions of hard taskmasters, are added to servitude. On this account, I am happy in being able to say, that the lot of slaves among us is, in general, much more tolerable than that of those in some other parts even of our own country. But still they are both in bondage. However favoured the situation of either, they are both deprived of that blessing, in possession of which the barren rock has its joys, and without which Eden itself would be a gloomy scene. . . .

But higher laws than those of common justice and humanity may be urged against slavery. I mean THE LAWS OF GOD, revealed in scriptures of truth. This divine system, in which we profess to believe and to glory, teaches us, that *God has made of one blood all nations of men that dwell on the face of the whole earth.*[17] It teaches us, that, of whatever kindred or people, we are all children of the same common Father; dependent on the same mighty power; and candidates for the same glorious immortality. It teaches us, that we should do to all men whatever we, in like circumstances, would that they should do unto us. It teaches us, in a word, that love to man, and a constant pursuit of human happiness, is the sum of all social duty.—Principles these, which wage eternal war both with political and domestic slavery— Principles which forbid every species of domination, excepting that which is founded on consent, or which the welfare of society requires. . . .[18]

But in vain is a large proportion of mankind addressed on the principles of morality and religion. These they will seldom regard, as long as they suppose *interest* and *policy* to deliver different precepts. For the sake of such, therefore, I add, with the utmost confidence, that slavery is not more opposed to justice, humanity, and religion, than it is to the INTEREST of individuals, and to the TRUE POLICY and HAPPINESS of that society in which it is suffered to exist.

Slavery will always be found, in proportion to the extent and severity with which it prevails, to INJURE THE MORALS of a people. That it tends to produce, on the one hand, haughtiness, a spirit of domination, cruelty, and lewdness, among the whites, appears probable, upon the slightest consideration of the subject, and is abundantly proved by experience. And, on the other hand, that it has an equal tendency, to produce and cherish almost every species of vice, among the slaves themselves, none, I presume, will hesitate to admit. Should any have a remaining doubt whether this be the case, let them compare the state of morals in those parts of our country, in which slavery is either unknown, or exists in the most lenient form, with that which is exhibited in those states in which slaves are more numerous and more degraded. . . .

In this State, as well as in most others in the union, the testimony of a slave cannot be admitted in judicial process, excepting in a few cases. What is the ground of this law? The answer is obvious,—"SLAVERY DEBASES THE MIND, AND CORRUPTS THE MORAL CHARACTER." The unhappy victims of oppression, feeling themselves precluded by violence, from enjoying the benefits of society, neglect the social virtues. Finding their own rights habitually invaded, they soon learn to disregard the rights of others. Living perpetually under the frowns of power, they are insensibly taught the arts of deception, treachery, and fraud, until every moral feeling is blunted or destroyed. Hence slaves, in all ages and countries, have generally exhibited the most odious moral depravity. . . .

Nor has slavery a more mischievous effect on the morals of society, than it has on NATIONAL INDUSTRY, POPULATION, AND GENERAL IMPROVEMENT. Men not only become lazy and idle when they can make others the servile instruments of their will; but labour will soon be esteemed disreputable and degrading, when it is chiefly performed by slaves. And whatever diminishes industry, discourages population, and sows the seeds of social weakness and disorder. . . .

In this part of the United States, indeed, the pernicious effects of slavery are displayed in a comparatively moderate degree. But even in our

State they are distinctly perceptible. Even here we should be a happier and a wealthier people, were every labourer a freeman, and, of consequence, the product of every man's labour his own property. . . .

Many have been the proposals of benevolent men to remedy this grand evil, and to ameliorate the condition of the injured negroes. . . . Immediately to emancipate *seven hundred thousand* slaves,[19] and send them forth into society, with all the ignorance, habits, and vices of their degraded education about them, would probably produce effects more unhappy than any one is able to calculate or conceive. Nor does the plan appear much more plausible, which some have proposed, to collect, and send them back to the country from whence they or their fathers have been violently dragged; or, to form them into a colony, in some retired part of our own territory. . . .

Perhaps no method can be devised, to deliver our country from the evil in question, more safe, more promising, and more easy of execution, than one which has been partially adopted in some of the states, and hitherto with all the success that could have been expected. This plan is, to frame laws, which will bring about emancipation in a GRADUAL MANNER; which will, at the same time, PROVIDE FOR THE INTELLECTUAL AND MORAL CULTIVATION of slaves, that they may be prepared to exercise the rights, and discharge the duties of citizens, when liberty shall be given them; and which, having thus fitted them for the station, will confer upon them, in due time, the privileges and dignity of other freemen. By the operation of such a plan, it is easy to see that slavery, at no great distance of time, would be banished from the United States; the mischiefs attending an universal and immediate emancipation would be, in a great measure, if not entirely, prevented; and beings, who are now gnawing the vitals, and wasting the strength of the body politic, might be converted into wholesome and useful members of it. Say not that they are unfit for the rank of citizens, and can never be made honest and industrious members of the community. Say not that their ignorance and brutality must operate as everlasting bars against their being elevated to this station. All just reasoning abjures the flimsy pretext. Make them freemen; and they will soon be found to have the manners, the character, and the virtues of freemen. . . .

The time, I trust, is not far distant, when there shall be no slavery to lament—no oppression to oppose in the United States: when the EMANCIPATING SPIRIT of our Constitution shall go forth . . . when she shall proclaim, even to the stranger and the sojourner, the moment he sets his foot upon American earth, that the ground on which he treads is sacred to LIBERTY; and that the air which he breathes, nourishes FREEMEN ONLY:—when every being, who bears the name MAN, whatever complexion an equatorial Sun may have burnt on him, and with whatever solemn injustice his rights may have been infringed, shall enjoy the privileges, and be raised to the dignity which belong to the human character.

*   *   *

E. H. Smith, April 11, 1798

THE occasion of our present meeting is solemn and affecting, melancholy but joyful. We are convened to celebrate the triumphs of benevolence; but we are convened also to the renewed exhibition of the long, extensive, and malignant usurpations of civil and domestic tyranny. . . . The justice, the humanity, the policy, the interest, of the enslavers of men have been eloquently appealed to; but with partial success! A few have listened and reflected; a few have felt and acted; but the many have continued unmoved, have persevered in the practice of their cruelties. Yet, startled and confused, in the midst of their career, by the surrounding progress of emancipation, they dread inquiry, are less assured of their future success, and have mitigated their severity, or doubled their precautions. In this state of public sentiment, our duty is obvious and simple—to preserve the vivid recollection of the enormities which mark the reign of oppression; of the efforts which have been made to shorten or destroy it; of the motives which should compel us to proceed in this exalted labour: to disseminate the knowledge of them far and wide, to the young as well as to the old, to the enslaved as well as to the free; and, for ourselves, to act with gentleness but with firmness, with zeal but with prudence. . . .

. . . Whether we regard the political or the social condition of the States that have authorized slavery, whether we consider its effects on their happiness or their power, the conclusion is equally against it. The safety and durable felicity of a government depend absolutely on the attachment of its subjects or citizens; and attachment can only be founded on a sense of the blessings it confers. Power can never be steadily maintained, nor effectually exercised, for a long period, but from the united exertions of a whole nation. This union must flow from mutual confidence, of the people and the government, of the citizens in each other. The only solid basis of confidence is morality. The same means which perpetuate power, secure happiness. . . . The degree of power is diminished with its extent, as its security is by its injustice; and as no nation has hitherto attempted to obtain universal dominion on equitable principles, so none has hitherto been able to preserve what little it has gained. . . .

The fate of the practice of oppression has been similar to that of every other vice; the more it has been investigated, the less defensible, the more odious has it appeared. Plea after plea has been suggested; each, in its turn, has been controverted and set aside. Few slave-holders, capable of comprehending truth, have attempted to refute the reasonings by which the justice, the humanity, the policy of the slave-trade, and the subserviency of slavery to national and individual interest, have been disproved. Yet, so much are men the slaves of habit, so closely does selfishness cling to our bosoms, so difficult is error of eradication, that, soiled in these topics of defence, the advocates of slavery have resorted to another.—We admit, say they, that slavery is unjust, abominable; an outrage on humanity; contrary to all found maxims of policy; and hostile to the interests of a people: but, then, what shall we do? Most sincerely do we wish that this curse had never visited our country. But it is entailed upon us by our fathers; it is interwoven with every part of our social organization; and we can not erase the blot, without destroying the fabric. *All things are just, but all things are not expedient.*—Alas! how multiform is error! . . . But, if slavery be a curse, let not time be lost in attempting to remove it. If its sudden removal be dangerous, let it be gradually accomplished; but let it be accomplished. What strange reasoning is that which would persuade us to continue and increase a mischief, because it has existence at this moment!—O men, free to acknowledge your errors, but indolent to reform them, put, at length, the axe to the root of this tree of evil! If you have fear lest its sudden fall bury you in its ruins, proceed with caution! Twig after twig, branch after branch, shall decay and fall; and your grateful posterity shall, without danger, cast down the bare and withered trunk. . . .

. . . It is the fate of error to lose strength and consistency by every examination; that all its pleas shall regularly diminish in effect, as they regularly succeed to each other. The moment that the slave-holder acknowledged the injustice of slavery, that moment the slow, but certain, death-wound was inflicted upon it. The apologists for this pernicious system of domestic oppression, have now reached to the extremity of subterfuge. . . . [H]enceforward they must maintain by force, what they can not support by reason. But what is this charge of *injustice* which they exhibit so vehemently against the assertors of the rights of the innocent? We did not, say they, commence the system of slavery. We found it already established. The laws of our country authorized the possession of a property in human flesh. They have hitherto maintained us in it. Is it not unjust to deprive us of that which the social regulations, you would now change, have conferred upon us? Will you, at once, despoil us of that which we have purchased on the faith of these regulations? Are you prepared, by a single vote, and without any compensation, to destroy so large a portion of all our wealth? Does not the law equally protect property, whether it exist in animate or inanimate substance? whether it be clothed with the bestial or human form? Dare you commit so horrid an injustice?—Miserable sophisters! were the law to authorize you to enslave your fellow-freemen of one State, or one County, should you act justly in availing yourselves of its sanction? Were you born to the inheritance of an ample estate in money, the fruits of your fathers' repeated thefts, could you vindicate your conduct in withholding it from the rightful proprietors, by any law of descents? Shall the legislators of a great nation be denied the power, which pertains to every individual of that nation, of acknowledging their errors, and labouring to correct them? Shall the most evident and inestimable interests of a whole community, not only its present, but its future interests, require the discontinuance of a system dangerous to our security, hostile to our property, and pernicious to our morals, and shall the short-sighted selfishness of a small, or even a considerable part of that community, determine its permanence? But, what is this compensation which you are denied? Is not the constant labour of a slave, for fifteen, or for ten, years, a sufficient compensation for the care of protecting his infancy? Would the tyrants demand triple recompence for their injustice? Recompence they shall have, and thrice threefold,—but let them tremble in the expectation!

In the existing circumstances of society, encumbered as we are with this mighty evil, which slavery has cast upon us, we are only free to chuse, amid variety of embarrassments. There is no fear that even this factitious right of property, so much insisted on, will not be sufficiently respected. Alas! there is no hope but that it long continue triumphantly to oppose all the efforts of benevolence. But, were it justly insisted on, what demons of malignant cruelty paralize the senses and the reason of legislators? Do they not see the ruin which surrounds us? Are they unconscious of the poison which hovers over every roof, lurks in every house, and infects every cup? Wait they till the venders of pestilence, till the manufacturers of plagues, relinquish their productive and desolating craft, before they labour for the restoration of health, for the prevention of disease? . . . You, yes you, Legislators of America, you are the real upholders of slavery! You, yes you, Legislators of this Commonwealth, you foster and protect it here! Is it not recognized by your laws? and in the very face of your Constitution? of that instrument which you maintained by your arms, and sealed by your blood? Have not those laws authorized, systematized, and protected, and do they not now protect it? If you fear the clamors of the enslavers of men, or if you acknowledge the justice of their claims to compensation, it is you who sanction, you who uphold the crime. It is you who are deaf to the demands of justice, the sighs of humanity, the representations of policy, the calls of interest, the suggestions of expediency, the warning voice of domestic tranquility. It is you who shut the ear, who close the eye, who clench the hand, insensible to every motive which should most determine men to hear, to see, and to act. You perpetrate, you perpetuate, you immortalize, injustice. . . . The opposers of justice do not read, think, reason, feel, they do not so much as listen. They admit but one idea, that of gain from the labour of their slaves; they are occupied but with one care, that of maintaining their authority. And you nourish that gain, you cherish that care, you defend with double mounds that monstrous authority, at the hazard, if not with the sacrifice, of all the dearest interests of society, of its very existence. These you hazard, when the remedy is obvious, certain, easy to be obtained, and safe to be applied. Mad insensibility! the little interests of the moment, the gratifications of vanity, and the contests of passion, a market, a palace, or a strip of land, engross your thoughts and dissipate your treasures, while the welfare of a nation sleeps unregarded, while thousands of your fellow-beings, children of the same father, and inheritors of the same destiny, eat the bitter bread of slavery, writhe under the lash of cruelty, and sink into the untimely grave amid the taunts of oppression!—Amen! so be it! and so shall be the retribution!

The conduct of men conscious of their villainy, is always and every where the same. Accused, they attempt their justification; but, failing here, they drive to overwhelm with censure those who have detected their baseness, and called upon them to repair their injustice. Their last efforts are directed to the destruction of the subjects of their oppression, in the vain hope of palliating its enormity, by proving it to have been merited. . . . Incapable of vindicating themselves, or of effectually misrepresenting the purity of our motives, the encouragers of slavery have fallen on the miserable Africans; as though their vices and their follies constituted a reason for subjecting them to bondage, and bending them with reiterated wrong. Shallow subterfuge! feeble malice! Every motive urged against them ought to interest us in their behalf. Are they dull and stupid, it is ours to startle them into thought, and rouze them to inquiry; are they ignorant, it is ours to cultivate and instruct them; base, ours to elevate; vicious, ours to reclaim them. The more forlorn and hopeless their condition, the more energetic and persevering should be our efforts. The measure of our benevolence should be capacious as their wants; and our zeal commensurate with their insensibility. Stupidity, ignorance, folly, vice, have each its several remedy; and our security as well as interest, our duty as well as happiness, demand the application. What must be the texture of his heart who can find reason in the ignorance, in the vices, and in the sufferings of men, in all that most can render them objects of compassion and of charity, for insuring that ignorance, augmenting those vices, and adding to these sufferings the yoke of bondage, and the sting of torture? Call you him man, or demon?

The experience of many years, evidence palpable to the most hardened and obstinate sense, has demonstrated the capacity of the Blacks. The very vices of which they stand so bitterly accused, demonstrate it. They, like all men else, are the creatures of education, of example, of circumstance, of external impressions. Make them outcasts and vagabonds, thrust them into the society of drunkards and of thieves, shut from them the fair book and salutary light of knowledge, degrade them into brutes, and trample them in the dust, and you must expect them to be vile and wretched, dissolute and lawless, base and stupid. . . .

But, not withstanding the degraded condition of the Africans, and their descendants, among us,—a condition to which they have been reduced, or in which they have been retained, by those who reproach them with it, and would offer it as an excuse for their own inhumanity and injustice,—still they exhibit many examples of humble, but of cheering virtue. We not only see them irreproachably employed in various mechanic occupations, but, in some few instances, elevated to the illustrious offices of instructors of learning, and inculcators of morality. The desk, and the pulpit, have witnessed their triumphs over all the efforts of blind and malignant prejudice. Already they begin to feel their own worth as men; already are they impressed with some just sense of the nature of those exertions which are making in their behalf; already have they attained to some conception of that prudent and virtuous conduct which is the best reward for all our toils; already may they challenge the palm from many of their whiter brethren. Perceive you not that spirit of improvement, slow though it be, yet visible, which diffuses itself among them? Observe you not their growing knowledge, their increasing industry, their softening manners, their correcter morals? Hear you not that sigh, wakened by your benevolent sympathy? Mark you not that tear of grateful joy, silently descending? See you not that sable figure, that cast himself at your feet, that kisses your hand, that clasps your knees, "fathers and benefactors of our race," that exclaim "the sons of Africa feel your virtue at their souls;—their hearts, their hands, their lives, are devoted to your service."

"Go! hapless progeny of a violated parent! cultivate peace, order, knowledge. Let your patience grow with your wrongs. Let your hearts learn forgiveness, your hands labour for your tyrants, your lives refute their calumnies. Go! assured, that, as for us, we have well considered what awaits us,—the extent of surrounding obstacles, and their duration, and have resolved, never to quench our zeal, to withhold our care, to intermit our labours, never to drop the language of persuasion, and forge the tone of justice, till we behold you disenthralled of bonds, reinstated in your rights, blessed with science, and adorned with virtue."

Sources: Samuel Miller, *A Discourse Delivered April 12, 1797, at the Request of and before the New-York Society for the Promoting the Manumission of Slaves, Protecting Such of Them as Have Been or May Be Liberated* (New York, 1797); E. H. Smith, *Discourse, Delivered April 11, 1798, at the Request of and before the New-York Society for Promoting the Manumission of Slaves, and Protecting Such of Them as Have Been or May Be Liberated* (New York, 1798).

F. Gradual Abolition Act, 1799

In an achievement at once partial and profound, New York finally enacted a gradual abolition law in March 1799. Efforts to pass an emancipation had failed to clear the state senate in each of the previous two years. After laboring over the precise details, the upper and lower houses of the state legislature reached consensus in March 1799. When Governor Jay and the other members of the Council of Revision gave their consent, gradual abolition became the official policy of New York. After July 4, 1799, the lengthy process of transforming a former slave society into a free state could begin in earnest.

Political conditions for abolition were ripe in 1799. The slaveholding regions of the Hudson Valley and Long Island, which had most consistently sought to preserve slavery, were losing ground in their fight against abolition, or at least to secure direct financial compensation for the anticipated loss of slave labor. New York City's growing delegation was stalwart in its support for abolition, as were representatives from newer northern and western counties. These former frontier regions saw their proportion of the legislature increase dramatically when the state decided to expanded the legislature in 1796. In these newer counties, there were virtually no slaves or free blacks. These regions had little interest in maintaining the institution of slavery and steadfastly opposed proposals for compensating distant slaveholders for the losses they allegedly would incur as a result of gradual abolition. Thus, a major stumbling block to emancipation was removed.

The bill that passed followed a formula for manumission that Pennsylvania had established in 1780 and that had been the working model in New York ever since. Granting immediate freedom to people already enslaved never received serious consideration in the New York legislature.[20] Under the 1799 law, only children born to enslaved mothers after July 4,

1799, would be deemed free. Those children, however, were required to serve their mothers' masters well into adulthood, in essence cushioning the blow of emancipation to slaveholders and dulling the blade used to break the shackles of slavery. The law included several provisions regarding the registration and maintenance of children born under the terms of the law. Considerable attention was given to who would bear the financial cost of raising those children that white masters did not wish to retain as servants. In an age during which state government spending was quite low and local governments were held accountable for the upkeep of the poor, assigning responsibility for the maintenance of free children was a matter of no small importance to lawmakers.

Despite the law's severe shortcomings, the ultimate goal of the law was unmistakable. An institution that had grown deep roots in New York's soil over the previous 170 years was forced into permanent decline. The actual pace of emancipation and the quality of freedom to be experienced by black New Yorkers would be determined in the next century.

Laws typically contain many revealing technicalities; this law is no exception. There are several questions to consider when examining the 1799 gradual emancipation law: Why did New York commit itself to this form of gradual emancipation? Whose interests did the legislature try to protect most? Why were males and females treated differently in this legislation? Why was there no mention of race, color, or the future status of the people ultimately freed by this law? Would this law have satisfied the critics and supporters of emancipation whom you encountered in documents B, C, D, and E?

* * *

Be it enacted . . . That any child born of a slave within this state after the fourth day of July next shall be deemed and adjudged to be born free: *Provided nevertheless,* That such child shall be the servant of the legal proprietor of his or her mother until such servant, if a male, shall arrive at the age of twenty-eight years, and if a female, at the age of twenty-five years.

And be it further enacted, That such proprietor, his, her or their heirs or assigns, shall be entitled to the service of such child until he or she shall arrive to the age aforesaid, in the same manner as if such child had been bound to service by the overseers of the poor.[21]

And be it further enacted, That every person being an inhabitant of this state who shall be entitled to the service of a child born after the fourth day of July as aforesaid, shall, within nine months after the birth of such child, cause to be delivered to the clerk of the city or town whereof such person shall be an inhabitant, a certificate in writing containing the name and addition of such master or mistress, and the name, age and sex of every child so born, which certificate shall be by the said clerk recorded in a book to be by him for that purpose provided, which record shall be good and sufficient evidence of the age of such child; and the clerk of such city or town shall receive from said person twelve cents for every child so registered; and if any such person neglects to make a return of every such child as aforesaid to said clerk within nine months after the birth thereof, such person shall forfeit and pay five dollars for every such offence, to be sued for and recovered by the clerk of the city or town in which such person resides, the one half for his own use and the remainder for the use of the poor of the said city or town: *Provided nevertheless*, that it shall be and is hereby made the duty of the town clerk to register the certificate of any such child at any time after nine months from its birth; and every master or mistress, masters or mistresses of every such child shall forfeit and pay the sum of one dollar for every month he, she or they shall neglect to deliver such certificate to the town clerk.

And be it further enacted, That the person entitled to such service may, nevertheless, within one year after the birth of such child, elect to abandon his or her right to such service, by a notification of the same from under his or her hand, and lodged with the clerk of the town or city where the owner of the mother of any such child may reside; in which case every child abandoned as aforesaid shall be considered as paupers of the respective town or city where the proprietor or owner of the mother of such child may reside at the time of its birth; and liable to be bound out by the overseers of the poor on the same terms and conditions that the children of paupers were subject to before the passing of this act.

And be it further enacted, That every child abandoned as aforesaid shall be supported and maintained till bound out by the overseers of the poor as aforesaid, at the expence of this state: *Provided however*, That the said support does not exceed three dollars and fifty cents per month for each child; and the comptroller is hereby authorized and directed to draw his warrant on the treasurer of this state for the amount of such account, not exceeding the allowance above prescribed.[22] . . . *And provided also*, That the person so abandoning as aforesaid, shall, at his own expence, support and maintain every such child till it arrives at the age of one year, and every owner omitting to give notice in due form as aforesaid shall be answerable for the maintenance of every such child until the arrival of the respective periods of servitude specified in the first section of this act.

And be it further enacted, That it shall be lawful for the owner of any slave, immediately after the passing of this act, to manumit such slave by a certificate for that purpose under his hand and seal.

Source: Chap. 62, "An Act for the gradual abolition of Slavery," March 29, 1799, in *Laws of the State of New-York, Passed at the Twenty-Second Meeting of the Legislature Begun . . . the Second Day of January, 1799* (Albany, 1799), 721–723.

G. African American Political Oration, 1809

The free black population of New York City tripled between 1790 and 1800 and more than doubled again during the course of the decade after the gradual emancipation statute.[23] Indeed, slavery declined much faster in New York than would have been the case if the only path to freedom had been the law itself. Running away, negotiating for release from bondage, and private manumissions contributed to the growth of free black communities, especially in Manhattan, the state's burgeoning port, to which many newly free rural African Americans migrated.

African Americans in New York City seized both the opportunity and the necessity of building their own institutions. Black New Yorkers founded several churches in the late eighteenth and early nineteenth centuries to service the spiritual and social needs of the community free of the second-class status accorded them in white churches. Black New Yorkers also established mutual aid and relief societies to care for members of the community impoverished as a result of illness or death. Among these organizations was the Wilberforce Philanthropic Association, named in honor of William Wilberforce (1759–1833), a leading voice in Britain's Parliament for the abolition of the slave trade and, later, for the abolition of slavery throughout the British Empire.

Black self-help organizations had another function besides tending to community members in need. These societies also proudly asserted the presence of the free black community in the polity and public life of New York City. Thus, African Americans marked the anniversaries of historic milestones such as America's abolition of the slave trade (January 1, 1808) with public speeches like the one below, as well as with parades. Black New Yorkers asserted their rights of citizenship and their right to the streets. Such activities often alarmed not only openly racist whites but also their alleged allies in the white philanthropic community. The NYMS fretted that such assertions of autonomy would alienate the broader public. Such activities also undermined NYMS authority over the black community, as African Americans demonstrated that they were not the subordinated clients of white philanthropy.

Nothing in the gradual abolition law denied blacks access to the same voting rights under the same terms as white New Yorkers (see document A). As the following speech indicates, black New Yorkers took seriously their rights as voters, as well as the partisan divisions that had emerged both locally and nationally during the 1790s. Even though the 1799 vote in New York's legislature for the gradual abolition had not reflected division between the state's Republicans and Federalists, black New Yorkers did not view their interests in politically neutral terms. African American New Yorkers identified their interests with the Federalist Party for a variety of reasons. Revered Federalist figures such as New Yorkers John Jay and Alexander Hamilton (see the introduction to document E) had championed the cause of manumission. Although comfortable with social hierarchy rather than democracy, Federalist Party politicians viewed the relatively small free black community as political allies, while viewing the potential masses of white voters as a threat to social and political order.

The Republican Party, more populist in orientation, took a dim view of any black claim to equality. Nationally, the Republicans were the party of Thomas Jefferson and James Madison, Southern slaveholders who, despite some personal misgivings about slavery, identified their political fortunes with slavery and its expansion to the south and the west. Moreover, Jefferson had publicly expressed his belief in alleged black racial inferiority and the incompatibility of free blacks and free whites in American society, hoping instead that African Americans would be settled someplace else, such as Africa. As president, he also vigorously pursued the isolation of Haiti, the Caribbean republic founded by former French slaves.

Why did Joseph Sidney, whose speech appears below, discuss politics and black political participation in this oration marking the end of U.S. participation in the African slave trade? What specific reasons did he give for black support of the Federalist Party? How did Sidney regard the abolition of slavery? What other advice did he give to his fellow African Americans in this speech? Do you see any reason why this speech might have worried members of the NYMS? Compare this speech to the white antislavery orations excerpted in document E.

* * *

Friends, Countrymen, and Fellow-Citizens,
DEEPLY affected with the various sensations and emotions which the occasion is so peculiarly calculated to excite, I rise to address you. We, together with our fellow-citizens at large, this day celebrate the commencement of a *new year*. . . . But in addition to the general joy which this day
occasions to the American empire, and in which *we*, in common with our
fellow-citizens, participate; I say, in addition to the cause of general rejoicing, the return of this day opens to *us*, my countrymen, a newly discovered source of joy, of which ourselves, and the sympathizing friends of
suffering humanity, are the exclusive partakers. On this auspicious day,
we celebrate the anniversary of that glorious era, which, in these United
States, put a period to that inhuman species of traffic, that, with relent-
less cruelty, had so long plundered unhappy *Afric* of her sons.

My friends, 'tis not an illusion of fancy, 'tis a truth recorded in the annals, and enrolled among the statutes, of the United States, that no
African, nor a single individual descended from *African* ancestors, shall
henceforth be imported into this country as a slave.—What a stride is this
towards the total abolition of slavery in America! what a progress towards the consummation of our fondest hopes! what a presage that the
exertions, the good wishes, and the prayers of the humane and benevolent, will finally triumph!—And with what transports of joy may we not
hail the return of this memorable, this auspicious day, this jubilee of freedom!! . . .

Since, then, the *Slave-trade* is by law for ever abolished, may we not,
my countrymen, without incurring imputation of rashness or presumption, look forward to the period when slavery, in this land of freedom,
will be unheard of and unknown? Yes! this is what we most ardently desire, what we fondly anticipate, and what, I think, we may with certainty
expect to realize.

The *immediate emancipation* of all our brethren in the United States,
is an event which we cannot reasonably expect; and, perhaps, ought not
to desire. For it is a lamentable fact, that our brethren in the South are in
a state of deplorable ignorance. Uneducated as they are, and unacquainted with every thing except the plantations on which they toil, and
from which they are never suffered to depart, it is incredible that they can
possess sufficient information to render their *immediate* emancipation a
blessing either to themselves, or to society at large. But a want of information, on the part of our southern brethren, cannot be urged as an argument against their *gradual* emancipation. . . .

New-York, and several other of the middle states, actuated by a spirit similar to that which animated the sages of New-England, have obeyed the voice of humanity; and are gradually abolishing slavery. Would to God that I could say the same of the southern states! but truth compels me to observe, that in the southern section of the United States, and particularly in Virginia, slavery still exists in all its horrors, unrelieved by the slightest degree of mitigation!

Alas! what is man, and of what is he formed! How contradictory in his professions! how strangely inconsistent in his actions!

No people in the world make louder pretensions to "*liberty, equality, and the rights of man,*" than the people of the South! And yet, strange as it may appear, there is no spot in the United States, where oppression reigns with such unlimited sway! . . .

Heaven grant that some WILBERFORCE, some champion of African freedom, whose warm, whose expanded, whose benevolent heart, is capable of beating in unison with their sufferings, may arise in Virginia; assert the long neglected and abused rights of Afric's sons; and institute that plan of gradual emancipation, which has been so successfully adopted and pursued in New-England and New-York! . . .

But I shall wave these reflections, and proceed, my countrymen, to suggest to you, some of those duties which have devolved on us, in consequence of our having recently obtained our freedom, and which appear to me peculiarly proper to be called to mind, on the present occasion.

Freedom has broken down that wall of separation, which formerly distinguished our rights and duties, from those of the white inhabitants. Our rights and duties have, of course, assimilated to theirs. And, permit me to add, that the judicious exercise of these rights, and the punctual performance of these duties, involve considerations, which are all-important, both to ourselves and to our country.

Among the most valuable of our newly acquired rights, is that of *suffrage*. This right is particularly valuable, inasmuch as it enables us to express our choice with respect to our rulers. Good rulers are a blessing, but bad rulers are, and must be considered, a curse to any nation. The *right* of suffrage, brings with it a *duty* of the highest obligation. For as this *right* gives us the power of voting, so it devolves on us the indispensable *duty*, of bestowing our votes on those, and on those only, whose talents, and whose political, moral, and religious principles, will most effectually promote the best interests of America.

My countrymen, you cannot be unacquainted with the fact, that there has existed, for some time past, in our country, two great political parties. At the head of the *Federal Republican Party*[24] was the immortal WASHINGTON, the Father of his country. Hamilton, Jay, Adams, Pinckney, King, and Pickering,[25] together with most of our old revolutionary officers and soldiers, were among the illustrious characters, who attached themselves, through principle and patriotism, to this party.

After achieving the independence of their country, this distinguished band of patriots formed the *federal* constitution; and from that circumstance, were denominated *Federalists*, or *Federal Republicans*. The single object of this party was, to preserve the liberty, to promote the happiness, to increase the prosperity, and to extend the respectability of the United States. Being satisfied as to the immense advantages which are to be derived from commerce, and knowing, that the interests of the middle and eastern States are intimately connected with it, this party, while in office, gave to commerce every possible encouragement. To this end, a small navy was built to protect our vessels from the armed ships of foreign nations. So long as Federalists remained in office, so long this country enjoyed an uninterrupted state of increasing prosperity—And so long as this happy state of things continued, so long did agriculture and commerce unite hand in hand, to diffuse their riches, and to extend their blessings to every class of citizens. . . .

Such was the state of our affairs, when the *Anti-federal* or *Democratic party*, consisting of a set of ambitious, designing, and office-seeking men, first adventured from its native cave of filth and darkness, into open day. A number of abandoned printers, mostly foreigners, enlisted in the service of this party: and from that moment, commenced a persecution against *federal men, and federal measures;* which persecution, for cool and malignant cruelty, can never be exceeded. To destroy the reputation of distinguished federalists, calumnies the most vile, were daily circulated through the country. Even the virtues and services of WASHINGTON did not prove a shield sufficiently broad, to protect him against the envenomed shafts of malice. . . .

Thus feeding on detraction, and fattening on the mangled reputation of federalists, the democratic party became a majority—and thus their leader, Mr. Jefferson, became *the President of the United States.* And from that inauspicious day, though the current could not instantly leave its wonted channel, yet, the tide of American prosperity soon ceased to flow, and all our goodly prospects vanished.

One of the first acts of the present administration, was to *displace* those revolutionary officers whom Washington had placed in office, as a small reward for all their labours, toils, and dangers. Washington placed in office real patriots and statesmen, who fought to procure our independence; others have bestowed these high dignities on *foreigners*, probably as a reward for their *insurrection* and *slander*.

Our infant navy, the protector of our commerce, fell an early victim to the *fury* of the *Virginian Junto*. Nor could that *fury* be appeased, until our commerce itself had received the stroke of death. Yes, my countrymen! an *unlimited embargo*, wielded by the mad democracy of the southern states, has, like the besom of destruction, swept our commerce from the ocean! . . .[26]

Nor is it in the eastern states only, that this rash measure is felt. We all, my countrymen, most sensibly feel it. The poor and the labouring class of people, in every state, are peculiarly its victims. Yes, we do feel, and we shall indubitably continue more and more to feel, its hard and partial operation. Nor do we find a probability of relief, in the partiality of our democratic rulers for undeserving emigrants to our shores. . . .

. . . Now, the southern states, which comprise the great body of the democratic party in our country, being hostile to commerce, and this party having laid the embargo, and being still the ruling party, we cannot rationally expect that commerce will again flourish, until the general government shall be administered by federalists, the real friends of commerce, and the genuine disciples of Washington. It is not within the limits of probability, that a *change of measures for the better*, will be effected, in any other way than by a *change of men*.

How important then, that we, my countrymen, should unite our efforts with those of our *Federal friends*, in endeavouring to bring about this desirable change—this change, so all-important to commerce, to our own best interests, and to the prosperity and glory of our country!

But there is another consideration, which appears to me worthy of being suggested. The great hotbed of democracy[27] is Virginia, and the other southern states. All the democratic members of Congress, who have any considerable influence in directing the machine of government, belong to the South. And almost all the free inhabitants of the southern section of the United States, are of the democratic party. And these are the very people who hold our African brethren in bondage. These people, therefore, are the *enemies* of our *rights*. And as the democrats in this state are acting with these, our *enemies*, we should not only be wanting in duty to ourselves, but we should be destitute of the *spirit* of *freemen*, were we not to turn our backs upon democracy, and unite with our *federal friends*, to place men in office possessed of humanity, justice, firmness, and *American* patriotism.

Besides, is the great idol of democracy[28] *our* friend? That he is not, is evident; else he would respect the rights of our African brethren; several hundreds of whom he keeps as *slaves* on his plantations. What did WASHINGTON? This illustrious and humane man, feeling that slavery was incompatible with the principles for which he fought, most generously emancipated every slave that he owned, and gave to each a portion sufficiently large to answer his exigencies, until he could procure employment.[29]

Can you then, my countrymen, for a moment hesitate in choosing between your enemies and your friends? between slavery and freedom? Will you run into the camp of your enemies? Will you flock to the *Slavery-pole* of democracy?—Or will you patriotically rally round the *standard of liberty?*—a standard which was erected by IMMORTAL WASHINGTON; and which has been consecrated by the blood of the MARTYRED HAMILTON.[30]

Before I conclude, permit me, my countrymen, to impress on your minds a duty, which it is our highest interest ever to observe. This duty consists in endeavouring unceasingly, by pure and upright conduct, to convince the world that we are not only capable of self-government, but also of becoming honourable citizens and useful members of society. Let it be our business to demonstrate to the conviction, even of the enemies of our freedom, that *sobriety, honesty,* and *industry,* are among the distinguishing traits of our characters; that we know too well the value of liberty, ever to abuse her inestimable privileges; and that although the "Ethiopian cannot change his *skin,*" yet his *heart* may, nevertheless, become an habitation for all the virtues which ever adorn the human character.

A conduct, on our part, in all respects dignified and proper, will effectually put to silence every cavil which may be offered against African emancipation, and must eventually convert our enemies into friends.

I need scarcely to remind you, my countrymen, on an occasion like this, that all those whose exertions have, in any degree, contributed to bring about the interesting event which we this day celebrate, and, in particular, "The Manumission Society of the City of New-York," whose kind interference has greatly ameliorated our condition, are all eminently entitled to our warmest gratitude.—Long may they all be remembered, and amply rewarded for their "labours of love!"—May they have the satisfaction of realizing that their efforts for our happiness and usefulness in life, have been crowned with success! And may we always be possessed of *that evidence* of gratitude to these our benefactors, which springs from *pure* and *upright conduct!*

And let me add, that such a *conduct* is the best evidence which we can possibly produce, of that gratitude which we owe to the GOD OF MERCIES, for his interposition in our behalf. HE has ever been our kindest benefactor; and, as such, we owe him a debt of gratitude, which we can never cancel. While we therefore, my countrymen, in unison, lift up our voices in praise and thanksgiving to this GOD of mercies, let us supplicate, that by a more general extension of freedom and of pure patriotism throughout our country, every return of this anniversary may be accompanied with additional causes for JOY AND REJOICING.

Source: Joseph Sidney, *An Oration Commemorative of the Abolition of the Slave Trade in the United States; Delivered Before the Wilberforce Philanthropic Association of the City of New-York, on the Second of January, 1809* (New York, 1809).

H. An Act Regulating Black Suffrage, 1811

For twelve years, gradual abolition proceeded without any overt statutory restrictions on black voting in state elections. Race and suffrage were not legally linked. Then, in 1811, the state legislature passed a law designed in large part to harass potential black voters. All blacks seeking to vote had to prove that they were, in fact, free men, not slaves. Moreover, would-be black voters were required to pay the fees associated with registering proof of eligibility.

The law reflected racial and political calculations. Competition between New York's Federalist and Republican Parties was intense and cutthroat in the early years of the nineteenth century. The law, passed by a Republican state legislature, served the partisan purpose of reducing the size of the African American voting bloc, which was particularly large in New York City.

The law, formally titled an "Act to Prevent Frauds and Perjuries at Elections," purported to combat voter fraud, specifically the participation of ineligible voters in New York's elections. Partisanship combined with the state's complicated voter eligibility requirements (see document A) to make illegal voting a commonplace. One historian notes, "In their competition for votes, Federalists and Republicans made voting fraud an integral part of New York politics and illegally expanded the electorate."[31] In other words, the parties encouraged supporters who fell short of the state's property requirements to vote anyway. Democracy spread—or at least the number of voters increased—due to loose enforcement of the law. The lengthy first section of the law provided the wording of oaths to be administered to would-be voters who were challenged as not qualified to vote—based on insufficient property, citizenship, age, or having already cast a ballot elsewhere—in a particular election. Several further clauses of this anticorruption law, sponsored by Republicans, who had returned to control of the state legislature in 1811 after briefly being supplanted by the Federalists, specifically targeted African Americans. Illegally voting pro-Republican Irish immigrants were not similarly singled out.

Endorsed again in 1813 and modified in 1815, the law was designed to depress black voter turnout by raising obstacles not confronting other voters. The law also set an ominous precedent for future revisions of the voter qualifications.

The law claimed to target slaves. What evidence is there that legitimate black voters were actually the target? In what ways did this law make it more difficult for African Americans to vote? Compare this document to documents A, B, and C. Were the provisions of this law consistent with earlier thinking on black voting?

*   *   *

III. *And be it further enacted*, That whenever any black or mulatto person shall present himself to vote at any election in this state, he shall produce to the inspectors or persons conducting such election, a certificate of his freedom, under the hand and seal of any one of the clerks of the counties of this state, or under the hand of a clerk of any town within this state.

IV. *And be it further enacted*, That it shall and may be lawful for every black or mulatto person within this state, to make and exhibit proof before any one of the justices of the supreme court, any mayor, recorder, or judge of any court of common pleas within this state, of his freedom, such proof to be reduced to writing and exhibited in the county where the person producing the same shall reside. And provided the said justice, mayor, recorder or judge be of opinion, that the person producing the same is free according to the laws of this state, he shall certify the same in writing, stating therein a brief description of the person so adjudged to be free, his age, the place of his birth, and the time when he became free, as nearly as the same can be ascertained, and it shall be the duty of the said black or mulatto person to cause the said proof to be filed, and the certificate of the said justice, mayor, recorder or judge, to be entered of record, either in the clerk's office of the said county, or in the clerk's office of some one of the towns in the said county, and a copy of the said record, certified under the hand of the clerk in whose office the same shall be recorded, shall be the certificate of freedom required by the preceding section, to be produced at all such elections, and unless such certificate shall be produced, no black or mulatto person shall be permitted to vote at any such election.

V. *And be it further enacted*, That the officer taking such proof shall be entitled, as a compensation for taking the same, twenty-five cents, and for giving such certificate, the further sum of twelve and an half cents, to be paid by the person applying for the same; and the clerk for filing such proof and recording such certificate shall be entitled to such fees as are usual for like services.

VI. *And be it further enacted*, That every black or mulatto person producing such certificate, shall, if required by any one of the inspectors of such election, or if challenged by an elector, make oath or affirmation, that he is the identical person named and intended in such certificate, and if any person shall be guilty of false swearing in taking such oath or affirmation, he shall be adjudged guilty of wilful and corrupt perjury, and shall upon conviction thereof, suffer the punishment now directed by law in cases of wilful and corrupt perjury.

VII. *And be it further enacted*, That it shall be lawful for such justice of the supreme court, mayor, recorder, or judge, on application by any black or mulatto person, to issue a summons, requiring any person residing within the county wherein such application shall be made, to appear and make affidavit of all such matters and things as he or she may know concerning the freedom of such black or mulatto person; and whenever any person shall refuse to appear and make affidavit in pursuance of such summons, a warrant shall issue from such justice, mayor, recorder or judge, to compel his or her appearance, and if on his or her appearance, he or she shall refuse to make affidavit or affirmation, as the case may require, of the facts which may be within his or her knowledge, touching the matter to be enquired into, he or she may be committed to the common gaol of the county, there to remain without bail or mainprize[32] for a term not exceeding one calendar month.

Source: "Act to prevent frauds and perjuries at elections, and to prevent slaves from voting," in *Laws of the State of New-York Passed at the Thirty-Fourth Session of the Legislature, Begun and Held at the City for Albany the Twenty-Ninth Day of January, 1811* (Albany, 1811), 370–373.

I. Act Declaring 1827 as the End of Slavery in New York, 1817

Although second to last among states north of Maryland to commence gradual abolition,[33] New York was the first to pass a law fixing a precise date for slavery to end. Yet even this final round of abolition was gradual. New York's law declared all slaves free as of July 4, 1827. Children born in the interim ten years would have to serve their mothers' masters until age twenty-one. Children born between 1799 and 1817 meanwhile had to continue serving their mothers' masters under the provisions of the original gradual abolition law. The last servant would receive his or her full freedom under the terms of this act in 1848.

As with all New York's laws regarding slavery and defining African American rights, a mix of humanitarian, political, and selfish motives was at work. One of the gravest dangers facing African Americans in New York after the passage of the gradual abolition law in 1799 was kidnapping and sale out of state. Although selling slaves out of New York State had been illegal since 1788, untold numbers— perhaps several thousand—of African Americans were shipped out of state in the early nineteenth century. With slavery slowly but inevitably approaching its end, unscrupulous whites had an incentive to cash in on the value of their human property by selling them southward, to regions of the country where slavery was thriving. The nominally free children of slaves could be sold south by the masters who inherited the right to their service under the provisions of the 1799 law. Moreover, free blacks were targets of kidnappers, who could ship their unwilling human cargo as far away as New Orleans or Havana, Cuba. Judges also had discretion to transport convicted slave felons out of state.

Both New York's free black community and the Manumission Society fought against these insidious threats to meaningful emancipation. Some kidnappings could be prevented when blacks and whites caught wind of particular plots. Ultimately, the NYMS concluded that a definitive emancipation was necessary to counteract these conditions.

Daniel Tompkins, the Republican governor of New York and an NYMS member, began advocating a new abolition law in 1812. He did not receive satisfaction until 1817, just before he took up his new post as vice president of the United States. Tompkins argued that the law would answer "the dictates of humanity" while enhancing "the reputation of the state." He also noted, accurately, that slaveholders paid a low price for the state's humanitarianism: since the law effectuated the freedom of slaves born before July 5, 1799, many masters would be losing only the services of women and men no longer in their prime working years. Moreover, the law would not go into effect for a decade.[34]

The law reflected the ambiguity of even this final abolition. The provision fixing a date for slavery's end came at the end of a lengthy law affirming and qualifying various aspects of existing slave and manumission law. African Americans would continue to be subject to a separate set of rules governing their peculiar, albeit now officially transitional, status. The state remained preoccupied with the public costs of emancipation, including the freeing of elderly slaves and cases in which the free children of slave mothers might become burdens of public charity, should their masters choose to abandon them. Meanwhile, the law in theory offered protections to New York's blacks from the rest of the slave-trading and slaveholding world.

Compare this law to the original gradual abolition law (document F). Why did New York repeatedly choose July 4 as the day for changing its laws governing slavery? How effectively did this new law address the problems faced by African American New Yorkers and their white allies in the NYMS? Why did the law so carefully reaffirm previous slave law at such great length, introducing the clause for the final abolition of slavery only at the very end?

* * *

I. . . . every negro, mulatto or mustee, within this . . . state, who is now a slave, shall continue such, unless such slave shall be manumitted according to law; and that the baptizing of any such slave, shall not be deemed a manumission of such slave: *Provided always*, that every person born a slave within the United States, and who hath heretofore been, or shall hereafter be manumitted, shall be deemed, taken and adjudged to have been capable of taking by devise, descent or otherwise, all estates, real or personal, in the same manner as if he or she had been born free, and shall and may at all times hereafter, and in all courts, have the like remedy for the recovery of such estates, or for injuries done to the same, as if such person had been born free; but this act shall not be construed to create a cause of action against the former owner of such slave or his representatives.

II. . . . all marriages contracted, or which may hereafter be contracted, wherein one or both of the parties was, were or may be slaves, shall be considered equally valid as though the parties thereto were free, and the child or children of any such marriage shall be deemed legitimate: *Provided*, that nothing in this section contained, shall be deemed or construed to manumit any such slave or slaves.

III. . . . no slave shall be a witness in any case, except for or against another slave, in criminal cases.

IV. *And be it further enacted*, That every child born of a slave within this state, after the fourth day of July, in the year of our Lord one thousand seven hundred and ninety-nine, shall be free, but shall remain the servant of the owner of his or her mother, and the executors, administrators or assigns of such owner, in the same manner as if such child had been bound to service by the overseers of the poor, and shall continue in such service, if a male, until the age of twenty-eight years, and if a female, until the age of twenty-five years; and that every child born of a slave within this state after the passing of this act, shall remain a servant as aforesaid until the age of twenty-one years and no longer.

V. . . . every person entitled to the services of any child, under and by virtue of this act, shall, before such child arrive at the age of eighteen years, teach such child, or cause to be taught, to read, so that it may be able to read the holy scriptures, or shall give such child, between the ages of ten and eighteen, four quarters schooling; and if the person so entitled to such service, shall neglect to cause such child so to be taught, or to have such schooling, then such child shall be released from its servitude when it shall arrive at the age of eighteen years, any thing herein contained to the contrary notwithstanding: *And further*, that in every such case, the overseers of the poor of the city or town in which such child shall or may be or reside, may, and it shall be their duty, forthwith to bind out such child, until it shall have arrived at the age of twenty-one years. . . .

VII. . . . it shall be lawful for the owner of any slave, to manumit such slave, by last will and testament, or by any such instrument in writing under his hand; but if such slave, at the time of such manumission, be above the age of forty-five years, or within that age and not of sufficient ability to provide for his or her support, the person manumitting such slave, and his or her heirs, executors and administrators, shall respectively be liable for the maintenance of the slave so manumitted, in case such slave shall become a charge to any city or town within this state. . . . *Provided nevertheless,* that if the owner of such slave, at or immediately before the time of manumission, shall obtain a certificate . . . certifying that such slave appears to be under the age of forty-five years, and of sufficient ability to provide for himself or herself, or that the parent or parents of such slave is or are willing and able to maintain and provide therefor. . . .

[*IX through XII ban the importation of slaves into New York and define the exceptions to this rule, originally established by state law in 1785.*]

XIII. . . . if any person shall send to sea, or export, or attempt to export from this state, or send or carry out of, or attempt to send or carry out of this state, except as is by this act provided, any slave or servant, every person so exporting, or attempting to export, or sending or carrying out of this state, or attempting to export, or sending or carrying out of this state, such slave or servant; and every person aiding or consenting to such exportation, or attempt to export; or to such sending or carrying out of this state, or to such attempt to send or carry out, shall be deemed guilty of a public offence, and forfeit the sum of five hundred dollars. . . .

XIV. . . . it shall be lawful for every person who shall have resided ten years within this state, and who shall be about to remove permanently therefrom, to carry with him or her every such slave as shall have been the property of such person during the ten years next preceding. . . .

XV. . . . it shall be lawful for any person not an inhabitant of this state, who shall be travelling to or from, or passing through this state, to bring with him any slave, and take such slave with him from this state, provided such slave shall not reside or continue in this state more than nine months; and it shall also be lawful for any inhabitant of this state, going [on] a journey to any other part of the United States, to carry with him or her any such slave or servant as aforesaid: but such inhabitant shall bring back such slave or servant, and in default thereof shall be deemed to have committed a public offence. . . .

[*Sections XVI. and XVII. extend the principle of gradual abolition to slaves born after July 4, 1799, who were brought into the state with their masters.*]

XXII. . . . if any person shall employ, harbor, conceal or entertain, any slave, or such servant as aforesaid, knowing such slave or servant to belong to any other person, without the consent of such owner, such person shall forfeit to the owner of such slave or servant, the sum of twelve dollars and fifty cents for every twenty-four hours. . . .

XXIII. . . . if any person shall trade or traffic with any such slave or servant, knowing them to be such, either in buying or selling, without the consent of the owner of such slave, or the master or mistress of such servant, such person shall, for every such offence, forfeit treble the value of the articles so bought or sold. . . .

XXIX. . . . if any person shall, without due process of law, seize and forcibly confine, or inveigle or kidnap, any negro, mulatto, mustee or other person of color, with intent to send or carry him out of this state against his will, or shall conspire with any person or persons, or aid, abet, assist, hire, command or procure any other person to commit the said offence, or any captain of a vessel or other person, shall sell or dispose of in any foreign port or place any negro, mulatto, mustee or other person of color, and shall be duly convicted of any of the said offences . . . shall be fined or imprisoned, or both. . . .

Whereas persons of color, owing service or labor in other states, sometimes secrete themselves on board of vessels while such vessels are lying in the ports or harbors of other states . . .

XXX. *Be it further enacted,* That it shall be lawful for all such captains or commanders . . . to seize such person of color and take him before any magistrate of a county . . . and upon proof by oath or affirmation, to the satisfaction of the said magistrate or justice, that such person of color did, without his consent or knowledge, secrete himself on board his vessel, such magistrate or justice shall give a certificate . . . which shall be sufficient warrant to send or carry such person of color to the port or place from which such person was so brought: *Provided,* that nothing in this section contained shall prevent such person of color, when brought before such magistrate or justice, from proving he does not owe service or labor in any other state.

XXXII. . . . That every negro, mulatto or mustee within this state, born before the fourth of July, one thousand seven hundred and ninety-nine shall, from and after the fourth day of July, one thousand eight-hundred and twenty-seven, be free.

Source: "An Act relative to slaves and servants," March 31, 1817, in *Laws of the State of New-York Passed at the Fortieth Session of the Legislature, Begun and Held at the City of Albany, the Fifth Day of November, 1816* (Albany, 1817), 136–144.

Part II

The Convention of 1821
and the Politics of Disfranchisement

Context

Four decades after their birth, both the United States and New York State arrived at a crossroads. An older set of political, economic, and social arrangements no longer seemed adequate to cope with present conflicts or future ambitions. Directly and indirectly, the constitutions written by the state's and the nation's founding fathers became fragile. Nationally, the Republicans had all but vanquished their Federalist political rivals. But regional rivalry not only threatened to undermine whatever good feelings the War of 1812 and the decline of partisanship inspired. The Missouri Territory's application for statehood under a proslaveholding constitution precipitated a bitter North-South split in Congress that threatened the political nation.

In fast-growing New York, competition for political power created a shifting constellation of alliances that kept alive much of the heat generated by the old Federalist-Republican rivalry, even as the ranks of the Federalist Party continued to thin. Such open competition fueled demands that the state reconsider constitutional provisions written by a previous generation to limit the right to vote to men of property. The nation's and the state's economic ambitions matched the political ambitions of leading and ordinary men alike. Governor DeWitt Clinton, who already had spearheaded plans for New York City to swallow the whole of Manhattan Island, now set his sights on building a canal that would traverse his state from Lake Erie to the Hudson River, a plan that would stimulate massive commercial and geographic expansion for both state and nation.

Meanwhile, as the date for New York's final abolition approached, congressional debates about the future of slavery in the Missouri Territory had their ominous parallels in the popular politics of white male enfranchisement and the hardening rhetoric of racism. The crises, conflicts, and transformations underway by the 1820s set the terms for the impending disfranchisement of New York's black citizens and the institutionalization of "jim crow New York."

Like slavery, the persistence into the nineteenth century of property qualifications to determine voting rights seemed, in the eyes of many Northerners, to contradict core American political values. Ironically, the 1800 election of Southern slaveholder Thomas Jefferson as president of the United States legitimated a more democratic vision of American politics, in which the common man should rule rather than show political deference to those who occupied the heights of the social and economic hierarchy.

Even in Federalist strongholds such as Connecticut, citizens increasingly clamored to liberalize voting eligibility and pressed against traditional political and cultural authorities, embodied in the alliance between the Congregational Church and the Federalist Party. Yet, in the early years of the nineteenth century, political competition and political corruption were the more likely methods for increasing voter participation in the Northeast. Federalists and Republicans sought to bring supporters to the polls, whether or not they actually qualified. For example, Republicans tapped into the growing pool of immigrants in New York City, while rural upstate Federalist landowners marshaled the votes of tenants. The momentum for more fundamental changes in the rights of suffrage increased during the following decade. In Connecticut, opponents of property-holding suffrage restrictions achieved a series of breakthrough victories in the years after the War of 1812, culminating in the 1818 Constitutional Convention.

While New Yorkers may have been inspired in part by constitutional conventions in neighboring Connecticut and Massachusetts, New York's 1821 convention was very much a product of unique personalities and partisan divisions that emerged during the early nineteenth century. The rivalry between Federalists and Republicans was increasingly eclipsed by a split within the dominant Republican Party. Martin Van Buren, the ambitious political operative and state attorney general from Ostego County, built a network of so-called Bucktail Republicans to challenge the political dominance of Republican governor DeWitt Clinton. To stave off the Bucktails, the Clintonians reached out to Federalists for support. This alliance was enough to secure Clinton's reelection to the governor's office in 1820. But it also angered Bucktails, who rallied popular support for a constitutional convention to rewrite the state's constitution, revise the suffrage requirements, and, they hoped, drive their rivals from power.

The statewide referendum for the proposed constitutional convention won easily. Eligibility to vote in the referendum was not governed by the property-holding restrictions that defined the electorate in ordinary state elections. The expanded criteria allowed males age twenty-one or older to vote even without significant property, as long as they paid taxes, worked on the state roads, served in the state militia, or were legally exempted from these responsibilities. As in the 1777 state constitution, no mention was made of race or skin color as a defining requirement.

The convention's massive Bucktail Republican majority and the clear public mandate for expanding voting rights in a new constitution masked other important divisions among the delegates and in the state as a whole. The Bucktail majority contained a range of political temperaments, with some of the delegates much more favorably disposed toward universal white male suffrage than others. Moderates such as Martin Van Buren and U.S. Vice President Daniel Tompkins may have held the balance of power, but their views were not uncontested from the left or the right. Indeed, though small in number, the Federalist faction contained some of the most prominent and learned delegates in attendance. Although these avowedly conservative delegates did not have the votes to stop the convention's majority from enfranchising white men or disfranchising black ones, they did possess the ability to frame the convention's debates in revealing ways. Deeming race a fundamental qualification for citizenship would not be done quietly or without demands for an explanation.[1]

Another division that bore directly on the debate over citizenship and African American voting rights concerned the role of New York City in the future political landscape of the state. The city's population had expanded at a rapid rate during the first two decades of the nineteenth century. That population was swelled both by people from the countryside moving to the city and through immigration, primarily from Ireland and England. The city also had a large free black population, although as the city grew, African Americans made up an ever smaller proportion of the total—just under 9 percent in 1820.[2] In any case, the outline of New York City's future was clear to many observers: manufacturing would take its place alongside shipping and commerce to shape the city's economic life. Thus, the city would be home to masses of working men with little accumulated wealth or property.

Any plan to change the rules governing suffrage, including the reduction or elimination of property-holding requirements, could dramatically affect the city's political power and influence within the state. At the convention, delegates from around the state and from various political factions repeatedly employed the image of New York City to make arguments on a variety of questions, including suffrage and the apportionment of representation to the state legislature. Delegates determined to disfranchise African Americans imputed to blacks the worst characteristics and alleged vices of city-dwellers to make their case against full black citizenship. Republicans also reminded one another that black voters had been reliable supporters of their Federalist—and, by implication, Clintonian—rivals.

The politics of race also was on the minds of convention delegates because the crisis provoked by Missouri's admission to the Union as a slave state had only recently been resolved. During the Missouri crisis, New York's representatives in Congress as well as state politicians had played an active role in Northern opposition to the Missouri constitution—which not only supported slavery but also denied the rights of equal citizenship to free blacks. Despite its ultimate resolution, the crisis had alarmed many observers. Former president Thomas Jefferson, in retirement at his Monticello plantation, likened it to "a fire-bell in the night," as it portended future threats to Southern slavery and national unity. Aspiring political leaders such as New York's Martin Van Buren saw the crisis as a threat to the ascendant national Republican Party, which was predicated on alliances between like-minded politicians in the North and South and their commitment to a popular politics based on commercial growth and geographical expansion. By 1820, slavery was well on its way to extinction as a practical reality and an internal political issue in New York; but the growth of Southern slavery permanently threatened national political harmony, unless Northerners could be persuaded not to challenge Southern prerogatives.

The demise of slavery in New York and its continued strength in the South and portions of the West intensified the relationship between race and culture. The emergence of freedom and the changing character of racism had significant political implications for New York's African American population. Nowhere was slavery's slow, now certain end more obvious than in New York City. Indeed, by 1821, Manhattan hosted the largest single community of free blacks in the entire Western Hemisphere. As documents in the part I indicate, this community built its own cultural institutions and asserted its own voice in public affairs. In the eyes of some whites, black people exercising citizenly independence grew to be simply "intolerable."

In the nineteenth century, opponents of black equality used, in new and powerful ways, stereotypes and ridicule traditionally employed to police the cultural and political boundaries between black and white. Both popular culture and intellectual discourse legitimated the politics of racial resentment. Although the origins of racism as a system of thought stretch back several centuries, the language and the methods of allegedly enlightened science employed to justify social distinctions and explain physical difference were relatively new. In 1785, Thomas Jefferson expressed a suspicion that blacks and whites were so inherently different that the two populations could not possibly live in freedom together. At first repudiated by many American religious and intellectual commentators, Jefferson's racist suspicions developed into scientific and sociological orthodoxy in the nineteenth century. National groups were presumed to have inborn characteristics that defined individual members. By mid-century, the most extreme racial theorists went so far as to argue that blacks and whites had been created separately or were part of a separate species.

Intellectualized racism and popular racism mirrored each other. Free blacks were mercilessly mocked in print, while some elite well-wishers sought to have free blacks colonized in Africa. Thus, a blend of personal prejudice and political opportunism placed the concept of equal citizenship under extreme duress as the delegates gathered in Albany to rewrite New York's constitution.

The presumption that suffrage reform applied only to men further weakened the position of free blacks at the convention. Women did not have the right to vote in New York. Moreover, emerging ideas in the early Republic cast women as a separate class of citizens, who supported public virtue through their private roles as mothers and wives but not as direct participants in public life. At the convention, condescending remarks about the special role of women in society were less relevant than the related assumption that women, like children, were a dependent group whose exclusion from political life was entirely normal. Legal limitations on the property-holding rights of married women underscored that dependency. Delegates argued that, given the unfranchised status of women, children, and foreigners, proposed rules denying black males the vote were nothing extraordinary. The exclusion of women, by this circular logic, proved the legitimacy of setting other sorts of limits on access to voting rights. At the same time, advocacy of militia service, another white male prerogative, as a qualification for voting established an implicit link between gendered and racial exclusion at the convention.

Extending the right of suffrage and black disfranchisement were hardly the only items on the agenda of the 1821 New York Constitutional Convention. The 1777 document was to receive a thorough revision, with committees appointed to reconsider the three major branches of state government. High on the convention's reform agenda was the need to abolish two of the most unusual and least democratic features of New York's constitution—the manner in which appointments to state government offices were made and the Council of Revision, which reviewed all legislation before it could become law.

Nevertheless, an expansion of the rights of suffrage was at the heart of the convention's business: indeed, one historian has commented that the 1821 New York Constitutional Convention "was the seat of one of the great suffrage debates in American history."[3] And, as it turned out, redefining the relationship between race, citizenship, and voting rights lay at the heart of that discussion. It is easier to sort out who won and who lost as a result of the convention's debates than to determine precisely what combination of racism and political self-interest drove the convention to deny one of the most crucial components of citizenship to African American New Yorkers. Whatever the case, a new era of mass-participation white democracy dawned, even as an era of abolition and strides toward black citizenship came to a close.

Chronology

1818   The Nation: Connecticut enacts new state constitution, including clause denying the franchise to African Americans not already voting.

1819   The Nation: Missouri application for statehood, with a proslavery constitution, provokes national controversy.

1820   The Nation: After much difficulty, U.S. Congress forges Missouri Compromise.

1821   New York: State legislature authorizes a state constitutional convention, contingent on approval in a statewide referendum (March); New York voters provide overwhelming endorsement of a constitutional convention (April); elections for convention delegates conducted (June); convention commences in Albany (August); convention adjourns after approving a new constitution (November).

1822   New York: Voters ratify the new constitution in a January election.

Figure 2 Map of New York State in 1824
Reflecting the state's dramatic expansion, New York assumed its modern political contours during the first decades of the nineteenth century. [Map of the State
of New York in 1824, based on A. Finley, *Map of the State of New York*
(Philadelphia, 1824).] *Courtesy of the Boston College Center for Media and Instructional Technology.*

J. Connecticut Constitution
Confirms Disfranchisement, 1818

In the first three decades of the nineteenth century, several states called constitutional conventions to revise substantially their state charters. Among the most important results of this constitutional reform was the sweeping away of property requirements that had governed voter eligibility since colonial times. Doing so proved to be a critical step toward enfranchising all adult white men throughout the nation. The process of extending the full rights of citizenship to white men was coupled with a restriction of those same rights for African American men. In essence, citizenship was racialized more or less explicitly in several states. At the end of the antebellum era, African American males could vote under the same terms as white men in just five states—Massachusetts, Rhode Island, Maine, New Hampshire, and Vermont, all New England states, the last three with tiny black populations.

The political context stimulating constitutional revision differed from state to state. New York's neighbor to the east, Connecticut, was one of the first to rewrite its constitution, doing so in 1818.[4] Republicans in this Federalist political stronghold had pushed for a democratized suffrage for more than a decade. The Federalist Party successfully resisted attacks on property requirements that had survived the American Revolution virtually unchanged. But the Federalists' vigorous opposition to the War of 1812 and continued opposition to the separation of church and state provided a new opening for reform. In addition to a greater democracy, reformers sought to undermine elite power by instituting secret ballots. Property requirements were also viewed as a tool of manipulation and corruption because officials could enforce such requirements selectively. Moreover, an expanded franchise, some thought, would discourage many of Connecticut's young men from emigrating westward. At the same time that reformers challenged property requirements, laws passed by the Connecticut legislature in 1814 and 1818 began to define citizenship and voting rights in racially exclusive terms.

The groundswell of support for reform led to new franchise laws and the calling of a constitutional convention to confirm them. The Connecticut delegates to that meeting sanctioned new franchise rules in dry, legal language that was relatively conservative. Connecticut replaced old property-holding requirements with rules that permitted white males of twenty-one years of age or older to vote, as long as they paid taxes or served in the militia. The convention voted down an attempt to have the word *white* removed from the constitution's elections clause. As written, the new Connecticut constitution did not appear to strip already-voting African Americans of their rights but rather to limit the new version of voting rights to white males. But as Connecticut's legal code already had made it virtually impossible for blacks to vote, the constitution confirmed disfranchisement.

Connecticut's push for franchise reforms set a precedent for neighboring New York and Massachusetts. Indeed, the Connecticut constitution would be cited by both proponents and opponents of black enfranchisement in New York three years later. As with New York's constitution, the Connecticut constitution signaled the beginning of a period of legal discrimination, segregation, and public violence against blacks in the state.[5]

What principles did Connecticut use to determine eligibility for voting? Did the law explicitly bar blacks from voting in future elections? Why didn't the law strip the right to vote from anyone previously holding that right? Compare the language of the Connecticut constitution to New York's 1811 law (document H) regarding black voting rights.

* * *

Article VI. Of the Qualifications of Electors

Sect. 1. All persons who have been, or shall hereafter, previous to the ratification of this constitution, be admitted freemen, according to the existing laws of this state, shall be electors.

Sect. 2. Every white male citizen of the United States, who shall have gained a settlement in this state, attained the age of twenty-one years, and resided in the town in which he may offer himself to be admitted to the privilege of an elector, at least six months preceding; and have a freehold estate of the yearly value of seven dollars in this state; or having been enrolled in the militia, shall have performed military duty therein, for the term of one year next preceding the time he shall offer himself for admission, or being liable thereto, shall have been, by authority of law, excused therefrom; or shall have paid a state tax within the year next preceding the time he shall present himself for such admission; and shall sustain a good moral character, shall, on his taking such oath as may be prescribed by law, be an elector.

Sect. 3. The privileges of an elector shall be forfeited, by a conviction of bribery, forgery, perjury, duelling, fraudulent bankruptcy, theft, or other offence for which an infamous punishment is inflicted.

Sect. 4. Every elector shall be eligible to any office in this state, except in cases provided for in this constitution.

Sect. 5. The selectmen, and town clerk, of the several towns, shall decide on the qualifications of electors, at such times, and in such manner as may be prescribed by law.

Sect. 6. Laws shall be made to support the privilege of free suffrage, prescribing the manner of regulating and conducting meetings of the electors, and prohibiting, under adequate penalties, all undue influence therein, from power, bribery, tumult, and other improper conduct.

Sect. 7. In all elections of officers of the state, or members of the general assembly, the votes of electors shall be by ballot.

Sect. 8. At all the elections of officers of the state, or members of the general assembly, the electors shall be privileged from arrest, during their attendance upon, and going to, and returning from the same, on any civil process.

Sect. 9. The meetings of the electors for the election of the several state officers, by law annually to be elected, and members of the general assembly of this state, shall be holden on the first Monday of April in each year.

Source: *Journal of the Proceedings of the Convention of Delegates Convened at Hartford, August 26, 1818, for the Purpose of Forming a Constitution of Civil Government for the People of the State of Connecticut* (Hartford, 1901), 111–113.

K. Resolution Opposing the Missouri Constitution, 1820

The 1819 application of Missouri for statehood touched off a major national political crisis. Missouri intended to maintain slavery as a legal institution. The first state to be created from the massive Louisiana Purchase,[6] Missouri's proposed admission to the United States threatened to set a dangerous precedent for future state creation. Of more immediate concern, Missouri's entry as the twenty-third state would tip the even balance in the U.S. Senate between those states that had outlawed slavery, or at least were well on their way to doing so, and those states where slavery's legal future remained secure. The Senate was politically crucial to both North and South because the Northern states had more representatives in the House of Representatives, while Southerners had controlled the presidency for all but four years since 1789.

Missouri's statehood application exposed deep sectional rifts between North and South. Attempts to impose a gradual abolition plan on Missouri as a condition for statehood attracted overwhelming support from Northern members of the House of Representatives and even greater opposition from Southern representatives. With help from a handful of Northern senators, the gradual abolition amendments that passed the House failed in the Senate. Ultimately, Congress found a way out of the crisis, by admitting Maine, which had previously been part of Massachusetts, as a nonslave state and Missouri as a slave state, unencumbered by restrictions on slavery. In addition, Congress agreed to exclude slavery from any other states carved from the Louisiana Purchase, except those below a line that began at Missouri's southern border and extended westward.

New York's representatives in Washington, D.C., played an active role in the crisis. It was New York congressman James Tallmadge Jr. who had proposed the controversial amendment to ban further slaves from coming to Missouri and freeing those born after Missouri achieved statehood at age twenty-five. And it was New York Senator Rufus King who most forcefully defended the antislavery amendments in the upper house of congress.

The Empire State's antislavery position in the national political arena appeared to have broad political support at home in New York. A massive 117–4 majority of the New York State assembly supported a resolution instructing the state's congressional delegation to oppose the Missouri constitution, which not only permitted slavery but also denied free blacks the right to move to Missouri.

Despite the compromise reached in Washington, D.C., the Missouri crisis served as a sobering reminder of how delicately the nation was stitched together and how readily slavery might slice through that stitching. Leading New York politician Martin Van Buren, who in 1821 embarked on a national political career that would eventually make him U.S. president, worked assiduously to solidify a Republican Party alliance between Northerners and Southerners, in large part by working to protect Southern slaveholding interests and muting public debate over slavery.

Why did New York's politicians so overwhelmingly oppose Missouri's constitution and take a leading role in the Missouri crisis? Was such a stance consistent with laws concerning and practices toward African Americans in New York over the previous forty-five years? Were Van Buren's concerns about the division between North and South warranted?

*   *   *

THURSDAY, NOVEMBER 23, 1820

Mr. Sanford communicated the following resolutions, passed by the legislature of the state of New York; which were read.

State of New York
In Assembly, *November* 13, 1820

Whereas the legislature of this state, at the last session, did instruct their Senators, and request their Representatives in Congress, to oppose the admission, as a state, into the Union, [of] any territory not comprised within the original boundaries of the United States, without making the prohibition of slavery therein an indispensable condition of admission:

And whereas this legislature is impressed with the correctness of the sentiments so communicated to our Senators and Representatives; therefor,

Resolved, (if the honorable the Senate concur herein,)[7] That this legislature does approve of the principles contained in the resolutions of the last session; and further, if the provisions contained in any proposed constitution of a new state, deny to any citizens of the existing states the privileges and immunities of citizens of such new state, that such proposed constitution should not be accepted or confirmed; the same, in the opinion of this legislature, being void by the constitution of the United States. And that our Senators be instructed, and our Representatives in Congress be requested, to use their utmost exertions to prevent the acceptance and confirmation of any such constitution.

Resolved, (if the honorable the Senate concur herein,) That the President of the Senate and the Speaker of the Assembly do cause copies of these resolutions, duly certified by them, to be transmitted to the Senators and Representatives in Congress from this state.

Ordered, That the Clerk deliver a copy of the preceding resolutions to the honorable the Senate, and request their concurrence to the same.

PETER SHARPE, *Speaker*

Attest, Dl. Van du Weyder, *Clerk of Assembly*

State of New York
In Senate, *November* 15, 1820

Resolved, That the Senate do concur with the honorable the Assembly, in their said resolutions and recitals.

Ordered, That the Clerk deliver a copy of said resolutions of concurrence to the honorable the Assembly.

JOHN TAYLER, *President*

Attest, JOHN F. BACON, *Clerk of Senate*

Source: *Journal of the Senate of the United States of America, Being the Second Session of the Sixteenth Congress: Begun and Held, at the City of Washington. November 13, 1820, and in the Forty-Fifth Year of the Independence of the Said States* (Washington, D.C., 1820), 26–27.

L. Antiblack Article,
National Advocate, 1821

In the weeks before the constitutional convention opened, political activists and editors around New York wrote in anticipation of the coming debates. The state's newspapers were filled with various essays, letters, and articles detailing the issues at stake and the arguments that would be pressed. Not all preconvention journalism, however, focused explicitly on questions of policy and matters of administration. Quite often in that summer's newspapers, New Yorkers prepared for the convention by indirectly debating race, suffrage, and citizenship.

On the pages of Mordecai Noah's *National Advocate*, advocacy of black disfranchisement was at first submerged as part of a more wideranging attack on the African American presence in Manhattan's public life. Noah was a particularly complex figure in the creation of "jim crow New York." A pioneering Jewish public servant, he was the sheriff of New York City in addition to serving as editor of the *National Advocate*.[8] At least one theater historian also considers Noah "the father of Negro minstrelsy."[9] Noah's preeminent Tammany, pro-Republican newspaper repeatedly mocked and denounced the growing black population of New York City during the summer of 1821.

As the convention convened in Albany, the *Advocate*'s rhetoric grew more inflammatory. This article is illustrative of Noah's sustained criticism of the presence of free African Americans in New York's public spaces. The *Advocate*'s editor was particularly concerned with the African Grove Theatre and its growing popularity in the late summer of 1821. This anxiety carried over after the success of suffrage restriction, as Noah and other Tammany supporters grew even bolder in their attacks on the theater and other free black institutions. A year later, Noah encouraged white attacks on the black theater, which resulted in the August 10, 1822, riot.

By the time the 1821 convention sat down to debate the suffrage clause in the constitution, Noah had perfected his argument, claiming that the "intolerable" free black community, with its theaters, promenades, and accompanying claims to urban equality, merited disfranchisement. In a September 24 editorial addressed to Tammany delegates in Albany and Tammany readers in Manhattan, Noah asserted that "it is perfectly ridiculous to give [blacks] the right of suffrage—a right which they cannot value, and which in this city, particularly in the federal wards, is a mere vendible article." Here, Noah united partisan fears of black Federalism and traditional notions of African American dependency.[10]

How did Noah seek to delegitimate black claims for political equality? How are we to account for the peculiar mix of dialect and fantasy at work in these articles? How does this antiblack text compare to earlier anti-abolition writings? (See document C.)

*   *   *

Africans—People of colour generally are very imitative, quick in their conceptions and rapid in execution; but it is in the lighter pursuits requiring no intensity of thought or depth of reflection. It may be questioned whether they could succeed in the abstruse sciences, though they have, nevertheless, some fancy and humour, and the domestics of respectable families are complete facsimiles of the different branches of it, not only in dress but in habits and manners.

Among the number of ice cream gardens in this city, there was none in which the sable race could find admission and refreshment. Their modicum of pleasure was taken on Sunday evening, when the black dandys and dandizettes, after attending meeting, occupied the side walks in Broadway, and slowly lounged towards their different homes. As their number increased, and their consequence strengthened; partly from high wages, high living, and the elective franchise; it was considered necessary to have a place of amusement for them exclusively.—Accordingly, a garden has been opened somewhere back of the hospital[11] called African Grove; not spicy as those of Arabia, (but let that pass) at which the ebony lads and lasses could obtain ice cream, ice punch, and hear music from the big drum and clarionet. The little boxes in this garden were filled with black beauties "making night hideous"; and it was not an uninteresting sight to observe the entree of a happy pair. The gentleman, with his wool nicely combed, and his face shining through a coat of sweet oil, borrowed from the castors; cravat tight to suffocation, having the double faculty of widening the mouth and giving a remarkable protuberance to the eyes; blue coat fashionably cut; red ribbon and a bunch of pinchback seals; wide pantaloons; shining boots, gloves, and a tippy rattan. The lady, with her pink kid slippers; her fine Leghorn, cambric dress, with open work; corsets well fitted; reticule, hanging on her arm. Thus accoutered and caparisoned, these black fashionables saunter up and down the garden, in all the pride of liberty and unconsciousness of want. In their address; salutations; familiar phrases; and compliments; their imitative faculties are best exhibited. After a vile concerto by the garden band, a company of four in a box commenced conversation, having disposed of a glass of ice cream each.

"You like music, Miss? Can't say I like it much. I once could play Paddy Cary, on the piano; our young ladies learnt me. Did you eber hear Phillips sing, 'Is dare a heart dat neber lov'd'? I sing xactly like him; Harry tell us some news. De Greeks are gone to war wid de Turks. O! Dat's bery clever; and our gentlemen said at dinner yesterday, dat de Greeks had taken Constantinople, and all de wives of de Dey of Algiers. O shocking! Vell, Miss, ven is de happy day; ven vill you enter de matrimony state? Dat's my business: Gentlemen musn't meddle with dese delicate tings. Beg pardon Miss. O! no offence—Harry, who did you vote for at de election? De fedrilists to be sure; I never wotes for de mob. Our gentlemen brought home tickets and after dinner, ve all vent and woted. Miss how you like to go to de springs? I shouldn't like it; too many negers from de suthard, and such crowd of folks, that decent people can get no refreshments."

Thus they run the rounds of fashions; ape their masters and mistresses in everything; talk of projected matches; rehearse the news of the kitchen, and the follies of the day; and bating the "tincture of their skins," are as well qualified to move in the *haut ton*, as many of the white dandies and butterflies, who flutter in the sun shine. They fear no Missouri plot; care for no political rights; happy in being permitted to dress fashionable, walk the streets, visit African Grove, and talk scandal.

Source: "Africans," *National Advocate*, August 3, 1821.

M. Extended Excerpts from the Convention of 1821

The frankness with which delegates addressed the future of full citizenship for African American New Yorkers is what makes the transcript of the 1821 Constitutional Convention such an appealing and appalling document. Delegates attempting to couple white enfranchisement with black disfranchisement masked neither their intentions nor their motives. Defenders of African American civil rights made their own racial and class biases clear. Delegates, moreover, conducted this racial debate within the context of conflicting assessments about the desirability and limitations of democracy itself. Those who dissented from the main thrust of the convention did so openly, forcing the architects of New York's new white man's democracy to articulate with clarity their own views. Thus, the convention's transcript rewards careful reading and ambitious interpretations by students of American political culture, as well as students of race and society.

The constitutional degradation of black citizenship was a drama with a prologue, three main acts, and an epilogue. The prologue to the actual debate of black suffrage established procedural and philosophical precedents for subsequent proposals. The liberal rules for selecting delegates to the convention foreshadowed the movement to jettison property holding as a qualification for voting. The creation of committees to draft language for various parts of the proposed constitution set the stage for the ensuing debate on suffrage. So, too, did the discussion of whether the constitution was the proper place to confirm or even accelerate the state's 1817 commitment to end slavery in New York.

Direct debate over the franchise and race began on September 19, when the suffrage committee reported to the convention as a whole its draft proposal for defining voter eligibility. The proposal to extend suffrage for white male citizens—and only white male citizens—quickly became a debate about the place of free blacks in New York's expanding political landscape, occupying the attention of delegates for much of September 19 and September 20.

Once the convention rejected a strict racial bar to nonwhite voting, a second act opened, in which the convention delegates discussed over the course of several days the nature of New York's representative government and whether the existing property-holding standards for voting served any useful purpose. The debates spanning from September 21 to September 28 at times prompted sharp, revealing references to race. As important, these debates confirmed an emerging consensus on a refurbished, nineteenth-century definition of citizenship. Generous notions of participation in and contributions to the civic life and civil order left scant grounds for excluding male New Yorkers from the right to vote. Tax paying, militia service, even work on the public roads appeared to entitle a man to help select his representatives.

The third act of the drama, primarily taking place on October 6 and October 8, indicated that opponents of black rights had suffered only a temporary setback in mid-September. Advocates of racial disfranchisement sought a political middle ground from which to take measures to strip blacks of the vote. In the middle act of the drama, conservatives had taken great pains to explain the virtues of property-holding requirements; the dangers to the future political order of vice-ridden urban masses collecting in New York City, the state's burgeoning metropolis; and the evils of so-called universal suffrage. Nevertheless, these conservatives often had advanced the most persuasive defense of existing black rights, strenuously objecting to color as grounds for qualifying or disqualifying voters. Conservatives saw the tables turned on them when the issue of black voting returned to the convention's agenda. Even as the convention thoroughly repudiated the freehold standard for white voting, it affixed this standard on potential black voters, effectively disfranchising existing black voters and making it impossible for other African Americans to help swell the ranks of the expanding electorate. Appeals to history and morality were impotent in the face of racial animus and political and philosophical expediency.

Having approved the broad outlines and some of the details of disfranchisement, the convention, in the epilogue to the drama, filled in the final details of voting rights, confirmed its commitment to racial

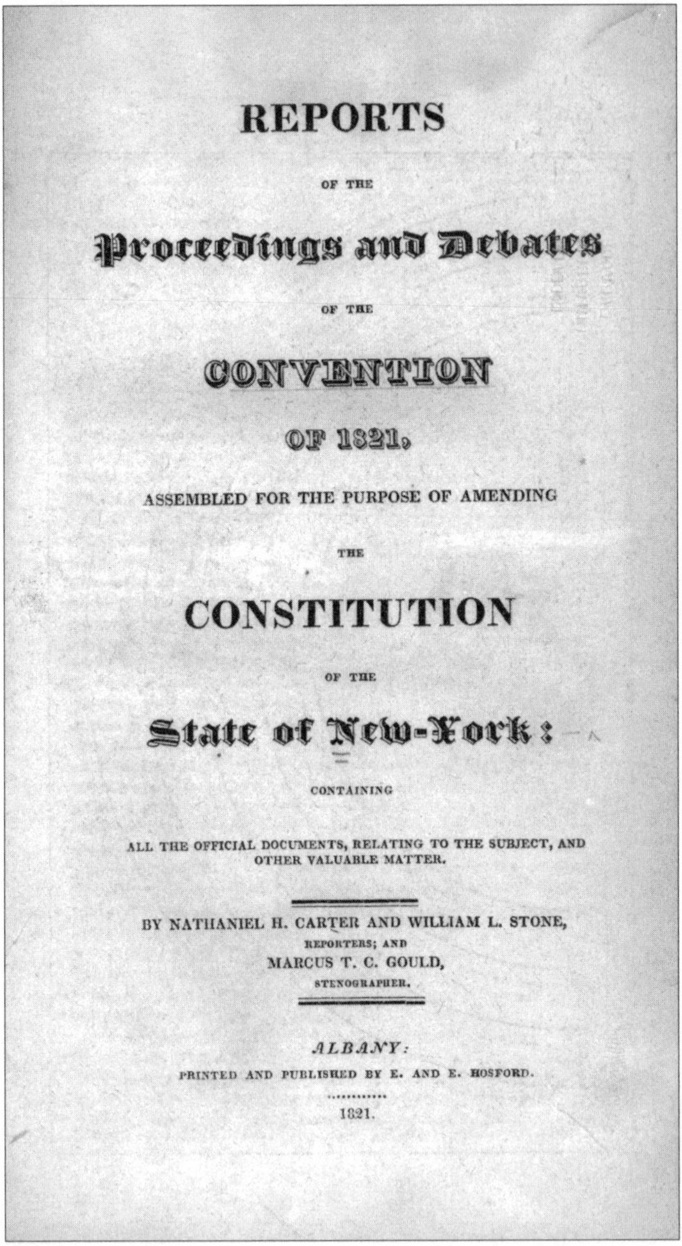

REPORTS

OF THE

Proceedings and Debates

OF THE

CONVENTION

OF 1821,

ASSEMBLED FOR THE PURPOSE OF AMENDING

THE

CONSTITUTION

OF THE

State of New-York:

CONTAINING

ALL THE OFFICIAL DOCUMENTS, RELATING TO THE SUBJECT, AND
OTHER VALUABLE MATTER.

BY NATHANIEL H. CARTER AND WILLIAM L. STONE,
REPORTERS; AND
MARCUS T. C. GOULD,
STENOGRAPHER.

ALBANY:
PRINTED AND PUBLISHED BY E. AND E. HOSFORD.
....
1821.

Figure 3 Cover Page of Carter and Stone, *Proceedings and Debates*
Cover page of Nathaniel H. Carter and William L. Stone, *Reports of the Proceedings and Debates of the Convention of 1821* (Albany, 1821). *Reprinted by permission of the President and Fellows of Harvard College.*

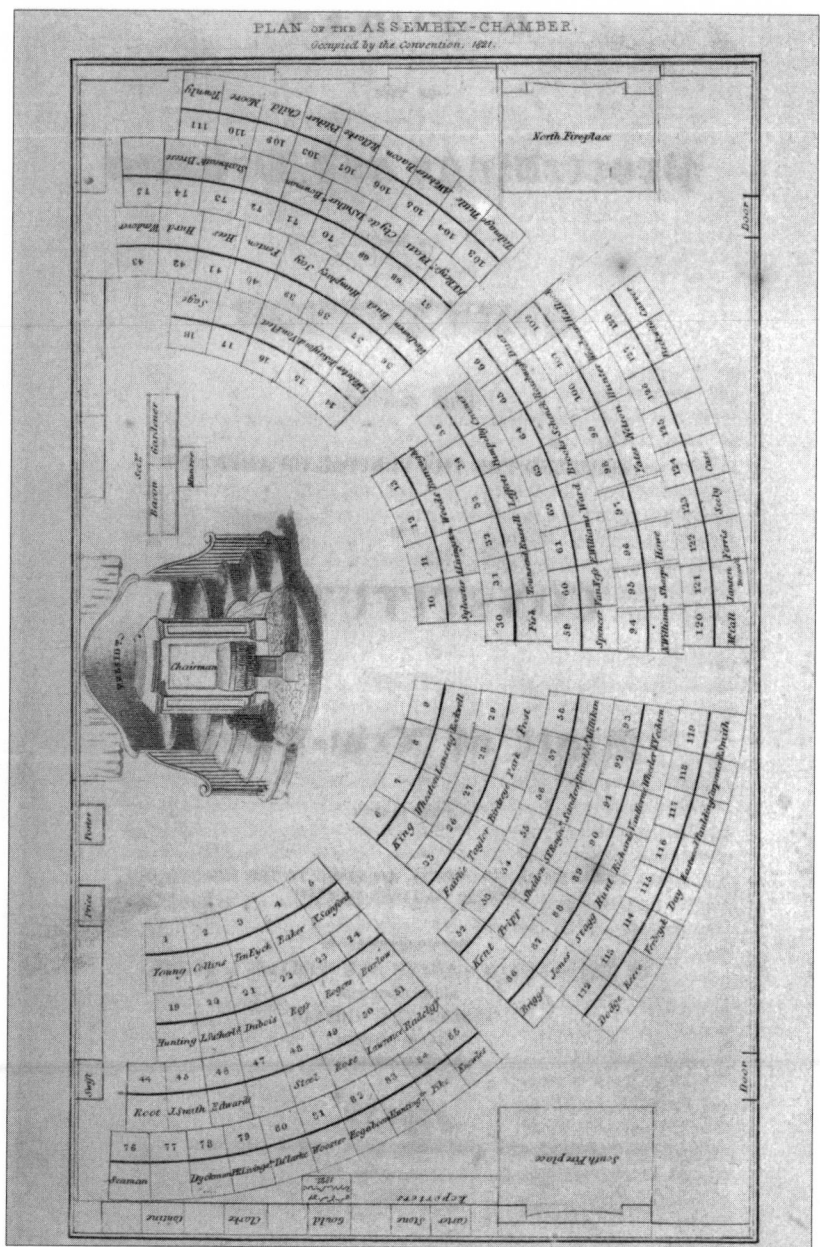

Figure 4 Seating Chart of 1821 Convention

Seating chart of the 1821 convention, which met in the New York state assembly chamber in Albany. [Nathaniel H. Carter and William L. Stone, *Reports of the Proceeding and Debates of the Convention of 1821* (Albany, 1821).] *Reprinted by permission of the President and Fellows of Harvard College.*

exclusion, and declined to alter the pace of or constitutionally to legitimate the abolition of slavery. The final draft of the new state constitution instituted the new voting rights regime, which would shape discussions of race and citizenship in New York for decades to come.

The document that follows is excerpted from an almost seven hundred-page transcript published shortly after the close of the convention. Transcriptions of this kind did not have the benefit of sound recording but rather were composed by reporters in the audience and disseminated to the press during the course of the convention. According to the transcript's reporter-editors, Nathaniel H. Carter and William L. Stone, delegates sometimes had the opportunity to offer corrections to the texts of their speeches as previously published in newspapers.

Carter and Stone had professional and political interests in the proceedings of the convention. Carter operated an Albany newspaper and Stone, a veteran of New York State journalism, had recently taken a leading role in the publication of New York City's *Commercial Advertiser*. Both men had ties to DeWitt Clinton, whose supporters and allies were so thoroughly outnumbered at the convention.

In their introduction to *Reports of the Proceedings and Debates of the Convention of 1821*, Carter and Stone asserted the professional goals of accuracy and thoroughness, disavowing any partisan agenda. Accordingly, they expressed a desire to aid the public in judging for themselves the merits of the proposed constitution. Carter and Stone also wished to establish a historical record of the proceedings more permanent than what newspapers could provide. Perhaps giving a hint of concern over the direction of the convention, they noted how thoroughly the proposed constitution had rewritten the fundamental rules of New York politics. And without question, the massive Carter and Stone transcript provided significant room for the words of dissenters and critics to be heard. Nevertheless, the document excerpted extensively below achieved Carter and Stone's professed object to make a broad contribution to the public and historical record. Their transcript offers a thorough record of the spectrum of arguments advanced by the delegates who, during the late summer and fall of 1821, debated New York's political future.

The 1821 convention debates raise a variety of questions: Why were delegates willing to declare their opinions about African Americans so openly? What recent and historical experiences and events informed the views of various participants in the suffrage debates? In what ways does the transcript echo earlier documents? In what ways did the delegates' remarks diverge from the rhetoric of prior decades? How did the absence of black voices at the convention affect the course of the debate?

Why did some delegates both criticize liberalizing franchise rules and defend the principle of black voting rights? How did those who favored enfranchising white men justify setting up new barriers to black voting? What attitudes did delegates hold toward one another? How effectively did they respond to the substance of one another's arguments? Did the ultimate outcome of these debates—the constitutional provisions disfranchising black New Yorkers—represent a culmination of previous events or a departure from them?

Prologue: Principles and Procedures

Before New York could define black citizenship and respond to debates over race, slavery, and suffrage occurring in other parts of the country, a constitutional convention had to be authorized and a means for choosing delegates established. And once the convention itself met, a method for dividing responsibility for rewriting the constitution according to the presumed will of the people had to be established. The convention formed committees to revise specific portions of the constitution, including one on the right of suffrage. This panel reflected the Bucktail composition of the convention and, presumably, its priorities and biases.

Shortly before taking up the report of the suffrage committee, the convention considered whether the abolition of slavery ought to be affixed to a proposed bill of rights. The convention decided to postpone consideration of the bill of rights, and with it the possible constitutional abolition of slavery. Yet the brief rhetorical skirmish over abolition indicated the almost inevitable surfacing of race-related subjects in the broader discussion of the state's future political character. This initial discussion of slavery also exposed the potential political pitfalls of debating race and slavery in relation to the state's constitution.

This introductory material raises a number of questions: Why did the law establishing a referendum on a possible constitutional convention open suffrage to people excluded from ordinary elections under the existing constitution of 1777? How thorough a revision of the previous constitution did the legislature authorize and the convention delegates contemplate? How did delegates justify allowing slavery to continue under the new constitution? Why did purported opponents of slavery believe that no constitutional action was necessary?

* * *

The Convention Act

The law recommending that the state call a constitutional convention received overwhelming support from New York's voters. Eligibility requirements for those voting in the referendum were significantly broader than the standards for determining voter eligibility in ordinary state elections. Also noteworthy is the fact that no mention of race or skin color was made in defining voter eligibility for the referendum.

AN ACT
Recommending a Convention of the People of this State.
Passed March 13, 1821.

I. *Be it enacted by the People of the State of New-York, represented in Senate and Assembly*, That the inspectors at each poll, in the several towns and wards of this state, at the annual election, to be held on the last Tuesday in April next, shall provide a proper box, to receive the ballots of the citizens of this state, in relation to the convention herein after provided for. On which ballots shall be written or printed, by those voters who are in favour of the proposed convention, the word *Convention*, and by those voters who are opposed thereto, the words *No Convention*, and that all free male citizens of this state, of the age of twenty-one years or upwards, who shall possess a freehold within this state, or who shall have been actually rated, and paid taxes to this state, or who shall have been actually enrolled in the militia of this state, or in a legal volunteer or uniform corps, and shall have served therein, either as an officer or private; or who shall have been, or now are by law exempt from taxation, or militia duty; or who shall have been assessed to work on the public roads and highways, and shall have worked thereon, or shall have paid a commutation therefor, according to law; shall be allowed, during the three days of such election, to vote by ballot as aforesaid, in the town or ward in which they shall actually reside.

II. *And be it further enacted,* That it shall be lawful for either of the inspectors of such election, of his own accord, and it shall be the duty of such inspectors, when thereto required by any citizen entitled to vote as aforesaid, to administer to any person offering to ballot as aforesaid, the following oath or affirmation: "I _____, do solemnly swear or affirm, (as the case may be,) that I am a natural born, or naturalized citizen of the state of New-York, or of one the United States, (as the case may be,) of the age of twenty-one years, or upwards: that I am the owner of a free-hold within this state; or that I have been actually rated and paid taxes to this state; or that I actually have been enrolled, and have served in the militia of this state, or in a legal volunteer or uniform corps, either as an officer or private; or that I have been or now am by law exempt from taxation or militia duty; or that I have been actually assessed to work on public roads and highways, and have worked thereon, or have paid a commutation therefor, according to law: and that I now am an actual resident and inhabitant of the town or ward in which I offer my ballot; and that I have not before voted and will not again vote at this election." And it is hereby declared, that if any person, so being required to take the said oath or affirmation, shall refuse to take the same, he shall not be allowed to vote at such election, until he shall take such oath or affirmation.

III. *And be it further enacted,* That the said election shall, in all respects, be conducted, and the poll lists shall be kept, in the manner prescribed by law, for the election of senators; that the said votes shall be canvassed by the inspectors of the several polls of the said election, and the returns thereof made by such inspectors, to the clerks of the respective towns and counties, at the same time, and in the same manner, as the canvass and return of votes for senators are by law directed to be made; that the certificates of the returns of the said votes, shall be recorded by the clerks of the several towns and counties, and transcripts thereof shall be certified, and be transmitted to the secretary of this state, at the same time and in the same manner, as certificates of the votes for senators, are now by law required to be recorded, transcribed, and transmitted to the secretary of this state; that the said transcripts received by the secretary of this state as aforesaid, shall remain in his office of record, and the votes so given, shall be canvassed at the same time, by the same persons, and in the same manner, and the result thereof shall be published as is prescribed by law, in relation to the election of senators.

IV. *And be it further enacted,* That if it shall appear by the said canvass, to be made as aforesaid, that a majority of the ballots or votes, given in, and returned as aforesaid, are for *No Convention,* then and in such case, the canvassers are hereby required to certify and declare that there shall be no further proceedings under this act, in relation to the calling of a convention. But that if it shall appear by the said canvass, that a majority of the ballots or votes are for a *Convention,* that then and in such case, the canvassers shall certify and declare, that a convention will be called accordingly, and that a copy of the said certificate shall be transmitted by the secretary of this state, to the sheriffs of the respective cities and counties of this state, and shall be by them published, and copies delivered to the supervisors of the several towns, within the respective counties, in the same manner as notices for the election of senators are now by law required to be published and delivered.

V. *And be it further enacted,* That in case the said canvassers shall certify and declare a majority of such ballots or votes to be for a *Convention,* it shall and may be lawful, and it is hereby recommended to the citizens of this state, on the third Tuesday of June next, to elect by ballot, delegates to meet in convention, for the purpose of considering the constitution of this state, and making such alterations in the same as they may deem proper; and to provide the manner of making future amendments thereto.

VI. *And be it further enacted,* That the number of delegates to be chosen, shall be the same as the number of members of assembly, from the respective cities and counties of this state; and that the same qualifications for voters shall be required on the election for delegates, as is prescribed in the first section of this act, and none other; and that the oath prescribed in the second section of this act, shall be likewise taken by all the voters under this section, if required; and that all persons entitled to vote by this law for delegates, shall be eligible to be elected; and that the election for such delegates shall be held at such places as the inspectors herein after mentioned, shall for that purpose notify, and shall take place on the said third Tuesday of June next, and shall continue and be held on that day, and on the two succeeding days. . . .

VIII. *And be it further enacted,* That the delegates so to be chosen, shall meet in convention at the capitol, in the city of Albany, on the last Tuesday of August next, from whence they may, if they think proper, adjourn to any other place; and they, and their attendants and officers, shall be allowed the like compensation for their travel and attendance, as the members of the legislature are allowed by law. . . .

IX. *And be it further enacted*, That the proceedings of the said convention, shall be filed in the office of the secretary of this state, and the determination and propositions of the said convention shall be entered of record in the same office. And that it shall be the duty of the said convention, to submit their proposed amendments to the decision of the citizens of this state, entitled to vote under this act, together, or in distinct propositions, as to them shall seem expedient. . . . And the propositions of such convention, which shall be approved by a majority of the votes at such election, shall be deemed and taken to be a part of the constitution of this state; and that the propositions which shall not be so approved, shall be considered void and of none effect.

Thursday, August 30 — Saturday, September 1, 1821

At the prompting of U.S. senator and Queens County delegate Rufus King, the convention adopted a committee system for the proposal of various changes to the state's constitutional structure. King argued that such an approach would minimize personal "jealousies" and encourage "a calm, temperate and wise deliberation." The venerable Federalist, who in 1787 had represented Massachusetts at the U.S. Constitutional Convention, expressed his wish "that the Convention may proceed with great caution and moderation" and to "inspire our constituents with confidence in the prudence of this body." Leavening his conservative tone with egalitarian values, King concluded by stating for his colleagues principles that would be tested and redefined during the course of the convention:

[T]hese great principles of free government, which arise from, and can only be sustained by, the intelligence and virtue of the people, are not only denied by the great nations of the old world, but a contrary and most slavish doctrine is proclaimed and enforced by them—a doctrine which falsely assumes, that a select portion of mankind only are set apart by Providence, and made solely responsible for the government of mankind.

In contradiction to this theory, it is our bounden duty to make it manifest to all men, that a free people are capable of self-government; that they can make, and abate, and remake their constitution; and, at all times, that our public liberties, when impaired, may be renovated, without destroying those securities which education and manners, our laws and constitutions have provided.

A committee of thirteen delegates, appointed by Convention President and U.S. Vice President Daniel Tompkins, reported the creation of ten committees charged with drafting new constitutional language. The convention convened committees to consider each of the three major branches of government—executive, legislative, and judicial—as well as committees to consider a bill of rights and to review unusual features of the 1777 state constitution governing the appointment of state officials and the vetoing of legislation. Each committee comprised six or seven members. The overall Bucktail Republican majority generally was reflected in the makeup of each committee.

The suffrage committee had seven members. All but Stephen Van Rensselaer, a Federalist from Albany County, were Bucktail Republicans. Two of the committee members—Nathan Sanford, the committee's chairman, and James Fairlie—represented New York City. Two, Samuel Young and John Cramer, represented Saratoga County. Peter Livingston represented Dutchess County. Doctor John Z. Ross of Genesee County was the lone delegate from western New York on the panel. Fairlie recommended that the committee charged with drafting new language to define the scope and character of the future electorate be referred to as the "right of suffrage" committee rather than the "elective franchise" committee.

MONDAY, SEPTEMBER 17, 1821

In the midst of a debate over the specific provisions of a proposed bill of rights, Dutchess County delegate James Tallmadge proposed to make the abolition of slavery a part of the constitution. Tallmadge, who had precipitated the Missouri crisis as a member of the U.S. Congress, sought a constitutional guarantee of abolition that also would have accelerated the timetable established in 1817, which deferred abolition until 1827. Other delegates endorsed Tallmadge's principles but sought to modify his plan.

GEN. TALLMADGE[12] . . . wished to add the following clause—That slavery and involuntary servitude shall not exist, nor be allowed in this state, except for the punishment of crimes, whereof the party shall have been duly convicted, and except in cases of children born of slaves after the 4th of July, 1799, and of minors, indentured apprentices, and servants.

He wished merely to explain his views in offering this amendment, without entering, however, into any debate. The first object was to produce that universal emancipation, which it was due to our country to effect. As to the exception, they who are under the act of '99 are in a state of infancy and subject to involuntary servitude, shall be left as they are— but to all others, he wished to extend immediate emancipation. With regard to the words "involuntary servitude," they are necessary, for in Ohio, where *slavery* is abolished, from the omission of the words in question, hundreds and hundreds, nay, thousands of slaves from neighbouring slave states, are carried over and bound to a perpetual apprenticeship.

THE PRESIDENT [Daniel Tompkins], wished the provision to be so amended, as to make the emancipation take place in 1827, the term now contemplated by our laws, and proposed the following—"There shall be neither slavery nor involuntary servitude in this state, otherwise than in the punishment of crimes, of which the party shall have been duly convicted, after the 4th of July, in the year one thousand eight hundred and twenty seven."

MR. VAN BUREN wished the proposition to lie on the table till to-morrow, as it embraced important provisions and considerations.

MR. CRAMER wished to extend the benefits of emancipation, so as to prohibit the sale of slaves out of the state, and proposed the following substitute—"that the law of this state, passed April 9, 1813, providing for the abolition of slavery, shall not be altered or repealed by any subsequent legislature."

TUESDAY, SEPTEMBER 18, 1821

The next day, Peter R. Livingston, Tallmadge's colleague from Dutchess County, questioned whether the challenges of forging a bill of rights were worth the effort. Livingston saw as daunting the technical debates over certain aspects of a bill of rights, while he believed that the rights of the people were safeguarded through the system of checks and balances and, ultimately, the people at large. As for slavery, Livingston warned that Tallmadge "would carry you to the meridian of Washington, and arouse and mingle in this debate all those feelings which grew out of the Missouri question." Tallmadge claimed he could not imagine the convention getting embroiled in the issues of the Missouri crisis because he presumed that his stance against slavery in that instance still represented the consensus view of New York's leading politicians. Tallmadge then admonished Livingston, "But, sir . . . are we to shrink from the controversy? No, sir. I think it fair to say, that, while my life lasts, the oppressed people who gave rise to that discussion, shall receive my support, in every place, and every situation where I may . . . introduce it." The convention, soon after these remarks, postponed further consideration of the bill of rights and, thus, the slavery question.

A month later, when the constitutional abolition of slavery resurfaced for discussion, the character of black freedom in New York had been significantly redefined. Tallmadge himself, despite his purported devotion to abolition, voted more than once in favor of disfranchising language as the discussion of race merged with debates over the future character of New York's democracy.

Act One: The Debate over Racial Disqualification

Delegates did not take long to establish that the suffrage committee's proposal to limit voting rights to whites alone was one of the report's most remarkable and controversial features. From this point forward, the status of free blacks in New York would weave itself in and out of debates over suffrage. In this phase of the debate, battle lines were sharply drawn between unapologetic racists and those who would explain alleged African American deficiencies in environmental terms, those who wished to treat blacks as a special category within the population and those who did not, those who deemed alleged popular beliefs and demands the sole standard by which to define black citizenship and those who sought in the historical record protection for future black rights. At the end of two days of debate, opponents of black disfranchisement won a narrow and temporary victory.

How did some delegates justify the suffrage committee's plan to extend the suffrage among whites while erecting a racial bar to black voting? What dangers did these delegates ascribe to black voting? What characteristics did various delegates attribute to people worthy of full citizenship? On what grounds did delegates attack the plan to make voting an exclusively white privilege? What concessions did the defenders of African American suffrage make to popular prejudices against black people? What role did history—including the history of slavery in New York—play in the debate over suffrage?

*   *   *

WEDNESDAY, SEPTEMBER 19, 1821

Twenty-two days after the start of the convention, the suffrage committee formally proposed language to broaden eligibility for all state elections. The committee proposed to do away with property holding as the sole criterion for male enfranchisement. Instead, the payment of taxes or, in lieu of taxes, work on the public roads or service in the militia would make an adult male eligible to vote in state elections. The committee also proposed to make uniform the criteria for voting in state assembly, state senate, and gubernatorial elections. At the same time, the committee sought to strip African Americans of the vote, based at least in part on an unabashedly racist logic. Thus, while extolling the need to reward the bravery and patriotism of ordinary white New Yorkers of modest means, committee member John Z. Ross denigrated black New Yorkers as unworthy or "incapable" of full citizenship. Ross deemed it appropriate that each state had the sovereign right to determine according its own public interest who should be allowed to vote and should not be constrained by abstract principles.

MR. SANFORD[13] moved that the Convention go into committee of the whole, on his report relative to the right of suffrage. . . .

The report having been read—

MR. N. SANFORD took the floor. The question before us is the right of suffrage—who shall, or who shall not, have the right to vote. The committee have presented the scheme they thought best; to abolish all existing distinctions, and make the right of voting uniform. Is this not right? Where did these distinctions arise? They arose from British precedents. In England, they have their three estates,[14] which must always have their separate interests represented. Here there is but one estate—the people. To me, the only qualifications seems to be, the virtue and morality of the people; and if they may be safely entrusted to vote for one class of our rulers, why not for all? In my opinion, these distinctions are fallacious. We have the experience of almost all the other states against them. The principle of the scheme now proposed, is, that those who bear the burthens of the state, should choose those that rule it. There is no privilege given to property, as such; but those who contribute to the public support, we consider as entitled to a share in the election of rulers. The burthens are annual, and the elections are annual, and this appears proper.

To me, and the majority of the committee, it appeared the only reasonable scheme that those who are to be affected by the acts of the government, should be annually entitled to vote for those who administer it.
Our taxes are of two sorts, on real and personal property. The payment
of a tax on either, we thought, equally entitled a man to a vote, and thus
we intended to destroy the odious distinctions of property which now
exist. But we have considered personal service, in some cases, equivalent
to a tax on personal property, as in work on the high roads. This is a burthen, and should entitle those subject to it to equivalent privileges. The
road duty is equal to a poll tax on every male citizen of 21 years, of 62 1-
2 cents per annum, which is about the value of each individual's work on
the road. This work is a burthen imposed by the legislature—a duty required by rulers, and which should entitle those subject to it, to a choice
of those rulers.

Then, sir, the militia next presents itself; the idea of personal service, as
applicable to the road duty, is, in like manner, applicable here; and this
criterion has been adopted in other states. In Mississippi, mere enrolment
gives a vote. In Connecticut, as is proposed here, actual service, and that
without the right of commutation, is required. The duty in the militia is
obligatory and onerous. The militia man must find his arms and accou-
trements, and lose his time. But, after admitting all these persons, what
restrictions, it will be said, are left on the right of suffrage? 1st. The voter
must be a citizen. 2d. The service required must be performed within the
year, on the principle that taxation is annual, and election annual; so that
when the person ceases to contribute or serve, he ceases to vote.

A residence is also required. We proposed the term of six months, because we find it already in the constitution; but we propose this residence
in the state, not in the county or town, so that wherever a voter may be
at the time of election, he may vote there, if he has been a resident of the
state for six months. The object of this was to enable those who move, as
very many do, in the six months preceding an election, out of the town or
ward in which they have resided, to retain the right of voting in their new
habitations. The term of six months is deemed long enough to qualify
those who come into our state from abroad, to understand and exercise
the privileges of a citizen here. Now, sir, this scheme will embrace almost
the whole male population of the state. There is perhaps no subject so
purely matter of opinion, as the question how far the right of suffrage
may be safely carried. We propose to carry it almost as far as the male
population of the state. The Convention may perhaps think this too

broad. On this subject we have much experience; yet there are respectable citizens who think this extension of suffrage unfavourable to the rights of property. Certainly this would be a fatal objection, if well founded; for any government, however constituted, which does not secure property to its rightful owners, is a bad government. But how is the extension of the right of suffrage unfavourable to property? Will not our laws continue the same? Will not the administration of justice continue the same? And if so, how is private property to suffer? Unless these are changed, and upon them rest the rights and security of property, I am unable to perceive how property is to suffer by the extension of the right of suffrage. But we have abundant experience on this point in other states. Now, sir, in many of the states the right of suffrage has no restriction; every male inhabitant votes. Yet what harm has been done in those states? What evil has resulted to them from this cause? The course of things in this country is for the extension, and not the restriction of popular rights. I do not know that in Ohio or Pennsylvania, where the right of suffrage is universal,[15] there is not the same security for private rights and private happiness as elsewhere.

Every gentleman is aware that the scheme now proposed, is derived from the law calling this Convention, and in the constitution of this body, we have the first fruits of the operation of the principle of extensive suffrage—and will any one say that this example is not one evincing the discretion with which our people exercise this right? In our town meetings too, throughout the state, we have the same principle. In our town elections we have the highest proof of the virtue and intelligence of our people; they assemble in town meetings as a pure democracy, and choose their officers and local legislatures, if I may so call them; and if there is any part of our public business well done, it is that done in town meetings. Is not this a strong practical lesson of the beneficial operation of this principle? This scheme has been proposed by a majority of the committee; they think it safe and beneficial, founded in just and rational principles, and in the experience of this and neighbouring states. The committee have no attachment, however, to this particular scheme, and are willing to see it amended or altered, if it shall be judged for the interest of the people.

MR. ROSS . . . The subject now submitted, may be viewed as one of deep and interesting importance; inasmuch as it discriminates who among our fellow citizens shall be allowed to exercise the high privilege of designating, by their votes, who shall represent them in their wants and their wishes, in the various and multiplied concerns of legislation and civil government. In every free state, the electors ought to form the basis, the soil from which every thing is to spring, relating to the administration of their political concerns. Otherwise it could not be denominated a government of the people. This results from the immutable principle, that civil government is instituted for the benefit of the governed. Consequently all, at least, who contribute to the support or defence of the state, have a just claim to exercise the elective privilege, if consistent with the safety and welfare of the citizens. It is immaterial whether that support or defence of the state be by the payment of money, or by personal service, which are precisely one and the same thing, that of taxation. Assuming this, then, as the basis, as being the least objectionable of any other, we are furnished with certain data by which the right to vote can be determined. By entering them in a register, we are able to test the qualification of electors, without resorting to the multiplication of oaths, which under the present constitution had grown into a most corrupting and alarming evil. After the most full and attentive consideration of the subject, the committee were led to the conclusion, that this would be the most simple and practical mode of ascertaining, with certainty, who are entitled to the privilege of electors. At the same time, it gives a liberal extension to that privilege, which, unquestionably, a vast majority of our constituents will demand at our hands, and which we can have no wish to withhold, unless to perpetuate those odious distinctions which have hitherto so long and so justly been complained of.—This is one of the crying evils for which we were sent here to provide a remedy. It is not to be expected, sir, that any general rules can be devised, that will extend to every possible case that it would be desirable to include, nor is it possible to exclude all who might abuse the privilege. Where evils must necessarily exist, the great object of this Convention, I trust, will be to choose the least—to settle down on such general principles as will result in conferring on the people of this state, the greatest possible sum of happiness and prosperity.

That all men are free and equal, according to the usual declarations, applies to them only in a state of nature, and not after the institution of civil government; for then many rights, flowing from a natural equality, are necessarily abridged, with a view to produce the greatest amount of security and happiness to the whole community. On this principle the right of suffrage is extended to white men only. But why, it will probably be asked, are blacks to be excluded? I answer, because they are seldom, if ever, required to share in the common burthens or defence of the state. There are also additional reasons; they are a peculiar people, incapable, in my judgment, of exercising that privilege with any sort of discretion, prudence, or independence. They have no just conceptions of civil liberty. They know not how to appreciate it, and are consequently indifferent to its preservation.

Under such circumstances, it would hardly be compatible with the safety of the state, to entrust such a people with this right. It is not thought advisable to permit aliens to vote, neither would it be safe to extend it to the blacks. We deny to minors this right, and why? Because they are deemed incapable of exercising it discreetly, and therefore not safely, for the good of the whole community.—Even the better part of creation,[16] as my honourable friend from Oneida, (Mr. N. Williams,) stiles them, are not permitted to participate in this right. No sympathies seemed to be awakened in their behalf, nor in behalf of the aborigines,[17] the original and only rightful proprietors of our soil—a people altogether more acute and discerning, and in whose judicious exercise of the right I should repose far more confidence, than in the African race. In nearly all the western and southern states, indeed many others, even in Connecticut, where steady habits and correct principles prevail, the blacks are excluded.[18] And gentlemen have been frequently in the habit of citing the precedents of our sister states for our guide; and would it not be well to listen to the decisive weight of precedents furnished in this case also?

It is true that in many of the states the black population is more numerous than in ours. Then, sir, if the exclusion be unjust or improper, that injustice would be of so much greater extent. The truth is, this exclusion invades no inherent rights, nor has it any connection at all with the question of slavery. The practice of every state in the union, is to make such exceptions, limitations, and provisions in relation to the elective privilege, under their respective constitutions, as are deemed to be necessary or consistent with public good—varied in each according to the existing circumstances under which they are made. It must therefore necessarily rest on the ground of expediency. And, sir, I fear that an extension to the blacks would serve to invite that kind of population to this state, an occurrence which I should most sincerely deplore. The petition presented in their behalf, now on your table, in all probability has been instigated by gentlemen of a different colour, who expect to control their votes. But whether this be so or not, next the blacks will claim to be represented by persons of their own colour, in your halls of legislation. And can you consistently refuse them? It would be well to be prepared for such a claim.

On the whole, sir, let your constitution, at a proper period, declare their emancipation; exempt them from military service as the United States government directs, and from other burthens as heretofore; give them the full benefits of protection; and there, in mercy to themselves, and to us, let us stay our hands.

Sir, as to the propriety and justice of extending the elective privilege to all who perform military duty, and render services upon the public highways, I apprehend that it can easily be shewn that public policy, as well as justice, require this extension. In fact, those who have no other qualification to entitle them to vote, contribute more in proportion to their ability to pay, towards the defence and improvement of the state, than the wealthy. They are required to be at the expense of equipping themselves, and to serve three or four days in the year, and for what? Why to be ready to defend the lives and property of the wealthy. And this must be done, however oppressive their poverty, or urgent their business. If not, they must be subject to fine, and to imprisonment too, if they happen to be destitute of money to pay it. In time of war, the burthen is still more unequal; they must be shoved into the front of the battle; no money to procure them a substitute; their families, if they have any, must be left unprotected and unprovided for; themselves exposed to disease, slaughter, and death; and this too, in defence of a country which now denies them the only true badge of freemen, the right of suffrage. Deprive them of this badge, and where is the pledge that ensures their fidelity in defence of the state?

Does not true policy, then, enforce the propriety of strengthening their attachment to their country, by clothing them with the habiliments[19] of freemen? I know, sir, the venerable gentleman from Albany (Gen. S. Van Rensselaer) with whom I had the honour to be associated on that committee, is apprehensive that by extending the right of suffrage to all who perform these services, that we extend it to too many, who will not exercise it with independence and judgment. Sir, many of this description may be found among all orders of men, rich as well as poor. However trifling he may suppose the burthen imposed on persons living in the cities, to comply with military requisitions, he may be assured, that in the country it amounts to a very serious burthen.

I have a deference and respect for that gentleman's opinions, his virtues, and his philanthropy, to which all bear testimony. And, sir, I am the more surprised that he should be averse to conferring this privilege on men he has once led on to battle, as he himself must have witnessed their privations and their sufferings. In his operations upon the Niagara frontier during the late war, a great part of the forces under his command were composed of men who, with the provisions here reported, would be excluded from the right of suffrage.[20] I have no wish, sir, to endanger the rights of property, by advocating the extension of this privilege. On the contrary, I am anxious those rights should be guaranteed by every necessary precaution. Let them be made amply secure; require, if you please, that persons to be elected to office shall possess a certain amount of freehold estate. At the same time extend the right of suffrage to every citizen who is compelled to bear arms; for remember, that we are not always to be in a state of peace, and let us estimate the rights of the militia accordingly.

During the late war, frequent were the calls on the militia, and as often were they promptly obeyed. They subjected themselves to immense sacrifices; exposed themselves to every hardship and danger incident to the vicissitudes of war, for the protection and defence of the state, and for the preservation of that privilege which they now claim a right to enjoy. Let me ask, sir, what would have been the fate of the brave army of Gen. Brown when pent up in Fort Erie, had not the militia fled to their relief, and averted their impending ruin? Enclosed by a superior force of the enemy, whose incessant and destructive fire from his batteries continually thinned their ranks, and wasted away our veteran little army, unable to secure a retreat, and too much weakened to advance. In this perilous crisis, the militia, without waiting to receive orders, but on appealing to their patriotism, instantly hurried to their protection. They crossed the Niagara in opposition to the pressing advice of their disaffected, but more wealthy neighbours; and, under the command of Gen. Porter, they rescued the remains of that army which had survived the glorious conflict at Bridgewater from inevitable destruction.[21] The militia, on that occasion, achieved what would have given lustre to the best disciplined troops. They met, and drove the enemy from his strong intrenchments; liberated our army, and saved the western part of the state from plunder and conflagration. It has since been well said, in allusion to that event, that the militia of New-Orleans[22] have done much; the militia of other places have done much: but it remained for the militia of Genesee, and the Niagara frontier, to successfully storm and take possession of the enemy's batteries.

Considering, sir, the perilous situation of our country at this momentous period, the general government literally destitute of men and of money, pressed by a veteran foe on every side, a part of the union yielding to the contaminating spirit of disaffection—in this direful dilemma, the nation turned its last hope upon the militia, particularly of New-York. That hope, sir, was not disappointed. The then governor or commander in chief, by his patriotic and unexampled exertions, infused a universal spirit of emulation, and twenty thousand hardy champions of liberty rushed into the field at once from this single state. It was the militia, sir, that snatched the trembling liberties of the nation from the malignant grasp of the enemy. But for them, we might all of us at this moment have been compelled to deplore the loss of that high privilege, the right of suffrage. And what do they now ask? Simply to be allowed to participate with you in the rights of self-government. And shall they be denied? I trust not, sir. If their services are duly appreciated, I indulge the hope that no honourable gentleman of this Convention will resist the justice of their claims.

Two dissenting members of the suffrage committee explained their desire not to extend the right to vote so broadly, proposing alternative language. Delegates not on the suffrage committee, however, quickly reinserted the issue of racial exclusion into the debate. Peter Jay vigorously criticized the idea of stripping African Americans of the vote, appealing to recent events, to history, as well as to moral and political principle. He rejected the racist assumptions about inborn black inferiority.

GEN. S. VAN RENSSELAER[23] felt called upon, as dissenting from the opinion of the committee, and as particularly pointed at by the gentleman last up, to state his motives for that dissent. He was willing to permit all who contributed in money to the state, or county, or town, who have residence in the towns, or a legal settlement, to vote; but he was not willing to give a wandering population, men who are no where to be found when the enemy, or the tax gatherer, comes, the same privileges as those who actually contribute to the support and the defence of the government. The gentleman has referred to the services of the militia which I had the honour to command—does the gentleman suppose that that militia was composed of this wandering population? No, sir; they were farmers and farmers' sons. I am not anxious to discuss this subject at large, but beg to submit a substitute for the first clause, which goes as far as I think it safe or proper to go. To extend the right of suffrage beyond this, would, in my judgment, at some future time, when the number of inhabitants in this state not owning land, will be vastly greater than that of the land owner, subject the rights of landed property to imminent danger. Mr. Van Rensselaer then submitted the following substitute:

"Every male citizen, of the age of 21 years, who shall have resided in the state one year, and in the city or county where he may claim to vote six months preceding an election; and within the last two years shall have been assessed and paid a state, county, or town tax, together with the sons of citizens qualified as aforesaid, above the age of 21 years, and not exceeding ____ years, who may neither have been assessed nor paid any such tax, shall be entitled to vote for governor, lieutenant-governor, senators, members of assembly, and for every other officer to be elected by the people."

MR. FAIRLIE felt himself called upon by the unusual and improper reference of the gentleman from Genesee, (Mr. Ross,) to the views of the minority in the select committee, and particularly to those of the honourable gentleman from Albany, (Mr. S. Van Rensselaer) to state, that the gentleman from Albany was not alone in that committee in his opposition to the admission to the right of suffrage of militiamen, and persons working on the roads. He had concurred in that opposition, though he did not mean to be understood as saying, that after a full discussion of the question, he might not feel himself at liberty to vote for the clause as reported.

COL. YOUNG moved to amend the substitute offered by the gentleman from Albany, by inserting the word "white" before citizens.

MR. JAY.[24] The chairman of the select committee has given a fair and candid exposition of the reasons that induced them to make the report now under consideration, and of the motives by which they were governed. He has clearly stated why they were desirous of extending the right of suffrage to some who did not at present enjoy it, but he has wholly omitted to explain why they deny it to others who actually possess it. The omission, however, has been supplied by one of his colleagues, who informed us that all who were not white ought to be excluded from political rights, because such persons were incapable of exercising them discreetly, and because they were peculiarly liable to be influenced and corrupted. These reasons, sir, I shall notice presently. When this Convention was first assembled, it was generally understood that provisions would be made to extend the right of suffrage, and some were apprehensive that it might be extended to a degree which they could not approve. But, sir, it was not expected that this right was in any instance to be restricted, much less was it anticipated, or desired, that a single person was to be disfranchised. Why, sir, are these men to be excluded from rights which they possess in common with their countrymen? What crime have they committed for which they are to be punished? Why are they, who were born as free as ourselves, natives of the same country, and deriving from nature and our political institutions, the same rights and privileges which we have, now to be deprived of all those rights, and doomed to remain forever as aliens among us? We are told, in reply, that other states have set us the example. It is true that other states treat this race of men with cruelty and injustice, and that we have hitherto manifested towards them a disposition to be just and liberal. Yet even in Virginia and North-Carolina, free people of colour are permitted to vote, and if I am correctly informed, exercise that privilege. In Pennsylvania, they are much more numerous than they are here, and there they are not disfranchised, nor has any inconvenience been felt from extending to all men the rights which ought to be common to all. In Connecticut, it is true, they have, for the last three years, adopted a new constitution which prevents people of colour from acquiring the right of suffrage in future, yet even there they have preserved the right to all those who previously possessed it.[25]

Mr. Chairman, I would submit to the consideration of the committee, whether the proposition of the gentleman from Saratoga is consistent with the constitution of the United States. That instrument provides that "citizens of each state shall be entitled to all the privileges and immunities of citizens in the several states."[26] No longer ago than last November, the legislature of this state almost unanimously resolved, that "if the provisions contained in any proposed constitution of a new state, deny to any citizens of the existing states the privileges and immunities of citizens of such new state, that such proposed constitution should not be accepted or confirmed; the same in the opinion of this legislature being void by the constitution of the United States." Now, sir, is not the right of suffrage a privilege? And can you deny it to a citizen of Pennsylvania who comes here and complies with your laws, merely because he is not six feet high, or because he is of a dark complexion?

But we are told by one of the select committee, that people of colour are incapable of exercising the right of suffrage. I may have misunderstood that gentleman; but I thought he meant to say, that they laboured under a physical disability. It is true that some philosophers have held that the intellect of a black man, is naturally inferior to that of a white one; but this idea has been so completely refuted, and is now so universally exploded, that I did not expect to have heard of it in an assembly so enlightened as this, nor do I now think it necessary to disprove it. That in general the people of colour are inferior to the whites in knowledge and in industry, I shall not deny. You made them slaves, and nothing is more true than the ancient saying, "The day you make a man a slave takes half his worth away." Unaccustomed to provide for themselves, and habituated to regard labour as an evil, it is no wonder that when set free, they should be improvident and idle, and that their children should be brought up without education, and without prudence or forethought. But will you punish the children for your own crimes; for the injuries which you have inflicted upon their parents? Besides, sir, this state of things is fast passing away. Schools have been opened for them, and it will, I am sure, give pleasure to this committee to know, that in these schools there is discovered a thirst for instruction, and a progress in learning, seldom to be seen in the other schools of the state. They have also churches of their own, and clergymen of their own colour, who conduct their public worship with perfect decency and order, and not without ability.

This state, Mr. Chairman, has taken high ground against slavery, and all its degrading consequences and accompaniments. There are gentlemen on this floor, who, to their immortal honour, have defended the cause of this oppressed people in congress, and I trust they will not now desert them. Adopt the amendment now proposed, and you will hear a shout of triumph and a hiss of scorn from the southern part of the union, which I confess will mortify me—I shall shrink at the sound, because I fear it will be deserved. But it has been said that this measure is necessary to preserve the purity of your elections. I do not deny that necessity has no law, and that self-preservation may justify in states, as well as in individuals, an infringement of the rights of others. Were I a citizen of one of the southern states, I would not (much as I abhor slavery) advise an immediate and universal emancipation. But where is the necessity in the present instance? The whole number of coloured people in the state, whether free or in bondage, amounts to less than a fortieth part of the whole population.

When your numbers are to theirs as forty to one, do you still fear them? To assert this, would be to pay them a compliment which, I am sure, you do not think they deserve. But there are a greater number in the city of New-York. How many? Sir, in even that city, the whites are to the blacks as ten to one. And even of the tenth which is composed of the black population, how few are there that are entitled to vote? It has also been said that their numbers are rapidly increasing. The very reverse is the fact. During the last ten years, in which the white population has advanced with astonishing rapidity, the coloured population of the state has been stationary. This fact appears from the official returns of the last and the preceding census, and completely refutes the arguments which are founded upon this mis-statement. Will you, then, without necessity, and merely to gratify an unreasonable prejudice, stain the constitution you are about to form, with a provision equally odious and unjust, and in direct violation of the principles which you profess, and upon which you intend to form it? I trust, I am sure, you will not.

Erastus Root of Delaware County likened African Americans to resident foreign-born aliens, who paid taxes, were not required to serve the nation in war, and did not possess the ballot. He also questioned the relevance of New York's emphatic antislavery stance during the Missouri crisis, distinguishing between the state's domestic interest and its national political posture. Root, perhaps seeking to expose lingering wounds over Federalist opposition to the War of 1812, claimed that New York City blacks simply did the bidding at the polls of the same wealthy people who employed them for personal service. Then, questioning the patriotism of African Americans, he proposed language that would disfranchise this class of people by stating that only those eligible for service in the militia, as defined by federal law, be eligible for the franchise. Federal law specifically identified whites as eligible for militia service, and thus, in Root's formula, blacks would be excluded from the franchise.[27]

GEN. ROOT[28] . . . proceeded to explain his views of the social compact.

Sir . . . in the formation of a social compact, which generally grows out of exigency, when the people are but a little removed from their barbarous and rude state, they are not particular in enumerating the principles upon which they thus unite; but when they become more enlightened, they will undertake to say who shall belong to their family.

In my judgment, every one who is taken into the bosom of that family, and made to contribute, either in property or personal service, to the benefit of that family, should have a voice in managing its concerns. It cannot be denied, that the preservation of property is a much less consideration, than that of a security in our liberty and independence. Every member of this political family, who is worthy to be one of its members, will prize much higher the freedom of the country, than the preservation of property.

Sir, for the preservation, or protection of property, you require a contribution in property towards the public fund—you do this in the case of an alien, who may hold property and be protected by the laws of your country, in the enjoyment of that property; but he is not allowed to vote. An alien is sometimes permitted, by a particular law to hold property; and if he is an able bodied man, he is required to fight in defence of this country, yet he is not allowed to vote. The reasons are, that notwithstanding he may live among us and enjoy the benefit of our freedom, he may have a partiality for some foreign country; therefore, he is not to partake fully of our privileges till after a certain probationary season. The black population have a right to hold property, and are protected in the enjoyment of it by our laws: but, sir, in case of an invasion or insurrection, neither the alien nor black man is bound to defend your country. They are not called on, because it is supposed there is no reliance to be placed in them, they might desert the standard and join your enemy— they have not any anchorage in your country which the government is willing to trust.

Then under this view of the subject, it appears to me they cannot complain at being excluded from voting, inasmuch as they are not bound to assist in the defence of the country; but have their liberty secured to them. It would be improper that they should come forward and vote for the election of a commander in chief, whom they were not bound to obey. We have been told by the honourable gentleman from Westchester, (Mr. Jay) and shall be again told, that we are about to deprive these people of a franchise, with which they are now vested. Sir, it is impossible to remoddle [*sic*] your constitution without changing the relative rights of your citizens. It is said that these people are now entitled to vote under our constitution, and that it is proposed to deprive them of this privilege—Are there not others who are in a measure disfranchised by the report of this committee, which requires nothing but a residence, and to have paid taxes, to qualify a man to vote for governor and senators?

I am not disposed to follow the gentleman, who has referred us to the resolutions of the legislature for the two years past, instructing our members in congress on the subject of the Missouri question. Whatever our legislature may have done, it is not to affect the operations of this Convention, in deciding upon the great question before us. Their wisdom may be considered as worthy of some consideration, still I flatter myself it will not materially vary the result of the question. It is not necessary that we should enquire whether there is a just cause of alarm, for fear that these blacks will hereafter disturb our political family. At present the number of blacks who are voters is so small, that if they were scattered all over the state, there would not be much danger to be apprehended; but if we may judge of the future by the past, I should suppose there was some cause of alarm—when a few hundred free negroes of the city of New-York, following the train of those who ride in their coaches, and whose shoes and boots they had so often blacked, shall go to the polls of the election, and change the political condition of the whole state. A change in the representation of that city may cause a change in your assembly, by giving a majority to a particular party, which would vary your council of appointment who make the highest officers of your government—Thus would the whole state be controlled by a few hundred of this species of population in the city of New-York.[29]

This is not all, in time of war these people who are not called on to fight your battles, may make the majority of your legislature, which will defeat every measure for the prosecution of that war; so that instead of being an "organized corps" to fight your battles, they may be an "organized corps" to defeat the energies of the state with all its patriotic exertions.

But although he was in favour of retaining some of the principles of the propositions submitted by the honourable gentleman from Albany, yet there were others which he disapproved. He, therefore, proposed to amend it (Mr. Young having withdrawn his motion to insert) in the following manner:—

But no person shall be allowed to vote for any elective officer in this state, who would not if an able bodied man, and within the proper age prescribed by the laws of the United States, be liable to the performance of militia duty, unless exempted by act of congress, or the laws of this state, on account of some public office, or being employed in some public trust, or particular business, deemed by the legislative authority to be specially beneficial to the

United States or this state, or unless he shall have paid within the year next preceding his offering his vote, a fair equivalent in money for his personal services and equipments, to be determined by the legislature, according to the estimated expense in time and equipments, of an ordinary, able bodied and efficient militiaman; *Provided* that any such person, above the age required by law for the performance of militia duty, and who shall have, before arriving at that age, paid such equivalent, or been liable therefor, if an able bodied man, and then resident in this state, may be permitted to vote at any such elections.

Mr. R. thought this provision would meet the views of gentlemen who entertained the same sentiments in relation to the black voters that he did, and at the same time preserve the delicacy of language which is observable in the constitution of the United States, which no where uses the word slave.[30]

Root's fellow Bucktail delegate from Delaware County, Robert Clarke, drew together the equality enshrined in the Declaration of Independence and the mechanisms of the U.S. Constitution to argue against disfranchisement. He also attempted to harness images of patriotism on behalf of black New Yorkers, citing African American service in the War of 1812. Ultimately, he argued that protecting black civil rights was the least that whites owed the victims of slavery. Samuel Young, of the suffrage committee, responded by unapologetically articulating his support of racial restrictions on voting. Young denied that there were any principles or fundamental rights at stake. Citing popular prejudice against blacks, he claimed that it was the convention's prerogative to deny access to the ballot as the public saw fit.

MR. R. CLARKE said he rose with considerable embarrassment, knowing the weight of experience, talent, and elocution opposed to him. I am, said Mr. C. opposed to my honourable colleague (Mr. Root) on this question, to whose judgment and experience I have generally been willing to pay due deference. I am unwilling to retain the word "*white*," because its detention is repugnant to all the principles and notions of liberty, to which we have heretofore professed to adhere, and to our declaration of independence, which is a concise and just expose of those principles. In that sacred instrument we have recorded the following incontrovertible truths—" *We hold these truths to be self-evident—that all men are created equal; that they are endowed by their Creator with certain unalienable rights; that among these are life, liberty, and the pursuit of happiness."*

The people of colour are capable of giving their consent, and ever since the formation of your government they have constituted a portion of the people, from whence your legislators have derived "their just powers;" and by retaining that word, you deprive a large and respectable number of the people of this state of privileges and rights which they have enjoyed in common with us, ever since the existence of our government, and to which they are justly entitled. Sir, to this declaration we all profess to be willing to subscribe, yet by retaining this word you violate one of the most important maxims it contains.

It has been appropriately observed by the honourable gentleman from Westchester, (Mr. Jay,) that, by retaining this word, you violate the constitution of the United States. Besides the clause quoted by that honourable gentleman, I think there is another upon which it crowds very hard. Free people of colour are included in the number which regulates your representation in congress, and I wish to know how freemen can be represented when they are deprived of the privilege of voting for representatives. The constitution says, "representatives and direct taxes shall be apportioned among the different states, according to the inhabitants thereof, including all free persons," &c.[31] All colours and complexions are here included. It is not free "white" persons. No, sir, our venerable fathers entertained too strong a sense of justice to countenance such an odious distinction.—Now, sir, taking this in connection with the declaration of independence, I think you cannot exclude them without being guilty of a palpable violation of every principle of justice. We are usurping to ourselves a power which we do not possess, and by so doing, deprive them of a privilege to which they are, and always have been, justly entitled— an invaluable right—a right in which we have prided ourselves as constituting our superiority over every other people on earth—a right which they have enjoyed ever since the formation of our government—the right of suffrage. And why do we do this? Instead of visiting the iniquities of these people upon them and their children, we are visiting their misfortunes upon them and their posterity unto the latest generation.[32] It was not expected of us, that in forming a constitution to govern this state, we should so soon have shewn a disposition to adopt plans fraught with usurpation and injustice. Because we have done this people injustice, by enslaving them, and rendering them degraded and miserable, is it right that we should go on and continue to deprive them of their most invaluable rights, and visit upon their children to the latest posterity this deprivation? Is this just? Is it honest? Was it expected by our constituents? Will it not fix a foul stain upon the proceedings of this Convention which time will not efface.

My honourable colleague has told us "that these people are not liable to do military duty, and that as they are not required to contribute to the protection or defence of the state, they are not entitled to an equal participation in the privileges of its citizens." But, sir, whose fault is this? Have they ever refused to do military duty when called upon? It is haughtily asked, who will stand in the ranks, shoulder to shoulder, with a negro? I answer, no one in time of peace; no one when your musters and trainings are looked upon as mere pastimes; no one when your militia will shoulder their muskets and march to their trainings with as much unconcern as they would go to a sumptuous entertainment, or a splendid ball. But, sir, when the hour of danger approaches, your "white" militia are just as willing that the man of colour should be set up as a mark to be shot at by the enemy, as to be set up themselves. In the war of the revolution, these people helped to fight your battles by land and by sea. Some of your states were glad to turn out corps of coloured men, and to stand "shoulder to shoulder" with them. In your late war they contributed largely towards some of your most splendid victories. On Lakes Erie and Champlain, where your fleets triumphed over a foe superior in numbers, and engines of death, they were manned in a large proportion with men of colour. And in this very house, in the fall of 1814, a bill passed receiving the approbation of all the branches of your government, authorizing the governor to accept the services of a corps of 2000 free people of colour.[33] Sir, these were times which tried men's souls.[34] In these times it was no sporting matter to bear arms. These were times when a man who shouldered his musket, did not know but he bared his bosom to receive a death wound from the enemy ere he laid it aside; and in these times these people were found as ready and as willing to volunteer in your service as any other. They were not compelled to go, they were not drafted. No, your pride had placed them beyond your compulsory power. But there was no necessity for its exercise; they were volunteers; yes, sir, volunteers to defend that very country from the inroads and ravages of a ruthless and vindictive foe, which had treated them with insult, degradation, and slavery. Volunteers are the best of soldiers; give me the men, whatever be their complexion, that willingly volunteer, and not those who are compelled to turn out; such men do not fight from necessity, nor from mercenary motives, but from principle. Such men formed the most efficient corps for your country's defence in the late war; and of such consisted the crews of your squadrons on Erie and Champlain, who largely contributed to the safety and peace of your country, and the renown of her arms. Yet, strange to tell, such are the men whom you seek to degrade and oppress.

There is another consideration which I think important. Our government is a government of the people, supported and upheld by public sentiment; and to support and perpetuate our free institutions, it is our duty and our interest to attach to it all the different classes of the community. Indeed there should be but one class. Then, sir, is it wise, is it prudent, is it consistent with sound policy, to compel a large portion of your people and their posterity, forever to become your enemies, and to view you and your political institutions with distrust, jealousy, and hatred, to the latest posterity; to alienate one portion of the community from the rest, and from their own political institutions? I grant you, sir, that in times of profound peace, their numbers are so small that their resentment could make no serious impression. But, sir, are we sure; can we calculate that we are always to remain in a state of peace? that our tranquillity is never again to be disturbed by invasion or insurrection? And, sir, when that unhappy period arrives, if they, justly incensed by the accumulated wrongs which you heap upon them, should throw their weight in the scale of your enemies, it might, and most assuredly would, be severely felt. Then your gayest and proudest militiamen that now stand in your ranks, would rather be seen "shoulder to shoulder" with a negro, than have him added to the number of his enemies, and meet him in the field of battle.

By retaining the word "white," you impose a distinction impracticable in its operation. Among those who are by way of distinction called whites, and whose legitimate ancestors, as far as we can trace them, have never been slaves, there are many shades of difference in complexion. Then how will you discriminate? and at what point will you limit your distinction? Will you here descend to particulars, or leave that to the legislature? If you leave it to them, you will impose upon them a burden which neither you nor they can bear. You ought not to require of them impossibilities. Men descended from African ancestors, but who have been pretty well white-washed by their commingling with your white population, may escape your scrutiny; while others, whose blood is as pure from any African taint as any member of this Convention, may be called upon to prove his pedigree, or forfeit his right of suffrage, because he happens to have a swarthy complexion. Are you willing, by any act of this Convention, to expose any, even the meanest, of your white citizens, to such an insult? I hope not.

But it is said these people are incapable of exercising the right of suffrage judiciously; that they will become the tools and engines of aristocracy, and set themselves up in market, and give their votes to the highest bidder; that they have no will or judgment of their own, but will follow implicitly the dictates of the purse-proud aristocrats of the day, on whom they depend for bread. This may be true to a certain extent; but, sir, they are not the only ones who abuse this privilege; and if this be a sufficient reason for depriving any of your citizens of their just rights, go on and exclude also the many thousands of white fawning, cringing sycophants, who look up to their more wealthy and more ambitious neighbours for direction at the polls, as they look to them for bread. But although most of this unfortunate class of men may at present be in this dependent state, both in body and mind, yet we ought to remember, that we are making our constitution, not for a day, nor a year, but I hope for many generations; and there is a redeeming spirit in liberty, which I have no doubt will eventually raise these poor, abused, unfortunate people, from their present degraded state, to equal intelligence with their more fortunate and enlightened neighbours.

Sir, there is a day now fixed by law, when slavery must forever cease in this state. Have gentlemen seriously reflected upon the consequences which may result from this event, when they are about to deprive them of every inducement to become respectable members of society, turning them out from the protection, and beyond the control of their masters, and in the mean time ordaining them to be fugitives, vagabonds, and outcasts from society.

Sir, no longer ago than last winter, the legislature of this state almost unanimously resolved, that their senators be instructed, and their representatives requested, to prevent any state from being admitted into this union, which should have incorporated in her constitution any provision denying to the citizens of "each state all the rights, privileges, and immunities of citizens of the several states." These instructions and requests, it is well known, particularly referred to Missouri; and were founded upon a clause in her constitution, interdicting this very class of people "from coming to, or settling in, that state, under any pretext whatsoever." Whether these instructions and requests were proper and expedient at that time or not, is not necessary for me to inquire; and I only refer to them to shew, how tenacious the representatives of the people were, at

that time, of even the smallest rights of this portion of their citizens—
rights of infinitely less importance to the free people of colour of this state,
than those of which you now propose to deprive them. About the same
time, my honourable colleague, then a member of the assembly of this
state, introduced a bill, declaring that, according to our declaration of independence and form of government, "slavery cannot exist in this state."
I shall give no opinion upon the propriety of passing such a law at this
day; but I will say, that even the advocating such a humane proposition,
gave honourable testimony of the benevolence of his heart. And is it possible, that the representatives of the same people should be found, in a few
short months afterwards, entertaining a proposition which virtually and
practically declares, that freedom, that liberty cannot exist in this state;
and this proposition receiving support from the same individual who last
winter was the champion of African emancipation.

Sir, I well know that this subject is attended with embarrassment and
difficulty, in whatever way it may be presented. I lament as much as any
gentleman, that we have this species of population among us. But we have
them here without any fault of theirs. They were brought here and enslaved by the arm of violence and oppression. We have heaped upon them
every indignity, every injustice; and in restoring them at this late day, (as
far as is practicable) to their natural rights and privileges, we make but a
very partial atonement for the many wrongs which we have heaped upon
them; and in the solemn work before us, as far as it related to these people, I would do them justice, and leave the consequences to the righteous
disposal of an all-wise and merciful Providence.

The honourable gentleman from Genesee (Mr. Ross) has said that they
were a *peculiar* people. We were told the other day that the people of
Connecticut were a *peculiar* people. Indeed this is a *peculiarly* happy
mode of evading the force of an argument. I admit that the blacks are a
peculiarly unfortunate people, and I wish that such inducements may be
held out, as shall induce them to become a sober and industrious class of
the community, and raise them to the high standard of independent electors.

COL. YOUNG expressed his intention to vote against the amendment
proposed by the gentleman from Albany (Mr. Van Rensselaer) on the express ground that it did not contain the limitation of *white*. He should use
no circumlocution nor disguise. He was willing to express his opinion
openly and fully, and to record his name in the journals of the Conven-

tion, and thereby transmit it to posterity. He was disposed to discharge the duty which he owed to the people without fear or favor.

The gentleman who had just sat down had adverted to the declaration of independence to prove that the blacks are possessed of "certain unalienable rights." But is the right of voting a natural right? If so, our laws are oppressive and unjust. A natural right is one that is born with us. No man is born twenty-one years old, and of course all restraint upon the natural right of voting, during the period of nonage, is usurpation and tyranny. This confusion arises from mixing natural with acquired rights. The right of voting is adventitious. It is resorted to only as a means of securing our natural rights.

In forming a constitution, we should have reference to the feelings, habits, and modes of thinking of the people. The gentleman last up has alluded to the importance of regarding public sentiment. And what is the public sentiment in relation to this subject? Are the negroes permitted to a participation in social intercourse with the whites! Are they elevated to public office! No, sir—public sentiment forbids it. This they know; and hence they are prepared to sell their votes to the highest bidder. In this manner you introduce corruption into the very vitals of the government.

A few years ago a law was made requiring the clerks of the respective counties to make out a list of jurymen. Was a negro ever returned upon that list? If he were, no jury would sit with him. Was a constable ever known to summon a negro as a juror, even before a justice of the peace in a matter of five dollars amount? Never,—but gentlemen who would shrink from such an association, would now propose to associate with him in the important act of electing a governor of the state.

This distinction of colour is well understood. It is unnecessary to disguise it, and we ought to shape our constitution so as to meet the public sentiment. If that sentiment should alter—if the time should ever arrive when the African shall be raised to the level of the white man—when the distinctions that now prevail shall be done away—when the colours shall intermarry—when negroes shall be invited to your tables—to sit in your pew, or ride in your coach, it may then be proper to institute a new Convention, and remodel the constitution so as to conform to that state of society.

It has been urged, however, that it is not their fault that they do not serve in the militia. Granted—but state authority cannot compel them to serve. That subject is left to the general government, which directs the enrolment of *white* citizens only. *Expressio unius, est exclusio alterius.*[35]

An argument has been raised that the proposition in the report of the committee would deprive them of *vested rights*.

It has been correctly remarked in reply, by the gentleman from Delaware, (Mr. Root,) that you cannot vary or extend the rights of one class, without infringing upon those of another. Formerly, no residence was required for a voter. Now it is proposed to require the residence of a year; and perhaps by that provision the rights of four or five hundred emigrants may be affected, and by this, we may possibly exclude four or five hundred black freeholders. The argument in the one case will apply to the other.

If we look back to the time when our constitution was formed, we find that there were then few or no free blacks in the state. The present state of things was not contemplated, and hence no provision was made against it. The same was the case in Connecticut. In their recent constitution they have provided for the exclusion of the blacks.

If you admit the negroes, why exclude the aborigines?[36] They have never been enslaved. They were born, free as the air they breathe. That want of self-respect which characterises the negroes, cannot be imputed to them.

It is said that the negroes fought our battles. So did aliens—the French. But were the French on that account entitled to vote at our elections? No, sir. It is a question of expediency; and believing as I do, that the blacks would abuse the privilege if granted, I am disposed to withhold it.

After some procedural discussions, Peter Jay made a motion to remove the word white *from the suffrage committee's original proposal. Jay's motion met with the approval of Albany delegate James Kent, a conservative Federalist. The distinguished chancellor of New York's courts questioned whether it would permissible under the federal Constitution to ban black voting and mocked the entire notion of color as a meaningful distinction among men. Young, unmoved, cited disfranchisement in Connecticut as precedent and engaged in some mockery of his own.*

MR. KENT[37] . . . We did not come to this Convention to *disfranchise* any portion of the community, or to take away their rights. Suppose a negro owning a freehold and entitled to vote in Vermont, removes to this state. Can we constitutionally exclude him from enjoying that privilege? The constitution of the United States provides that "the citizens of each state shall be entitled to all the privileges and immunities of citizens in the several states;" and it deserved consideration whether such exclusion would not be opposed to the constitution of the United States.

There was much difficulty in the practical operation of such a principle. What shall be the criterion in deciding upon the different shades of colour? The Hindoo and Chinese are called yellow—the Indian *red!* Shall these be excluded should they come to reside among us? Great efforts were now making in the Christian world to enlighten and improve their condition, and he thought it inexpedient to erect a barrier that should exclude them forever from the enjoyment of this important right.

COL. YOUNG replied, and enforced the reasons which he had previously urged against the amendment that had been withdrawn.

It had been objected that the measure would be a hardship upon the blacks. But it had been recently and soberly done in the land of "steady habits" [*Connecticut*]. And are we more wise, more sober, more correct, than they? We ought to make a constitution adapted to *our* habits, manners, and state of society. Metaphysical refinements and abstract speculations are of little use in framing a constitution. No white man will stand shoulder to shoulder with a negro in the train band or jury-room. He will not invite him to a seat at his table, nor in his pew in the church. And yet he must be placed on a footing of equality in the right of voting, and on no other occasion whatever, either civil or social.

It had been said that there was no criterion to determine questions of fact in relation to the various shades of colour. That will be left for the legislature to define and settle. And although there may be some difficulty in individual cases, yet that circumstance furnishes no argument against the establishment of the principle.

The minds of the blacks are not competent to vote. They are too much degraded to estimate the value, or exercise with fidelity and discretion that important right. It would be unsafe in their hands. Their vote would be at the call of the richest purchaser. If this class of people should hereafter arrive at such a degree of intelligence and virtue, as to inspire confidence, then it will be proper to confer this privilege upon them. At present emancipate and protect them; but withhold that privilege which they will inevitably abuse. Look to your jails and penitentiaries. By whom are they filled? By the very race, whom it is now proposed to cloth with the power of deciding upon your political rights.

If there is that natural, inherent right to vote, which some gentlemen have urged, it ought to be further extended. In New-Jersey, females were formerly allowed to vote; and on that principle, you must admit *negresses* as well as *negroes* to participate in the right of suffrage. Minors, too, and aliens must no longer be excluded, but the "era of good feelings" be commenced in earnest.

Responding to remarks by New York City delegate Jacob Radcliff and addressing questions of citizenship posed by the debate, Rufus King spoke. King, the most nationally prominent active Federalist in the state, had been a leading opponent of admitting Missouri to the Union as a slave state. King concurred with Kent that the racially exclusive constitutional language under consideration in New York violated the federal compact. Yet his remarks also revealed his own prejudices and anxieties regarding race and citizenship.

MR. KING . . . The constitution of the United States is beyond the control of any act of any of the states. It is a compact, to which the people of this state, in common with those of other states, are parties, and cannot recede from it without the consent of all. With this understanding, what, let me ask, is the meaning of the provision quoted by the gentleman from Albany, (Mr. Kent.) Take the fact that a citizen of colour, entitled to all the privileges of a citizen, comes here. He purchases a freehold; can you deny him the rights of an elector, incident to his freehold? He is entitled to vote, because, like any other citizen, he is a freeholder; and every freeholder your laws entitle to vote. He comes here, he purchases property, he pays you taxes, conforms to your laws; how can you then, under the article of the constitution of the United States which has been read, exclude him. The gentleman from New-York (Mr. Radcliff) thinks, that the meaning of this provision in the United States' constitution extends only to *civil* rights: such is not the text, it is to all rights. This seems to me to lay an insuperable barrier in our way. But I am, at the same time free to confess, that I am fully alive to the difficulties of this question, though I do not feel that they do now press upon us. I am not sure how a black, unless born free, may become a citizen; a man born a slave cannot be a citizen: a red man cannot be a citizen; they cannot even be naturalized, for naturalization can only be effected under the laws of the United States, which limit to the whites. The subject is evidently full of difficulties, though, as I before said, they are not now pressing. But the period is not distant when they must be. As certainly as the children of any white man are citizens, so certainly the children of the black men are citizens;

and they, may in time, raise up a progeny, which will be disastrous to the other races of this country. I will not trouble the Convention further; but I thought it due to the occasion to express my opinion of the constitutional barriers which interpose, to prevent our retaining the word "white" in the clause.

After further remarks by Young and Root, the Convention adjourned until the following morning.

THURSDAY, SEPTEMBER 20, 1821

Albany Federalist and former New York attorney general Abraham Van Vechten began the day's discussion by questioning why a convention called to expand the franchise was attempting to strip blacks of the vote. African Americans, he reminded the convention, had held the right of suffrage for almost fifty years. He asserted that the principles of New York's gradual abolition of slavery included black citizenship and enfranchisement.

MR. VAN VECHTEN[38] observed, that the question before the committee was of importance, and one on which he should be happy to see a unanimous vote. It had been said that the people looked for an extension of the right of suffrage, but he had not heard it suggested that they desired the disfranchisement of any class of electors.—The amendment reported by the select committee contemplated to deprive electors of colour of a right which they have enjoyed since the adoption of the constitution. He asked why this should be done? Those electors are freemen, and have been recognized as citizens of the state nearly half a century; have under the sanction of our constitution and laws duly acquired the legal qualifications of electors. Have they done any thing to forfeit their right of suffrage? This has not been shewn. It was indeed urged that they are a degraded people, wanting intelligence, integrity, and independence, who sell their votes to the highest bidder, and that many commit perjury to make themselves voters. But what evidence have the committee to fix those imputations on that class of electors, which does not fix the same imputation, on as numerous a class of white electors? Is perjury, moral degradation, ignorance, and want of independence confined to the electors of colour? Have they the capacity to acquire and take care of the property which is necessary to constitute them electors, and are they incapable of enjoying the privileges which the acquisition of property entitles them to?

Is it competent for us to prescribe what moral and intellectual qualifications will constitute an honest and independent elector? I presume not, (said Mr. Van Vechten,) nor has the select committee attempted to do so, except by excluding persons duly convicted of infamous crimes.

—It seems that some gentlemen entertain doubts whether any of our people of colour are in a legal sense citizens, but those doubts were in his opinion unfounded.—We are precluded from denying their citizenship, by our uniform recognition for more than forty years—nay some of them were citizens when this state came into political existence—partook in our struggle for freedom and independence, and were incorporated into the body politic at its creation. As to their degradation, that had been produced by the injustice of white men, and it does not become those who have acted so unjustly towards them, to urge the result of that injustice as a reason for perpetuating their degradation.—The period has elapsed when they were considered and treated as the lawful property of their masters. Our legislature has duly recognized their unalienable right to freedom as rational and accountable beings. This recognition, and the provision made by law for the gradual amelioration of their condition, by necessary implication, admit their title to the native and acquired rights of citizenship. Indeed the report of the select committee considers them to be citizens—why else are the words *white citizens* used in the report? If there are no citizens of colour the term *white* by way of distinction is unmeaning. Again, the law under which the members of this Convention were elected, expressly gives the right of voting not only for calling the Convention, and at the election of its members, but on the amendments which the Convention may propose to the constitution. Are not these unequivocal and conclusive concessions of their citizenship?

But it is said that they are by law exempted from sharing the public burthens of militia service, and serving as jurors, because public sentiment is against an intermixture with them in those services. Mr. Van Vechten remarked that their exemption from militia duty, was the gratuitous act of the government of the United States, in which the free people of colour were not consulted. With respect to serving on juries there is no legal exemption in favour of the people of colour who have the qualifications prescribed by law for jurors. It is true that in compliance with the prejudices of the community they are practically excluded from jury service, and probably their exemption from militia duty was induced by the same motive. But is this a just ground for defranchising them? Are they not liable, whenever the government shall see fit to require them, to render the same services that white citizens are enjoined to perform? Are they not taxable, and do not many of them pay their proportion of taxes in common with white citizens? This cannot be denied. How then can we in framing a permanent form of government, justly deny them the rights of free citizens, on account of their present exemption by law from militia duty, and their practical exemption from serving as jurors? Do our prejudices against their colour destroy their rights as citizens? Whence do those prejudices proceed? Are they founded in impartial reason, or in the benevolent principles of our holy religion? Nay, are they indulged in cases where the services of men of colour are desirable? Do we not daily see them working side by side with white citizens on our farms, and on our public highways? Is it more derogatory to a white citizen to stand by the side of a citizen of colour in the ranks of the militia, than in repairing a highway, or in labouring on a farm? Again, are not people of colour permitted to participate in our most solemn religious exercises—to set down with us at the same table to commemorate the dying love of the Saviour of sinners? This will not be denied by any one who has been in the habit of attending those exercises, and those religious solemnities—And what is the conclusion to which this fact directs us? Is it not that people of colour are our fellow candidates for immortality, and that the same path to future happiness is appointed for them and us—and that in the final judgment the artificial distinction of colour will not be regarded.—How then can that distinction justify us in taking from them any of the common rights which every other free citizen enjoys?

There is another, and to my mind, an insuperable objection, said Mr. V. V., to the exclusion of free citizens of color from the right of suffrage, arising from the provision in the constitution of the United States, "that the citizens of each state shall be entitled to all privileges and immunities of citizens in the several states." The effect of this provision is, to secure to the citizens of the other states, when they come to reside here, equal privileges and immunities with our native citizens. Suppose, then, that a free citizen of colour should remove from the state of Connecticut into this state, could we deny him the right of suffrage when he obtained the legal qualification of an elector? Is not the constitution of the United States paramount to ours on the subject? and if it is, will it be wise or fit to incorporate an amendment in our constitution, by which we deny to our own citizens of colour, a privilege which we cannot withhold from the same description of citizens of other states, when they migrate into this state.

It has been stated by the gentleman from Saratoga, (Mr. Young) that by the constitution of Connecticut, which has been recently adopted, the right of suffrage is confined to white male citizens. But on looking into the constitution it will be seen that the first section relative to the qualifications of electors, expressly saves and confirms the right of suffrage to all who had been or should be made freemen of that state before the ratification of the constitution. It will not be denied that citizenship was necessary to enable any person to become a freeman in Connecticut, nor can it be disputed that there are and have long been freemen of colour in that state. We have therefore the authority of the framers of the constitution of Connecticut against the principle of disfranchising our present electors of colour.

The gentleman from Saratoga, as well as the gentleman from New-York, (Mr. Radcliff) contend that the provision in the constitution of the United States which has been quoted, relates to civil rights, and not to the political privileges. On what is the distinction founded? Is not the language of the constitution "all privileges and immunities" broad enough to comprehend both civil rights, and political privileges? Are there any qualifying words to support the distinction? Is not the right of suffrage admitted on all sides to be an important privilege? Surely the gentleman's distinction is not only unfounded, but inconsistent with the clear and unequivocal language of the constitution, as well as with the obvious policy which induced to the provision in question in its broadest sense. . . .

Mr. V. V. concluded by repeating that he had understood that it was expected by a considerable portion of the people of this state, that the right of suffrage would be extended, but he had not heard that it was expected or desired (except by some of the citizens of New-York) that any of the present electors of this state should be disfranchised. He should therefore vote for striking out the word *white* in the amendment before the committee, in order to reserve inviolate the present constitutional rights of all the electors.

Representing Albany, New York Supreme Court chief justice Ambrose Spencer spoke in defense of the right of the convention to define the rights of suffrage to safeguard the interests of "the majority of the community" by defining particular groups as ineligible to vote. He denied that the U.S. Constitution interfered with this principle. But the conservative jurist argued further that the interests of the state would suffer from too generous an expansion of suffrage laws for white people as well. He raised the specter of poor voters acting not as independent citizens but as pawns of their wealthy employers and providers.

CHIEF JUSTICE SPENCER[39] said, it was the duty of every man to contribute his aid in arriving at a just result in this important question. He thought he might say he had not wasted much of the time of this Convention. The subject was a momentous one—not merely the proposition before the committee, but the subject matter of it; and certainly he could not justify himself in remaining silent on this important question. He should lay it down as a fundamental maxim, that in proceeding to amend the constitution, this Convention had an unquestionable right to protect and guard the rights of the majority of the community, although it may seemingly invade the rights of others; that the community has a right to secure its own happiness and prosperity, and that we are authorized to adopt all means that shall conduce to that end. If we find existing in this community any particular class of people, who cannot with propriety and safety exercise and enjoy certain privileges, we have a right to abridge them by placing them in the hands of the majority. We have in our constitution determined that no man under twenty-one years shall exercise the right of suffrage, upon the presumption that they do not possess mature understandings, and therefore have not a right to enjoy this privilege. Has the correctness of this principle ever been doubted? He believed not, although many arrive at maturity of understanding, and are ornaments of society, before they reach that age. It is necessary in establishing laws, to have general rules. He therefore had no hesitation to say, that with regard to the blacks, whatever we have to accuse ourselves of, from our own fault, or the fault of our ancestors, we have the unquestionable right, if we think the exercise of this privilege by them will contravene the public good; we have a right to say they shall not enjoy it. This is consistent with the feelings of every man.

Sir, difficulties have been urged, and it has been supposed by some gentlemen, that it is an infringement of the constitution of the United States, which says "the citizens of each state shall be entitled to all the privileges and immunities of citizens in the several states." Now, sir, said Mr. Spencer, I have two answers to this: First, If by adopting this principle we shall not be able to exclude men of colour from coming from states, where they enjoy that privilege, the committee know that any thing we may do, inconsistent with the constitution of the United States, would be ineffectual; if it be competent for us to do so, it would be inoperative. This

is one answer. We therfore need not be deterred on that ground. I go farther; and must be permitted, with great deference to those distinguished
gentlemen who are opposed to me on this subject, to express my own
views of the construction of that article. My own opinion is, that this
clause regards mere personal rights. It was intended by the constitution
to admit persons of other states to purchase property, and enjoy all the
personal rights, as in the states whence they came. Let us look at it in relation to the constitutions of the several states. We have declared that a
person to be eligible to the office of governor must have been a resident
of this state a certain number of years, before he is qualified. Now, I ask,
whether an emigrant from the state of Vermont would contend, that he
was eligible to that office, in the same manner as if he had always resided
in this state? A residence of six months is required to entitle a person to
vote; but a person coming from Vermont, upon the principle here contended for, would say that he had a right to vote, because he had been enrolled in the militia, without reference to the question how long he had
resided in the state. . . . [A] person of colour coming from another state,
would have the privileges as one of the same class here. He should forbear to enlarge upon this part of the subject; but he did hope that gentlemen would concur with him in believing that this clause in the constitution regarded personal rights, and no other.

In arranging its municipal affairs, any government may adopt such
regulations as it may think fit. A citizen has no more right to claim to be
an elector, than to be elected.—The regulation of the right of voting is an
arrangement for the public good; and upon the principal question, if we
would conscientiously decide, he believed we should say, that persons of
colour do not possess the requisite qualifications for exercising this privilege with discretion. They are a degraded race—it is in part our fault. It
had been considered since his day by good and pious individuals, that
slavery was lawful—that it was justified by scripture. That opinion has
changed—the contrary is believed by all classes of people; and we ought
not to deprive them of rights, if by permitting them to enjoy those rights,
we do not injure ourselves. Provision has been made in this state for the
abolition of their bondage; but in other states slavery exists.—Gradual
emancipations may take place; and the truth is not to be disguised, that
slaves, thus emancipated, are flocking into this state, and particularly into
the metropolis. This consideration ought to arrest the attention of this
committee.

He did verily believe, that this description of persons lacked intelligence. It was not owing to their nature altogether, but partly to the manner in which they had been brought up, that they were not capable of judging discreetly in matters of government. Though he should vote against this motion, yet he must connect it with other propositions reported by the committee. He admitted that we have a right to do so for our own safety and security. It has been said by some gentlemen, that by their enjoying these privileges, others were to be abridged—this is not the test; and yet with regard to the report of this committee, they admit a large number of persons to vote, merely because they contribute to the support of the government by their personal services. On this subject how stands our constitution now, with regard to the most numerous branch of the legislature? [Here Mr. Spencer read the clause of the constitution, regulating the votes for members of assembly.] The first inquiry will now be, how many persons will be admitted to the right of suffrage, who do not at present enjoy it, under the existing constitution. The second, whether extending this right in so great a degree, as is proposed, would be compatible with the interests of this state. The report says, that all white male citizens, who within the year immediately preceding the election, have worked on the highways, have been enrolled in the militia, &c. shall be allowed to vote. This will be on the ground of their contributing to the public fund.

Let me ask, said Mr. S. to whom this right will be extended? It will principally be extended to single persons, who have no families, nor permanent residence; to those who work in your factories, and are employed by wealthy individuals, in the capacity of labourers. Now, I hold, and I do it with all deference to the opinions of others—for I do not mean to charge any thing upon this committee—but I do hold, that it will be one of the most aristocratic acts that was ever witnessed in this community—under the pretence of giving the right to them, we in fact give it to those who employ, clothe, and feed them. I appeal to this Convention, whether they do not believe, that a man who employs twenty, thirty, or fifty of these persons, if, on the approach of an election, he tells them that he wishes them to vote for this or that candidate, whether they will not feel themselves bound to comply with his wishes. That man who holds in his hands the subsistence of another, will always be able to control his will. Such a person will forever be the creature of the one who feeds, shelters, clothes, and protects him. This class of persons, would be as subservient to the will of their employers, as persons of colour. In truth, it would seem to me, that under the notion that there is a call for extending the right of suffrage, this report goes to the most extravagant length.

He said he would explain what he believed to be the origin of this sentiment in favour of extending the elective franchise. The western part of this state has increased with an almost unexampled rapidity, with a virtuous and intelligent people—I speak of those who hold lands by virtue of contracts. They have gone on improving their estates, and paying as far as they could; but in very few cases have they completed their payments, and merely for the want of a form of a deed, they have been excluded from the right of voting. A short time since, attempts had been made in the legislature to invest them with the privilege of voting, as being equitable freeholders, but the attempt did not succeed; and their condition certainly does appear to call for some relief.

I have believed, and do still believe, said Mr. S. that we are called on to extend the right of suffrage, as far as the interests of the community will permit; but I do think we cannot contemplate carrying it to the full extent recommended in the report, without knowing that we are not giving it to those people who will nominally enjoy the right, but to those who feed and clothe them. I shall vote against striking out the word white, on the ground that it is necessary for securing our own happiness. I cannot say I would deprive those people, who have acquired property, of the privilege of voting; but I cannot consent to extend it to others, in whose hands it will be as much abused as by these coloured people. I am willing to extend the right of suffrage as far as my conscience will admit; but I never can agree to extend it so far, as to deprive the agricultural interests of this state of the rights which they ought to enjoy. I never can consent to extend this right, and make an aristocracy by giving the man who has the longest purse, the power to control the most votes.

Following Justice Spencer's remarks, three delegates elaborated on issues raised in the previous day's debate. James Tallmadge Jr. offered data to suggest that black voter turnout in New York City was so low that he wondered "whether the evil complained of was of a magnitude to require the disfranchisement of this unfortunate race." Jacob Radcliff of New York City sought to bolster the argument for constitutional legitimacy of disfranchisement by noting numerous other states that had imposed racial restrictions on voting. Leading Bucktail Republican delegate Peter

R. Livingston of Dutchess County then launched a broad assault against
black voting rights. After reviewing New York's history to show that the
original New York constitution was written under the presumption that
blacks were slaves, not potentially enfranchised citizens, Livingston as-
serted that it was present needs, not past precedent, that should determine
the convention's course of action. He emphasized the allegedly low pub-
lic morals of the New York City black community and the potential size
and influence of an urban black electorate.

MR. RADCLIFF[40] . . . The constitutions of Kentucky, Ohio, Louisiana,
Indiana, Mississippi, Illinois, Alabama, and Missouri, all new states, contain similar provisions. These having been formed since the original association, were required to submit their respective constitutions to congress for their approbation, as preliminary to their admission into the political family. They did so—and this question has therefore been decided
by congress no less than eight times without a single objection ever having been raised against the unconstitutionality of such a provision. The
Missouri question was of a political nature, and altogether different from
the present.

Mr. R. further illustrated the arguments that had been offered in support of the report of the committee, and answered the objections that had
been raised. In reply to the remark, that whites were often as profligate as
the blacks, he admitted it; but the same could not be said of them as a
class: and if gentlemen could draw a line of distinction that should divide
the profligate from the virtuous, he would cheerfully give it his support
without reference to colour. He contended that it would be conferring no
benefit upon the blacks to allow them to vote. It only led to scenes of dis-
sipation and expense. The principle of extension, as reported by the committee, would give us 2,500 negro votes in the city of New-York—and he
hoped that gentlemen from the country would not, merely because they
felt no pressure from the evil, let loose upon that city a host of voters that
might give law to the whites, and in the consequences affect the remotest
corners of the state.

MR. LIVINGSTON. The Convention, sir, have arrived at that part of
their business which is the most interesting to the public at large. The
questions relating to the legislative and executive branches are less important, because they are at all times in the hands of the people, who can

dispose of them at their pleasure. But we have now come back to the right of suffrage—a right which comes home to the business and bosom of every man.

It may be expedient to review our constitutional history. When these states separated from the mother country, and formed constitutions of government, they declared that all men were free and equal; and yet in the next breath they gave a practical refutation of the doctrine they had advanced, by depriving their citizens of equal rights, in granting privileges to the rich which were denied to the poor. And why did they exclude the latter from the right of suffrage? Public policy required it. The wealth of this state was comparatively in the hands of a few individuals. Four or five families could almost control the wealth of the state, and it was necessary to conciliate the rich to avail themselves of their influence and wealth. What was then the situation of the people of colour? They were slaves. A free negro was a phenomenon in the state. They were recognized only as property. Since that time various acts hare been passed ameliorating their condition—providing for their gradual emancipation—and prohibiting their exportation to foreign states as slaves. But after having thus provided for their emancipation, and welfare, it behoves us to have regard to the safety of ourselves. Grant them emancipation. Grant them the protection of your laws, and the enjoyment of their religion. But if they are dangerous to your political institutions, put not a weapon into their hands to destroy you. It is indeed painful to review their condition. But look at that people, and ask your consciences if they are competent to vote. Ask yourselves honestly, whether they have intelligence to discern, or purity of principle to exercise, with safety, that important right. Look at their memorial on your table. Out of about fifty petitioners, more than twenty could not even write their names—and those petitioners were doubtless of the most respectable of the colour. Such persons must always be subject to the influence of the designing; and when they approach the ballot boxes, they are too ignorant to know whether their vote is given to elevate another to office, or to hang themselves upon the gallows.

It is said, indeed, that the danger consists only in the city of New-York. And is not that city entitled to our protection? A city which embraces one-tenth of the population, and two-thirds of the wealth of the state? a city that is your boast, and the sinew of your prosperity, and which, if it takes a wrong direction, jeopardizes the dearest interests of the state. Sir, I remember that in 1801, the political complexion of our national government depended upon, and was changed by, the vote of a single ward in the city of New-York.

My honourable colleague has told you that at a recent election, there were but 163 black votes given in that city. I believe he has been misinformed. But whatever may have been the number *admitted*, there were more than 500 that *applied* for admission; and if they are not excluded, the principle of the report will let in upon that devoted city a horde of voters whom I will forbear to describe. Description could not do justice to the picture—but I ask this Convention what intercourse they, as individuals, would hold with them? Aside from all considerations of colour, what has been their conduct that should entitle them to your hospitalities and association? What privilege have you conferred—what protection have you granted them, that has not been abused? I refer to documents that can give the answer. Look into your calendars. Survey your prisons—your alms-houses—your bridewells[41] and your penitentiaries, and what a darkening host meets your eye! More than one-third of the convicts and felons which those walls enclose, are of your sable population. Sir, I wish to excite no hostile feelings towards them. I pity them from my heart. I lament their condition. I am disposed to amend it; but I cannot consent to invest them with a power that may be wielded to the destruction of all we hold dear.

We have been told by the honourable gentleman from Albany, (Mr. Van Vechten) that we were not sent here to deprive any portion of the community of their vested rights. Sir, the people are here themselves. They are present in their delegates. No restriction limits our proceedings. What are these *vested* rights? Sir, we are standing upon the foundations of society. The elements of government are scattered around us. All rights are buried, and from the shoots that spring from their grave, we are to weave a bower that shall overshadow and protect our liberties. Our proceedings will pass in review before that power that elected us; and it will be for the people to decide whether the blacks are elevated upon a ground which we cannot reach. Sir, we, all of us, entered into the government subject to the implied condition that our constitution was liable to revision and alteration; and that the blacks, in this particular, have vested rights exempt from the power of abridgment or alteration, which the whites have not, I have yet to learn.

But, sir, look to the savages that inhabit your western counties. You have governed them by your laws. You have legislated over them. You have taken their property into your keeping. But where have you allowed them to vote? And why will you debar them a privilege to confer it upon a race infinitely beneath them in all those properties and attributes that give worth and dignity to man?

But, sir, we are presented with a constitutional impediment. I shall not stop to discuss the technical construction, it may bear; but I hold that it is incompetent for the general government to interpose in the regulation of our municipal affairs. It is a privilege incident to that state sovereignty which has been reserved. Has congress the right to dictate to the state of New-York what shall be the qualifications of her voters? It cannot be pretended. Suppose the legislature of this state should enact, as they have an undoubted right to do, that no black man shall be admitted as a witness; and suppose a suitor in a court of justice should demand that a black man, who had been imported from a neighbouring state where no such law existed, should be admitted to testify in defiance of your law, would his demand avail him? And yet if the construction contended for be correct, that suitor might rest himself upon the constitution of the general government, and give your law to the winds. No sir, the constitution of the United States does not—nor was it ever intended that it should, interfere with the local regulations of the several states. Such a construction would annihilate our sovereignty and prostrate our independence forever.

Peter Jay responded to the attacks on black citizenship with a series of pointed criticisms. First, he debunked the argument that black disfranchisement was analogous to New York's constitutional provision barring clergy from holding state office. He then lectured his colleagues that permanent racial disfranchisement was an abuse of public power. Jay also addressed the relationship between slavery, emancipation, and citizenship, denying that New York had any more to fear from black citizenship than they did from emancipation itself and mocking the notion that New York should fear the unlikely event of Southern emancipation flooding New York with free black people. The Westchester County Federalist concluded by attacking the color prejudice upon which plans for disfranchisement ultimately rested.

MR. JAY in reply—Mr. Chairman—I am sensible that little remains to be gleaned, in a field which has been so well reaped. Still, there are some arguments which deserve a reply, and some points which have been discussed, upon which a few rays of light may perhaps yet be thrown. It has been repeatedly urged, that since the whole body of the clergy, have, from reasons of political convenience, been disfranchised, we may with equal justice, and for the same reasons, disfranchise the people of colour. But is it true that the clergy are disfranchised? or that their case is similar to that of the people whose rights we are now considering? The clergy have a right to vote, and do vote; they have a right to be represented, and they are represented. The only restriction put upon them, is, that while they exercise the pastoral office, they shall exercise no other. If this be disfranchisement, the chancellor and chief justice of the state are equally disfranchised. Neither of those high officers can be a representative in the legislature unless he resigns his judicial office. But if he resigns it, he immediately becomes eligible; so a clergyman, while he exercises his pastoral office, may not be elected, but if he resigns that office and ceases to be a minister of the gospel, he may, for any thing that I know to the contrary, accept any other appointment which the people shall please to bestow upon him. History proves, that the interference of the clergy in secular concerns, has usually been prejudicial to the public: that when they mingled in the heats and asperities of political parties, they impaired their own dignity and usefulness, and occasioned dissensions and distrusts among the flocks committed to their charge. The Convention, therefore, which framed our constitution, thought it wise to set them apart, and to confine them to the high and honourable office of instructing the people in their most important duties, and to exempt them from all those offices which would expose them to the rancour of political contests. But what analogy is there between these provisions, and that by which all people of a certain complexion are to be excluded from the right of suffrage? A clergyman has that right; a black is to be excluded from it. A clergyman may not be elected, a black man may be. The disability of the clergyman is annexed to the clerical character, and ceases with it; the disability of the black man is to be annexed to his blood, is never to be removed, and is to be inseparable from him and his posterity to the latest generation. Again it has been urged, that the case of the people of colour is similar to that of the Indians. This also is a mistake. The Indian tribes are considered by us as independent nations. We send to them ambassadors, we receive ambassadors from them, and make treaties with them. They are aliens to us, and we to them.

Under these circumstances, they are no more entitled to vote at our elections, than Englishmen, Frenchmen, or other foreigners. But should an Indian forsake his tribe and settle in the county of Dutchess, his child, born there, would be as much a citizen, as either of the members from that county, and as much entitled to a vote. Another argument, sir, has been strongly pressed by the gentleman from whom I have the misfortune to differ upon this occasion. It is insisted, that this Convention, clothed with all the powers of the sovereign people of the state, have a right to construct the government in the manner they think most conducive to the general good—If, sir, right and power be equivalent terms, then I am far from disputing the rights of this assembly. We have power, sir, I acknowledge, not only to disfranchise every black family, but as many white families also as we may think expedient. We may place the whole government in the hands of a few, and thus construct an aristocracy; nay, I do not perceive why the reasons of some gentlemen would not prove, that we have power to confine the government to a single family, and then a monarchy might be the result. But, sir, right and power are not convertible terms. No man, no body of men, however powerful, have a right to do wrong. And if it be unjust to exclude from all participation in the government of their country, those who are the free born natives of its soil, and who possess all the qualifications required from others to whom we secure the right of suffrage, merely because their complexion displeases us, then, whatever may be our powers we have no right to commit this injustice.

Mr. Chairman, we have often heard the term legitimate, and we have been taught to abhor it. What is the meaning of this term? It means, in the language of courts, that by the ancient constitutions of certain countries, all power is vested in a few families, some royal, others noble, and that none other have a right to interfere in the government. We consider this doctrine at once odious and absurd, and we call upon the citizens of those countries, to resist it even unto blood. And yet, sir, we now sit here debating whether we shall confine the government of this state to certain families, and whether all the other families in the state shall not be forever excluded from any share of it. To this, my opponents answer, that the safety of the people is the supreme law and that the moral condition of the people of colour, renders their exclusion an act of duty—and a gentleman opposite has asked me, whether, notwithstanding my abhorrence to slavery, I would advise the state of South-Carolina, or of Georgia, to adopt the measures of an immediate emancipation. I had already given a distinct answer to this question in the observations which I first addressed to the committee on this subject—I then said, that an immediate and universal emancipation of the slaves in those states, would be productive of more misery, and probably of more crime, than a continuance of the present state of things, and that therefore, I should not advise it—and I admitted, that great and imperious public necessity would justify a sacrifice of private right to the public good—But, sir, I appeal to the candour of the gentlemen themselves, whether they have made out a case of such necessity. It had not been, nor could it be, asserted, that the votes of the coloured population have ever occasioned the smallest inconvenience, or the slightest discontent, in a single county of the state, except New-York. And it appears that even in that city, the number of those votes at the last contested election were less than two hundred—and is it possible that you will violate a single principle of justice, or of equal liberty, in order to obviate the inconvenience of this contemptible number of votes?

I am told, sir, that the southern states are about to emancipate their slaves, and that we shall then be overrun by an emigration of free blacks from those parts of the union. Happy should I be, sir, if this intelligence were confirmed. But where is the evidence of this approaching emancipation? I have heard, indeed, that the southern planters were adopting measures to rivet more firmly the fetters of slavery, but never that they were beginning to break them. I have heard of laws that forbade the ministers of the gospel to proclaim them the glad tidings of salvation. I have heard of laws to prohibit any man from imparting to them a knowledge of letters, and of the first rudiments of literature. I have heard of laws which prohibited manumission—But I have not heard of a single measure which tended to prepare them for the enjoyment of freedom, or which indicated an intention of granting it.

I have yet, sir, to notice the arguments of the gentleman from Saratoga, (Col. Young)—these were avowedly addressed, not to our reason, but to our prejudices, and so forcibly have they been urged, that I feel persuaded they have had more influence on the committee, than all that has been said beside on this occasion. Though repeated in various forms, they may all be summoned up in this: that we are accustomed to look upon black men with contempt—that we will not eat with them—that we will not sit with them—that we will not serve with them in the militia, or on juries, nor in any manner associate with them—and thence it is concluded, that they ought not to vote with us—how, sir, can that argument be answered by reason, which does not profess to be founded on reason? Why do we feel reluctant to associate with a black man? There is no such reluctance in Europe, nor in any country in which slavery is unknown. It arises from an association of ideas. Slavery, and a black skin, always present themselves together to our minds—But with the diminution of slavery, the prejudice has already diminished, and, when slavery shall be no longer known among us, it will perhaps disappear— But, sir, what sort of argument is this? I will not eat with you, nor associate with you, because you are black; therefore I will disfranchise you. I despise you, not because you are vicious, but merely because I have an insuperable prejudice against you;—therefore I will condemn you, and your innocent posterity, to live forever as aliens in your native land. Mr. Chairman, I do trust, that this committee will not consent to violate all those principles upon which our free institutions are founded, or to contradict all the professions which we so profusely make, concerning the natural equality of all men, merely to gratify odious, and I hope, temporary prejudices—Nor will they endeavour to remove a slight inconvenience by so perilous a remedy as the establishment of a large, a perpetual, a degraded, and a discontented *caste*, in the midst of our population.

After Jay's remarks, the convention voted sixty-three to fifty-nine to eliminate the word white *from the suffrage language under consideration. The convention had not been deaf to calls for justice or appeals to history. Joining a solid core of fifteen Federalists to defeat an absolute racial bar to full black citizenship were approximately thirty-five Bucktail Republicans. Subsequent developments would demonstrate that this alliance against explicitly racist language would be fleeting.*

Undaunted by this setback to racial exclusion, Root attempted to rally support for disfranchisement around his earlier proposal to link voting eligibility to federal laws barring blacks from militia service. Another delegate objected that this would place too much authority over New York's voting rules in the hands of the federal government. The day's discussion of suffrage closed with a brief debate over whether the constitution should require formal voter registration prior to each election.

Act Two: Citizenship versus Property

During the next extended phase—spanning more than a week—of the suffrage drama, delegates debated the core principles behind major revision of voting rights in New York State. Although the impetus for the convention in large part had been to sweep away property holding as a qualification for voting in state elections, proponents of the old constitutional order insisted on laying bare their objections to democratizing suffrage. Conservatives especially sought to articulate a case for preserving a distinction between those eligible to vote in state assembly elections and state senate elections and clearly expressed a growing concern about the future place of New York City in the state's politics.

Futile though these efforts were to stem the tide, the arguments raised against widening the suffrage forced supporters of an expanded electorate to clarify their own core principles with regard to citizenship in a democratized political culture. Meanwhile, conservatives unwittingly provided the democratizers with arguments that would later be pivotal when the convention returned to the issue of African American citizenship. These debates over the political rights of property, moreover, circled back to the prior debate on black voting, revealing how this subject lingered just beneath the surface of other discussions. In sum, during this phase of the convention, delegates established a working definition of citizenship that ultimately most delegates would be unwilling to apply to African Americans. The convention clearly indicated its approval of a uniform set of voter qualifications for all elections and of expanded suffrage no longer linked to landholding.

On what basis did some delegates defend the freehold property standard for full voting rights? Why did other delegates ultimately deem conservative arguments unpersuasive? Why and in what contexts did delegates invoke the subject of African American voting rights? Why did some of those delegates who defended the African American suffrage also staunchly support property qualifications for senatorial elections? What did delegates mean by "universal suffrage," and why did some of those who favored an expanded suffrage hope to avoid universalizing the franchise—even among all adult white men?

* * *

Friday, September 21, 1821

The convention resumed discussion regarding technical aspects of voter qualification, voter registration, and voting procedure. Several delegates commented on the necessity of retaining the constitutional guarantee that state elections be conducted by paper ballots, not voice vote.

After comment from several delegates, the convention declined to include language requiring legislators to swear an oath against dueling, in part for fear that this would open the door to a range of other requirements regarding religious and political convictions. Erastus Root then spoke on a variety of unresolved issues. His concern about what he called "strolling voters" prompted his desire that voters must live for six months in the town or county where they would vote, so that parties did not undermine elections by encouraging supporters from neighboring counties to flood into counties just prior to a contest. He then returned to militia service as a qualification for voting, defending his desire to bar blacks from voting by adhering to the U.S. government's racially exclusive militia rules: "With regard to the militia, Congress is supreme, and when by it the negroes are made to train, then let them vote." Next, Root commented on the exception made for Quakers and Shakers—pacifist religious sects that did not allow their members to take up arms. Root urged that the fee imposed on such pacifists to maintain their right to vote in lieu of military service be substantial enough to cover the full cost of service and equipment for a militia member:

> On paying such a commutation, Quakers and Shakers will be entitled to vote; and so they will, after the age of forty-five [*the age at which a man's militia obligation expired*]. But this last advantage is not extended to Negroes. Sir, those who are withdrawn from the world and the world's people, those who are set apart, and who refuse all present service, and all commutation towards the defence of the country, should have no voice in electing "the commander in chief of all the land and naval forces." . . . Sir, in time of peace, I am told, and believe, that those people seldom vote, but when war comes they are active enough!—and if they are active in voting, I would warm them into activity in paying too.

Root clearly sought to fuse military obligation and full citizenship in his remarks. Root's comments also may have prompted some colleagues and readers to recall the long-standing opposition to slavery of Quakers in New York and elsewhere.

Federalist supreme court justice Jonas Platt from Oneida County criticized many of Root's observations, reiterating his fear that applying federal rules on militia service would cede New York's own authority. Included in the federal government's power, under Root's provision, would be the possibility of enfranchising African Americans in New York in order to influence the results of future elections.

JUDGE PLATT . . . it seems to me utterly inadmissible, that in defining the right of suffrage in our state, we should adopt a test, which is to depend on the fluctuating will of another government, over which we have no control.—This is the chief corner stone of our political edifice; and shall we refer it to congress to determine its shape and size, and in what manner it shall be laid? My constituents are intelligent, and jealous of the least invasion of their rights. They sent me here to aid in fixing and defining, within reasonable and certain limits, the inestimable right of suffrage. Should the proposition now before us prevail, I may be asked, when I return home, whether we have secured the electoral franchise to those who ought to enjoy it? If I should answer that we have fixed and established it, as to some persons, but that we have referred it to congress to determine whether other persons should or should not have the right of voting in our elections; I fear, sir, the answer would not be satisfactory. If my neighbour should enquire whether, by our new constitution, he has a right to vote; I might answer, you have no such right at present; but perhaps congress will grant it to you hereafter; or, I might say, you are entitled to vote now, but congress may disqualify you next year. I must refer you to Washington for information on that point. It is very uncertain what the members of congress from other states may judge proper in the case; but I can inform you, for your satisfaction, that in Virginia no man is allowed to vote unless he has a large freehold estate; and in South Carolina, no person can be elected as a member of the legislature, unless he be a proprietor of 500 acres of land, and ten slaves. Whether the delegates from those states will think proper to allow such a man as you, to vote in this state, is uncertain. Perhaps, if you are disposed to vote according to their wishes, you may be permitted to enjoy the privilege.

Mr. Chairman, I hope and believe there is not one of my constituents, who would not be indignant at such an explanation.

The gentleman from Delaware lately told us, that no free negro ought to be allowed to vote; and I agree with him, that most of them are at present unfit to exercise that privilege. That gentleman also stated, that the votes of three hundred free negroes in the city of New-York, in 1813, decided the election in favour of the federal party, and also decided the political character of the legislature of this state. He now proposes to confer the right of suffrage on all who train in the militia. By the existing law of congress, no black man can be enrolled in the militia. But suppose an important state election is about to take place here, or that an election of president and vice president is to be made, by electors who are to be appointed by our next legislature; is it not possible that congress might wish to control the choice of forty presidential electors in this state? If so, they have only to enlarge or control the description of persons who are to be taxed, or enrolled in the militia; and our right of suffrage must be enlarged or abridged accordingly. By the census of 1820, it appears there are 10,368 free people of colour in the city of New-York. By including free black men in the militia, which congress have an undoubted right to do, they would thereby create at least one thousand voters in the city of New-York, which might very probably determine the political character of our state legislature, and of course would determine the choice of presidential electors.

The report of the select committee, and the amendment offered by the gentleman from Delaware, are both liable to this objection. In my judgment, they adopt a principle, which undermines the foundation of state sovereignty: and I therefore revolt at the proposition.

Several delegates rose to make both substantive and procedural remarks on Root's proposals without specifically engaging the issue of African American citizenship. The convention then adjourned for the day.

SATURDAY, SEPTEMBER 22, 1821

Chief Justice Spencer opened the next day's consideration of the suffrage with an attempt to rescue the principle of property-holding requirements, which the convention seemed poised to abandon almost entirely. Spencer proposed that the new constitution, like the 1777 constitution, establish a higher standard of eligibility for voting in state senate elections: one year of residency in the state, instead of six months, and landholdings or tenements worth at least $250. A wife's property would be included toward the value of the potential male voter's property. In seeking to revive property as a qualification, Spencer purported to protect "a barrier in legislation, which the wisdom of the sages and patriots of the revolution have erected for our protection." Spencer argued that the large numbers of men moving to the western part of the state would be enfranchised based on the valuable improvements they made on lands they had contracted to purchase at a later date. He distinguished between the popular desire to expand voting rights and the need to maintain the distinction between the upper and lower houses of the assembly. Spencer asserted that the two branches were "charged" with different functions— the lower house was entrusted "with the protection and preservation of

*the personal rights, the lives and liberties of the citizens," while the upper
house "was intended as the guardians of our property generally, and especially of the landed interest, the yeomanry of the state." Spencer ce-
mented his conservative vision by raising concerns about the future,
trumpeting the wisdom and effectiveness of past arrangements, and
saluting the contributions of property holders to the state's present
virtues.*

CHIEF JUSTICE SPENCER . . . This state, within a century, must contain a population of many millions. Are we amending our constitution to
last our own lives only? Are we establishing fundamental principles for
this and the next generation only? No, sir. If we are wise, we must take a
prospective view, and we must endeavour, as far as humanity will allow,
to impress on our doings the seal of immortality—We must fashion our
constitution to suit the present and future times. In this view, as we have
repeatedly been admonished upon this floor, we must contemplate, that
the condition of the community will change, that other interests will
spring up; that we are to become a manufacturing state; that commerce
and the mechanical arts will be widely and extensively established. At
present the agricultural interest predominates; but who can foresee, that
in process of time, it will not become the minor body? And what is there
to protect the landed interests of the state, the cultivators of the soil, if the
wide and broad proposition on your table be adopted; admitting the
whole mass of the adult male population of the state to vote not only for
governor, lieutenant-governor, and assembly, but senators also? He
would venture to predict, that the landed interests of the state will be at
the mercy of the other combined interests; and thus all the public burthens may be thrown on the landed property of the state.

It may be said that the smallness of the number, and the duration of the
office of senators for four years, will give the requisite dissimilarity between the two branches, and thus obviate the necessity of a distinction in
the qualification of the electors. This he conceived to be a mistake. The
duration of the office may make the senators somewhat more independent, but it can neither alter nor change the identity of their composition;
and the smallness of the number can have no other effect than to promote
a more familiar discussion.

However subdivided the legislature may be in its several branches, if it
be composed of persons exactly similar in qualifications, and be elected
by persons having the same qualifications, it will be virtually one and the

same body. Put one body in an upper house, the other in a lower house; call one lords, and the other commons, it avails nothing; they are but one body, possessing the same feelings, the same sympathies, and the same objects. It was a conviction of this immutable truth, which led the framers of our constitution to establish a difference in the qualification of the electors; and I may confidently appeal to the intelligence of this Convention, that hitherto its operation has not been injurious to the interests of society; on the contrary, we have lived securely, we have enjoyed every protection, and we have prospered beyond example.

Let me ask, sir, whether this great, this radical, this fundamental change, which goes to break down a barrier of our constitution, has been demanded by the sober sense of this community? I again say, that I have no knowledge of any disposition existing to any considerable extent, to make this deep, and, as I firmly believe, dangerous innovation.

Is it desirable that we should remove the safeguards of property, and destroy the incentive to acquire it, by rendering it insecure. By removing these guards, we repress industry, frugality, temperance, and all those exertions to the acquisition of landed property, which make good citizens. Are we jealous of property, that we should leave it unprotected? To the beneficence and liberality of those who have property, we owe all the embellishments and the comforts and blessings of life. Who build our churches, who erect our hospitals, who raise our school houses? Those who have property. And are they not entitled to the regard and fostering protection of our laws and constitution? Let me not be suspected of a disposition to infringe or curtail the rights of any portion of the community. I would impart the right of electing the assembly, the most numerous branch of legislation, to every man whom we believe will exercise the right with independence and integrity; and thus the rights of every portion of the people will be protected. I have said on a former occasion, that the rule adopted must necessarily be a general rule; but let us take care, whilst we nominally give the right of voting to a particular description of our citizens, that we do not in reality give it to their employers. The man who feeds, clothes, and lodges another, has a real and absolute control over his will. Say what we may, the man who is dependant on another for his subsistence, is not an independent man, and he will vote in subservience to his dictation. Let us, then, take care, whilst we abominate aristocracy, that we do not actually organize it, by giving to the rich an undue influence, and by creating venal votes to be bought.

Another staunchly conservative voice, that of Chancellor Kent, rose to further elaborate the defense of property holding as a qualification for voters in state senate elections. Kent, too, emphasized that the current system had produced a remarkably healthy society, characterized by "unexampled progress in the career of prosperity and greatness." Kent feared, however, that New York might become a victim of its own growth, by allowing the landless masses already beginning to aggregate in New York City, to vote on an equal footing with propertied citizens.

CHANCELLOR KENT . . . Our financial credit stands at an enviable height; and we are now successfully engaged in connecting the great lakes with the ocean by stupendous canals, which excite the admiration of our neighbours, and will make a conspicuous figure even upon the map of the United States.

These are some of the fruits of our present government; and yet we seem to be dissatisfied with our condition, and we are engaged in the bold and hazardous experiment of remoddelling [*sic*] the constitution. Is it not fit and discreet: I speak as to wise men; is it not fit and proper that we should pause in our career, and reflect well on the immensity of the innovation in contemplation? Discontent in the midst of so much prosperity, and with such abundant means of happiness, looks like ingratitude, and as if we were disposed to arraign the goodness of Providence. Do we not expose ourselves to the danger of being deprived of the blessings we have enjoyed?—When the husbandman has gathered in his harvest, and has filled his barns and his granaries with the fruits of his industry, if he should then become discontented and unthankful, would he not have reason to apprehend, that the Lord of the harvest might come in his wrath, and with his lightning destroy them?

The senate has hitherto been elected by the farmers of the state—by the free and independent lords of the soil, worth at least $250 in freehold estate, over and above all debts charged thereon. The governor has been chosen by the same electors, and we have hitherto elected citizens of elevated rank and character. Our assembly has been chosen by freeholders, possessing a freehold of the value of $50, or by persons renting a tenement of the yearly value of $5, and who have been rated and actually paid taxes to the state. By the report before us, we propose to annihilate, at one stroke, all those property distinctions and bow before the idol of universal suffrage. That extreme democratic principle, when applied to the legislative and executive departments of government, has been regarded

with terror, by the wise men of every age, because in every European republic, ancient and modern, in which it has been tried, it has terminated
disastrously, and been productive of corruption, injustice, violence, and
tyranny. And dare we flatter ourselves that we are a peculiar people, who
can run the career of history, exempted from the passions which have disturbed and corrupted the rest of mankind? If we are like other races of
men, with similar follies and vices, then I greatly fear that our posterity
will have reason to deplore in sackcloth and ashes, the delusion of the
day.

It is not my purpose at present to interfere with the report of the committee, so far as respects the qualifications of electors for governor and
members of assembly. I shall feel grateful if we may be permitted to retain
the stability and security of a senate, bottomed upon the freehold property of the state. Such a body, so constituted, may prove a sheet anchor
amidst the future factions and storms of the republic. The great leading
and governing interest of this state, is, at present, the agricultural; and
what madness would it be to commit that interest to the winds. The great
body of the people are now the owners and actual cultivators of the soil.
With that wholesome population we always expect to find moderation,
frugality, order, honesty, and a due sense of independence, liberty, and justice. It is impossible that any people can lose their liberties by internal
fraud or violence, so long as the country is parcelled out among freeholders of moderate possessions, and those freeholders have a sure and
efficient control in the affairs of the government. Their habits, sympathies, and employments, necessarily inspire them with a correct spirit of
freedom and justice: they are the safest guardians of property and the
laws: We certainly cannot too highly appreciate the value of the agricultural interest: It is the foundation of national wealth and power. According to the opinion of her ablest political economists, it is the surplus produce of the agriculture of England, that enables her to support her vast
body of manufacturers, her formidable fleets and armies, and the crowds
of persons engaged in the liberal professions, and the cultivation of the
various arts.

Now, sir, I wish to preserve our senate as the representative of the
landed interest. I wish those who have an interest in the soil, to retain the
exclusive possession of a branch in the legislature, as a strong hold in
which they may find safety through all the vicissitudes which the state
may be destined, in the course of Providence, to experience. I wish them
to be always enabled to say that their freeholds cannot be taxed without

their consent. The men of no property, together with the crowds of dependants connected with great manufacturing and commercial establishments, and the motley and undefinable population of crowded ports, may, perhaps, at some future day, under skilful management, predominate in the assembly, and yet we should be perfectly safe if no laws could pass without the free consent of the owners of the soil. That security we at present enjoy; and it is that security which I wish to retain.

The apprehended danger from the experiment of universal suffrage applied to the whole legislative department, is no dream of the imagination. It is too mighty an excitement for the moral constitution of men to endure. The tendency of universal suffrage, is to jeopardize the rights of property, and the principles of liberty. There is a constant tendency in human society, and the history of every age proves it; there is a tendency in the poor to covet and to share the plunder of the rich; in the debtor to relax or avoid the obligation of contracts; in the majority to tyranize over the minority, and trample down their rights; in the indolent and the profligate, to cast the whole burthens of society upon the industrious and the virtuous; and *there is a tendency in ambitious and wicked men, to inflame these combustible materials.* It requires a vigilant government, and a firm administration of justice, to counteract that tendency. Thou shalt not covet; thou shalt not steal; are divine injunctions induced by this miserable depravity of our nature. Who can undertake to calculate with any precision, how many millions of people, this great state will contain in the course of this and the next century, and who can estimate the future extent and magnitude of our commercial ports? The disproportion between the men of property, and the men of no property, will be in every society in a ratio to its commerce, wealth, and population. We are no longer to remain plain and simple republics of farmers, like the New-England colonists, or the Dutch settlements on the Hudson. We are fast becoming a great nation, with great commerce, manufactures, population, wealth, luxuries, and with the vices and miseries that they engender. One seventh of the population of the city of Paris at this day subsists on charity, and one third of the inhabitants of that city die in the hospitals; what would become of such a city with universal suffrage? France has upwards of four, and England upwards of five millions of manufacturing and commercial labourers without property. Could these kingdoms sustain the weight of universal suffrage? The radicals in England, with the force of that mighty engine, would at once sweep away the property, the laws, and the liberties of that island like a deluge.

The growth of the city of New-York is enough to startle and awaken those who are pursuing the *ignis fatuus*[42] of universal suffrage.

In 1773	it had	21,000 souls.
1801	"	60,000 do. [*ditto*]
1800	"	76,000 do.
1820	"	123,000 do.

It is rapidly swelling into the unwieldy population, and with the burdensome pauperism, of an European metropolis. New-York is destined to become the future London of America; and in less than a century, that city, with the operation of universal suffrage, and under skilful direction, will govern this state.

The notion that every man that works a day on the road, or serves an idle hour in the militia, is entitled as of right to an equal participation in the whole power of the government, is most unreasonable, and has no foundation in justice. We had better at once discard from the report such a nominal test of merit. If such persons have an equal share in one branch of the legislature, it is surely as much as they can in justice or policy demand. Society is an association for the protection of property as well as of life, and the individual who contributes only one cent to the common stock, ought not to have the same power and influence in directing the property concerns of the partnership, as he who contributes his thousands. He will not have the same inducements to care, and diligence, and fidelity. His inducements and his temptation would be to divide the whole capital upon the principles of an agrarian law.

Liberty, rightly understood, is an inestimable blessing, but liberty without wisdom, and without justice, is no better than wild and savage licentiousness. The danger which we have hereafter to apprehend, is not the want, but the abuse, of liberty. We have to apprehend the oppression of minorities,[43] and a disposition to encroach on private right—to disturb chartered privileges—and to weaken, degrade, and overawe the administration of justice; we have to apprehend the establishment of unequal, and consequently, unjust systems of taxation, and all the mischiefs of a crude and mutable legislation. A stable senate, exempted from the influence of universal suffrage, will powerfully check these dangerous propensities, and such a check becomes the more necessary, since this Convention has already determined to withdraw the watchful eye of the judicial department from the passage of laws.

We are destined to become a great manufacturing as well as commercial state. We have already numerous and prosperous factories of one kind or another, and one master capitalist with his one hundred apprentices, and journeymen, and agents, and dependents, will bear down at the polls an equal number of farmers of small estates in his vicinity, who cannot safely unite for their common defence. Large manufacturing and mechanical establishments, can act in an instant with the unity and efficacy of disciplined troops. It is against such combinations, among others, that I think we ought to give to the freeholders, or those who have interest in land, one branch of the legislature for their asylum and their comfort. Universal suffrage once granted, is granted forever, and never can be recalled. There is no retrograde step in the rear of democracy. However mischievous the precedent may be in its consequences, or however fatal in its effects, universal suffrage never can be recalled or checked, but by the strength of the bayonet. We stand, therefore, this moment, on the brink of fate, on the very edge of the precipice. If we let go our present hold on the senate, we commit our proudest hopes and our most precious interests to the waves.

It ought further to be observed, that the senate is a court of justice in the last resort. It is the last depository of public and private rights; of civil and criminal justice. This gives the subject an awful consideration, and wonderfully increases the importance of securing that house from the inroads of universal suffrage. Our country freeholders are exclusively our jurors in the administration of justice, and there is equal reason that none but those who have an interest in the soil, should have any concern in the composition of that court. As long as the senate is safe, justice is safe, property is safe, and our liberties are safe. But when the wisdom, the integrity, and the independence of that court is lost, we may be certain that the freedom and happiness of this state, are fled forever.

I hope, sir, we shall not carry desolation through all the departments of the fabric erected by our fathers. I hope we shall not put forward to the world a new constitution, as will meet with the scorn of the wise, and the tears of the patriot.

The argument for maintaining a property-holding standard in senatorial elections received strong criticism from delegates much closer to mainstream opinion at the convention. Before launching into specific criticisms of the Spencer and Kent arguments, Erastus Root declared, "I

rejoice that this proposition has presented itself distinctly to the commit-
tee, and hope that its rejection may be had in a plain and unequivocal
manner." Root reminded the convention that in a society of "common-
ers" without "privileged orders" the idea of using different branches of
government to protect different interests did not apply. He questioned
both the logic and the practicality of a system based on two different sets
of voter qualifications. Root believed that the state senate would effec-
tively balance the legislature by virtue of senators' longer terms in office
and the smaller size of this upper house: he summarized this last argu-
ment by stating that "these are the only wholesome and necessary checks
that the nature of our government requires."

Root's colleague, Peter R. Livingston, was equally critical of the con-
servative case for property-holding requirements. Livingston invoked
both the American Revolution and the French Revolution as evidence
that the people had both a right to participate in the government that
taxed them and an interest in not placing political privilege in the hands
of wealthy property holders. Livingston made an explicitly populist ap-
peal, embracing the virtues historically embodied by the common men of
the republic and dismissing as vain pretensions the claims of elites. After
Livingston, Jacob Radcliff added brief but pointed remarks impugning
the logic behind the proposed property-holding qualification. Abraham
Van Vechten, in a lengthy speech not included in the present text, de-
fended the Spencer proposal, arguing that property was a distinct right in
need of protection, particularly as nonlandholding urban dwellers in-
creased their share of the state's population and wealthy manufacturers
increased their power in the years to come. Shortly after Van Vechten
spoke, the convention adjourned for the day.

MR. P. R. LIVINGSTON . . . It is said that wealth builds our churches,
establishes our schools, endows our colleges, and erects our hospitals. But
have these institutions been raised without the hand of labour? No, sir;
and it is the same hand that has levelled the sturdy oak, the lofty pine, and
the towering hemlock, and subdued your forests to a garden. It is not the
fact, in this country, that money controls labour; but labour controls
money. When the farmer cradles his wheat and harvests his hay, he does
not find the labourer on his knees before him at the close of the day, so-
licitous for further employment; but it is the farmer who takes off his hat,
pays him his wages, and requests his return on the morrow.

Apprehensions are professed to be entertained, that the merchant and manufacturer will combine to the prejudice of the landed interest. But is not agriculture the legitimate support of both? And do gentlemen really suppose that they will madly combine to destroy themselves? If the title to land contributed to the elevation of the mind, or if it gave stability to independence, or added wisdom to virtue, there might be good reason for proportioning the right of suffrage to the acres of soil. But experience has shewn that property forms not the scale of worth, and that character does not spring from the ground. It seems, indeed, to be thought, that poverty and vice are identified. But look to the higher classes of society. Do you not often discover the grossest abuse of wealth? Look to the republics of Greece. They were all destroyed by the wealth of the aristocracy bearing down the people.

And how were the victories of Greece achieved in her better days? By the militia. How were the liberties of Rome sustained? By her militia. How were they lost? By her standing armies. How have we been carried triumphantly through two wars? By the militia—by the very men whom it is now sought to deprive of the inestimable privilege of freemen. And whom do you find in your armies in time of war? The miser? The monied Shylock?[44] The speculator? No, sir; it is the poor and hardy soldier who spills his blood in defence of his country; the veteran to whom you allow the privilege to fight, but not to vote. If there is value in the right of suffrage, or reliance to be placed upon our fellow citizens in time of war, where, I ask, is the justice of withholding that right in times of peace and safety?

MR. RADCLIFF was not in the habit of declaiming on popular rights, but he thought there should be an equality, whatever qualifications might be fixed on.

He was opposed to the proposition now under consideration, because he could perceive no utility that was likely to grow out of its adoption; and if useless, it was of course injurious. Propositions of an affirmative character, ought always to be accompanied by proofs of their probable utility.

Gentlemen have referred to the theories of learned statesmen; but Mr. R. thought it would be found that those theories rested upon no better basis than speculative opinion, or analogies derived from countries, between which and our own, there is no relation. We know that those statesmen were mistaken on some important points. They said our government would vanish in twenty years, that it did not possess intrinsic strength, adequate to its support. But forty years experience has shewn us the fallacy of their predictions.

Property will always carry with it an influence sufficient for its own protection. And shall we give it an artificial aid, that may be dangerous to the rights of the community? But we are told that property is entitled to representation. If the principles of the social compact are likened to a partnership stock, it follows that each partner is entitled to vote according to the amount of his state in that partnership, like shares in a monied institution:—of course upon the ratio of $250 proposed by the mover of the amendment under consideration, every freeholder having $500 worth of property would be entitled to two votes, and if he has $5000 worth he would be entitled to twenty votes.

MONDAY, SEPTEMBER 24, 1821

The convention resumed discussion of the Spencer proposal to limit state senate elections to voters with a $250 freehold. President of the convention Daniel Tompkins placed his objections to property-holding qualifications in the context of the devoted service of New York's militia during the War of 1812. The sitting U.S. vice president, who had served as governor of New York during that war, interjected race back into the discussion by comparing "degraded, ignorant and vicious" black men, whose voting rights had been protected by the convention a few days before, with white soldiers whose own rights were imperiled by the proposed amendment. Tompkins's use of race made a distinction that he had not made as governor, when, during the War of 1812, he lobbied U.S. Secretary of State James Monroe to accept New York's offer to raise regiments from the state's black population. After the war, then-governor Tompkins had urged the legislature to enact an accelerated gradual abolition (see document I). The selective historical memory exhibited in Tompkins's brief remarks foreshadowed the convention's imminent denial of black citizenship and the deterioration of white support for black rights during the first quarter of the nineteenth century.

MR. TOMPKINS observed that his ill health would preclude him from entering at length on the present discussion. He regretted the introduction of this amendment. . . . [A]fter the principle of the original proposition had been agreed to, in relation to an uniform system of voting, it was unfortunate that its repose should have been disturbed. . . .

Property, sir, when compared with our other essential rights, is insignificant and trifling. "Life, liberty, and *the pursuit of happiness*"—not of property—are set forth in the declaration of independence as cardinal objects. Property is not even named. It is said, however, that the man of property should have some peculiar safeguard on which he can rely for its protection. But is not property represented in the executive? Is it not provided that he shall be a freeholder?

It is not to be disguised, that we are about to become a naval power. The late war bore triumphant testimony to the fact, that we are under no necessity of maintaining a standing army. The militia is sufficient to repel incursions of the savages, to suppress insurrections or to repel an invading force. Give them something, then, to fight for. How was the late war sustained? Who filled the ranks of your armies? Not the priesthood—not the men of wealth—not the speculators: the former were preaching sedition, and the latter decrying the credit of the government, to fatten on its spoil. And yet the very men who were led on to battle, had no vote to give for their commander in chief. Gentlemen were very sensitive the other day on the question of excluding the blacks—a class confessedly degraded, ignorant and vicious; and now little sympathy is felt for the white man—the patriot soldier, who shed his blood in the defence of your soil, and whose bones whitened the shore of a foreign enemy.

Mr. T. related the case of a sailing master in the battle on Lake Champlain, who, when the crew, in the severity of the action, had retreated below, called them back to their duty by an artifice, pretending that the British vessel had struck. Animating them by his example, he inspired them with confidence, and the victory was achieved.—His fidelity and heroism would have done honour to Washington; and yet this man died of poverty and a broken heart. He had not a right to vote! We give to property too much influence. It is not that which mostly gives independence. Independence consists more in the structure of the mind and in the qualities of the heart.

Why is the judiciary independent? Because, by the tenure of its office, it is out of the reach of momentary impulse—not because the members of it are rich themselves, or chosen by the rich. We have yielded to property as much as it deserves. It remains, also, that we should look to the protection of him who has personal security and personal liberty at stake. It is the citizen soldier who demands the boon, and he rightfully demands it. It is a privilege inestimable to him, and "only formidable to tyrants."

Suffrage committee member John Cramer, of Saratoga County, attacked at much greater length the attempt by conservatives at the convention to reinsert a property-holding standard into the plan for an expanded franchise. He suggested that defenders of a more restrictive voter eligibility misread both the historical record and the convention's popular mandate. Like Root and Tompkins, Cramer invoked the virtues, in war and peace, of ordinary New Yorkers to fortify his case for the expanded suffrage offered by the committee.

MR. CRAMER: I had supposed that the great fundamental principle, that all men were created equal in their rights, was settled, and forever settled, in this country. I had supposed, sir, that there was some meaning in those words and some importance in the benefits resulting from them. I had supposed from the blood and treasure which its attainment had cost, that there was something invaluable in it: and that in pursuance of this principle it ought to be the invariable object of the framers of our civil compact, to render all men equal in their political enjoyments as far as could be, consistent with order and justice. . . .

After disputing the claims of delegates Spencer and Kent, Cramer turned his fire on Abraham Van Vechten, who two days before had questioned whether "public opinion" was committed to an elimination of the freehold requirement. Cramer responded:

He knew nothing of any public meetings, entitled to any weight, in sanctioning this alteration! There were some, sir, of which I have heard, held on the last Tuesday of April last, in every town and county in this state, and at which a majority of seventy thousand demanded and [*sic*] alteration in this feature of our constitution; there was, sir, another meeting, in June last, of the people, on this subject, and they, by their ballots, elected the members of this Convention, and demand, at their hands, the extension of equal rights and equal enjoyments, without distinction as to property. This was one of the great objects, which induced the people to call a Convention; but for this, sir, and for the purpose of having your government made cheaper and more economical in all its departments, this Convention would not have been called by the honest yeomanry of the country. . . .

But it has been said, that the landed interest of this state, bears more than its equal proportion of the burthens of taxation. This, sir, I deny. All property, real and personal, is equally taxed, and bears its just proportion of the public burthens; but, sir, is not life and liberty dearer than property, and common to all, and entitled to equal protection? No, sir. That gentleman appeared to be impressed with the idea, that the *turf* is of all things the most sacred, and that for its security, you must have thirty-two grave turf senators from the soil, in that *Sanctum Sanctorum*,[45] the senate chamber, and then all your rights will be safe. No matter whether they possess intelligence, if they are selected by your rich landholders, all is well.—But it is alledged by gentlemen, who have spoken on that side of the house, that the poor are a degraded class of beings, have no will of their own, and would not exercise this high prerogative with independence and sound discretion if entrusted with it; and, therefore, it would be unwise to trust them with ballots.—This, sir, is unfounded: for more integrity and more patriotism are generally found in the labouring class of the community than in the higher orders. These are the men, who add to the substantial wealth of the nation, in peace. These are the men, who constitute your defence in war. Of such men, consisted your militia, when they met and drove the enemy at Plattsburgh, Sacket's Harbour, Queenston, and Erie;[46] for you found not the rich landholder or speculator in your ranks; and are we told, that these men, because they have no property, are not to be trusted at the ballot boxes! Men, who in defence of their liberties, and to protect the property of this country, have hazarded their lives; and who, to shield your wives and children from savage brutality, have faced the destructive cannon, and breasted the pointed steel? All this they could be trusted to do. They could, without apprehension, be permitted to handle their muskets, bayonets, powder and balls; but, say the gentlemen, it will not answer to trust them with tickets at the ballot boxes.

I would admonish gentlemen of this committee, to reflect, who they are about to exclude from the right of suffrage, if the amendment under consideration should prevail.—They will exclude your honest industrious mechanics, and many farmers, for many there are who do not own the soil which they till. And what for? Because your farmers wish it? No, sir, they wish no such thing; they wish to see the men who have defended their soil, participate equally with them in the election of rulers. Nay, now you exclude most of the hoary headed patriots, who achieved your independence, to whom we are indebted for the very ground we stand upon, and for the liberties we enjoy. But for the toil and sufferings of these men, we should not now be here debating as to forms of government. No, sir, the legitimates would soon have disposed of all this business. And why are these men to be excluded? Not because they are not virtuous, not because they are not meritorious; but, sir, because they are poor and dependant, and can have no will of their own, and will vote as the man who feeds them and clothes them may direct, as one of the honourable gentlemen has remarked. I know of no men in this country, who are not dependant. The rich man is much dependant upon the poor man for his labour, as the poor man is upon the rich for his wages. I know of no men, who are more dependant upon others for their bread and raiment, than the judges of your supreme court are upon the legislature, and who will pretend that this destroys their independence, or makes them subservient to the views of the legislature. Let us not, sir, disgrace ourselves in the eyes of the world, by expressing such degrading opinions of our fellow citizens. Let us grant universal suffrage, for after all, it is upon the virtue and intelligence of the people that the stability of your government must rest. Let us not brand this constitution with any odious distinctions as to property, and let it not be said of us as has been truly said of most republics, that we have been ungrateful to our best benefactors.

In debating the property-holding requirement, delegates contended with one another over to what context the consideration of this question properly belonged. Speakers reviewed the historical record from New York, as well as from other states and nations, to make their cases. David Buel Jr., a lawyer from Rensselaer County, summarized his remarks by saying:

The national government is founded on the principle of diffusive suffrage. Most of the states have adopted the principle: and as our fortunes are embarked with theirs in one common ship, we cannot expect that our government under any regulation of the right of suffrage, will survive the union of the states. If that government is safe without a distinction in the electors founded on property, we need not fear to abolish a distinction which, if retained, will cause much uneasy feeling among the people, and bring an unnecessary odium upon the landed interest. A distinction which will have a tendency to excite combinations unfriendly to the interest of the land holders, and which, but for the distinction in the right of suffrage, will probably never exist.

John Ross, a member of the suffrage committee, also asserted the existence of a national trend to abandon freehold requirements and cited a popular mandate for such action in New York.

Elisha Williams, a lawyer from Columbia County, warned his fellow delegates against turning this debate into a partisan contest on his way to asserting the principle that all political communities limit entry to full citizenship according to one standard or another. Although Williams was a Federalist and a consistent opponent of racial disfranchisement at the convention, he enunciated principles that delegates ultimately employed to attack black citizenship at the convention. Williams specifically used the accepted exclusion of females from the polls to defend the concept of a selectively limited suffrage. The leap from sexual qualifications for voting rights to racial qualifications for voting rights was perhaps shorter than Williams might have imagined. Similarly, the anti-urban imagery evoked by Williams and other conservatives in their last-ditch effort to save the freehold qualification was folded into the Republican case against black voting.

Mr. E. Williams . . . Mr. Chairman, the friends of rational liberty in all quarters of the globe have their attention fastened upon independent, confederated America; in the front rank of this confederacy, in the most conspicuous station, stands the great state of New-York, and the result of this Convention will decide her fate, perhaps for ever. . . . Our proceedings, our opinions and votes, are placed on never-dying records; our character as patriots and statesmen, will be determined by the measures we adopt; if those measures be stamped with wisdom; if they be conceived in the spirit of disinterested regard for the common good, and bear the impress of impartial justice, then that character will hold us in grateful remembrance. . . . The constitution, sir, is the heart of the republic—the source of political life; from it issues the blood that nourishes and warms the remotest members of the political body: it is the sun in the center of the political system; around it the legislative, executive, and judicial powers revolve in their proper orbits, imparting light and life to the great elements of social prosperity and happiness—the manners, habits, and customs, the education, morals, and religion of the people, giving to them protection and perpetuity.

We are not, Mr. Chairman, now just emerging from the savage state; we have a government, founded on social compact: a portion of our natural rights has been surrendered, and sovereignty, which in the state of nature equally appertained to all, has been concentrated, and vested in a portion of the people, for the common benefit and protection of the whole. The sovereign power of the state is, indeed, comprised with, but it is by no means accurately described by the term, the people. This term in its general and most comprehensive signification, embraces the whole population—all that portion of the human family, which is comprised within the limits of the state. But as the great object of the exercise of sovereignty is the general good, it never has been, in fact, and all will admit that it never ought to be, in theory, committed to the people, in this extended acceptation of the term. It ought not to be so committed, because the young and inexperienced, those who are helpless and dependant, by nature and inevitable necessity, as well as by civil institution and legal contract, cannot be, and never have been supposed, in the most extravagant theories of equality, capable of expressing their wills independently and intelligently. Thus, by the universal consent of mankind, one half, and truth no less than politeness, compels me to add, the better half of the whole human family, is at once and utterly excluded from any participation of sovereignty. The male population we again divide, excluding all infants; and from the remaining portion we subtract all foreigners, all paupers, and all felons; until we find sovereignty reduced, and that too, by common consent and universal custom, from a population, in the case of our own state, of upwards of thirteen hundred thousand souls, into the hands of about one hundred and fifty thousand free male citizens, who are the actual, legitimate sovereigns of the state, and who constitute but about one tenth of its entire numbers. If it be true that all persons are born equal in political rights, possessing equal portions of legitimate sovereignty, how happens it that nine-tenths of our fellow legitimates are dethroned, and we, the one-tenth, are declared the rightful sovereigns of this free and independent state? If the right of self-government were, as some gentlemen seem to consider it, not only a natural, but an unalienable right, it would follow that, by nature and by Providence, it had been bestowed equally upon every individual of the human race, and that by no act could a portion lawfully assume to itself the attribute of sovereignty conferred alike on all; it would be usurpation; it would be tyranny.

In this country, and in this state, the people have selected, from all the forms of government known to civilized man, an elective republic. No doubt they have selected with unrivalled wisdom; but, in establishing a constitution and fundamental laws, they have found it necessary even here to limit the number of those, in whom the sovereign power shall rest, and to pronounce what portion of the whole, will be most likely to exercise it with wisdom, with justice, and for the promotion of the public welfare.

. . . But, most surely, it does not follow that all who are protected by government, or entitled to its protection, are also entitled to a voice in the designation of the men who administer that government. All have lives to be protected; but all living are not, therefore, entitled to become electors. All are entitled to civil and religious liberty—the minor as extensively as the adult—the female as extensively as the male—yet they have not all a voice in choosing their rulers; many a female, as well as many a legal infant, is in possession of large estates, but they cannot vote. . . .

. . . Vivid and impressive as was the picture drawn by our President [*convention President Daniel Tompkins*] of the gallant officer, who died of a broken heart because, as it would seem, he was not an elector, even a limited fancy might add to the apparent injustice of our country.—Suppose the gallant hero had been a youth of twenty years of age; is it proposed to embrace his case and make brave infants voters? Suppose him a foreigner, shedding blood in defence of his adopted country; is it proposed to give him the right of suffrage? Suppose our hero the only son of his mother, and she a widow—her husband had fallen, in the establishment of the independence of his native land, and his son had laid down his life for its preservation—her property is all that Providence has permitted her to retain; is it proposed to permit her to guard that property with the electoral ballot? . . .

The gentleman from New-York, (Mr. Radcliff,) has contended that, by nature all were endowed with the right of suffrage; and he calls upon us to show universal suffrage would be dangerous to the best interests of the state. Sir, the burden of proof rests upon the gentleman himself, not on us; the constitution on this occasion, holds the negative; and I call upon him to point out the danger to be apprehended from the exercise of this elective power by the yeomanry of the country. Have the freeholders exercised it tyrannically? Let their wide liberality—their expanded charities—give the answer.

We are called upon to confer this power on those who may exercise it discreetly. Do the freeholders wish to participate with those who merely do no hurt? . . . For what end introduce them? If they vote *with* the free-holders, they are not wanted; if they vote *against* them, their power will be injurious to freehold rights. And who are these people who are to aid the freeholders in electing their senate? On this subject, sir, I know I am liable to be misrepresented, and have already been so by anticipation, by those who have "the people" ever on their *tongues*, but, who, I fear, have seldom carried them much lower. Who are they who will protect the landed interest of this state, better than its owners; or better determine when a direct tax is necessary and proper to be imposed on their farms; and better judges what laws are calculated to advance the agricultural in-terests of the state? Sir, they are the ring streaked and speckled population of our large towns and cities, comprising people of every kindred and tongue. They bring with them the habits, vices, political creeds, and na-tionalities of every section of the globe; they have fled from oppression, if you please, and have habitually regarded sovereignty and tyranny as iden-tified; they are men whose wants, if not whose vices, have sent them from other states and countries, to seek bread by service, if not by plunder; whose means and habits, whose best kind of ambition, and only sort of industry, all forbid their purchasing in the country and tilling the soil. Would the state be better governed—would the landed interest be better protected, by the suffrages of such men, than by the ballots of freehold-ers? Mr. Jefferson has said, sir, that great cities were upon the body politic great sores. . . . I would not, certainly I would not, if I could prevent it, carry, by absorption, the contents of those sores through the whole polit-ical body. These cities are filled with men too rich, or too poor to frater-nize with the yeomen of the country; and I warn my fellow freeholders of the dangers which must attend the surrender of this most inestimable of privileges—this attribute of sovereignty.

On whom do the burthens of government fall, in peace and in war? On you. Your freeholds cannot escape taxation—they cannot elude the vigi-lance of the assessor, and though encumbered to their whole value, they must pay on their entire amount. When danger threatens, to whom must you look for support? Is your militia called for, he who has no interest in your soil, swings his pack, and is away, leaving the farmer and the farmer's son, to abide the draft, and defend the life, liberty, and property of themselves and the community. They are identified with the interest of the state. I would to heaven, the entire mass of the freeholders of this state were here present, to decide upon this all-important question—to determine whether they would wantonly cast away this saving power—

this long-enjoyed attribute of sovereignty, granted to them, at first, by the whole population, and which would constitute the richest inheritance they could transmit to posterity. Among the blessings which a moderate portion of property confers, the right of suffrage is conspicuous; and the attainment of this right, holds out a strong inducement to that industry and economy, which are the life of society. If you *bestow* on the idle and profligate, the privileges which should be purchased only by industry, frugality, and character, will they ever be at the trouble and pains to *earn* those privileges? No, sir; and the prodigal waste of this invaluable privilege—this attribute of sovereignty—like indiscriminate and misguided charity, will multiply the evils which it professes to remedy. Give the people, to the extent contended for, one department of the government, as a means of security from possible oppression; but preserve, I conjure you, to the faithful citizen, as his best recompense—as the richest gem he can hoard—and as the sheet-anchor of the republic, the freehold right of suffrage for the senate.

TUESDAY, SEPTEMBER 25, 1821

In response to the Spencer amendment to limit suffrage in senatorial elections, Bucktail Republican leader and Ostego County delegate Martin Van Buren spoke at length for more inclusive standards. Van Buren contrasted the alarmist rhetoric of conservatives with the reality that the property-holding requirement would bar thousands of small freeholders from the polls.

MR. VAN BUREN . . . If a stranger had heard the discussions on this subject, and had been unacquainted with the character of our people, and the character and standing of those, who find it their duty to oppose this measure, he might well have supposed, that we were on the point of prostrating with lawless violence, one of the fairest and firmest pillars of the government, and of introducing into the sanctuary of the constitution, a mob or a rabble, violent and disorganizing. . . .

By the census of 1814, it appeared, that of 163,000 electors in this state, upwards of 75,000 were freeholders, under $250, and all of them householders, who may possess any amount of personal property—men who have wives and children to protect and support; and who have every thing but the mere dust on which they trod to bind them to the country. And the question was, whether, in addition to those who might, by this Convention, be clothed with the right of suffrage, this class of men, composed of mechanics, professional men, and small landholders, and constituting the bone, pith, and muscle of the population of the state, should be excluded entirely from all representation in that branch of the legislature which had equal power to originate all bills, and a complete negative upon the passage of all laws. . . . This was the grievance, under which so great a portion of the people of this state had hitherto laboured. It was to relieve them from this injustice, and this oppression, that the Convention had been called. . . .

Van Buren reminded the convention that among the staunchest defenders of black suffrage were the conservatives who sought to impose a freehold requirement. Thus, Van Buren implied, conservatives protected the rights of the vice-ridden and disregarded the rights of the virtuous. Van Buren also connected a unified non-property-holding standard to the rhetoric of the American Revolution and to the wishes of farmers throughout the state.

It was . . . but yesterday, that they afforded the strongest evidence of their continued hold upon our feelings and our judgments, by the triumph they effected, over the strongest aversions and prejudices of our nature—on the question of continuing the right of suffrage to the poor, degraded blacks. Apply . . . for a moment, the principles they inculcate to the question under consideration, and let its merits be thereby tested. Are those of your citizens represented, whose voices are never heard in your senate? . . . Was it not even less than the *virtual representation*, with which our fathers were attempted to be appeased by their oppressors?[47] It was even so; and if so, could they, as long as this distinction was retained, hold up their heads, and, without blushing, pretend to be the advocates for that special canon of political rights, that taxation and representation were, and ever should be, indissoluble? He thought not.

. . . Who, he asked, had hitherto constituted a majority of the voters of the state? The *farmers*—who had called for, and insisted upon the Convention. *Farmers and freeholders!* Who passed the law admitting those, who were not electors, to a free participation in the decision of the question of *Convention* or *No Convention*, and also in the choice of delegates to that body. A legislature, a majority of whom were farmers, and probably every one of them freeholders, of the value of two hundred and fifty dollars and upwards! The farmers of this state had, he said, by an overwhelming majority admitted those who were not freeholders, to a full participation with themselves in every stage of this great effort to amend our constitution, and to ameliorate the condition of the people: Could he, then, ought he to be told, that they would be disappointed in their expectations, when they found that by the provisions of the constitution as amended, a great proportion of their fellow citizens were enfranchised and released, from fetters which they themselves had done all in their power to loosen? He did not believe it. . . . If any thing, (said Mr. Van Buren,) could render this invaluable class of men dearer and more estimable than they were, it was this magnanimous sacrifice which they had made on the altar of principle, by consenting to admit those of their fellow citizens, who, though not so highly favoured as themselves by fortune, had still enough to bind them to their country, to an equal participation in the blessings of a free government. . . .

The next consideration which had been pressed upon the committee by the honourable mover of the amendment, was, the apprehension that the persons employed in the manufactories which now were, or which, in the progress of time, might be established amongst us, would be influenced by their employers. . . . [I]t was a sufficient answer to the argument, that if they were so influenced, they would be enlisted on the same side, which it was the object of the amendment to promote, on the side of property. If not—if they were independent of the influence of their employers, they would be safe depositories of the right. For no man, surely, would contend that they should be deprived of the right of voting on account of their poverty, except so far as it might be supposed to impair the independence, and the consequent purity of the exercise of that invaluable right. . . .

If he could possibly believe . . . that any portion of the calamitous consequences could result from the rejection of the amendment, which had been so feelingly pourtrayed by the honourable gentleman from Albany, (Mr. Kent,) and for whom he would repeat the acknowledgment of his respect and regard, he would be the last man in society who would vote for it. But, believing, as he conscientiously did, that those fears were altogether unfounded; hoping and expecting that the happiest results would follow from the abolition of the freehold qualification, and hoping too, that caution and circumspection would preside over the settlement of the general right of suffrage, which was hereafter to be made, and knowing, besides, that this state, in abolishing the freehold qualification, would but be uniting herself in the march of principle, which had already prevailed in every state of the union, except two or three . . . he would cheerfully record his vote against the amendment.

Despite the remarks of one last Federalist speaker, lawyer William Van Ness of Columbia County, who attempted to provoke concern about landless masses of urban voters in New York City and eventually elsewhere in the state, the Convention dealt the amendment an overwhelming defeat, one hundred to nineteen. The principle of a liberal and uniform standard for suffrage in state elections had cleared a crucial hurdle with ease, setting the stage for further debate over whether those standards would be applied equally to black and white citizens.

WEDNESDAY, SEPTEMBER 26, 1821

With the principle of broad, uniform suffrage requirements established, delegates sought to determine precisely how universal male suffrage should be. Conservatives were scarcely more successful in pruning back the extent of suffrage than they had been in defining the senatorial electorate the previous day. An amendment brought by Peter Jay to reject militia service as a criterion for voting lost by an overwhelming margin. Race, as brief remarks by Peter R. Livingston revealed, hovered in the background, as it had the day before.

Those who sought to limit the expansion of suffrage garnered more widespread support for rejecting work on the public roads as a qualification for voting. Federalist delegates such as Rufus King were joined in opposition to the roadwork clause by Republican Martin Van Buren. The latter hoped to strike roadwork out as a qualification, remarking, "The people were not prepared for universal suffrage."

MR. DUER[48] observed, that it had been yesterday decided, in effect, that, the qualifications of electors should be the same for whatever public officer was the subject of their choice. He had fully concurred in that measure. . . .

MR. D. was not one of those who believed that every person has an absolute right to elect his rulers; still less, that they derive such right from social compact or grant. The object of all government was the security and happiness of the governed. No right could exist inconsistent with that object. It was a question of expediency only, and not at all dependent on abstract principle.

Mr. D. was heretic enough to believe that there was no peculiar abstract excellence in a republican form of government. Its excellence depended on its adaptation to the habits and manners of the people. Where the people were sunk in vice and profligacy, it was perhaps the worst government that could be instituted. But where the body of the people were intelligent and moral—where there existed habits of attachment to liberty and subordination to law, a republican government, was, of all others, the most excellent.

It was not to be denied, that there were some among ourselves, who did not possess the discretion or independence necessary for the due and proper exercise of the invaluable privilege of the right of suffrage. There was no necessary connexion between poverty and vice. Yet as a general rule—in a country like ours, where the acquisition of property is within the reach of all, where the labourer to-day may be a freeholder tomorrow, it was but too generally the fact, that those who remained in poverty, were continued in it by idleness or vice. And it was a melancholy reflection, that by an inscrutable law of nature, this class were sure to increase with the advance of population.

Can it then be questioned, if the principle and the fact be admitted, that it is our duty to prohibit, or limit the exercise of a right that is sure to be abused? The sober minded people of this state are not prepared for the new and untried principle of universal suffrage; and the introduction of this principle would necessarily result from an adoption, either of the report of the committee, or of the amendment of the gentleman from Delaware [*Erastus Root*]. . . .

King: . . . [T]here should be a common rule agreed upon, by which to include and by which to exclude.

In Mr. K's opinion, every man should be excluded who has not the *capacity* to give an impartial and independent suffrage, or who was habitually and necessarily influenced by other men.

The great and difficult question is how to apply this rule. Mr. K then proceeded at considerable length to show that those who merely performed military service and labour on the roads, did not ordinarily compose that class of electors that could be deemed independent; and that although we were bound to extend to them all the charities of our nature, and although it could be no object or desire of any member of the Convention, to depress any class of our fellow citizens, yet it well deserved reflection whether they were not so commonly dependant on others, as to render it unsafe to extend to them a privilege so precious to us, and which, if abused, would be dangerous to the very existence of our liberties. . . .

Mr. P. R. Livingston . . . . spoke against the rule, which had been proposed by the gentleman from Queens [*Rufus King*]; and remarked, that if the principle would apply in any case, it would be in that of the blacks, in favour of whom that gentleman had voted.

THURSDAY, SEPTEMBER 27, 1821

The convention continued to debate just how broad to make the franchise, with various delegates offering to tinker with language regarding length of residency, military service, and payment of taxes for the public roads. Despite the technicalities of the matter, the larger principle at stake was whether suffrage should be made truly universal for all adult males. An amendment offered by Melancton Wheeler of Washington County seemingly universalized the suffrage by enfranchising all adult men not already eligible by virtue of paying taxes if they had resided in the state for three years and in the town where they were to vote for one year. Many convention delegates were hesitant to go that far, although arriving at a precise formula for limiting the franchise in some way proved vexing. In the midst of these discussions, Jacob Sutherland, a lawyer from of Schoharie County, offered an intellectual architecture for the middle ground sought by Van Buren and his followers between universal suffrage and extensive franchise restrictions. Sutherland's fears about the rise of dangerous urban classes perhaps exceeded the mainstream view of the convention. Yet his logic ultimately bore dangerous implications for African Americans, whose future as voters was particularly vulnerable to a combination of racism, partisanship, and political expediency.

MR. J. SUTHERLAND. I have taken no part in the discussion of the different questions, in relation to the right of suffrage, not, because I have not felt the importance of the subject, but because I was sensible that most of the considerations which would influence its decision, would be more forcibly urged by others. I have felt the great importance of the subject. It lies at the very foundation of every representative government; and the decision which we shall finally pronounce upon it, must most essentially affect the future character of all our institutions. I could not enter into the feelings of those gentlemen who, thought that in parting with the freehold qualification for senatorial electors, we gave up our only guarantee for the unmolested enjoyment of life, liberty, and property—that we were committing the sacred institutions of our forefathers, under which we have lived and prospered for more than forty years, to the winds and to the waves of a turbulent and unbalanced democracy. If I could have thought so, I should have united my feeble efforts to theirs in endeavouring to preserve that feature of our constitution. But without entering into the argument of that question, I did believe with the honourable gentleman from Queens, that public opinion called for the abolition of the freehold qualification. By public opinion, I do not mean popular clamour, which in truth is often produced by a very few individuals: I mean the calm and deliberate judgment of the people, pronounced upon a subject on which they are competent to think and to decide, after it has been fairly proposed, and temperately and fully discussed. To public opinion thus understood, I would yield everything: To popular clamour nothing. I will not detain the committee by attempting to show that the question to which I have alluded, is one on which the people are capable of thinking or deciding; nor with an enumeration of the circumstances, which have induced me to believe, that a large majority of those who are interested in the question, wish the freehold qualification abolished. I will only advert to the fact of the great unanimity with which that question was decided by the Convention, which contains perhaps as fair and respectable a representation of the freehold interest of the state as could be assembled.

He thought gentlemen did not realize, how far they have already extended the right of suffrage. We have given to that large and respectable portion of our fellow citizens, who under our present constitution, can vote only for members of assembly, the privilege of voting for governor and senators also; they have now an equal participation with the freeholders of the state in the choice of all the officers of government. He believed, that the people of this state would be satisfied with the extension—that they did not wish nor expect that portion of our population, to whom it has heretofore been thought unsafe or unwise to entrust the right of suffrage, even for a single branch of the government to be admitted to the great and responsible privilege of choosing all its departments: It was making a violent, and, he believed, an unexpected stride—It was vibrating from one extreme to the other. It is not to be denied—it is a fact, which all observation and all history teaches, that there is and must be, in every great community, a class of citizens, who, destitute alike of property, of character, and of intelligence, neither contribute to the support of its institutions, nor can be safely trusted with the choice of rulers; and that this class increases in a geometrical ratio, with the increase of its wealth and its population. That, that description of persons ought not to enjoy the right of suffrage, all must admit; and the only difficulty seems to be, in fixing upon a rule which will exclude them, without at the same time excluding a different and better class of citizens. There is no general rule which is not subject to particular exceptions; and I am free to admit, that none can be fixed upon in relation to this subject, which will not exclude some who ought to be admitted, and admit others who ought to be excluded. But shall we therefore have no restrictions at all? . . . .

FRIDAY, SEPTEMBER 28, 1821

The convention continued to debate the precise details of the voting clause of the constitution and whether or not the emerging language was tantamount to universal suffrage. Delegates reiterated and elaborated upon earlier arguments. Martin Van Buren continued to urge that the convention resist the tidal pull of "universal suffrage." By contrast, other delegates, including U.S. Vice President Daniel Tompkins and Jacob Radcliff of New York City, thought the fear of so-called universal suffrage misplaced.

MR. TOMPKINS . . . thought too much alarm had been created by the bug-bear universal suffrage. Taxation as connected with representation, meant liability to taxation. How was it when no taxes were imposed in this state? Was there no representation? The property qualification had always been an odious feature in the constitution; and as it would bear away with it a vast proportion of the perjuries, slanders, &c. that had often disgraced our elections, he hoped it would be abolished. . . .

MR. RADCLIFF was for universal suffrage. Public sentiment called for it. Provision had been made for nearly all, and the remnant ought not to be excluded. Authorities cited from foreign writers, and precedents drawn from other governments, were wholly irrelevant—the people of this country, above all others, were intelligent and virtuous—he was not afraid of them. The argument drawn from the rise of populous cities was fallacious—town and country increase in the same ratio.

Ultimately, efforts by conservatives and some moderates to block the Wheeler amendment failed in a close vote. Residency for a sufficient length of time was, under certain conditions, deemed sufficient to qualify adult males for the franchise.

Saturday, September 29, 1821

Having debated many of the broad principles as well as the specific details of future suffrage rules, the convention, prompted by Ogden Edwards of New York City, resolved to form a select committee of delegates to reformulate the actual constitutional language. The select committee of thirteen was expressly charged with revisiting the issue of black suffrage. After the convention appointed the new committee, delegates offered a number of resolutions regarding suffrage language for the committee to consider, including a variety of proposals to reinsert some sort of racial exclusion into the suffrage provisions of the new constitution. Of the thirteen members of the new select committee on suffrage, only Samuel Young of Saratoga, a staunch supporter of a racial bar to voting, had been a member of the original suffrage committee. Of the remaining twelve members, eight had voted originally to exclude all blacks from voting, while four had opposed the earlier measure.

Mr. Edwards offered the following resolution:

Resolved, That the committee of the whole be discharged from the further consideration of the report of the select committee appointed to consider the right of suffrage and the qualification of persons to be elected, and that the same, together with the amendments made thereto in committee of the whole, be referred to a select committee consisting of thirteen members, and that the committee also report their opinion upon the expediency of excluding people of colour from the right of suffrage.

In explanation of the reason which induced him to offer the resolution, Mr. Edwards remarked, that the object of this Convention, was to form such a constitution as would meet the approbation of the whole community—a constitution that would be deeply rooted in the affections of the people. All were in favour of granting to every man who was qualified to vote the elective privileges; but there were certain limits, beyond which we ought not to go. A select committee might embody the sentiments of all the members, and harmonize their different views.

COL. YOUNG said he was about to move, that the committee of the whole be discharged from the further consideration of the report on the right of suffrage, with a view that it might be referred back to the select committee. It was his intention to offer, at a proper time, an amendment by inserting the word "white," so as to read "white male citizens." The committee had settled that the right of suffrage shall be extended; the vote was a strong one. . . . Sir, many of the gentlemen in the majority upon this question are from the country; and know more about the feelings of the yeomanry, than those who, from their wealth, habits, and official stations, do not mingle among the people.

The convention referred a variety of amendments for the consideration of the new select committee. Aside from proposals by some delegates still holding out for a property requirement, the focus of these resolutions was on making only whites eligible for the broadest, most expansive clauses in the proposed suffrage article to the future constitution. Clauses making residency and militia service sufficient to qualify white voters would not, under the proposals forwarded to the select committee, apply to black voters.

Act Three: Compromising Black Citizenship

When the convention as a whole returned to the suffrage question a week later, delegates zeroed in on black New Yorkers as the group whose explicit exclusion from the full rights and obligations of citizenship would provide legitimacy for expanded suffrage. Having swept away the broad property requirements of the 1777 constitution, delegates affixed exclusionary restrictions on potential black voters. The language that emerged allowed twenty-one-year-old white men who lived in the state for a year to vote if they paid any tax or served in the militia. Black males had a state residency requirement of three years. Only whites too poor to pay taxes but who worked on the public highways had to fulfill a similar three-year residency. Unlike poor whites, potential black voters would be required to own and pay taxes on real estate property, free and clear of debts, worth at least $250. Thus, the convention applied to African Americans—and only African Americans—the repudiated formula of an electorate limited to property-holders.[49]

Martin Van Buren helped guide his colleagues toward this compromise, which, from the standpoint of its supporters, combined principle and expediency, exclusion and justice. The convention, Van Buren and others could claim, did not indiscriminately universalize suffrage. By the same token, the convention made racial exclusion conditional, releasing most blacks from the obligation to pay taxes and allegedly creating incentives to ascend to the ranks of full citizenship through property holding. The fundamentally racist assumption of these provisions, as critics noted, was that blacks required "inducements" to demonstrate qualities deemed virtually universal among white men. In essence, the vices of the city that conservatives warned about during the convention were imputed to the portion of the population most vulnerable to political assault— African Americans.

How did proponents of special language regulating potential black voters justify the proposed compromise over black suffrage? Did these delegates reckon the removal of property requirements for white voters with the extension of property requirements for black voters? How did the debate over black suffrage connect to concerns about the possibility of so-called universal suffrage? What arguments did critics of black disfranchisement make in their final attempts to forestall it? Why did the convention find these anti-disfranchisement arguments, effective against the ban on black voting proposed in mid-September, unpersuasive in October?

*　　*　　*

Thursday, October 4, 1821

The select committee charged with considering suffrage requirements and racial disfranchisement proposed language for the Convention's consideration:

I. Every male citizen of the age of twenty-one years, who shall have been one year an inhabitant of this state, preceding the day of the election, and for the last six months a resident of the town, county, or district, where he may offer his vote, and shall have been, within the next year preceding, assessed, and shall have actually paid a tax to the state or county, or shall be by law exempted from taxation: And also, every male citizen of the age of twenty-one years, who shall have been for three years, a resident in the town, county, or district where he may offer his vote, and shall have been, within the last year, assessed to labour, or paid an equivalent therefore, according to law, shall be entitled to vote in the town or ward where he actually resides, and not elsewhere, for all officers that now are, or hereafter may be, elective by the people: *Provided*, That no male citizen, other than white, shall be subject to taxation, or entitled to vote at any election, unless, in addition to the qualifications of age and residence, last above mentioned, he shall be seized and possessed, in his own right, of a freehold estate of the value of two hundred and fifty dollars, over and above all debts and incumbrances charged thereon, and shall have been, within the year next preceding the election, assessed, and shall have actually paid a tax to the state or county.

SATURDAY, OCTOBER 6, 1821

Before turning to racial disfranchisement, delegates addressed provisions for qualifying voters on the basis of taxation, militia service, and work on the highways. Jacob Van Rensselaer launched one last defense of the conservative vision of suffrage, seeking to protect the prerogatives of landholding against the allegedly looming encroachments of the ever-expanding urban population. The convention then debated the method of disfranchisement and racialized obligations and privileges of citizenship envisioned by the select committee. Last-ditch appeals to reject racial exclusion as immoral and incompatible with the state's post-Revolutionary history failed.

GEN. J. R. VAN RENSSELAER . . . There is in every community, a portion of idle, profligate, and abandoned men; and it is unjust and impolitic, that this description of people should have it in their power to control the government and the property of the industrious, the virtuous and moral part of the community. The object of all good governments is the protection of life, liberty, and property. The two first, are always safe, under a government of laws, because no laws can be passed which shall operate partially as to them. All will be protected or injured alike by any general provision; but the introduction of universal suffrage, would operate unequally as it regards to the latter object, because it would afford to him who possesses no property, who has none to be affected by any law which may be enacted, as much political power as the freeholder or farmer who contributes from ten to fifty dollars per year towards its support. The farmers and mechanics who own portions of property procured by the practice of all the moral virtues, are uniformly and constantly bound to afford support and protection, in peace and in war to your government— in times of peace by contributions in money, and in war by their personal services also; while the first description of persons never afford either. Whenever their situation can be improved, they emigrate to some other state, or evade the operation of your laws: as mere mercenaries they sometimes enter your armies and fight your battles, but seldom, if ever, from any higher motive than the mere pecuniary consideration they re- ceive—While the farmer, whose property is always visible, always bound to contribute according to the value, to the support of government, is fas- tened to the soil almost as much as the oak, whose roots have penetrated it—and in the proportion as the measures of your administration are bad and injurious, the more is his difficulty of escaping their effects increased. The effect and operation of this widely extended suffrage, would be but partially felt, were the whole population of the state composed of farm- ers and ordinary mechanics, as the influence of the parent would be ex- ercised over the son, and all would feel an immediate interest in the pros- perity, and welfare of their country. But the case of this state is wisely dif- ferent from this. Already have we in the city of New-York, about one tenth of the whole population of the state. . . .

. . . Man has been, and probably always will be, subject to the same passions and feelings; and, under like circumstances, the future will strongly resemble the past. And it is, therefore, the province of prudence and wisdom, by some slight property qualification for electors, to exclude those from a participation in the political power of this government, who have nothing to lose by the enactment of bad laws, and who may feel per- haps too strong a desire to violate private rights for the gratification of their cupidity.

Various delegates commented on Van Rennselaer's defense of the prop- erty-holding standard, including James Fairlie of New York City, who quipped, "The city of New-York he thought was not quite so bad as the gentleman represented. As it was larger than other places, so it contained more vice, in the same proportion." Shortly after Van Rensselaer's pro- posed amendment was defeated, Olney Briggs, a radical Bucktail from Schoharie County who listed his occupation as "mechanic," reintroduced the notion of making the franchise an exclusively white privilege.

MR. BRIGGS . . . He said that it had been substantially decided by the Convention, that property was not the standard of qualification for a vote. Of course it ought not to be so, with respect to the blacks, any more than the whites. He was therefore opposed to the proviso, and wished to insert this provision in its stead [*limiting suffrage to whites only*].

COL. YOUNG was in favour of the motion.

CHANCELLOR KENT was opposed to the motion of the gentleman from Schoharie, and in favour of the proviso reported by the committee. He had already expressed his sentiments on this subject, and he should not trouble the committee with a repetition of them. It was true, that the blacks were in some respects a degraded portion of the community, but he was unwilling to see them disfranchised, and the door eternally barred against them. The proviso would not cut them off from all hope, and might in some degree alleviate the wrongs we had done them. It would have a tendency to make them industrious and frugal, with the prospect of participating in the right of suffrage.

MR. VAN BUREN was in favour of the plan proposed by the select committee, and opposed to the amendment.

MR. SHARPE remarked that the report of the select committee proposed to make the blacks a privileged order, inasmuch as they were not liable to pay taxes, in certain cases, and were exempted from the performance of jury and military service. It was, therefore, but fair that some privilege should be withheld as an equivalent for these exemptions.

MR. BRIGGS wished to make the constitution consistent in all its parts. The black man was a degraded member of society, and would, therefore, be always ready to sell his vote; nor would real estate make him a better man. The whites can never take them to their bosoms.

GEN. TALLMADGE was opposed to the motion. He was prepared to vote, for the proviso which the committee had reported, because he considered it as a compromise of conflicting opinions. He also thought it held out inducements to that unfortunate class of our population to become industrious and valuable members of the community.

MR. JAY said, this subject had already been fully discussed, and once disposed of by the Convention; and he had hoped that it would not again be made a question for debate. It was not his intention to revive the discussion of it; and he rose merely to make some reply to the remarks which had fallen from the gentleman from Schoharie, (Mr. Briggs.) He could wish that gentleman had assigned some reasons why persons of colour might not be as intelligent and virtuous as white persons. Had nature interposed any barriers to prevent them from the acquisition of knowledge, or the pursuit of virtue? It was true they were now in some measure a degraded race; but how came they so? Was it not by our fault, and the fault of our fathers? And because they had been degraded, the gentleman from Schoharie was for visiting the sins of the fathers upon the children,[50] and for condemning them to eternal degradation. He could not but think there were too many unfounded prejudices; too much pride of democracy on this subject. However we may scorn, and insult, and trample upon this unfortunate race now, the day was fast approaching when we must lie down with them in that narrow bed appointed for all the living. Then, if not before, the pride of distinction would cease. There the prisoners rest together; they hear not the voice of the oppressor. The small and the great are there; and the servant is free from his master. In commingled and undistinguished dust we must all repose, and rise together at the last day. God has created us all equal; and why should we establish distinctions? We are all the offspring of one common Father, and redeemed by one common Saviour—the gates of paradise are open alike to the bond and the free. He hoped the committee would never consent to incorporate into the constitution a provision which contravened the spirit of our institutions, and which was so repulsive to the dictates of justice and humanity.

MR. BUEL said it was not correct, as had been suggested on a former day by the honourable gentleman from Saratoga, (Mr. Young,) that no provision for the exclusion of the blacks had been made by the framers of our constitution, because they were then so few and inconsiderable as to have been overlooked by them. It would be found that as long ago as 1730, a special law of this state was enacted to prevent the concealing of slaves. Statutes had been on the same subject down to the time of the revolution, which evinced that the people of this state were not ignorant of the tendency or extent of the effect and progress of emancipation. In the period of the revolutionary war, a statute had been passed for the encouragement of enlisting blacks into the service, which provided that at the expiration of three years the slave should be entitled to his freedom, and the master to the military bounty.

He had previously suggested the difficulty of discrimination which would arise from such a provision. Philosophers had distinguished the human race by five colours, the white, black, brown, olive, and red. By the amendment, four of the races would be excluded. In the West Indies a man became white *according to law*, when only one sixteenth part of African blood ran in his veins. These questions might lead to unpleasant elucidations of family history, and ought to be avoided.

COL. YOUNG replied to the observations of Mr. Buel, and admitted that the theory of philosophers might be correct; but he contended that in forming a constitution, reference was to be had, not to speculation, but to the common sense of mankind. That would sufficiently direct, who were to be admitted, and who were to be excluded, by such a general provision.

MR. BRIGGS made three unsuccessful efforts to take the floor.

MESSERS. ROSS and R. CLARKE addressed the committee on the subject, when

MR. BRIGGS replied to the objections that had been raised by the honourable gentleman from Westchester, (Mr. Jay.) That gentleman had remarked that we must all ultimately lie down in the same bed together. But he would ask that honourable gentleman whether he would consent to lie down, in life, in the same feather bed with a negro? But it was said that the right of suffrage would elevate them. He would ask whether it would elevate a monkey or a baboon to allow them to vote? No, it would be to sport, and trifle, and insult them, to say they might be candidates for the office of president of the United States. But gentlemen whose opinions he respected, had advised him to withdraw his motion, and therefore he withdrew it.

The question was then taken on the first part of the section, as amended, in the following words:

"Every male citizen of the age of twenty-one years, who shall have been one year an inhabitant of this state preceding the day of the election, and for the last six months a resident of the town, county, or district where he may offer his vote, and shall have paid a tax to the state or county within the year next preceding the election, assessed upon his real or personal property; or shall be by law exempted from taxation."

This opening clause of the proposed constitutional language governing suffrage passed by an overwhelming majority with only two delegates dissenting. The convention then took up the clause extending the franchise to all adult males who worked on or paid taxes to support public roads and had established a relatively stable residence in their communities. The clause read:

And also, every male citizen of the age of twenty one years, who shall have been, for three years next preceding such election, an inhabitant of this state; and for the last year a resident in the town, county, or district, where he may offer his vote; and shall have been, within the last year, assessed to labour upon the public highways, and shall have performed the labour, or paid an equivalent therefor, according to law, shall be entitled to vote in the town or ward where he actually resides and not elsewhere, for all officers that now are, or hereafter maybe, elective by the people.

After an explanation by Martin Van Buren as to why he had once opposed such language but now approved it, and after unsuccessful attempts by two other delegates to delete significant portions of this clause, the convention approved it.

The *Proviso* [*concerning black voting*] was next in order.

GEN. ROOT moved to rise and report. He hoped they would not (it being 3 o'clock) take up the negroes upon an empty stomach. . . .

MR. BACON said that he objected to this mode of excluding the black population from voting, because, in the first place, it was an attempt to do a thing indirectly which we appeared either to be ashamed of doing, or for some reason chose not to do directly, a course which he thought every way unworthy of us. This freehold qualification is, as it applies to nearly all the blacks, a practical exclusion, and if this is right, it ought to be done directly. By the adoption of this too, we involved ourselves in the most obvious inconsistency, declaring thereby, that although property either real or personal, was no correct test of qualification in the case of a white man, it was a very good one in that of a black one, that although as gentlemen had maintained it conferred neither talents, integrity, or independence on the one, it imparted them all to the other. If we were determined to exclude them at all, it would be more correct and honourable to do it directly.

In relation to that general question he would take this opportunity for the first time, to explain, in a few words, his general views. He had as little fondness as any one for either legislating or forming systems of government wholly upon those general sweeping theories of the universal and inalienable rights of man, of which we have heard so much here,— and whoever attempted to bottom all his measures upon any general theories, without alluding to the practical limitations and exceptions to which they were always subject, shewed himself a very crude statesman, and a rash and dangerous legislator. One of our first general principles is, that we recognize no distinct casts [*sic*] or orders of men, having distinct and fixed personal or political rights,—and nothing but a strong political necessity can authorise a violation of this principle, could it be made to appear that any such necessity existed in the present case, he would not hesitate to yield to it. But what are the facts adduced to make out such a case? The documents before us shew an entire black population of hardly forty thousand of all ages and sexes, both slaves and free, scattered through a white population of nearly a million and a half; and that so far from the former gaining upon us, it has for the thirty years past sensibly diminished when compared with the latter. Whence then the apprehended danger, when an experience of forty years has brought with it none. The exclusion from the right of suffrage, of aliens, of females and others, alluded to by gentleman from Saratoga, all stand on grounds of public safety, or high political inconvenience. The exclusion of the blacks from militia duty and from juries, is founded only on considerations of feeling and of taste in the whites, and adopted for the sole convenience of the latter, but it is not on any such principles, that we can justify withholding from them the first of our general political rights, where its exercise is forbid by no considerations of public safety, or political necessity.

MR. EASTWOOD said he was not in favour of letting in black *vagabonds* to vote, but felt more liberal than the select committee; he therefore moved to strike out $250 and insert $100.

The question was thereupon taken on Mr. Eastwood's motion and lost.

The provision to exclude all black voters, except for men with over $250 of freehold property, then passed by a vote of seventy-two to thirty.[51] This roll-call vote on racially defined suffrage, and roll-call votes two days later, revealed a considerable bloc of swing voters among Bucktail Republicans. A total exclusion of black voters had been defeated in September with support of delegates holding a variety of ideological and factional identities, including Bucktail Republicans. But arguments that emphasized present-day concerns rather than historical obligation and precedent midwifed support for a formula that stopped short of a blunt denial of African American voting rights. Ultimately, more than two-thirds of the delegates found a racially defined property requirement for black suffrage a suitable mix of practical compromise and principled moderation, thereby embracing a blend of racism and political populism that would inform the debate over black citizenship in New York and the nation for the next two generations.

MONDAY, OCTOBER 8, 1821

Having voted on individual sections of the proposed suffrage provisions for a new state constitution, the convention then discussed the article as a whole, first debating the section calling for the registration of eligible voters. The convention eliminated this language, apparently persuaded by Erastus Root that preelection registration was burdensome, particularly in rural areas where would-be voters would suffer great inconvenience simply to register themselves in advance of each election. This expensive and unwieldy process, Root argued, would depress voter turnout. Having settled this question, Jonas Platt offered an impassioned critique of racial disfranchisement, indicting its proponents as guilty of patent hypocrisies that the mantle of democratic patriotism could not obscure. Supporters of racial exclusion once again defended their positions. A vote on the proviso governing African American voters produced an almost identical tally to the vote two days before. The convention reaffirmed the principle of racially defined access to full citizenship.

MR. PLATT moved to expunge the proviso in the first section, which declares that no person, "*other than a white man,*" shall vote, unless he have a freehold estate of the value of $250. He said, I am not disposed,

sir, to turn knight errant in favour of the men of colour. But the obligations of justice are eternal and indispensable: and this proviso involves a
principle which, upon reflection, I cannot concede, or compromise as a
matter of expediency. I am aware of the intrinsic difficulty of this subject.
The evils of negro slavery are deep rooted, and admit of no sudden and
effectual remedy. In the act of doing justice, we are bound to consider
consequences. With such a population as that of Virginia, or the Caroli-
nas, a sudden emancipation, and permission to the negroes to vote, would
be incompatible with the public safety: and necessity creates a law for itself. But, sir, in this state there is no grounds for such a plea. I admit, that
most of the free negroes in our state, are unfit to be entrusted with the
right of suffrage; they have neither sufficient intelligence, nor a sufficient
degree of independence, to exercise that right in a safe and proper manner. I would exclude the great mass of them, but not by this unjust and
odious discrimination of colour. We are under no necessity of adopting
such a principle, in laying the foundation of our government. Let us attain this object of exclusion, by fixing such a uniform standard of qualification, as would not only exclude the great body of free men of colour,
but also a large portion of ignorant and depraved white men, who are as
unfit to exercise the power of voting as the men of colour. By adopting the
principle of universal suffrage, in regard to white men, we create the necessity, which is now pleaded as an excuse for this unjust discrimination.

Our republican text is, that all men are born equal, in civil and political rights; and if this proviso be ingrafted into our constitution, the practical commentary will be, that a portion of our free citizens shall not
enjoy equal rights with their fellow citizens. All freemen of African
parentage, are to be constitutionally degraded: no matter how virtuous or
intelligent. Test the principle, sir, by another example. Suppose the proposition were, to make a discrimination, so as to exclude the descendants of
German, or Low Dutch, or Irish ancestors; would not every man be
shocked at the horrid injustice of the principle? It is in vain to disguise the
fact; we shall violate a sacred principle, without any necessity, if we retain
this discrimination. We say to this unfortunate race of men, purchase a
freehold estate of $250 value, and you shall then be equal to the white
man, who parades one day in the militia, or performs a day's work on the
highway. Sir, it is adding mockery to injustice. We know that, with rare
exceptions, they have not the means of purchasing a freehold: and it
would be unworthy of this grave Convention to do, *indirectly*, an act of
injustice, which we are unwilling openly to avow. The real object is, to ex-

clude the oppressed and degraded sons of Africa; and, in my humble judgment, it would better comport with the dignity of this Convention to speak out, and to pronounce the sentence of perpetual degradation, on negroes and their posterity for ever, than to establish a test, which we know they cannot comply with, and which we do not require of others.

The gentleman from Saratoga, who, as chairman of the committee, reported this proviso, (Mr. Young,) has exultingly told us, that ours is the only happy country where freemen acknowledge no distinction of ranks—where real native genius and merit can emerge from the humblest conditions of life, and rise to honours and distinction. It sounded charmingly in our republican ears, and I have but one objection to it, which is that, unfortunately for our patriotic pride, it is not true. I abhor the vices and oppressions which flow from privileged orders as much as any man, but it is a remarkable truth, that in England, the present *Lord Chancellor Elden*, and his illustrious brother, *Sir William Scott*, are the sons of a *coal-heaver*; and the present Chief Justice Abbot, of the Kings Bench, is the son of a *hair-dresser*.[52] The gentleman from Saratoga, (Mr. Young,) began his philipic in favour of universal suffrage, by an eulogium on liberty and equality, in our happy state. And what then? Why, the same gentleman concluded by moving a resolution, in substance, that 37,000 of our free black citizens, and their posterity, for ever, shall be degraded, by our constitution, below the common rank of freemen—that they never shall emerge from their humble condition—that they shall never assert the dignity of human nature, but shall ever remain a degraded cast [*sic*] in our republic.

. . . I confess, sir, I feel some apprehension, when I anticipate, that the speeches of that honourable member, will be read by the proud English critic; who will boast, that "slaves cannot breathe English air;" that "they touch his country, and their shackles fall."[53] The gentleman from Saratoga will be justly considered, as a leading patriot and statesman in our republic; and if his text and his commentary, his precept and his practice, are at variance; we shall be nakedly exposed to the lash of criticism, from the hand of retaliation.

Before we adopt this proviso, I hope gentlemen will take a retrospect of the last fifty years. Consider the astonishing progress of the human mind, in regard to religious toleration; the various plans of enlightened benevolence; and especially the mighty efforts of the wise and the good throughout Christendom, in favour of the benighted and oppressed children of Africa.

In our own state, public sentiment has been totally changed on the subject of negro slavery. About sixty years ago, an act of our colonial assembly was passed, with this disgraceful preamble: "whereas justice and good policy require, that the African slave-trade should be liberally encouraged." And within the last forty years, I remember, in the sale of negroes, it was no uncommon occurrence to witness the separation of husband and wife, and parents and children, without their consent, and under circumstances which forbid all hope of their ever seeing each other again in this world. And this was done without apparent remorse or compunction, and with as little reluctance on the part of buyer and seller, as we now feel in separating a span of horses, or a yoke of oxen. But I thank God, that a sense of justice and mercy has in a good measure regenerated the hearts of men. A rapid emancipation has taken place; and we approach the era when, according to the existing law, slavery will be abolished in this state.

But, sir, we owe to that innocent and unfortunate race of men, much more than mere emancipation. We owe to them our patient and persevering exertions, to elevate their condition and character, by means of moral and religious instruction. And I rejoice that by the instrumentality of Sunday schools, and other benevolent institutions, many of them promise fair to become intelligent, virtuous, and useful citizens. Judging from our experience of the last fifty years; what may we not reasonably expect, in the next half century? Sir, if we adopt the principle of this proviso, I hope and believe, that our posterity will blush, when they see the names recorded in favour of such a discrimination.

I beseech gentlemen to consider the enlighted [sic] age in which we live! Consider how much has already been accomplished by the efforts of Christian philanthropy! During the last forty years, we have brought up this African race from the house of bondage: We have led them nearly through the wilderness, and shewn them the promised land. Shall we now drive them back again into Egypt? I hope not, sir. The light of science, and the heavenly beams of Christianity, are dawning upon them. Shall we extinguish these rays of hope? This is not a mere question of expediency. Man has no right to deal thus with his fellow man; except on the ground of necessity and public safety. It is not pretended that such a reason exists in this case. We shall violate a sacred principle, to avoid, at most a slight inconvenience:—and, if I do not deceive myself, those who shall live fifty years hence, will view this proviso in the same light as we now view the law of our New-England fathers, which punished with death all who were guilty of being Quakers, or the law of our fathers in the colonial assembly of New-York, which offered bounties to encourage the slave trade.

As a republican statesman, I protest against the principle of inequality contained in this proviso. As a man and a father, who expects justice for himself and his children, in this world; and as a Christian, who hopes for mercy in the world to come; I can not, I dare not, consent to this unjust proscription.

CHIEF JUSTICE SPENCER was opposed to the proviso, although on a former occasion he had voted to exclude the blacks altogether. His reasons were, that the rule contained in the proviso was incorrect, because it gave to the owner of real estate an advantage over a person who might, perhaps, possess a leasehold estate of the value of $1,000, or personal property to the amount of $20,000.

MR. VAN BUREN said he had voted against a total and unqualified exclusion, for he would not draw a revenue from them, and yet deny to them the right of suffrage. But this proviso met his approbation. They were exempted from taxation until they had qualified themselves to vote. The right was not denied, to exclude any portion of the community who will not exercise the right of suffrage in its purity. This held out inducements to industry, and would receive his support.

COL. YOUNG, would forbear remarks upon the uncourteous expression of the gentleman from Oneida (Mr. Platt) in pronouncing his (Mr. Y's) observations untrue. But he should repeat that they were true, and that the United States of America was the only country under heaven, where the humble poor could emerge from obscurity. . . .

MR. Y. considered the proviso as the result of compromise. It had been so considered and *advocated* on Saturday by an honourable gentleman from Albany (Mr. Kent) who a few minutes after *voted* against it. Another honourable gentleman from Albany has now given notice, that although a few days ago he voted for the *total* exclusion of the blacks, he is now opposed to their *qualified* exclusion. Gentlemen had an undoubted right to change their minds, but he would desire it to be specifically understood, that if this proviso was rejected, he should move to insert the word *white* in the report and exclude them altogether.

CHANCELLOR KENT explained. He said that slavery existed in this state at the time of the revolution, and yet it was not recognized in the constitution. There was no such thing known in the constitution of the non-holding states, with the exception of Connecticut, as a denial to the blacks of those electoral privileges that were enjoyed by the whites. In Europe the distinction of colour was unknown. The judges of England said even so long ago as the reign of Queen Elizabeth, that the air of England was too pure for a slave to breathe in. The same law prevails in Scotland, Holland, France, and most of the other kingdoms of Europe.

After Kent's remarks, the convention confirmed its support for black disfranchisement and for the new suffrage rules more generally in a series of three roll-call votes.

Epilogue: Losers and Loose Ends

Several issues relating to suffrage and citizenship remained to be resolved as the convention wound up its business on the franchise. Among these issues was whether those barred from voting should be counted toward population when apportioning representatives in the state legislature, the size of New York City's role in state politics, and whether to make final revisions to the language regulating black suffrage.

The convention also once more turned its attention to the lingering but still controversial subject of slavery. Proposals to accelerate or merely to confirm the impending abolition of slavery in New York met with little favor. The support for including antislavery language in the constitution did not mirror opposition to disfranchisement: conversely, some prominent opponents of disfranchisement voted and spoke against constitutional language with regard to slavery. The brief debate revealed the deep ambivalence of New York's political leaders on the meaning of slavery, race, and emancipation to the state's past and its future.

What principles did delegates think should govern the allotment of representatives? Why did African American voting once again surface in the debate over apportionment of legislative seats? How did the fear of the city mirror fears about black voters? Why did the convention decline to abolish slavery constitutionally? Why did some opponents of disfranchisement also oppose including abolition provisions in the constitution?

Why did the convention decline to make any further adjustments in the provisions restricting black voting?

*   *   *

THURSDAY, OCTOBER 11, 1821

Having defined the electorate in broad but far from universal terms— having in effect excluded most African Americans and all women—the convention debated whether representation in the state legislature should be apportioned to the counties based on numbers of voters or numbers of inhabitants. The power and influence of New York City was central to this debate, as in that burgeoning metropolis were gathered the largest numbers of people who would not qualify to vote. The debate, which continued into the next day, inevitably led to reflections on the racialized and gendered nature of citizenship in the democratizing political culture of the nineteenth century. These remarks thus provide further insight into the process of disfranchisement and the racialized definition of citizenship that resulted from it.

CHANCELLOR KENT thought the question of retaining the term "inhabitants," was entitled to much consideration. It had not indeed been distinctly brought before the select committee, of which he had the honour to be a member, but he was disposed to think it ought to be retained.

There now appeared to exist considerable alarm of the overbearing weight and influence of the city of New-York. He had been desirous to restrain the right of suffrage within such bounds as would exclude that kind of population which, in large cities especially, could not be expected to exercise it with purity and discretion. But after the limitation was made, the representatives came into the legislature not merely to represent the electors, but the inhabitants also, male and female—widows and minors—and the property that they might respectively possess.

The city of New-York was the pride and glory of the state, and although discretion was required in its governance, it was entitled, and ought to enjoy, its full and proportional weight and influence.

MR. EDWARDS. I presume, sir, that it is the intention of this Convention to distribute equal and exact justice to all the people of this state. This intention will be defeated by the adoption of the proposition of the honourable gentleman from Saratoga, (Mr. Young.) Consider, sir, for one moment, the operation upon the city of New-York, of the rule that representation is to be apportioned according to the number of electors: In that city, no person is bound by law to work on the highways, and they have but very few highways to work. In the country, every person above twenty-one years of age, is required by law to work on the highways; you have consequently adopted a rule, with respect to the right of suffrage, which must necessarily be partial in its operation. The consequence of it is, that multitudes are admitted to the enjoyment of the elective franchise in the country, when corresponding classes of society are excluded from it in the city. To make this subject still more plain, I will suppose that the elective franchise was confined to those alone who labour on the highways. The consequence of this would be, that not a man in the city of New-York would be permitted to vote. Then, if the proposition is adopted that representation is to be apportioned according to the number of electors, it would follow, that that city would not have a representation in either branch of the legislature. Now, sir, if this proposition is adopted, though that city will not be entirely disfranchised, yet it will be, so far as it goes to deprive it of the representation which it is entitled to in consequence of its comprising a population who are neither taxed nor perform military duty, and who, if they resided in the country, would be required to work on the highways. . . .

The patriotic, venerable, and venerated men who formed our constitution, did, to be sure, deem it wise to insert that provision. But, sir, we were then but just emerging from a state of subjugation to a monarchical government. The principles of civil liberty were then, as it were, in their cradle. We have had the benefit of practising upon them for nearly half a century; and I think I may now say, without giving offence, that they are now better understood. We have, by an overwhelming majority, expunged the freehold qualification from the constitution. We have disclaimed the supremacy of property, as well as of birth, and of privileged orders. We have proceeded upon the broad principle, "that all men are free and equal;" and in regulating the elective franchise, we have endeavoured to govern it by such rules as would only exclude those whom we were apprehensive would not exercise it with independence or integrity. We have proceeded upon similar principles with respect to them, which we have with respect to our wives and children. They were not included; not because their rights were not equally dear to us with our own, but because public feeling and their good, as well as the good of the whole, required it. And, sir, because we have not thought proper to invest them with the elective franchise, does it follow, that they are not to be duly represented through those who are their natural guardians? because they are not permitted to vote, that they are not to have any weight in the government? No, sir; they are represented by us. So all, who live in the same community with those who exercise the elective franchise, have a common interest with them, that the community should have a due representation in the legislature.

Laws must be equal in their operation; and all who live in the same community will be sure of having their rights equally respected. People, living in different parts of the state, in different states of society, and pursuing different avocations, have, of course, as communities, different interests; and it is equally important to them, whether they are voters or not, that the community in which they reside should be duly represented. Sir, have we deprived the freeholders of their exclusive privileges, upon the broad ground, that we would tolerate no privileged orders for the purpose of establishing another class, the electors? And are we now going to sanction the principle, that the government is made for the *electors*, and not for the people? Are we going to sanction the principle, that the government is not made for the people, but for a certain privileged class? If so, let the apportionment be according to the electors: if not, it must be according to the number of inhabitants. . . .

FRIDAY, OCTOBER 12, 1821

MR. PRESIDENT [*Daniel Tompkins*] hoped that the amendment offered yesterday by the gentleman from Saratoga, to make electors the basis of representation, would prevail. He certainly was not disposed to take from the city of New-York any portion of the representation to which she should be justly entitled; but it must be admitted, that there would always in that city, be a great number of foreigners who never contemplated to become citizens, and who, therefore, ought not to be taken into the account, in determining the representation to which that city should be entitled. Again—there was now in the city of New-York, a population of free people of colour, greater in amount than the whole white population of the county of Richmond—and this was a species of population which they had reason to believe would be very large in that city. He could not consent that this city, from a population of aliens and free blacks, should have a greater share in the representation of the state, than the county of Richmond would have for its whole number of white citizens. He should, he said, vote for the amendment, as affording a more just, and equitable rule than that proposed by the report of the select committee. . . .

Mr. KING. It was not the intention of the committee to have free people of colour, or aliens, taken into the account, but to limit to the free white *citizens*.

COL. YOUNG. The term inhabitant, used by the committee, would, he said, embrace both aliens and free blacks. . . . He hoped they [*delegates from New York City*] were not desirous of having this unsound and floating population of the city, placed on the same footing with the purer population of the country. He contended that the rule of taking the electors only, was the only just rule, and one which would operate more equally and uniformly. The population of the city of New-York would vary many thousands, depending on the state of its commerce and its health. When commerce flourished, they would be crowded with foreigners—when it languished, both foreigners and their own citizens would resort to other places. So also, in respect to its health—when sickly, great numbers would leave it, and the footing of a census of that city would vary many thousands, depending on the time when taken.

JUDGE VAN NESS . . . With respect to the apportionment, he thought a rule might be adopted which would be satisfactory to all. He would suggest the propriety of taking *free white citizens* only, into the account. By this, the large population of free blacks, and of aliens, in the city would be excluded, and the rule would operate equally over every other part of the state; and if the amendment of the gentleman from Saratoga, should be rejected, he would move an amendment conformable to the suggestions he had just made.

MR. VAN VECHTEN said, the question was, whether the representation should be determined by the number of inhabitants, or by the number of electors only. . . .

We all profess to have the same object in view, that of making an equal distribution of the privileges and burthens of the community, as far as constitutional provisions can accomplish it. It is alleged that if their representation is in proportion to their population, it will be greater than they are entitled to have, and because we have done them injustice in one respect, it is right to follow it up. This is not correct.

The rule of representation must always be more or less arbitrary; but the idea appears to have been entertained by some gentlemen present, that none are represented in our legislature, but those who have a right to a voice in the election of its members. This is a mistake—all classes are represented. There may be a vast amount of property owned by persons not possessing the right of suffrage; and is this to have no weight, or receive no consideration? All classes of the community have a right to representation—and having proceeded thus far in admitting a large portion of voters in the country, we are bound in duty to render an equivalent to the inhabitants of the city of New-York. He should, therefore, be opposed to the proposition of the gentleman from Saratoga, (Mr. Young.) . . .

Mr. RADCLIFF proposed to amend the amendment of Mr. Young, by appending thereto the following qualification: "according to the number of free inhabitants, excluding paupers, aliens, and persons of colour not taxed."

He contended that there was unquestionable injustice in admitting highway labour as a qualification, without any adequate equivalent to the corresponding class of citizens in New-York. He hoped that gentlemen would not be disposed to put their hands to a constitution that should contain such glaring and monstrous injustice. He claimed that the character of the people of the city was equally good with that of the towns and villages. He thought there was an unreasonable jealousy of that city. The history of the state would prove, that the city was comparatively retrograding in its population. Our houses were empty, and our people retiring to the country. Even in the most prosperous times, it was barely able to retain its ratio. Its good fortune was connected with and depended on the country. He asked for no advantage of the country in favour of the city—but he did ask, in the name of eternal justice, that the same measure should be meted out to the metropolis, which the counties in the country enjoyed.

The convention ultimately adopted language almost identical to that proposed by Radcliff. Thus, each county's representation in the state assembly was calculated based on "inhabitants," rather than only eligible voters, in its population. But "aliens, paupers, and persons of colour not taxed" were subtracted from each county's total population for the purpose of calculating representation. The eight senatorial districts established by the constitution were to be adjusted after each census in accordance with the formula for counting all inhabitants except the same three specified groups. This compromise reflected both the ambivalence frequently expressed at the convention toward the place of New York City within state politics and the murky ethics of racial disfranchisement.

FRIDAY, OCTOBER 19, 1821

After over a month's hiatus, the issue of slavery's future constitutional status returned to the convention's agenda with the proposal to make slavery unconstitutional. James Tallmadge, the author of the resolution, indicated particular concern with the status of children born to slaves, who, under the provisions of New York's laws, would still be obligated to serve their mothers' masters long after the official end of slavery in 1827. Delegates expressed a range of objections to constitutional abolition, including the perceived embarrassment of mentioning slavery in the document at all, the rights of masters, and allegedly practical concerns about provision for dependent and indigent emancipated slaves. The discussion revealed that the embrace in New York of antislavery principles was less than total and that the assumption of black dependency, a critical rationalization for black disfranchisement, was deeply ingrained. As in the suffrage debates, some delegates saw no reason to mask their contempt for African Americans. Meanwhile, even staunch critics of slavery and defenders of black voting rights argued that a constitutional provision was unnecessary. The convention defeated the antislavery amendment by more than a two-to-one margin.

GEN. TALLMADGE would make a few remarks explanatory of the resolution which he had the honour to submit. He alluded to the law of 1799, which enacted, that all children born of slaves after that time should be free,—males at the age of twenty-eight years, and females at the age of twenty-five. But the law of 1817, made no provision that would prevent the existence of slavery in this state until 1846, as it was to operate only prospectively. These acts, however, indicated the sentiment of the public, and were in the nature of a pledge, which ought to be redeemed by inserting this provision in the constitution. It was a mistake, he said, that slavery would, by the existing laws, cease in this state, in the year

1827; but he hoped the Convention would decide, that it should not continue after that time. In such case, the legislature would have an opportunity, before that period, to make proper provision for their support during their second infancy. . . .

GEN. ROOT . . . had objections of more importance. The first was, that it was unnecessary, as the legislature had already done what this provision contemplated their doing, and there was an act of that kind, that there was no probability they would ever recall. In the second place, he did not wish to deface and blacken the constitution by any provision in which slavery should be recognized.

MR. RADCLIFF regarded it as a proper subject for legislation. He was not an advocate for slavery, but he thought the legislature had advanced with equal pace in the progress of public opinion, on the subject of emancipation.

MR. BRIGGS thought that posterity would find out that we had slaves here, whether we blackened the features of the constitution with them or not.

MR. BUEL was in favour of the resolution. The gentleman from Delaware is disposed to omit this provision in the constitution, and is opposed to blackening that instrument by introducing it. But our public records recognize the fact of the existence of slavery, and it had already been inserted in the constitution in the distinction between white and black votes in the exercise of the right of the suffrage. It was an important provision, and the subject ought not to be left to legislative discretion. Justice required it, and public expectation would warrant its insertion.

MR. E. WILLIAMS opposed it. It was a clause in favour of common beggars. Nothing was more interesting to the people than the system of poor laws. Work-houses had been established with salutary effect, and he believed that these slaves turned loose would become strolling paupers, and would be willing to remain so if they could avoid labour.

MR. BRIGGS said, that if in the work-house they were compelled to labour, it was with their own consent.

MR. SUTHERLAND proposed to offer a substitute if this should be rejected, the purpose of which was, to confirm and make unalterable the existing laws on the subject of slavery.

MR. SHARPE observed, that this resolution would turn slaves out of the warm kitchens of the farmers, where they had lived comfortably, to perish in hovels. It was injurious to the slave. Slaves had been sold on the faith of the law as now existing. Formerly, if a slave ran away, $100 dollars reward was offered for his apprehension. Now the kitchens of Long-Island are emptied upon the city of New-York, and the reward offered is SIX CENTS, but not charges!

GEN. TALLMADGE asked, if in relation to the subject of work-houses, whether gentlemen intended to repeal the law providing for their liberation in 1827? If they did not, it was our moral duty, by a constitutional provision, to guaranty their emancipation. The law makes slaves of those children who were born of slaves after 1799, and before 1817, so that instead of a total emancipation in 1827, slavery might be continued in this state until 1846, unless this provision is adopted. . . .

MR. JAY professed himself to be zealous in the cause of emancipation, but he thought the law, as it now stands, was more wise and expedient than an immediate freedom. The cause of humanity would gain nothing by instant emancipation.

CHANCELLOR KENT . . . Slavery was universally reprobated, and no new constitutional provision was necessary to give that sentiment additional impulse. It would in his opinion be as proper to provide that the legislature should make no law to hang a man without a trial—or a law in favour of polygamy. . . .

MR. E. WILLIAMS remarked, that this was the first proposition that had been presented for the confiscation of vested rights. Masters had rights that ought not to be violated; and as to the slave it was a crusade against the last remaining hope of the miserable African. He has now a claim to support—a claim which the laws of God and man contribute to enforce. By this provision the master and the slave would be severed, and the rights of both essentially impaired.

SATURDAY, OCTOBER 20, 1821

Another group of delegates tried one last time to insert some sort of language regarding slavery in the constitution. Two resolutions, one introduced by Jacob Sutherland of Schoharie County and another introduced by Samuel Russell of Erie County, sought to affirm in the constitution the gradual abolition process established by the 1817 slavery law. The attempt by these two Bucktail delegates to seal off gradual emancipation from any further legislative adjustments failed. Rufus King spoke against the proposals, claiming that the end of slavery in the state was secure and expressing the hope that the memory of slavery in New York would someday be effaced as well. King's dream that slavery would be forgotten drew the convention's discussion of race and citizenship toward an ironic conclusion. King's allies, particularly Peter Jay, had argued against disfranchisement in large part by demanding that New Yorkers attend carefully to their own history.

MR. KING . . . It is now proposed to insert in the constitution, a provision confirming the law by which the slaves within this state will be free in 1827. By voting for this provision, those who the other day voted against immediate emancipation, will manifest their motives in doing so, to have been in kindness to the slaves, and the provision will also restrain the legislature from prolonging slavery beyond 1827.

Nothing concerning slavery is now contained in the constitution. The votes of those who with me were opposed to immediate emancipation, require no other explanation than the pernicious effects to the public, as well as to the slaves themselves, of such emancipation. On this account, therefore, the provision proposed to be inserted in the constitution is not requisite.

As a check on the legislature, it is equally unnecessary. The truth and force of public opinion on this subject, is a sufficient restraint on the legislature, and there is therefore no reason to apprehend that the legislature, from any motive, can be prevailed on to postpone the day of emancipation.

If a constitutional provision on this subject be not necessary, it should not be made, because every act of this character adopted by one of the states, does not fail to excite strong feelings in other states, which in these respects are less happy than ourselves.

Against this provision, it is moreover urged, that if we omit to mention it in our constitution, it may hereafter be forgotten that slavery once existed in the state. The suggestion may appear to be more specious than solid, though it is possible that we may be as fortunate as our ancestors.

It is now the proud boast of England, that the moment a slave stands upon her soil, or breathes her air, he becomes a free man. Yet we are informed that time was, when England sold English men into foreign bondage; and that so great was the number of English youths sent for sale to the Irish market, that Ireland passed a non-importation law to keep them out. If this practice of ancient times be almost sunk in oblivion, does not the circumstance encourage us to hope that the enslaving of black men may hereafter be forgotten: and should we not forbear to make our constitution a record thereof?

MONDAY, OCTOBER 29, 1821

As the convention began to finalize the suffrage provisions, delegates considered tinkering with the language governing black voting rights, briefly entertaining a motion that a substantial amount of personal property could serve as an alternative to a freehold. The convention also defeated a proposal "that all persons who shall have been previous to the ratification of this constitution, entitled to vote according to the existing laws of this state, shall be electors."

MR. R. SMITH moved as an additional qualification to persons of colour, to insert after the word "thereon," in the thirty-second line, the words "or other taxable property to the value of five hundred dollars."

MR. FAIRLIE hoped the subject would be suffered to rest in silence. It had been deliberately discussed, and distinctly voted upon.

CHIEF JUSTICE SPENCER was in favour of the amendment. He thought for the sake of consistency, it ought to be adopted. We had decided that real estate was not to have higher privileges than personal; and although he was not disposed to disturb the compromise on the question, yet he thought an accumulation of property to that amount, was such an evidence of the honesty and industry of the black man, that it ought to entitle him to vote, in the same manner as if his colour was white.

MR. BRIGGS said that a black man was not taxable for personal property to whatever amount, and therefore ought not to vote.

COL. YOUNG replied to the objection of inconsistency, and observed that the amendment would not get rid of the objection—for the man that can acquire $250 of personal property, could by the same act acquire the same amount of real property.

The question was then put on the amendment and lost.

The final language of the suffrage article approved by the convention and subsequently ratified by the voters as the second article of the New York Constitution read:

Sec. I. Every male citizen, of the age of twenty-one years, who shall have been an inhabitant of this state one year preceding any election, and for the last six months a resident of the town or county where he may offer his vote; and shall have within the year next preceding the election, paid a tax to the state or county, assessed upon his real or personal property; or shall by law be exempted from taxation; or being armed or equipped according to law, shall have performed within that year, military duty in the militia of this state; or who shall be exempted from performing military duty in consequence of being a fireman in any city, town, or village in this state: and also, every male citizen of the age of twenty-one years, who shall have been for three years next preceding such election, an inhabitant of this state; and for the last year, a resident in the town or county, where he may offer his vote; and shall have been within the last year, assessed to labour upon the highways, and shall have performed the labour, or paid an equivalent therefor, according to law; shall be entitled to vote in the town or ward where he actually resides, and not elsewhere, for all officers that now are, or hereafter may be, elective by the people: But no man of colour, unless he shall have been for three years a citizen of this state, and for one year next preceding any election, shall be seized and possessed of a freehold estate of the value of two hundred and fifty dollars, over and above all debts and incumbrances charged thereon; and shall have been actually rated, and paid a tax thereon, shall be entitled to vote at such election. And no person of colour shall be subject to direct taxation, unless he shall be seised and possessed of such real estate as aforesaid.

Sec. II. Laws may be passed, excluding from the right of suffrage, persons who have been, or may be convicted of infamous crimes.

Sec. III. Laws shall be made for ascertaining by proper proofs, the citizens who shall be entitled to the right of suffrage, hereby established.

Sec. IV. All elections by the citizens, shall be by ballot, except for such town officers, as may by law be directed to be otherwise chosen.

In January 1822, New York voters approved the new constitution by a vote of 74,732 to 41,402. Four years later, the first of eight amendments to the 1821 constitution would further extend the suffrage for white men. The amendment eliminated all qualifications for white men, except residence and citizenship.[54]

Part III

The Long Reconstruction, 1821–1877

Context

Three times in the half-century after 1821, New York voters went to the polls to decide whether to extend equal suffrage to the state's African American men. In 1846, in 1860, and again in 1869, the outcome was the same: the racially restrictive property qualification was maintained for men "of colour." Up until final enactment—and federal enforcement—of the Fifteenth Amendment in 1870, New Yorkers consistently opted to diminish the substance of black freedom. The Constitutional Convention of 1821's racialized construction of democracy cast a long shadow over the political culture of the nation's leading state. Through the Jacksonian period and into the era of the Civil War, the ideas and language of the 1821 constitution continued to resonate in New York debates over citizenship and suffrage. The dual transformations of the 1820s—the end of slavery and the ratification of the new Constitution—initiated a decades-long struggle, as New Yorkers wrestled with questions of democracy and segregation.

Repeated debates and elections on the 1821 property qualification provided a political foundation to New York's emerging segregated, society. For nineteenth-century New Yorkers, the primary legacy of 1821 was the achievement of a slaveless, yet segregated, democracy. The decades before the Civil War witnessed a gradually deepening separation of the races in New York, particularly in the state's cities. In the middle of the nineteenth century, African American New Yorkers faced employment discrimination and intensifying residential segregation. To a considerable degree, this process began in the public realm of the ballot box. "Jim crow New York", a world of increasing urban segregation in the

Figure 5 Five Points, 1827
Pictured in 1827, the year that the final abolition of slavery in New York went into effect, New York City's Five Points neighborhood was home to many former black slaves as well as impoverished white immigrants. ["Five Points, 1827," from *Manual of the Corporation of the City of New York* (New York, 1855).] *Reprinted by permission of the Houghton Library, Harvard University.*

half-century after 1821, was substantially designed by the delegates to the convention of 1821.

Political victory in Albany emboldened white supremacists around New York State. Disfranchisement narrowed the dimensions of black freedom and encouraged other nonpolitical forms of exclusion. On Hudson River steamers and on Broadway omnibuses, in theaters and at the almshouse, practices of black exclusion hardened. Pre-1821 New York City was a slave society; as such, there was little legal provision for separation of the races. By the middle of the nineteenth century, segregation had become the preferred method of dealing with emancipation.

African American New Yorkers knew that this growing segregation had many causes, but few disputed the idea that the property qualification of 1821 was especially important. Blacks organized numerous petition drives designed to persuade the state legislature to amend the constitution. In 1838, a number of ministers and journalists came together to form an umbrella organization for black New Yorkers. They chose to name their organization the New York Association for the Political Elevation and Improvement of the People of Color. The association's vice president, Henry Sipkins, had been a leading black voice against the property qualification back in 1821. Peter Vogelsang, another of the new group's leaders, explicitly linked disfranchisement in 1821 to the ensuing seventeen years of growing segregation.

New York City's black press and the local association expanded on their initial activities of the 1830s into a wave of statewide conventions in the 1840s and 1850s, all devoted to the elimination of the property qualification. Nearly every summer after 1840 found a group of black New Yorkers assembling to denounce the legacies of 1821 and to demand equal manhood suffrage. The first such meeting, held in Albany in 1840, occasioned a prolonged discussion of the caste society that had been designed nineteen years earlier; suffrage restriction had produced "a prevalent and unreasonable state of caste."[1] By the late 1850s, the statewide meeting had been renamed the Suffrage Convention.

The black freedom struggle in antebellum New York City was not alone in evoking memories of 1821. Over time, the city's Democratic Party grew more and more committed to a program of white manhood suffrage. At the 1846 constitutional convention in Albany, New York City delegates were not satisfied with the property qualification; rather, they sought disfranchisement for all black men. The Democratic defense of the property qualification for African Americans now argued that black suffrage would lead to black political control, or "negro masters." In the 1846 convention, such arguments provoked vigorous debate. All sides pointed back to 1821 to advance their cause. In the end, the Constitutional Convention of 1846 opted for separate submission, meaning that the voters of the Empire State would vote separately on the new constitution and on the proposal to remove the racially discriminatory property qualification. In the ensuing election, voters ratified the new constitution but overwhelmingly rejected equal manhood suffrage.

Even as white supporters of a racially exclusive polity carried the day a quarter of century after the Constitutional Convention of 1821, by the middle of the nineteenth century other New Yorkers came to articulate again a defense of interracial democracy and to assert for the first time a more expansive vision of universal suffrage. Abolitionists—black and white, male and female—challenged the racial order of the day; while attacking Southern slavery, antislavery New Yorkers often included criticism of local injustices. The Empire State was a central site for antebellum abolitionism. Numerous national organizations and journals were headquartered in the state's cities. The "Burned-Over District"—so named for the swatch of upstate communities deeply affected by the evangelical spirit of the Second Great Awakening—was especially hospitable territory for abolitionist organizing. Rochester, in particular, housed a vibrant local antislavery movement; it is no coincidence that Frederick Douglass chose that New York city as his new home in freedom. His July 5, 1852, oration, "What to the Slave Is the Fourth of July?" combined many strands of antislavery thought in antebellum New York to achieve a redefinition of American identity.

The linkage of the struggle for African American and women's rights was central to the mid-nineteenth-century campaign for full citizenship. Not only was Douglass's historic address delivered in antislavery Rochester, but the audience was the city's Ladies Anti-Slavery Society. Upstate New York had given rise to the first organized movement for women's rights in American history. Elizabeth Cady Stanton of Seneca Falls, Susan B. Anthony of Rochester, and other New York women came of age in a state where the politics of suffrage had been central since at least 1821. The historic Seneca Falls Convention of 1848 has conventionally been read as part of broader national and international histories of social change; it is important to keep in mind that by 1848, any public meeting in New York State organizing around the extension of suffrage necessarily had to confront the legacies of 1821. In the two decades after Seneca Falls, New York women's suffrage activists worked to connect their struggle to the fight against the property qualification. Only in the late 1860s, as the passage of the Fifteenth Amendment neared, did the alliance between some of the state's African American and women activists come undone.

The coming of the Civil War would change forever the political landscape in the Empire State. Early on, however, it was unclear just what the nature of that change would be. In February 1860, Abraham Lincoln addressed an audience of New Yorkers at Cooper Union in Manhattan; nine months later he was elected the sixteenth president. In that same election, as New Yorkers cast their ballots for Lincoln and the Republican Party, the state's voters for a second time voted to maintain the property qualification for African American suffrage. Even as the statewide Republican Party captured greater support in 1860, it was obvious that many in the Empire State were at best ambivalent about the coming struggle over slavery and freedom.

In July 1863, on the streets of Manhattan, the long reconstruction of New York exploded into a week of riotous violence. The Draft Riots revealed deep-seated resentments among many white New Yorkers about the Conscription Act of 1863 in particular and the war more generally. What began as focused attacks on the draft authorities and the Republican presence in the city expanded into a murderous wave of terror directed at Manhattan's few thousand blacks. Rioters attacked numerous African American citizens and set fire to the Colored Orphans' Asylum. Before it was over, this worst episode of civil disobedience in the nation's history left the Lincoln administration profoundly shaken and New Yorkers deeply divided once more over questions of race and citizenship.

That same month, with the Union army's victory at Gettysburg, the tide of war turned decisively, but the implications of peace remained uncertain. Dramatizing the uncertainty, April 1865 brought the surrender of the Confederacy and Lincoln's assassination. As the nation entered Reconstruction, the issues that New Yorkers had been contesting for a half century—equal citizenship, interracial democracy, manhood suffrage—came to define the national debate.

Once again, New Yorkers defined their place in the national political order through a constitutional convention. In 1867, New Yorkers elected delegates for the state's third constitutional convention of the nineteenth century. The proceedings, which were reflective of the national politics of the moment, dragged on into early 1868. What first seemed to promise a thorough Republican renovation of the New York constitution ended up in stalemate. Democrats seized on the issue of black suffrage—in particular, the maintenance of the property qualification of 1821—to regain momentum. In little time, the recently discredited Democratic Party would reestablish control in the state government. And in 1869, as in 1846 and 1860, the voters of New York State for a final time chose to maintain the African American property qualification for suffrage.

New York, however, was no longer the master of its political fate, at least with regard to race and suffrage. The New York vote to maintain restrictions on black voting came just as the Republican Congress in Washington passed the Fifteenth Amendment. That amendment—which became law in 1870—guaranteed equal manhood suffrage. In the fall of 1870, elections in New York State were held without the racially discriminatory property qualification. In New York City, the achievement of equal manhood suffrage brought with it a massive federal presence on election day. The Enforcement Acts of 1870 decreed that federal marshals would oversee ballot boxes in the nation's cities; in Manhattan, hundreds of armed federal authorities stood guard at polling places. Included among them were several African American deputy marshals. For the remainder of the nineteenth century, the nation's leading city witnessed a militarization of the ballot box.

The long Reconstruction of the North had begun not in 1865 but four decades earlier, at the Constitutional Convention of 1821. The delegates in Albany had taken the first step in determining the substance of black freedom. In New York, access to the ballot box gave shape to that half-century-long struggle over Reconstruction. Black activists of the late 1860s were still carrying on the debates of 1821. Suffrage restriction, as the black ministers of Manhattan pointed out in the fall of 1869, had been the political foundation of "jim crow New York."

Chronology

1822   The Nation: In South Carolina, authorities hang Denmark Vesey and over thirty other alleged slave insurrection co-conspirators.

1823   The World: British Anti-Slavery Society founded

1824   The World: Central America abolishes slavery.

1825   New York: Erie Canal completed, connects Buffalo and Albany.

1827   New York: *Freedom's Journal*, the nation's first African American newspaper, begins publication.

1829   The World: Mexico abolishes slavery.

1831   The Nation: Nat Turner's slave rebellion in Southampton, Virginia.

William Lloyd Garrison founds *The Liberator* in Boston.

The World: Slave revolt in Jamaica.

1832   The Nation: Nullification Crisis; South Carolina contests new federal tariff law.

1833   The Nation: American Anti-Slavery Society formed.

1834   The World: Britain converts status of Caribbean slaves to apprenticeship.

1836   The Nation: The House of Representatives adopts a gag rule to avoid debate on slavery; it remains in effect for eight years.

New York's Martin Van Buren elected U.S. president.

1837   The Nation: Panic of 1837 initiates six years of economic depression.

1838   The World: Britain abolishes apprenticeship in its Caribbean colonies; in effect, slavery in British colonies comes to an end.

1839   The Nation: Liberty Party formed, becoming the first antislavery political party.

1841   The Nation: Supreme Court decision in the *Amistad* case affirms the freedom of the escaped Africans.

1845   The Nation: *Narrative of the Life of Frederick Douglass* published.

1846   New York: State constitutional convention; equal manhood suffrage referendum rejected for the first time by the state's voters.

The Nation: The Wilmot Proviso, which would have barred slavery from all territories acquired in the Mexican-American War, divides the Congress along sectional lines and is finally defeated.

The World: Outbreak of Mexican-American War.

1847   New York: Fredrick Douglass establishes his first newspaper, the *North Star*, in Rochester, New York.

1848   New York: Women's Rights Convention in Seneca Falls.

The Nation: The Free Soil Party Convention, held in Buffalo in August, nominates Martin Van Buren as its presidential nominee.

The World: The United States and Mexico sign the Treaty of Guadalupe Hidalgo; the United States acquires approximately one-third of Mexico's prewar territory; the future states of New Mexico, Arizona, California, Nevada, Colorado, and Utah will be carved out of the new lands.

The World: France and Denmark abolish slavery in their colonies; Austrian Empire ends serfdom; revolutions in Europe.

1850   The Nation: The Compromise of 1850 attempts to defuse intensifying sectional divisions in the wake of the Treaty of Guadalupe Hidalgo; among several controversial provisions was the Fugitive Slave Act.

1852   New York: Frederick Douglass delivers his "What to the Slave Is the Fourth of July?" oration in Rochester.

The Nation: Publication of Harriet Beecher Stowe's *Uncle Tom's Cabin*.

1854 The Nation: Republican Party established amid Northern reaction against the Kansas-Nebraska Act, bringing together a coalition of former Whigs, Free Soilers, and Know-Nothings.

The World: Portugal abolishes slavery in its African colonies.

1857 The Nation: Supreme Court finds against Dred Scott in the case of *Scott v. Sanford*; Chief Justice Roger Taney not only denies Scott his freedom but goes on to deny U.S. citizenship to all African Americans.

1859 The Nation: John Brown leads raid on federal armory at Harpers Ferry, Virginia.

1860 New York: Referendum on equal manhood suffrage defeated by the state's voters.

The Nation: Abraham Lincoln elected president in November; one month later, South Carolinians convene in Charleston and declare themselves seceded from the United States.

1861 The Nation: With the Confederate attack on Fort Sumter, the Civil War begins; Congress enacts the first Confiscation Act, authorizing the seizure by the Union army of all Confederate property—including slaves—being used for the war effort.

The World: Czar Alexander II emancipates serfs in Russia.

1863 New York: New York City Draft Riots in July, the most violent incident of civil unrest in American history—in opposition to the nation's first military draft, rioters attacked Republican Party institutions and local African Americans; at least 119 died in the week of rioting.

The Nation: Emancipation Proclamation—President Lincoln commits the federal government to emancipating only those slaves living in Confederate-controlled territories. New York African Americans respond enthusiastically to the proclamation's call for the enlistment of black soldiers in the Union army.

1865 The Nation: The Civil War ends, and Abraham Lincoln is assassinated in the same week in April; the Thirteenth Amendment becomes law, abolishing slavery in the United States. Southern state governments enact repressive Black Codes, severely limiting the right of freedpeople.

1867 New York: Constitutional convention begins meeting in Albany; deliberations continue into early 1868.

The World: End of the Atlantic slave trade; British Parliament passes Reform Law, extending suffrage to men of the middle class as well as some from the working class.

1868 New York: Tammany Hall in Manhattan hosts the Democratic National Convention, where several Southern delegates were ex-Confederates; the former governor of New York, Horatio Seymour, is the party's nominee for the presidency.

The Nation: Fourteenth Amendment to the Constitution becomes law, guaranteeing equal protection before the law to all American citizens; along with other congressional legislation, citizenship is nationalized; war hero Ulysses S. Grant elected president.

1869 New York: For a third time, the voters of the state reject an equal manhood suffrage amendment to the state's constitution.

1870 New York: First elections held according to the principle of equal manhood suffrage.

The Nation: Fifteenth Amendment to the Constitution becomes law, guaranteeing equal manhood suffrage; Congress passes the first of the Enforcement Acts.

1871 The World: Paris Commune—radical government asserts authority in French capital after German victory in the Franco-Prussian War; Commune suppressed in brief but brutal civil war.

1873 The Nation: Panic of 1873 commences economic downturn, which lasts for the rest of the decade.

1877 New York: Tilden Commission issues its report.

The Nation: End of Reconstruction; wave of summertime strikes across the nation, originating among railway workers.

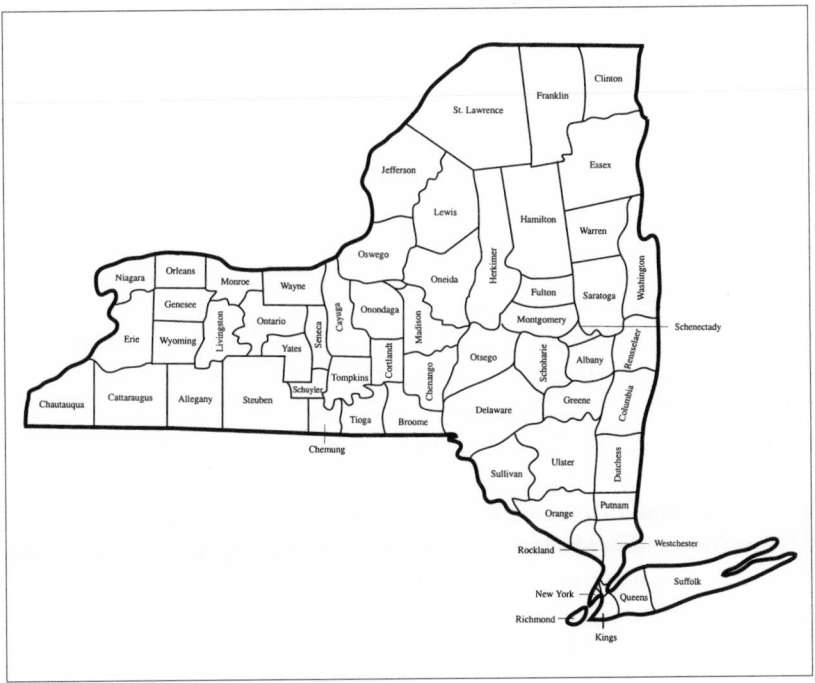

Figure 6 Map of New York State in 1864
Only minor changes, making room for four counties, occurred in the internal
contours of New York between the 1821 convention and the Civil War. [Map of
New York State in 1864, based on J. Calvin Smith, *Map of the State of New York
showing the location of boundaries of counties and townships, cities, towns and
villages, the courses of railroads, canals and stageroads* (New York, 1862).]
Courtesy of the Boston College Center for Media and Instructional Technology.

N. First African American Newspaper, 1827

Just months before the final emancipation of New York's slaves went into effect, the first African American newspaper in American history began publication. *Freedom's Journal* was founded by a group headed by editors Samuel Cornish and John Russwurm. Cornish, minister of the First Colored Presbyterian Church in New York City, had received his religious training in Philadelphia. Russwurm, the second black college graduate in the United States, had recently completed his studies at Maine's Bowdoin College.

The founding of the newspaper attested to the strength and diversity of New York City's black community, as well as the close ties between religious and secular concerns. In addition to churches and mutual aid societies (see introduction to document G), black New Yorkers worked in a variety of skilled trades, such as butchering and shoemaking. African Americans also founded a theater company, which offered productions attended by both blacks and whites, though assaults by white gangs drove this endeavor out of business.

As the demise of the African Grove Theater suggests, the founding of *Freedom's Journal* also exposed the stresses and strains of black life in New York City during the 1820s. Accompanying racial harassment was the exclusion of African Americans from a variety of occupations, thereby consigning increasing numbers of blacks to the most menial and unskilled jobs in the city. Besides racism, African Americans faced another threat to their tenuous hold on citizenship and security in New York. Colonization's program for removing free blacks from established American communities and settling them in Africa gained many prominent white advocates in New York and nationally. Even white philanthropists who would later lead the national campaign for the abolition of slavery initially supported the concept of black removal.

Freedom's Journal boldly sought to create an intellectual network of resistance to the growing assault on black freedom and dignity. The newspaper recruited subscribers in free black communities up and down the East Coast. Like other newspapers of its day, the *Journal* included a variety of material, including summaries of foreign events, historical profiles, letters from correspondents, and poetry.

In its introductory editorial, *Freedom's Journal* clung to the hope that blacks might still wield political influence at the polls, while more broadly asserting the need for African Americans to advocate the cause of racial justice on their own behalf and to describe black life in their own, non-racist terms. This effort proved to be no easy task. Despite attracting well over a thousand subscribers, the paper's forthright attacks on colonization alarmed white benefactors of Cornish's church. In response, he resigned his ministry there and, then, his editorship of the newspaper. Russwurm alienated readers by adopting the colonizationist cause and in 1829 quit the newspaper to run schools in Liberia, the colony established for black Americans on the western coast of Africa. Despite its relatively short lifespan, however, *Freedom's Journal* established an important precedent that black and white abolitionists would follow in publicizing their battle against slavery over the next three decades.

How did the editorial explain the need for a specifically African American newspaper? What particular threats to African Americans did the editorial identify? How did it propose to respond to those threats?

* * *

TO OUR PATRONS.

IN presenting our first number to our Patrons, we feel all the diffidence of persons entering upon a new and untried line of business. But a moment's reflection upon the noble objects, which we have in view by the publication of this Journal; the expediency of its appearance at this time, when so many schemes are in action concerning our people—encourage us to come boldly before an enlightened publick. For we believe, that a paper devoted to the dissemination of useful knowledge among our brethren, and to their moral and religious improvement, must meet with the cordial approbation of every friend to humanity.

The peculiarities of this Journal, render it important that we should advertise to the world the motives by which we are actuated, and the objects which we contemplate.

We wish to plead our own cause. Too long have others spoken for us. Too long has the publick been deceived by misrepresentations, in things which concern us dearly, though in the estimation of some mere trifles; for though there are many in society who exercise towards us benevolent feelings; still (with sorrow we confess it) there are others who make it their business to enlarge upon the least trifle, which tends to the discredit of any person or colour; and pronounce anathemas and denounce our whole body for the misconduct of this guilty one. We are aware that there many instances of vice among us, but we avow that it is because no one has taught its subjects to be virtuous: many instances of poverty, because no sufficient efforts accommodated to minds contracted by slavery, and deprived of early education have been made, to teach them how to husband their hard earnings, and to secure to themselves comforts.

Education being an object of the highest importance to the welfare of society, we shall endeavour to present just and adequate views of it, and to urge upon our brethren the necessity and expediency of training their children, while young, to habits of industry, and thus forming them for becoming useful members of society. It is surely time that we should awake from this lethargy of years, and make a concentrated effort for the education of our youth. We form a spoke in the human wheel, and it is necessary that we should understand our pendence on the different parts, and theirs on us, in order to perform our part with propriety.

Though not desirous of dictating, we shall feel it our incumbent duty to dwell occasionally upon the general principles and rules of economy. The world has grown too enlightened, to estimate any man's character by his personal appearance. Though all men acknowledge the excellency of Franklin's maxims, yet comparatively few practise upon them. We may deplore when it is too late, the neglect of these self-evident truths, but it avails little to mourn. Ours will be the task of admonishing our brethren on these points.

The civil rights of a people being of the greatest value, it shall ever be our duty to vindicate our brethren, when oppressed, and to lay the case before the publick. We shall also urge upon our brethren (who are qualified by the laws of the different states), the expediency of using their elective franchise; and of making an independent use of the same. We wish them not to become the tools of party.

And as much time is frequently lost, and wrong principles instilled, by the perusal of works of trivial importance, we shall consider it a part of our duty to recommend to our young readers, such authors as will not only enlarge their stock of useful knowledge, but such as will also serve to stimulate them to higher attainments in science.

We trust also, that through the columns of the FREEDOM'S JOURNAL, many practical pieces, having for their bases, the improvement of our brethren, will be presented to them, from the pens of many of our respected friends, who have kindly promised their assistance.

It is our earnest wish to make our Journal a medium of intercourse between our brethren in the different states of this great confederacy: that through its columns an expression of our sentiments, on many interesting subjects which concern us, may be offered to the publick: that plans which apparently are beneficial may be candidly discussed and properly weighed; if worthy, receive our cordial approbation; if not, our marked disapprobation.

Useful knowledge of every kind, and every thing that relates to Africa, shall find a ready admission into our columns; and as that vast continent becomes daily more known, we trust that many things will come to light, proving that the natives of it are neither so ignorant nor stupid as they have generally been supposed to be.

And while these important subjects shall occupy the columns of the FREEDOM'S JOURNAL, we would not be unmindful of our brethren who are still in the iron fetters of bondage. They are our kindred by all the ties of nature; and though but little can be effected by us, still let our sympathies be poured forth, and our prayers in their behalf, ascend to Him who is able to succour them.

From the press and the pulpit we have suffered much by being incorrectly represented. Men, whom we equally love and admire have not hesitated to represent us disadvantageously, without becoming personally acquainted with the true state of things, or discerning between virtue and vice among us. The virtuous part of our people feel themselves sorely aggrieved under the existing state of things—they are not appreciated.

Our vices and our degradation are ever arrayed against us, but our virtues are passed by unnoticed. And what is still more lamentable, our friends, to whom we concede all the principles of humanity and religion, from these very causes seem to have fallen into the current of popular feeling and are imperceptibly floating on the stream—actually living in the practice of prejudice, while they abjure it in theory, and feel it not in their hearts. Is it not very desirable that such should know more of our actual condition, and of our efforts and feelings, that in forming or advocating plans for our amelioration, they may do it more understandingly? In the spirit of candor and humility we intend by a simple representation of facts to lay our case before the publick, with a view to arrest the progress of prejudice, and to shield ourselves against the consequent evils. We wish to conciliate all and to irritate none, yet we must be firm and unwavering in our principles, and persevering in our efforts.

If ignorance, poverty and degradation have hitherto been our unhappy lot; has the Eternal decree gone forth, that our race alone, are to remain in this state, while knowledge and civilization are shedding their enlivening rays over the rest of the human family? The recent travels of Denham and Clapperton in the interior of Africa,[2] and the interesting narrative which they have published; the establishment of the republic of Hayti after years of sanguinary warfare; its subsequent progress in all the arts of civilization; and the advancement of liberal ideas in South America, where despotism has given place to free governments, and where many of our brethren now fill important civil and military stations, prove the contrary.

The interesting fact that there are FIVE HUNDRED THOUSAND free persons of colour, one half of whom might peruse, and the whole be benefitted by the publication of the Journal; that no publication, as yet, has been devoted exclusively to their improvement—that many selections from approved standard authors, which are within the reach of few, may occasionally be made—and more important still, that this large body of our citizens have no public channel—all serve to prove the real necessity, at present, for the appearance of the FREEDOM'S JOURNAL.

It shall ever be our desire so to conduct the editorial department of our paper as to give offence to none of our patrons; as nothing is farther from us than to make it the advocate of any partial views, either in politics or religion. What few days we can number, have been devoted to the improvement of our brethren; and it is our earnest wish that the remainder may be spent in the same delightful service.

In conclusion, whatever concerns us as a people, will ever find a ready admission into the FREEDOM'S JOURNAL, interwoven with all the principal news of the day.

And while every thing in our power shall be performed to support the character of our Journal, we would respectfully invite our numerous friends to assist by their communications, and our coloured brethren to strengthen our hands by their subscriptions, as our labour is one of common cause, and worthy of their consideration and support. And we do most earnestly solicit the latter, that if at any time we should seem to be zealous, or too pointed in the inculcation of any important lesson, they will remember, that they are equally interested in the cause in which we are engaged, and attribute our zeal to the peculiarities of our situation, and our earnest engagedness in their well-being.

THE EDITORS.

Source: *Freedom's Journal*, March 16, 1827.

O. Emancipation Addresses, 1827

Whatever its limitations, African American New Yorkers could not let the formal end of slavery in the state pass without remark. Although the 1821 state constitutional convention had imposed significant limits on the terms of black citizenship, African Americans had passed a symbolic milestone on the road to freedom. More concretely, thousands of slaves born before July 5, 1799, received their actual freedom from bondage in July 1827.[3]

During the long years prior to the Civil War, the Fourth of July was a source of ambivalence for African Americans. For both free and enslaved blacks, the independence of the United States, with its alleged emphasis on the "inalienable rights" to "life, liberty and the pursuit of happiness," was at best a cruel hoax and at worst the source of further racial degradation.[4] Even in the emancipation year of 1827, the pages of *Freedom's Journal* contained debate over how the holiday could be most meaningfully observed by African Americans. Complicating matters still further, even those whites who advocated for abolition were uncomfortable with public black celebrations (see document G). Meanwhile, more openly racist whites were not eager to share their streets and their holiday with African Americans. In New York City, emancipation was marked on both July 4 and July 5. William Hamilton delivered a formal oration in New York's African Zion Church, an African Methodist Episcopalian–affiliated congregation. On July 5, the city's black communities, including representatives of its leading benevolent organizations, staged a festive public march, with some participants in uniforms or on horseback, more on foot, accompanied by music and banners. The procession made its way past City Hall and concluded with a dinner and another speech. Elsewhere, black New Yorkers marked the end of slavery in churches throughout the state as well as in public spaces. As the following two speeches indicate, some focused their celebration on the historic achievement of freedom, while others looked ahead to the ongoing struggles for equal rights, full citizenship, and suffrage.

William Hamilton was a leading figure in organized black life in New York City. A house carpenter by trade, he was the first president of the New York City Society for Mutual Relief, which was founded in 1808. Hamilton served as a trustee of the African Zion Church, where he gave the address excerpted below. He also helped found *Freedom's Journal.* Later he played a leading role in national efforts to combat colonization, presiding over the 1834 Convention of the Free People of Colour, which met in New York City. Nathaniel Paul was pastor in the First African Baptist Society of Albany, New York.

Figure 7 John Street Methodist Church
Manhattan's John Street Methodist Church had a large black membership in the 1790s, before African Americans, tired of discrimination, left to form their own church. *Reprinted by permission of the I. N. Phelps Stokes Collection, Miriam and Ira D. Wallach Division of Art, Prints and Photographs, New York Public Library, Astor, Lenox and Tilden Foundations.*

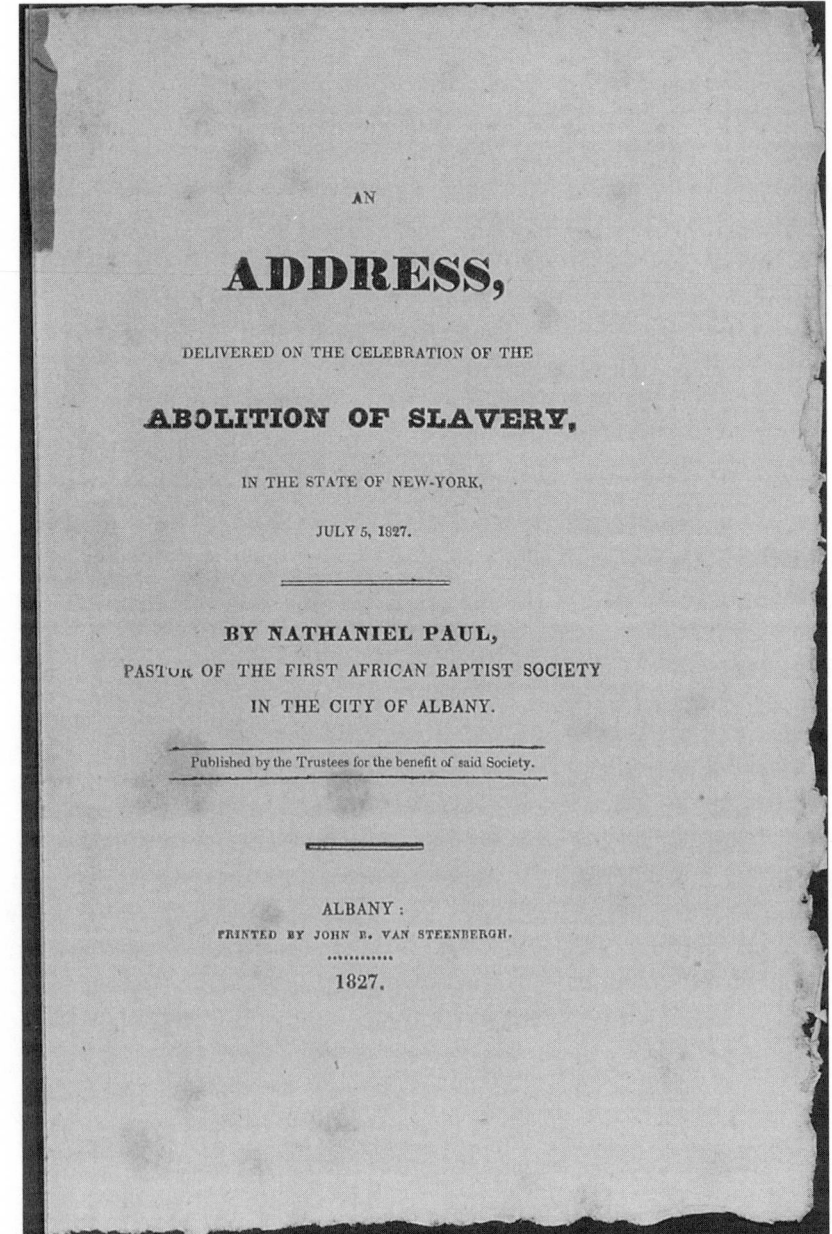

AN

ADDRESS,

DELIVERED ON THE CELEBRATION OF THE

ABOLITION OF SLAVERY,

IN THE STATE OF NEW-YORK,

JULY 5, 1827.

BY NATHANIEL PAUL,

PASTOR OF THE FIRST AFRICAN BAPTIST SOCIETY

IN THE CITY OF ALBANY.

Published by the Trustees for the benefit of said Society.

ALBANY:

PRINTED BY JOHN B. VAN STEENBERGH.

1827.

Figure 8 Cover page of Nathaniel Paul's *Address*
Cover page of Nathaniel Paul, *An Address, Delivered on the Celebration of the Abolition of Slavery, in the State of New-York, July 5, 1827* (Albany, 1827). *Reprinted by permission of the President and Fellows of Harvard College.*

How do these addresses elaborate on the themes presented in the *Freedom's Journal* editorial (document N)? In what ways do these addresses offer different perspectives on the end of slavery? How do they differ? How do they compare to earlier black and white addresses (documents E and G)? Did Hamilton and Paul view emancipation as an end or a beginning?

William Hamilton

LIBERTY! kind goddess! brightest of the heavenly deities that guide the affairs of men.

Oh Liberty! where thou art resisted and irritated, thou art terrible as the raging sea, and dreadful as a tornado. But where thou art listened to, and obeyed, thou art gentle as the purling stream that meanders through the mead: as soft and as cheerful as the zephyrs that dance upon the summer's breeze, and as bounteous as autumn's harvest.

To thee, the sons of Afric, in this once dark, gloomy, hopeless, but now fairest, brightest, and most cheerful of thy domain, do owe a double obligation of gratitude. Thou hast entwined and bound fast the cruel hands of oppression—thou hast by the powerful charm of reason, deprived the monster of his strength—he dies, he sinks to rise no more.

Thou hast loosened the hard bound fetters by which we were held: and by a voice sweet as the music of heaven, yet strong and powerful, reaching to the extreme boundaries of the state of New-York, hath declared that we the people of colour, the sons of Afric, are FREE!

My brethren and fellow-citizens, I hail you all. This day we stand redeemed from a bitter thraldom. Of us it may be truly said, "the last agony is o'er," THE AFRICANS ARE RESTORED! No more shall the accursed name of slave be attached to us—no more shall *negro* and *slave* be synonimous.

Fellow-citizens, I come to felicitate you on the victory obtained—not by a sanguinary contest with the foe—there are left no fields teeming with blood: not a victory obtained by fierce-flaming, death-dealing ordinance, vomiting forth fire and horrible destruction—no thousands made to lick the dust—no groans of the wounded and the dying. But I come to felicitate you on the victory obtained by the principles of liberty, such as are broadly and indelibly laid down by the glorious sons of '76; and are contained in the ever memorable words prefixed to the Declaration of

Independence of these United States: viz. "We hold these truths to be self-evident, that all men are created equal, and endowed by their Creator with certain inalienable rights; and that among these are life, liberty, and the pursuit of happiness." A victory obtained by these principles over prejudice, injustice, and foul oppression.

This day has the state of NEW-YORK regenerated herself—this day has she been cleansed of a most foul, poisonous and damnable stain. I stand amazed at the quiet, yet rapid progress the principles of liberty have made. A semi-century ago, the people of colour, with scarcely an exception, were *all slaves*. It is true, that many in the city, who remained here in the time of the revolution, (when their masters left at the approach of the British) and many too from the country, who became a kind of refugee, obtained their liberty, by leaving the country at the close of the war, or a few years respite from slavery: for such as were found remaining after the revolution, were again claimed by their masters. Yes, we were in the most abject state of slavery that can be conceived, except *that* of our brethren at the South, whose miseries are a little more enhanced. Without going back to the times of Negro plot, when a kind of fanaticism seized the people of New-York, something similar in its bearing and effect to the sad circumstances that took place among the people of *New-England*, in their more puritanic times, and about a half a century before the fancied plot, when they put to death the good people for being witches.[5]

Yes, my brethren, in this state we have been *advertised, and bought, and sold like any commodity*. In this state we have suffered cruelly: suffered by imprisonment, by whipping, and by scourging.

I have seen men chained with iron collars to their necks. I have seen——but hold! Let me proceed no farther. Why enter into the blood chilling detail of our miseries? It would only dampen those joys that ought to glow and sparkle on every countenance: it would only give vent to feelings that would not be reconcileable with the object of our assembling.

The cause of emancipation has ever had its votaries, but they stood single and alone. After the revolution, they drew nearer together.

That venerable body of religionists called FRIENDS, ought ever to be held in grateful remembrance by us. Their public speakers were the first to enter their protest against the deadly sin of slave-holding; and so zealous did its members become, that the church, or more technically, the meeting, passed laws; first forbidding its members from holding slaves for life, next forbidding the use of slaves altogether. But the most powerful lever, or propelling cause, was the MANUMISSION SOCIETY. Although many of its members belonged to the just-named society, yet very many were members of other religious societies, and some did not belong to any, but who were, philanthropists indeed. How *sweet it is to speak of good men!* . . .

These are the men that formed the Manumission Society, and stamped it with those best of principles, found in the preamble to the constitution, framed by them. It is too excellent to pass over, and is as follows: "The benevolent Creator, and Father of all men; having given to them all an equal right to life, liberty and property, no sovereign power on earth can justly deprive them of either but in conformity to impartial laws, to which they have expressly or tacitly consented; it is our duty both as *free citizens and Christians*, not only to regard with compassion the injustice done to those among us, who are held as slaves, but to endeavour by all lawful ways and means, to enable them to share *equally* with us, that civil and religious liberty, with which an indulgent Providence has blessed these states; and to which these our brethren are as much entitled as ourselves."

. . . The Manumission Society have laboured hard and incessantly, in order to bring us from our degraded situation, and restore us to the rights of men. It has stood, a phalanx, *firm and undaunted*, amid the flames of prejudice, and the shafts of calumny. How pleasing it is, they have a reward. Our Heavenly Father hath fixed the highest sensations of pleasure to good and virtuous actions.

My brethren, our enemies have assumed various attitudes: sometimes they have worn a daring front, and blasphemously have said, the *negroes have no souls, they are not men*, they are a species of the *ourang outang*. Sometimes, in more mild form, they say, they are a *species inferior to white men*. Then again they turn to blasphemy, and say, *God hath made them to be slaves.*

Let us look at them, and we shall see, with all their pomp, and pride, and hauteur, they are more the objects of pity and commiseration, than of anger and hate. Well may it be said, "the wicked are like the troubled sea."[6] *It is hard breathing in their atmosphere.* Are not deeds of injustice the harrowers up of fears of revenge, in proportion to their turpitude. We have a fair portrait in the Southern states. In order to see it more clearly, contrast the Southern and Northern sections of the union. Would the people of the North exchange situations for *the slaves of the South, ten times told?* . . . Do the people of the North, need nightly patroles to save them from insurrections? How sweet is the sleep of the virtuous! . . .

It would be foolishness in me, my brethren, to tell you that by all the rules laid down by naturalists, for determining the species of a creature, that we have souls, and are men. We too *irresistibly feel that we have, and are such*. We can more easily doubt that we *exist*, than doubt that we are *men*. To the second proposition, and my soul for it, if there is *any* difference in the species, that difference is in *favour* of the people of colour. . . .

I know that I ought to speak with caution; but an ambidexter [sic] philosopher, who can reason contrarywise, first tells you, "*that all men are created equal, and that they are endowed with the unalienable rights of life, liberty, and the pursuit of happiness*," next proves that *one class of men are not equal to another,* which by the bye, does not agree with axioms in geometry, that deny that things can be *equal*, and at the same time *unequal* to one another—suppose that such philosopher, should keep around him a number of slaves, and at the *same time* should tell you, that God hath no attribute to favour the cause of the master in case of an insurrection of the slaves.[7] Would not such a reasoner only show a heterogeneous mind? although he should be called an abstruse reasoner, what kind of superiority does he discover? Does he not reason, and act like one that battles with the elements? Does he reason like a man of true moral principles? Does he set a good example? Does he act in conformity to true philosophy? True philosophy teaches, that man should act in conformity to his reason, and *reason*, and the *law* of God and nature, declare that all men are equal, and that life, liberty, and the pursuit of happiness, are their unalienable rights.

It is a maxim among civilians, that the principles of government, and acts of the legislator, should be in unison. What ought to be considered the most vital principles of our general government, are contained in the words already mentioned, as standing in FRONT of the Declaration of Independence; and in that article of the constitution, that declares that *no person shall be deprived of life, liberty, or property, without due course of law*.[8] What a jargon does that law of the United States form with the principles here laid down, that gives to *one class of men* the right to arrest, wherever they may find them with its jurisdiction, *another class of men*, and retain them as their lawful property? This, no doubt is *superior* legislation, and bespeaks *superior* minds.

In these United States, among white men, there is an almost universal prejudice against the amalgamation of the blood of the white and black population, which goes so far as to create in them supercilious fear, or rather horrible sensation, that the pretty white, will be changed thereby to the dingy mulatto. Yes, true it is, and true though it is *white men masters*, do amalgamate the blood, and the *children of such amalgamation*, they *hold* as slaves; and worse, they *sell* as slaves. . . . [W]hite men sell the children of their own begetting, for sordid gold.

Authority and gold are their gods, their household gods, their sanctuary gods. . . . What titillation of soul they receive from these gods! How bold! how venturous! how stubborn! how pliant! how wise! how simple! how every thing *but virtuous* they are!

I am sorry to break from this unravelling so soon, for I did mean, to unravel this *mystery* of superiority. But it is necessary that we devote a few moments to a subject of vital interest to us. And here let me particularly address the youth. With you rests the high responsibility of redeeming the character of our people. White men say, you are not capable of the study of what may be called abstruse literature, and that you are deficient in moral character. I feel, I know, that these assertions are as false as hell. Yet I do know, you are sunk into the deepest frivolity and lethargy, that any people can be sunk. Oh Heavens! that I could rouse you. Has this frivolity taken from you all shame? Has this lethargy taken from you all ambition? YOUTH OF MY PEOPLE, I look to you. Shall this degrading charge stand unrepelled by contrary facts? Oh! that I could enflame you with proper ambition. Your honour, your character, your happiness, your well-being, all, all are at stake, and involved in the question at issue. And it is for you to retrieve or acknowledge that your fathers have been slaves deservedly.

First, my young friends, let me invite you to *the path of virtue*. It is a straight, open path, strewed with the sweetest aromatics: it is the path of pleasure, the path of honour, the path of respectability. Vice, from which I would call you, is its opposite; it is a crooked, thorny way, full of stinking weeds, the path of trouble, debasement, misery, and destruction.

Next, I would invite you to the *study of the sciences*. Here lies an open field of pleasure, that is increased at every step you take therein. If you have labour, be assured that your compensation is infinite. It has been the policy of white men, to give you a high opinion of advancement, when you have made but smattering attainments. They know that a little education is necessary, for the better accomplishing the menial services you are in the habit of performing for them. They do not wish you to be equal with them—much less superior. Therefore, in all advancements they assist in (I speak of them generally) they will take care that you do not rise above mediocrity.

My young friends, it is a laudable ambition that prompts us to the highest standing in literature. Is there any thing noble or praiseworthy obtained by sneaking conduct? Why look up to others, when we may obtain the highest standing ourselves? There is a height of knowledge which you may easily attain to, that when arrived at, you will look down with amazement, at the depth of ignorance you have risen from. I am sorry to say it; but I speak with the intention to quicken you, that *properly speaking*, there is none learned among us. If there is, now is the time to show themselves; it is worse than felony to keep back. It is too true, that men of prime genius among us, that have possessed high talents for improvement, have suffered improper considerations to keep them down. Therefore, my young friends, I look to you, and pray you, by all that *proper pride* you feel in being men, that you show yourselves such, by performing acts of worth equal with other men. Why not form yourselves into literary companies, for the study of the sciences? The expense would not be as great as you incur for useless gratifications, beside the advantage of receiving pleasure, infinitely beyond what those gratifications afford.

I would now turn to the female part of this assembly, particularly the young. *It is for you to form the manners of men.* My female friends, it is for you, not by proud, but modest conduct, to lead them in the true line of decorum and gentle manners. First, I would have you discountenance that loud vocability of gabble, that too much characterizes us in the street: I would look upon him, or her, that hailed me with too loud, or vulgar accents, as one who had forgot what is due to female modesty. Next, and most of consequence, I would have you prefer his affections and company most, who endeavours most to improve his mind. If you give preference to men of understanding, depend on it, they will endeavour to make themselves suitable to your wishes. But above all, endeavour *to improve your own minds*. I know that in the ability to improve, you are more than a match for white females, in all proper female education. Here, let me close, with our best thanks and wishes to the State of New-York.

Nathaniel Paul

THROUGH the long lapse of ages, it has been common for nations to record whatever was peculiar or interesting in the course of their history. . . . And as the nations which have already passed away, have been careful to select the most important events, peculiar to themselves, and have recorded them for the good of the people that should succeed them, so will we place it upon our history; and we will tell the good story to our children and to our children's children, down to the latest posterity, that on the *fourth day of July*, in the year of our Lord 1827, slavery was abolished in the state of New-York.

Seldom, if ever, was there an occasion which required a public acknowledgment, or that deserved to be retained with gratitude of heart to the all-wise disposer of events, more than the present on which we have assembled.

It is not the mere gratification of the pride of the heart, or any vain ambitious notion, that has influenced us to make our appearance in the public streets of our city, or to assemble in the sanctuary of the Most High this morning; but we have met to offer our tribute of thanksgiving and praise to almighty God for his goodness; to retrace the acts and express our gratitude to our public benefactors, and to stimulate each other to the performance of every good and virtuous act, which now does, or hereafter may devolve as a duty upon us, as freemen and citizens, in common with the rest of community. . . .

In contemplating the subject before us, in connection with the means by which so glorious an event has been accomplished, we find much which requires our deep humiliation and our most exalted praises. We are permitted to behold one of the most pernicious and abominable of all enterprises, in which the depravity of human nature ever led man to engage, entirely eradicated. The power of the tyrant is subdued, the heart of the oppressed is cheered[,] liberty is proclaimed to the captive, and the opening of the prison to those who were bound, and he who had long been the miserable victim of cruelty and degradation, is elevated to the common rank in which our benevolent Creator first designed, that man should move—all of which have been effected by means the most simple, yet perfectly efficient: Not by those fearful judgments of the almighty, which have so often fell upon the different parts of the earth; which have overturned nations and kingdoms; scattered thrones and sceptres; nor is the glory of the achievement, tarnished with the horrors of the field of battle. We hear not the cries of the widow and the fatherless; nor are our hearts affected with the sight of garments rolled in blood; but all has been done by the diffusion and influence of the pure, yet powerful principles of benevolence, before which the pitiful impotency of tyranny and oppression, is scattered and dispersed, like the chaff before the rage of the whirlwind.

I will not, on this occasion, attempt fully to detail the abominations of the traffic to which we have already alluded. Slavery, with its concomitants and consequences, in the best attire in which it can possibly be presented, is but a hateful monster, the very demon of avarice and oppression, from its first introduction to the present time; it has been among all nations the scourge of heaven, and the curse of the earth. It is so contrary to the laws which the God of nature has laid down as the rule of action by which the conduct of man is to be regulated towards his fellow man, which binds him to love his neighbour as himself, that it ever has, and ever will meet the decided disapprobation of heaven.

In whatever form we behold it, its visage is satanic, its origin the very offspring of hell, and in all cases its effects are grievous.

On the shores of Africa, the horror of the scene commences; here, the merciless tyrant, divested of every thing human, except the form, begins the action. The laws of God and the tears of the oppressed are alike disregarded; and with more than savage barbarity, husbands and wives, parents and children, are parted to meet no more: and, if not doomed to an untimely death, while on the passage, yet are they for life consigned to a captivity still more terrible; a captivity, at the very thought of which, every heart, not already biased with unhallowed prejudices, or callous to every tender impression, pauses and revolts; exposed to the caprice of those whose tender mercies are cruel; unprotected by the laws of the land, and doomed to drag out miserable existence, without the remotest shadow of a hope of deliverance, until the king of terrors shall have executed his office, and consigned them to the kinder slumbers of death. But its pernicious tendency may be traced still farther: not only are its effects of the most disastrous character, in relation to the slave, but it extends its influence to the slave holder; and in many instances it is hard to say which is most wretched, the slave or the master. . . .

Strange, indeed, is the idea, that such a system, fraught with such consummate wickedness, should ever be found a place in this the otherwise happiest of all countries—a country, the very soil of which is said to be consecrated to liberty, and its fruits the equal rights of man. But strange as the idea may seem, or paradoxical as it may appear to those acquainted with the constitution of the government, or who have read the bold declaration of this nation's independence; yet it is a fact that can neither be denied or controverted, that in the United States of America, at the expiration of fifty years after its becoming a free and independent nation, there are no less than fifteen hundred thousand human beings still in a state of unconditional vassalage.

Yet America is first in the profession of the love of liberty, and loudest in proclaiming liberal sentiments towards all other nations, and feels herself insulted, to be branded with any thing bearing the appearance of tyranny or oppression. Such are the palpable inconsistencies that abound among us and such is the medley of contradictions which stain the national character, and renders the American republic a by-word, even among despotic nations. But while we pause and wonder at the contradictory sentiments held forth by the nation, and contrast its profession and practice, we are happy to have it in our power to render an apology for the existence of the evil, and to offer an excuse for the framers of the constitution. It was before the sons of Columbia felt the yoke of their oppressors, and rose in their strength to put it off that this land become [sic] contaminated with slavery. Had this not been the case, led by the spirit of pure republicanism, that then possessed the souls of those patriots who were struggling for liberty, this soil would have been sufficiently guarded against its intrusion, and the people of these United States to this day, would have been strangers to so great a curse. It was by the permission of the British parliament, that the human species first became an article of merchandize among them, and as they were accessary to its introduction, it well becomes them to be, first, as a nation, in arresting its progress and effecting its expulsion. It was the immortal Clarkson,[9] a name that will be associated with all that is sublime in mercy, until the final consummation of all things, who first looking abroad, beheld the sufferings of Africa, and looking at home, he saw his country stained with her blood. He threw aside the vestments of the priesthood, and consecrated himself to the holy purpose of rescuing a continent from rapine and murder, and of erasing this one sin from the book of his nation's iniquities. . . . Happy for us, my brethren, that the principles of benevolence were not exclusively confined to the isle of Great Britain. There have lived, and there still do live, men in this country, who are patriots and philanthropists, not merely in name, but in heart and practice; men whose compassions have long since led them to pity the poor and despised sons of Africa. They have heard their groans, and have seen their blood, and have looked with an holy indignation upon the oppressor: nor was there any thing wanting except the power to have crushed the tyrant and liberated the captive. Through their instrumentality, the blessings of freedom have long since been enjoyed by all classes of people throughout New-England, and through their influence, under the Almighty, we are enabled to recognize the fourth day of the present month, as the day in which the cause of justice and humanity have triumphed over tyranny and oppression, and slavery is forever banished from the state of New-York.

Among the many who have vindicated the cause of the oppressed, within the limits of this state, we are proud to mention the names of Eddy and Murray, of Jay and Tompkins,[10] who, together with their fellow philanthropists embarked in the holy cause of emancipation, with a zeal which well expressed the sentiments of their hearts. They proved themselves to be inflexible against scorn, persecution and contempt; and although all did not live to see the conflict ended, yet their survivors never relaxed their exertions until the glorious year of 1817, when, by the wise and patriotic legislature of this state, a law was passed for its final extirpation. We will mourn for those who are gone, we will honour those who survive, until time extinguishes the lamp of their existence. When dead, they shall still live in our memory; we will follow them to their tombs, we will wet their graves with our tears; and upon the heart of every descendant of Africa, their deeds shall be written, and their names shall vibrate sweetly from ear to ear, down to the latest posterity. From what has already taken place, we are encouraged to expect still greater things. We look forward with pleasing anticipation to that period, when it shall no longer be said that in a land of freemen there are men in bondage, but when this foul stain will be entirely erased, and this, worst of evils, will be forever done away. The progress of emancipation, though slow, is nevertheless certain: It is certain, because that God who has made of one blood all nations of men, and who is said to be no respecter of persons, has so decreed; I therefore have no hesitation in declaring from this sacred place, that not only throughout the United States of America, but throughout every part of the habitable world where slavery exists, it will be abolished. However great may be the opposition of those who are supported by the traffic, yet slavery will cease. The lordly planter who has his thousands in bondage, may stretch himself upon his couch of ivory, and sneer at the exertions which are made by the humane and benevolent, or he may take his stand upon the floor of Congress, and mock the pitiful generosity of the east or west for daring to meddle with the subject, and attempting to expose its injustice: he may threaten to resist all efforts for a general or a partial emancipation even to a dissolution of the union. But still I declare that slavery will be extinct; a universal and not a partial emancipation must take place; nor is the period far distant. The indefatigable exertions of the philantrophists in England to have it abolished in their West India Islands, the recent revolutions in South America, the catastrophe and exchange of power in the Isle of Hayti, the restless disposition of both master and slave in the southern states, the constitution of our government, the effects of literary and moral instruction, the generous feelings of the pious and benevolent, the influence and spread of the holy religion of the cross of Christ, and the irrevocable decrees of Almighty God, all combine their efforts, and with united voice declare, that the power of tyranny must be subdued, the captive must be liberated, the oppressed go free, and slavery must revert back to its original chaos of darkness, and be forever annihilated from the earth. Did I believe that it would always continue, and that man to the end of time would be permitted with impunity to usurp the same undue authority over his fellow, I would disallow any allegiance or obligation I was under to my fellow creatures, or any submission that I owed to the laws of my country; I would deny the superintending power of divine providence in the affairs of this life; I would ridicule the religion of the Saviour of the world, and treat as the worst of men the ministers of the everlasting gospel; I would consider my Bible as a book of false and delusive fables, and commit it to the flames; nay, I would still go farther; I would at once confess myself an atheist, and deny the existence of a holy God.

But slavery will cease, and the equal rights of man will be universally acknowledged. Nor is its tardy progress any argument against its final accomplishment. But do I hear it loudly responded—this is but a mere wild fanaticism, or at best but the misguided conjecture of an untutored descendant of Africa. Be it so. I confess my ignorance, and bow with due deference to my superiors in understanding; but if in this case I err, the error is not peculiar to myself; if I wander, I wander in a region of light from whose political hemisphere the sun of liberty pours forth his refulgent rays, around which dazzle the star like countenances of Clarkson, Wilberforce, Pitt, Fox and Grenville, Washington, Adams, Jefferson, Hancock and Franklin; if I err, it is their sentiments that have caused me to stray.[11] For these are the doctrines which they taught while with us; nor can we reasonably expect that since they have entered the unbounded space of eternity, and have learned more familiarly the perfections of that God who governs all things that their sentiments have altered. Could they now come forth among us, they would tell that what they have learned in the world of spirits, has served only to confirm what they taught while here; they would tell us, that all things are rolling on according to the sovereign appointment of the eternal Jehovah, who will overturn and overturn until he whose right it is to reign, shall come and the period will be ushered in; when the inhabitants of the earth will learn by experience what they are now slow to believe—that our God is a God of justice, and no respecter of persons. But while, on the one hand, we look back and rejoice at what has already taken place, and on the other, we look forward with pleasure to that period when men will be respected according to their characters, and not according to their complexion, and when their vices alone will render them contemptible; while we rejoice at the thought of this land's becoming a land of freemen, we pause, we reflect. What, we would ask, is liberty without virtue? It tends to lasciviousness; and what is freedom but a curse, and even destruction, to the profligate? Not more desolating in its effects is the mountain torrent, breaking from its lofty confines and rushing with vast impetuosity upon the plains beneath, marring as it advances all that is lovely in the works of nature and of art, than the votaries of vice and immorality, when permitted to range unrestrained. Brethren, we have been called into liberty; only let us use that liberty as not abusing it. The day commences a new era in our history; new scenes, new prospects, open before us, and it follows as a necessary consequence, that new duties devolve upon us; duties, which if properly attended to, cannot fail to improve our moral condition, and elevate us to a rank of respectable standing with the community; or if neglected, we fall at once into the abyss of contemptible wretchedness: It is righteousness alone that exalteth a nation, and sin is a reproach to any people. Our liberties, says Mr. Jefferson, are the gift of God, and they are not to be violated but with his wrath. Nations and individuals have been blest of the Almighty in proportion to the manner in which they have appreciated the mercies conferred upon them: an abuse of his goodness has always incured his righteous frown while a right improvement of his beneficence has secured and perpetuated his gracious smiles: an abuse of his goodness has caused those fearful judgments which have destroyed cities, demolished thrones, overturned empires, and humbled to the dust, the proudest and most exalted of nations. As a confirmation of which, the ruinous heaps of Egypt, Tyre, Babylon, and Jerusalem, stand as everlasting monuments. If we would then answer the great design of our creation, and glorify the God who has made us; if we would avert the judgment of Heaven; if we would honor our public benefactors; if we would counter-

act the designs of our enemies; if we would have our own blessings perpetuated, and secure the happiness of our children and our children's children, let each come forward and act well his part, in whatever circle he
may move, or in whatever station he may fill; let the fear of God and the
good of our fellow men, be the governing principles of the heart. We do
well to remember, that every act of ours is more or less connected with
the general cause of the people of colour, and with the general cause of
emancipation. Our conduct has an important bearing, not only on those
who are yet in bondage in this country, but its influence is extended to the
isles of India, and to every part of the world where the abomination of
slavery is known. Let us then relieve ourselves from the odious stigma
which some have long since cast upon us, that we were incapacitated by
the God of nature, for the enjoyment of the rights of freemen, and convince them and the world that although our complexion may differ, yet
we have hearts susceptible of feeling; judgment capable of discerning, and
prudence sufficient to manage our affairs with discretion, and by example prove ourselves worthy the blessings we enjoy. . . . The wide field of
usefulness is now open before us, and we are called upon by every consideration of duty which we owe to our God, to ourselves, to our children, and to our fellow-creatures generally, to enter with a fixed determination to act well our part, and labour to promote the happiness and welfare of all.

There remains much to be done, and there is much to encourage us to
action. The foundation for literary, moral and religious improvement, we
trust, is already laid in the formation of the public and private schools,
for the instruction of our children, together with the churches of different
denominations already established. From these institutions we are encouraged to expect the happiest results; and while many of us are passing
down the declivity of life, and fast hastening to the grave, how animating
the thought, that the rising generation is advancing under more
favourable auspicies than we were permitted to enjoy, soon to fill the
places we now occupy; and in relation to them vast is the responsibility
that rests upon us; much of their future usefulness depends upon the discharge of the duties we owe them. They are advancing, not to fill the place
of slaves, but of freemen: and in order to fill such a station with honor to
themselves, and with good to the public, how necessary their education,
how important the moral and religious cultivation of their minds! Blessed
be God, we live in a day that our fathers desired to see, but died without

the sight: a day in which science, like the sun of the firmament, rising, darting as he advances his beams to every quarter of the globe. The mists and darkness scatter at his approach, and all nations and people are blessed with his rays; so the glorious light of science is spreading from east to west, and Afric's sons are catching the glance of its beams as it passes; its enlightening rays scatter the mists of moral darkness and ignorance which have but too long overshadowed their minds; it enlightens the understanding, directs the thoughts of the heart, and is calculated to influence the soul to the performance of every good and virtuous act. The God of Nature has endowed our children with intellectual powers surpassed by none; nor is there any thing wanting but their careful cultivation, in order to fit them for stations the most honorable, sacred, or useful. And may we not, without becoming vain in our imaginations, indulge the pleasing anticipation, that within the little circle of those connected with our families, there may hereafter be found the scholar, the statesman, or the herald of the cross of Christ: Is it too much to say, that among that little number there shall yet be one found like to the wise legislator of Israel, who shall take his brethren by the hand, and lead them forth from worse than Egyptian bondage, to the happy Canaan of civil and religious liberty; or one whose devotedness towards the cause of God, and whose zeal for the salvation of Africa, shall cause him to leave the land which gave him birth, and cross the Atlantic, eager to plant the standard of the cross upon every hill of that vast continent, that has hitherto ignobly submitted to the baleful crescent, or crouched under the iron bondage of the vilest superstition. Our prospects brighten as we pursue the subject, and we are encouraged to look forward to that period when the moral desert of Africa shall submit to cultivation, and verdant groves and fertile vallies, watered by the streams of Siloia,[12] shall meet the eye that has long surveyed only the wide spread desolations of slavery, despotism, and death. How changed shall then be the aspect of the moral and political world! Africa, elevated to more than her original dignity, and redressed for the many aggravated and complicated wrongs she has sustained, with her emancipated sons, shall take her place among the other nations of the earth. The iron manacles of slavery shall give place to the still stronger bonds of brotherly love and affection, and justice and equity shall be the governing principles that shall regulate the conduct of men of every nation. Influenced by such motives, encouraged by such prospects, let us enter the field with a fixed determination to live and to die in the holy cause.[13]

Sources: William Hamilton, *Oration Delivered in the African Zion Church, on the Fourth of July, 1827, in Commemoration of the Abolition of Domestic Slavery in This State* (New York, 1827); Nathaniel Paul, *An Address Delivered on the Celebration of the Abolition of Slavery in the State of New York, July 5, 1827* (Albany, 1827).

P. Address, African American
State Convention, 1840

The damage done by the property qualification was quickly apparent. Out of a statewide African American population of 29,701, only 298 men met the property-holding requirements.[14] The property qualification worked in concert with racial harassment to keep the vast majority of black men from the polls. In the early 1830s, a British visitor noted that "to be worth two hundred and fifty dollars is not a trifle for a man doomed to toil in the lowest stations; few negroes are in consequence competent to vote."[15]

As Jacksonians grew ever bolder in their celebrations of *herrenvolk* democracy and New York's Martin Van Buren was elected President, blacks across the Empire State began to organize politically. Beginning in 1837, the *Colored American*, a new African American weekly, regularly invoked the memory of betrayal in 1821. In the inaugural issue of March 4, 1837, the editors announced their intentions by publishing lengthy excerpts from the convention. For the next few years, the memory of 1821 was kept alive as the words of Erastus Root, Peter Jay, Martin Van Buren, and other delegates appeared.

Black agitation against the property qualification came of age in the 1830s and 1840s, as the legacies of 1821 became clearer. Residential segregation increased considerably in the quarter-century after black disfranchisement. Linked to this was the intensification of racial exclusion in the workplaces of the antebellum economy; as Richard Stott notes, "Blacks were almost totally excluded from manufacturing" by mid-century.[16]

In the two decades before the Civil War, African Americans across the North convened statewide meetings on a regular basis. Empire State blacks were especially dedicated to holding such conventions; in the 1840s and 1850s, such meetings continuously resolved to fight for the removal of the property qualification from the state's constitution. The first such meeting convened in Albany in 1840. As the following excerpt from the proceedings makes clear, this momentous act of black political organizing—one that set numerous precedents for later African American conventions—was founded upon anti-property-qualification activism.

How did the delegates to the 1840 convention invoke the history of New York and of the United States? In particular, how did this assembly remember the Constitutional Convention of 1821? On what bases did the delegates argue for the removal of the property qualification? Why, according to this address, was the right to vote so essential to black freedom?

* * *

Address of the New York State Convention of Colored Citizens, to the People of the State

FELLOW CITIZENS:—The State Convention of Colored Citizens assembled in Albany, August 18th, 19th and 20th, to consider their political condition, in behalf of their people in this state, would respectfully address you on a subject to them of the most vital import. They would call your earnest and unprejudiced attention to the unjust and withering policy that in 1821 led to the endorsing of an anti republican enactment, (Art. II. Sec. 1, State Constitution,) by which a portion of the citizens of this State were restricted in the exercise of a natural right, and refused an equal participation in its political arrangements. And they would also solemnly desire you to look around, and witness the multiplied evils that have for years weighed, and do now weigh heavily upon them, from not being allowed to use, on liberal and worthy terms, the all-important privilege of the elective franchise.

The patriotic framers of our State Constitution, in view of the then recent unwarrantableness of British jurisdiction, and pondering on the self-evident truths that had been made the solemn charter of their country's liberties, did, in 1777, (by suffrage and free choice appointed,) assemble in deliberative convention, and adopt such "acts and declarations as were calculated most efficiently to secure the rights and liberties of the good people of this State—most conducive to the happiness and safety of their constituents in particular, and of America in general."

Basing themselves upon the avowed principle of the democratic colonies, that taxation and representation should go together, and that governments receive their just power from the consent of the governed—they established in the Constitution, as a foundation guard to the plainest rights of the people, such provisions as were best designed to keep inviolate their undeniable prerogative to select their rulers—this being the first article of belief in their republican faith.

In so doing, they did not think it consistent with the principles they professed, to divide freemen; those who had shared with them the dangers of war; who had ever been willing to aid them in achieving their independence; we say, they did not divide these, their fellow citizens, into castes, and in the face of justice, confer privileges on one class that were refused to another. Every freeman, according to Art. VII of this firstly adopted instrument, who paid taxes, and hired a tenement worth forty shillings a year, was entitled to exercise the common right of voting.

In 1821, in opposition to the intellect, the philanthropy, and consistent republicanism of many noble men, who dignifiedly stood up and contended against the unprovoked intolerance that urged forward the measure, an act was passed, which, while it protected liberally others in the exercise of the franchise, made it incumbent upon every colored citizen to possess $250 freehold estate, in order to use the before common privilege. This requirement, as we have before declared, resulted most disadvantageously to us.

We now find ourselves existing in the chief division of the government, with no marks of criminality attached to our names, as a class; no spots of immorality staining our characters; no charges of disloyalty dishonoring our birthright; yet prevented (by an invidious complexional proscription) from being participants in those free born rights and sympathies that are bountifully guaranteed, not only to common humanity of this State, but also to foreigners, of whatever clime or language. We find ourselves the subjects, and not the objects of legislation, because we are prevented from giving an assenting or opposing voice in the periodic appointments of those who rule us and are made passive instruments of all laws, just or unjust, that may be enacted, to which we are bound to subscribe, even while we have no instrumentality, either in their formation or adoption.

We find ourselves crippled and crushed in soul and ability, because with all the longing that our spirits may possess to drink deeply of those pure waters that mentally and morally refresh and invigorate, we are thrust from the fountain with the cold treatment of aliens, having even that self-protecting instrument taken from us, which is the primary assurance and safeguard of citizenship.

We find ourselves shut out by the secondary influence of a monied restriction, from a right which is the basis of a people's liberties and prosperity; and by the withering influence of this, we are virtually and manifestly shut out from the obtainment of those resources of pecuniary and possessional emolument, which an unshackled citizenship does always ensure, and which very resources are held up before us as requirements for the use of a privilege, that, in accordance with the spirit of the government, should be the freest and most sacred.

This unequal participation in the privileges of the state, we consider invidious and proscriptive. It proceeds from no principles of justice; it is not predictable either from the position or character of the people upon whom it so unequally operates. The causes which were supposed to justify its enactment, or warrant its continuance, have either no existence, or are equally applicable to a large body of respectable voters of the state.

What are we, as a people, in the state? What is our condition? What is the character we have? What the reputation we sustain? We are native born citizens of the state—immediate descendants of men, held, not long since, as slaves. From this state we were *translated* into the partial enjoyment and limited possession of freedom. Cut off from the sympathies of our fellow citizens, almost abject in poverty, allowed, in many places, but a scanty, and inadequate participation in the privileges of education, and deprived almost entirely of the elective franchise, we have nevertheless, by the practical operation of common sense, by habits of industry, and the cultivation of the religious sentiments, been enabled to elevate ourselves above abasement, and possess ourselves of many of the advantages of RELIGION, INTELLIGENCE and PROPERTY.

We present the curious and acknowledged creditable spectacle of a people, bending under the weight of proscription, who yet will not suffer by a comparison with their more privileged fellow citizens of the same rank, in either religion, virtue or industry.

Although from the arbitrary distinctions that prevail throughout the community, we have been debarred entirely from collegiate education;

although, to a considerable extent, we have been excluded from the advantages of the common school system, yet we have been enabled, not only to sustain them among ourselves, but likewise, in many instances, select schools of our own. A spirit of intelligence pervades our entire people. Keeping pace with the progressive spirit of the age, and the continual intellectual progress of the nation, there are but few families in which books are not a common and necessary commodity.

In all parts of the state, from Montauk to Buffalo, literary and debating societies and clubs exist among our people, in city, town, and village. In some instances, these societies are adorned and made more useful by libraries and reading rooms. Our schools and associations are continually sending forth a host of youth, with strong determination and purpose of subserving the best and highest interests of their proscribed race. And not an inconsiderable number of the rising hope of our people, have sought, in some of the higher institutions of learning, either in this or a foreign land, the privileges of a classical education.

We have scattered, as bright spots all along the State, a number of young men, aspirants for the ministry, preparing for academical instruction; or entering, once in a while, the medical profession; with cultivated minds, and hearts devoted to the interests of man, and the great purposes of truth. The causes that have thrown a damp upon our literary ardor, have operated disadvantageously in our ecclesiastical relations. The prejudice against us in the community, has been more potent than the dictates of Christian equality. Not only are we debarred from the rightful exercise of ecclesiastical privileges, but we also meet with indignities and hindrances in the simplest forms of religious communion. We have often been driven from the quiet and peaceable enjoyment of those rights with which the death of a common Saviour invested us, in common with the rest of our fellow creatures of the human family.

Of necessity, then, have we been often forced to form religious societies of our own. Throughout the State, we have upwards of forty independent religious congregations, of the Presbyterian, Episcopal, Methodist and Baptist denomination; each with a temple erected to the worship of the Almighty; most with settled pastors under a regular yearly stipend; in connection with which there are about 6000 communicants, who, with the respective congregations in attendance with them, average in the aggregate not less than 15,000 of our people who statedly are under the influence of religion in connection with our own churches, besides those in attendance elsewhere.

The amount of energy and intellect brought out by these various projects, may be justly regarded as bespeaking much for the virtue and character of a disfranchised and oppressed people. Aside from this, a large body of our people are in partial communion with the various Christian communities throughout the State. From these sources, streams of religious influence and blessing are in continual flow, refreshing and invigorating our entire body.

An undue and disproportionate development of powers, produce unnatural effects. A continual enlargement of certain capacities, to the entire neglect of others, of equal, or it may be of more importance, produces deformity. In order to develope symmetry of either form or character, a full, general, healthy and vigorous exercise of *all* the powers, is absolutely necessary. In bringing forth the character of a people, this is clear and manifest. The history of the serfs, under the feudal system, the character of the same class in Russia, and the prominent traits of the disfranchised class in all communities at the present day, and especially the condition of enslaved men throughout the universe, give strong verity to the sentiment herein expressed. Human nature is complex in its formation. In proportion as the various powers of man are harmoniously educed, so is the nobleness and vastness of its capacity manifested. Free scope [. . .] given for the exercise of the physical and mental powers, to the detriment of the moral, a hideousness of character is evinced.—And so if the moral alone is cultivated, to the neglect of the mental and physical, the character is not symmetrical.

In a community, man sustains various relations, and possesses powers adapted to them—which, if not permitted a natural and legitimate exercise, are turned upon himself and follow with augmented and fearful capacity for evil, from the fact of having been diverted from a natural channel. It is thus with the possession or non-possession of the franchise in any state of society. Man is a creature of law—his nature adapted to government and its various functions. He sympathizes with its modes, and forms, and operations; and this, from the fact that there is not a single shade of revolution in the political aspect of a country, but it is felt to the extreme limits of the body politic; operating upon the individual being of all its subjects.

The deprivation of our people of the elective franchise, and a participation in the various rounds of public duty, shows the evil here spoken of. The powers that should have been thus employed, have not lain dormant. A trait which we possess in common with our common humanity, has been manifested in us. Powers will have exercise, either healthy or unhealthy. The impartial and proscriptive non-suffrage act, has been to us hurtful in the extreme. The powers that should naturally have been thus exercised, were wrested from their legitimate employment. It has been the source of evil, unmitigated, unalleviated; without even an approach to an adequate benefit. It is true we might become possessed of the immunities of citizens and voters by the property qualification. But this spur, this incitement as it is regarded by some, lost all its zest, in the bitter reflection, in the searing conviction, that we were made aliens and strangers in the country of our birth; a disfranchised class in the very land where lie the bones of our fathers—the land whose liberties they helped achieve by patriotic service, and whose soil is enriched by their purest and noblest blood!

But this is not all. When we were deprive[d] of the elective franchise, the blow was given which severed that hold, by which respect, deference, and consideration is obtained by the poorest and humblest citizen. Our fellow citizens saw they had nothing to expect from us. We became a proscribed, depressed class. We felt everywhere we went, in all our relations, that we had been made separate from the rest of our fellow citizens.

The pure and refreshing waters of literary excellence, were not allowed to flow by us, to quench the burning thirst of an eager and longing people. In the various religious bodies, they have not found their purity of Christian feeling powerful and universal enough to treat man, aside from arbitrary distinctions, "without respect of persons." In short, the means and facilities—the ways and avenues to wealth and influence were shut against us.

We ask, what might be expected of any people in such circumstances? What might be anticipated as legitimate results from such a condition?

Under like disabilities we perceive the sufferings of the Irish in Ireland, the degradation of the Greek, the besotted stupidity of the lower castes in India, and the abasement and continual decrease of the aborigines of our own country. So in this State; under like sufferings, under like injustice, the greater amount of crime and sufferings among our people, have proceeded from a non-participation in the prerogatives of citizenship.[17] Notwithstanding all these difficulties and depressions, calculated as they are to sicken to heart to a great extent, and make the soul give up, we have nevertheless been enabled to live above them.

We have been deprived of the elective franchise during the last twenty years. In a free country, this is ever a stimulant to enterprise, a means of influence and a source of respect. The possession of it sends life, vigor and energy through the entire heart of a people. The want of it in a community, is the cause of carelessness, intellectual inertness, and indolence. Springing above all these depressing circumstances, and exerting ourselves with unwonted alacrity, by native industry, by the accumulation of property, we have helped contribute, to a considerable extent, not only to the means of the state, but likewise to its character and respectability.

We claim, that there is no consideration what ever in existence, on account of which, the odious proscription of which we complain, should be continued. The want of intelligence, our misfortunes and the *crime* of others, which was once urged against us, does not now exist. Again: *we are the descendants of some of the earliest settlers of the State.* We can trace our ancestry back to those who first pierced the almost impenetrable forests that then lifted their high and stately heads in silent grandeur to the skies. When the vast and trackless wilderness, that had alone answered to the fierce roar of the roaming beast, or the whoop of the wild native, spread itself before the earlier settlers, our fathers were among those, who, with sinewy frame and muscular arm, went forth to humble that wilderness in its native pride. Since that time, our fathers, and we ourselves, have lent our best strength in cultivating the soil, in developing its vast resources, and contributing to its wealth and importance. Those who are the least acquainted with the history of the State, cannot but grant, that in this respect, we have contributed more than our proportionate part.

In times when patient toil and hardy industry were demanded, it will thus be seen, we have ever been present and active. Not only so. *In times of peril has our aid been called for, and our services as promptly given.* When the country, its interests, its best and most cherished rights and institutions, have been assailed, not unavailingly have we been looked to. When the shrill trumpet call of freedom was heard amid the mountains and the rocks, and along the rivers of the north, and a reverberating reply was heard from the broad fields and pine forests of the South; when the whole country, aroused by the injustice of British policy, arose as one man, for the maintenance of natural and unprescriptable rights; the dark browed man stood side by side with his fairer fellow citizen, with firm determination and indomitable spirit. During that memorable conflict, in severe and trying service, did they contend for those principles of liberty set forth in the Declaration of Independence, which are not of partial or local applicability, but which pertain alike to every being possessed of those high and exalted endowments that distinguish humanity.

Their blood is mingled with the soil of every battle field, made glorious by revolutionary reminiscence; and their bones have enriched the most productive lands of the country. In the late war of 1812, our people were again called upon to defend their country. The splendid naval achievements on Lakes Erie and Champlain, were owing mostly to the skill and prowess of colored men. The face of Perry was gained at the expense of the mangled bodies and bleeding veins of our disfranchised people. Not inconsiderably is it owing to them, that Americans of the present day can recur with pleasurable emotions, and pride of country, to the battle fields of Plattsburgh and Sacketts Harbor.[18]

We are Americans. We were born in no foreign clime. Here, where we behold the noble rivers, and the rich fields, and the healthful skies, that may be called American; here, amid the institutions that now surround us, we first beheld the light of the impartial sun. We have not been brought up under the influence of other strange, aristocratic, and uncongenial political relations. In this respect, we profess to be American and republican. With the nature, features and operations of our government, we have been familiarized from youth; and its democratic character is accordant with the flow of our feelings, and the current of our thoughts.

We have thus laid before you, fellow citizens, some considerations why we should never have been deprived of an equal suffrage, and why a just and impartial guarantee of this right, should soon be made.

But bating all these, we lay our claim on still higher ground. We *do* regard the right of our birthdom, our service in behalf of the country, contributing to its importance, and developing its resources, as favorable considerations—considerations adapted to banish all thought of proscription and injustice, from the power holding body of the country, and to lead them to a hearty and practical acknowledgment of the claims and rights of a disfranchised people.

Yet for these alone, we do not ask for the extension of the elective franchise. We would not, we do not predicate any right to it from any such basis. We would not fall into the error of basing rights upon grounds so untenable. We object to others placing our rights upon complexion. We ourselves would not lay our claims to consideration on this or any similar ground.

We can find no system of moral or political ethics in which rights are based upon the confirmation of the body, or the color of the skin. We can find no nation that has the temerity to insult the common sense of mankind, by promulgating such a sentiment as part of its creed. However individuals or nations may act, however they may assail the rights of man, or wrest from him his liberties, they all, equally and alike *profess* regard for natural rights, the protection and security of which they claim as the object of the formation of their respective systems.

Rights have an existence, aside from conventional arrangements or unnatural partialities. They are of higher origin and of purer birth. They are inferrable from the settled and primary sentiments of man's nature. The high dignities and exalted tendencies of our common humanity are the original grounds from which they may be deduced. Wherever a being may be found endowed with the light of reason, and in the exercise of its various exalted attributes, that being is possessed of certain peculiar rights, on the ground of his nature.

We base our claim upon the possession of those common and yet exalted faculties of manhood. WE ARE MEN. 1. Those sympathies which find their natural channel, and legitimate and healthy exercise in civil and political relations, have the same being and nature in us that they have in the rest of the human family. 2. Those yearnings and longings for the exercise of political prerogatives, that are the product of the adaptedness of man's social nature to political arrangements, strive with irrepressible potency within us, from the fact of our disfranchised condition, a prevalent and unreasonable state of caste, and the operation of laws and statutes not proceeding from, yet operating upon us. 3. Those indignities and wrongs which naturally become the portion of a disfranchised class, and gather accumulated potency from an increase and intenseness of proscription, naturally and legitimately revert to us. From possessing like sympathies for civil and political operations with others, and like susceptibilities for evil, when nature is hindered in any of its legitimate exercises—on the ground of our *common humanity,* do we claim equal and entire rights with the rest of our fellow citizens. All that we say here, meets with full sympathy from all connected with the history of the country, the nature of its institutions, the spirit of its Constitution, and the designs and purposes of its great originators.

We have no reason to think that the framers of the Declaration of Independence, in setting forth the doctrines it contains, regarded them as dogmas or idle theories. We believe they put full faith in them, as actual truths and living verities. This they evinced, by pledging to each other their lives, their fortunes, and their sacred honors. This they manifested, by an unswerving opposition to injustice and oppression.

It was in accordance with the views of that great charter of American freedom, that they framed the Constitution of the country. Setting aside the stale primogenital fallacies of the blood-dyed political institutions of the old world; repudiating the unnatural assumptions of the feudal system, and exploding the aged and destructive sophism of natural inequalities in the family of man, they clung with undying tenacity to the connecting chain that runs through the whole mighty mass of humanity, recognized the common sympathies and wants of the race, and framed a political edifice of such a nature and character as was congenial with the natural and indestructible principles of man, and as was adapted to secure to all under its broad AEGIS,[19] the purest liberty God ever conferred upon him.

That Declaration, and that Constitution, we think, may be considered as more fully developing the primary ideas of American republicanism, than any other documents. In these, individuals are regarded distinctly and respectively—each and every one as men, fully capacitated by the Creator for government and progressive advancement—which capacities, in a natural exercises, are not to be interfered with by government.

Republicanism, in these two documents, has an eye to individual freedom, without lets or hindrances. In her operations, she is impartial. She regards man—all men; and is indifferent to all arbitrary and conventional considerations. This we deem to be the character of the Declaration of Independence—and this, likewise, the character of the Constitution after which it was modelled. Republicanism was to be the distinguishing feature in its operations.

The Constitution of our own State, as it sprung from the clear head and pure heart of that incomparable patriot, JOHN JAY, in its preamble and several sections, was, in spirit, concordant with it. By this we mean, that although the qualifications for voting, *in general,* were higher than those prevailing at the present, yet the ground of the suffrage enactment was not based upon national peculiarities, or complexional distinctions. It is said that *any* man possessed of such and such qualifications should be a political denizen of the State.

As the State advanced in age, intelligence and population, augmented in wealth, and extended in resources, the call went forth for the extension of the franchise right. In accordance with the will of the people thus expressed, a convention was held in the city of Albany in 1821—2.

We beg that it may be remembered, that the convention was called for the purpose of *extending* the suffrage right. We would also call your attention to the fact, that the votes by which many of the delegates were elected to that convention, were cast by colored voters.[20] And more especially would we remind you, that during the proceedings of that convention, in its reports, addresses, &c., a peculiar deference is ever paid to the republican features of our common country, and its democratic tendencies. Yet in that convention, that portion of the citizens of the State whom we here represent, were shut out from an equal and common participation in the prerogatives of citizenship, in the operations of both State and National Governments, and thus placed under the operation of laws and statutes without our agency, and to which we are subjected without acquiescence.

We, the Colored Citizens of the State, in Convention assembled, representing 50,000 of the population, do ask your earnest attention, your deep reflection, your unbiased and conscientious judgment in this matter. We ask you, as a matter in which YOU are deeply concerned, to come forward and restore the fountains of political justice in this State to their pristine purity. We ask you to secure to us our political rights. We call upon you to return to the pure faith of your republican fathers. We lift up our voices for the restored spirit of the first days of the republic—for the great principles that then maintained, and that regard for man which revered the characteristic features of his nature, as of more honor and worth than the form and color of the body in which they dwell.

For no vested rights, for no peculiar privileges, for no extraordinary prerogatives, do we ask. We merely put forth our appeal for a republican birthright. We wish to be something more than political serfs and slaves. We fully believe in the fundamental doctrines set forth in the Declaration of Independence. We acquiesce in the sentiment that "governments derive their just power from the consent of the governed." And we say it is injustice of the most aggrieved character, either to deprive us of a just and legitimate participation in the rights of the state, or to make us bear the burdens, and submit to its enactments, when all its arrangements, plans, and purposes, are framed and put into operation utterly regardless of us, in their incipient state, than if we were nonentities; but which, in their practical operation, act upon us with destructive tendency, eat away our soul, and destroy our life. We ask for a living manifestation of belief in the above doctrine; we know already too much of its dead letter.

Fellow citizens! the Colored Citizens of this State, through us their representatives, respectfully and earnestly ask at your hands, the speedy adoption of such plans, and the formation of such measures, as may soon lead to the erasure of the odious proscriptive act of which we complain—we secured an equal suffrage, and the State freed from a stain upon its character.

A. STEWARD, Pres.

C. L. Reason,

H. H. Garnet, Secretaries.

Wm. H. Topp,

Source: *Colored American*, December 19, 1840.

Q. Excerpts from the Debate on Suffrage, New York State Constitutional Convention, 1846

One of the most striking features of nineteenth-century American politics was the regularity with which states came together to revise their constitutions. There was something of an expectation that each generation would hold a constitutional convention and debate anew first principles. By the early twentieth century, referenda and ballot initiatives would replace the older convention tradition.

For New Yorkers, 1846 brought the first state convention in a quarter century. That year's proceedings stand out for the range of issues that occupied the delegates' attention—notably antirent politics in the state's rural counties, demands for home rule in the state's cities, and prolonged debate over legal and judicial reforms.

The 1846 convention took place against a backdrop of sectional tension precipitated by conflict with Mexico. The Mexican-American War sparked one of the most divisive debates in our nation's history. Many Northerners were outraged by President James Polk's policies; the Massachusetts state legislature went so far as to denounce the war as unjust. A first-term Whig congressman from Illinois, Abraham Lincoln, risked his political career as he consistently denounced the foreign war. Many New Yorkers, especially abolitionists, were troubled by the war and its apparent proslavery implications. At the same time, Democratic New Yorkers were among the most enthusiastic supporters of the Mexican campaign and of Manifest Destiny more broadly.

In the convention, among the voices most interested in addressing the property qualification were New York City Democrats, men who were prowar and antiblack. Manhattan delegates were not satisfied with the property qualification; rather, they sought disfranchisement for all black men. John A. Kennedy, an Irish-born paint dealer, argued against "the last vestige of an odious, cruel, and unjust condition" (the property qualification) and proposed full black exclusion instead.

Compare the substance and tone of these debates with those at the convention of 1821 (see document L). What were the most important differences between the two convention debates? Conversely, what continuities are evident in the arguments being advanced?

* * *

1846 Convention

WEDNESDAY, SEPTEMBER 30, 1846

Benjamin Bruce, a thirty-four-year-old farmer from Lenox in Madison County, moved to strike out the word white *from the suffrage provision.*

In rising to address the Convention in support of the motion I have had the honor to submit, I find myself not a little embarrassed from the fact that I am surrounded by gentlemen of acknowledged talent and ability, who, I have reason to believe, will oppose the principles I have risen to advocate. But, convinced, as I am, of the truth and justice of the proposition, I am constrained to offer a few remarks on this question, which I consider one of the most important that has been under consideration during the protracted session of this Convention. Sir, the natural and acquired right of man has long since been *theoretically* settled in this government, but *practically*, a well settled and established theory has been to so great an extent repudiated, that at this period in our history, there are not a few among us that seem disposed to contest the theory that was established by our fathers at the very commencement of our National existence. Now, sir, let us go back in the history of the world to the eventful period when "the morning stars sang together,"[21] and when God, by his Almighty power said "let there be light." At this time, we are informed, "God created man in His own image, and breathed into his nostrils the breath of life," and then it was, that man's rights and privileges were clearly defined, and from that time to the present, they have remained unchanged, and man entitled to the full possession of them all, except what he forfeited to his creator by disobedience of divine commands.

And, sir, in the plan of redemption, Infinite wisdom has made no distinction, but on the contrary has said "whoever will, let him come and take of the waters of life."[22] That "of one blood all the nations of the Earth"[23] are created, is the declaration of holy writ, and the Declaration of our Nation's Independence boldly and unequivocally proclaims the same sentiment, that "all men are created equal, and endowed by their Creator with certain inalienable rights, among which is life liberty, and the pursuit of happiness." Sir, there is no distinction; and whether a man be born in the cold and barren regions of the North, or the warm and fruitful fields of the South, he is entitled to the same protection, and should be endowed with the same rights, and have secured to him the same privileges as any other citizen in this land of "equal rights and equal privileges." Sir, distinction in the exercise of the elective franchise, on account of color or complexion, is invidious and anti-republican. But such a distinction has existed in this state since 1820, to a great degree, and if the report from the honorable gentleman from Schoharie (Mr. Bouck)[24] is adopted, will exist in a still greater degree than has ever before been known. And in this conviction, sir, I propose to examine this report; for whatever other gentlemen may think of its merits, I confess there is at least one strange and unheard of position, and whether it is by design or by accident, I cannot say. It is sufficient for the argument that the provision is there. The first section provides that all *white* male citizens who have attained the age of 21 years and been one year a resident of the state, &c, shall have the right of the elective franchise. In the last section, he ostensibly proposes to give the same right to persons of color; but mark the language, which I will read—"*persons of color, possessing the qualifications named in the first section* of this article," shall have, &c. Now, sir, what are the qualifications to which this section of his report refers? Why, the first one is to be a *white* male citizen. So the persons of color must become, by some singular transformation, (I will not pretend to say what) *white* persons of color, to entitle them to the rights of citizens. . . .

England has repudiated and wiped out the institution of slavery. We retain it in its most odious forms. In the event of a war between the two most powerful nations of the civilised world, I ask if it would be unreasonable to expect that this class of our citizens might be induced (from motives of self-defence, which is the first law of nature) to yield to the temptation of the emissaries of a foreign power as they hold out to them the palm of emancipation? Sir, that "government derives their just power from the *consent* of the governed ["] is the plain, simple but positive language of our Declaration of Independence. But I ask where and how did these people give their "consent"? Sir it is all a mockery for you to boast of "equal rights and equal privileges" and deny the exercise of elective franchise to them, while you extend it to those who come to this from a foreign country, after a nominal or real residence of a single year, and in many cases a less period. I am one of those sir, who hold the truth to be self evident that "all men are created equal" and would reduce to *practice* what we all hold most tenaciously in theory. Now if "colored persons" are *men* then give them the rights and privileges of *men*, if they are not men, then make them *slaves, chattles* and *things*, and let us have no more of this "opposition to slavery" and desire "to benefit the colored man" that is so much *talked* in favor and voted *against*. . . .

John L. Russell, a lawyer from Saint Lawrence County, spoke in favor of the property qualification.

Mr. RUSSELL said the Convention had listened to much declamation, about natural rights of man. "All men are by nature equal, endowed with certain inalienable rights, among which are life, liberty and the pursuit of happiness," has been the text of all the preachers to the Convention, and they have all urged the very erroneous conclusion, that this Convention, in determining who should compose the electoral body—the only sovereign power and real governors of the state—are bound to admit negroes and Indians to an equal participation in this sovereign power and privilege. . . .

New Jersey, Pennsylvania, and Ohio, the only states between us and the slave population of the South, will not yield these privileges, because it would invite among them a dangerous proportion of another race of men.[25] But we are told, that New York should extend such invitation, by an offer of equal participation in the government of five-sixths of our own citizens, who cannot exercise the same privilege, and some gentlemen are pleased to take into their own hands, the thunderbolts of Almighty Power, and to wield its vengeance upon all who doubt the justice, or propriety, of extending the numbers of the electoral body, by an infusion of this new class with it. Mr. R. doubted, whether gentlemen had been legitimately ordained as ministers of Divine retribution. Many suspected that their motives, as well as their mission in this cause, were of the earth, earthly—and not of any Divine source, express or implied.

If we invite all the blacks, who are to come from the south, by giving them this political power, which they cannot have till they reach this state, the next ten years will bring thousands of them among us, if they have in fact the ambition of ruling with our race, which has been ascribed to them by their special friends on this floor.

Is such an accession to our population desirable? In the name of the people of St. Lawrence county, I answer, no! . . .

Suppose the thousands of emancipated blacks of the south, are, by an offer of all the privileges of citizenship, invited to settle in this state, must they not labor for their support? Will not their labor be brought in direct competition with that of our white laboring classes? It must of necessity, and one or two things must result.—Either, this competition must reduce the price of labor, or our white laborers must make room for our new black citizens, by emigrating to other states. In either view, this would be a political evil, and would work great injustice to the white laboring class—at least to nine-tenths of all our present voters. The few who live upon the profits of their capital, might not be seriously affected, except by the gradual degeneracy of the electoral body, and consequent insecurity of property. . . .

If the majority of the Convention doubted whether the present electors of the state desired to extend their franchise to the negro race, without restriction, Mr. R. would not object to have that question tested by a distinct, separate submission of the proposition; but he could go no further, to carry out the theories of any man, however philanthropic he may be.

This was one of the first suggestions of the possibility of separate submission. By this, Russell and his fellow disfranchisers sought to delink the new constitution from the question of retaining the property qualification. The goal was to have New Yorkers vote separately on whether to maintain a racially defined suffrage.

Thursday October 1, 1846

John A. Kennedy, a paint dealer from New York City, continued the argument for maintaining the 1821 property qualification.

Mr. Kennedy said, the absence of the chairman of committee No. 4, (Mr. Bouck,) and two others of its most intelligent members, had devolved on him, in part, the duty of explaining the views which influenced them in presenting the portion of the section under debate. This question had been very fully examined by the committee. Opportunity had been afforded to those who felt an interest in the subject, to lay their views and wishes before it. Among others a delegation from the colored population had appeared, and the same privilege was extended to them. After many meetings, and laborious application, the opinion prevailed in the committee, nearly unanimously, adverse to property qualification for an elector, in any case. The mere possession of property was deemed to be no test of political merit; that the colored man, whether possessed of property or not of a certain kind, and to a certain extent, was entitled to natural rights; and that if political privileges were extended to his race, they should not depend on his possessions, but on his manhood. The possession of property by the white man was no infallible evidence of either intelligence or patriotism. One dependent for his daily bread on his daily toil, might surpass him in both. And there was no good reason for believing that color would make an essential difference in these particulars. This article, therefore, was designedly put in the form in which it was, for the purpose of excluding from our fundamental compact, the last vestige of an odious, cruel and unjust condition for holding office, and exercising suffrage. If the colored man was worthy of being admitted to these privileges, it should be on a principle of perfect equality. He should be either excluded altogether from a participation in government, on account of his race; or admitted into full connexion for the sake of his humanity. The honorable and learned gentleman who occupied the floor yesterday, seemed determined to confuse rights with privileges, in discussing this question; and boldly claimed the elective franchise as a right.

In these views he could not concur. Rights were emanations from nature; born with him to whom they belonged, and alienable only for offences against society—and this under all forms of government. But on the contrary, privileges were acquired,—conventionally, or by grant of the governing power. When long possessed, they were sometimes denominated civil rights, but they never became naturalized. In considering a question of this kind, full of abstractions, it was, to say the least, disingenuous to endeavor to confound natural rights with civil franchises. It would not be disputed that civil rights or privileges were the constant subject of mutation, while natural rights were inalienable. Should it be conceded that the elective suffrage is not a franchise, but a natural right, to whom would it belong? and who would be entitled to its exercise? Not male citizens of natural age and diverse colors only. No, sir; natural rights recognized no more distinctions in age or sex, than in color or condition. Nor did they stop with our women and children: but fairly and honestly carried out, would extend the exercise to every human being who might happen to be on our soil on an election day, in the same manner in which they would be entitled to their personal liberty or the enjoyment of life. Gentlemen had made themselves merry in ridiculing the result to which their own arguments naturally conducted them; but declaim as they might against the results of their own reasoning, and ridicule as they must the extreme to which they were led by such perversion, if suffrage was a natural right, women and children were among your electors. . . .

To permit the Ethiopian race to become an important portion of the governing power of the state! To allow that race, the farthest removed from us in sympathy and relationship of all into which the human family was divided, to become a participant in governing, not themselves, but us! Nature revolted at the proposal.

We were informed by physiologists, that the human family was divided into five races, all of which had distinctive characteristics. Those two which had the fewest points of resemblance were the Caucasian and Ethiopian. Indeed in their purity, they were almost antipodes to each other, as well in habits and manners, as in complexion and physical organization. These variations were not made by man, nor by human government. It was the work of nature, and not without its object . . .

John Hunt, printer from New York City, continued the anti-black argument.

Mr. HUNT went into the subject of negro suffrage at some length. His doctrine, and that of his constituents, in relation to the right of suffrage, was briefly this. We (said he) want no masters, and least of all no negro masters, to reign over us. We contend for self-government. We hold that no man who is not a partizan of the republic's self—who is not a bona fide citizen, shall have any voice in the state. We also concede to all other persons, and all other nations, in their respective spheres, the same rights we claim for ourselves. The fact that all men had a right to form themselves, or rather are formed by the operation of circumstances and the law of necessity, into distinct nations or states—that every nation had the right of self-government without the interference of aliens or of other states, so long as it will take the trouble to exercise that right with any tolerable degree of wisdom and justice: we are entirely left out of sight by the advocates of negro suffrage. They forget that negroes were aliens—aliens, not by mere accident of foreign birth—not because they spoke a different language—not from any petty distinction that a few years association might obliterate, but by the broad distinction of race—a distinction that neither education, nor intercourse, nor time could remove—a distinction that must separate our children from their children for ever.

He regretted, as much as any one, that this class of irreclaimable aliens was fastened upon us. If any good could come of wishing, he could wish as heartily as any one, that the Ethiopian might change his skin, and become a part of our body politic. But all such wishes and all efforts to realize them, were idle. They might indicate a very good disposition, but they did not indicate a very good head. We might close our eyes in a fit of amiable enthusiasm, and try to dream their wool out of curl; but our dream did them no good. They knew and felt all the while, (that is, all the sane negroes,) that they were negroes and aliens by the act of God, and there was no remedy. The greatest injury that any man could inflict upon his fellow, was to place him in a false and unnatural position—to tempt him into a path which he could not travel, a sphere not his own; to seduce him into a war against his inevitable destiny, and thus destroy his powers of usefulness and his chances of happiness together. In his judgment, our negroes had thus been injured by their friends. They had been deluded with unreal hopes, and blinded to their true destiny, as he read it, far ignoble. For as they progressed in knowledge, their pride would incite them to return to the home of their race, where they could hold the position of superiors and teachers. They had gained much by the intercourse with civilized men. They were no longer idolators—no longer naked savages. They had made much progress in the arts and the learning of a superior race. They yet might—he believed they yet would—convey these arts and this learning to their uncivilized brethren. Such was the path he would point out to them—the destiny he would aid them to accomplish. As to the practical effect of negro suffrage in New York city, he predicted that it would be the exclusion of the race from Manhattan Island. Another consideration: The Jews were forbidden to yoke animals of different kinds together; and if it were wrong to unite the cow and the ass in the same yoke, would it be right to unite the Caucasian and the negro race in the same government? To conclude: The reason why his constituents refused to enter partnership with negroes in the business of government were, that they could perform all their political duties better without their help than with it. They did not wish to debase themselves by any hypocritical professions of fellowship.—They could not acknowledge as co-citizens a class of men more widely separated from them than any other race upon the globe, and who cannot be naturalized by any fiat of law or lapse of time.—We know (said he) that we put ourselves upon a par with negroes whenever we put negroes upon a par with us. We cannot enter into any political amalgamation with blacks. We will not meddle with their government in St. Domingo nor in Africa, and, if we can prevent it, they shall not meddle with ours.

Debate continued with several delegates rising up in opposition to Hunt's attack on black suffrage.

Elijah Rhoades, a merchant from Onondaga County, rose to denounce the property qualifications.

Mr. RHOADES said that he could but regret that a delegate from the great city of New York—the commercial emporium of this country—a city which professed to have a purer democracy than that in any other part of the world—should advocate in the deprivation of rights, simply on the ground of a difference in the complexion of the skin, or the curl of the hair. He also felt greatly disappointed when he heard the argument of the representative and mouth-piece of the committee (Mr. KENNEDY). Why, sir, so great is the democracy of the New-York progressives, that a negro is not even permitted to drive a cart there.[26] They are degraded to the lowest point of social and moral position there—as well as political. And yet one of the representatives of that city has based his argument on the statistics of crime committed by a class of men whom the democrats of that city have degraded so low.[27]

Debate continued for several days with a great deal of discussion focusing on immigrants and suffrage. Here was an important shift that would define the politics of suffrage in New York State for the remainder of the nineteenth century. Between 1850 and 1900, attempts to reform residency and literacy requirements shaped debates over democratic citizenship in the Empire State.

FRIDAY, OCTOBER 2

Bishop Perkins, a lawyer from Saint Lawrence County, attacked those who sought to remove the property qualification.

Mr. Perkins resumed his speech of yesterday on the extension of the right of suffrage to blacks. He ridiculed what he called the extreme apprehension in certain quarters lest a class of white voters, who were obliged often to change their residence, should commit frauds upon the ballot boxes, and might be bought or sold—and the great anxiety in the same quarter to let in a class of colored persons whose degradation and vices decreased their numbers annually, notwithstanding the large accession from other states.—It was the destiny of the black race ever to occupy an inferior social position to the white. It was the latent decree of the Almighty, and nothing could change it. Mr. P. laid it down as the economy of Providence that there should be separate races and grades of beings on the earth.—He asserted that the great offence which brought the flood on the earth was the intercourse between the sons of God and the daughters of men, the intercourse of one race with another that God had separated. When they commingled, he separated them again. A century after the dispersion at Babel profane history showed that this black history existed, with all the characteristics that now marked them. That climate should have done this was impossible. This mark was upon them as a warning that other nations should not commingle with them. Subsequently, when the Jews intermingled with other nations it was called whoredom, and was denounced by God.

You could not admit the blacks to a participation in the government of the country, unless you put them on terms of social equality with us—and that could only be done, by degrading our own race to a level with them. He adverted to Asia Minor, the garden of the world, and the three nations that were attempting to live there—the Jew, the Mahomedan, and the Christian—to the constant warfare going on between these nations, to the decrease in population which was the consequence. He adverted also to Mexico, where there were three races; with something like an equality of right, and yet nothing but a standing army could govern them. So in England, where there were distinct races, nothing but the bayonet kept the peace. He predicted that in the city of New York, negroes would never be permitted to come up to the ballot boxes, or if they did come, it would be only to be bought and sold like cattle in the market. Riots and violence would be the order of the day. Mr. P. closed by warning the Convention against adopting a provision which must disfranchise a large class of white voters—saying that they would hear from it at the polls of the election, as well as from the proposition to bring in the whole negro race at the polls.

By Friday, October 9, a growing number of delegates had come to support separate submission.

Colored Suffrage

The Convention next proceeded to the consideration of the report of the committee on revision submitting *separately* the proposition to extend the right of suffrage to colored citizens. . . .

Mr. Nicholas said this would unsettle the freehold suffrage of the colored people. The Convention had decided, by a strong vote, not to deprive them of this right, and that it should not be involved by this special submission of the question of equal suffrage. If the people decided in favor of equal suffrage, the present right would of course become a nullity, but should the special submission fail, he wished, and he believed that the Convention intended, that the present freehold suffrage should be continued in full force.

In the end, separate submission carried the day. The voters of New York State went on to defeat equal manhood suffrage by a vote of 224,336 to 85,406.

Source: William G. Bishop and William H. Attree, *Report of the Debates and Proceedings of the Convention for the Revision of the Constitution of the State of New York, 1846* (Albany, 1846).

R. Land Reform Proposal, 1846

Even as the voters of New York State were preparing to vote to maintain the property qualification, local abolitionists committed themselves to an unceasing campaign for equal citizenship. The work of the white abolitionist Gerrit Smith is particularly illuminating.[28]

Born in 1797 in Utica, Smith was a leading land owner in the village of Peterboro. His devotion to the antislavery cause intensified in the 1830s and 1840s, as he worked with the American Anti-Slavery Society. He was willing to use his own wealth to purchase the freedom of many enslaved blacks; in turn, he helped resettle these freedpeople in and around Peterboro. In the 1850s, Smith went on to serve a term in Congress before returning to upstate New York and aiding John Brown in the late 1850s as a member of the Secret Six.[29] In the mid-1840s, Smith's growing disenchantment with the course of national and state politics led him to conceive of a grand plan to circumvent the property qualification for African American would-be voters. Smith proposed to distribute over one hundred thousand acres of land in northern New York to the state's black citizens. Among many other goals, Smith aimed to enfranchise thousands of black men.

The following document is Smith's initial letter proposing his land-reform/suffrage-reform plan to prominent black activists in southern New York. James McCune Smith was a major African American writer, social critic, and physician; Charles Ray and Theodore Wright were both ministers. Dated August 1, the letter was sent on the anniversary of West Indian emancipation, a day celebrated by Northern abolitionists throughout the antebellum era. At no time did thousands—or even hundreds—of black settlers arrive to take Smith up on his offer. Smith grew frustrated by the early 1850s. However, the proposal did lead to the creation of the community of North Elba, New York, a black settlement that was the abolitionist firebrand John Brown's official residence from 1854 on.

In this letter, how did Gerrit Smith explain his plan of land redistribution? What special meanings did land ownership hold for Smith? How did he imagine his black audience and his intended beneficiaries?

* * *

Gerrit Smith to Rev. Theodore S. Wright, Rev. Charles B. Ray, and Dr. J. McCune Smith, August 1, 1846

Dear Friends,—For years, I have indulged the thought that, when I had sold enough land to pay my debts, I would give away the remainder to the poor.

I am an Agrarian. I would that every man who desires a farm, might have one; and I would, that no man were so regardless of the needs and desires of his brother men, as to covet the possession of more farms than one. Do not understand that I sympathize with lawless, violent and bloody Agrarianism.[30] "My soul, come not into their secret; unto their assembly mine honor, be not thou united."[31]

I have, with the Divine blessing, been able to make sales of land the present year, so extensive, as to inspire me with confidence, that my debts, very great as their sum still is, will be paid, in a few years. It is true, that, to make this event more certain, I must sell more land. Nevertheless, I feel it safe to make a beginning *now*, in the work of distributing land. I have, indeed, heretofore given tracts of land to public institutions, and a few small parcels to individuals: but I have now to enter upon the greater and better work of making large donations of land to the poor.

I will, at the present time give away but a part of the land, which I intend to give away. It will, perhaps, be better not to give away the remainder, until my debts are wholly paid. This land was accumulated principally by my father, the late Peter Smith.

I hope to be able to make, in all, some three thousand deeds—most of them now, and the remainder within two or three years. The deeds will generally convey from forty to sixty acres of land each.

To whom among the poor I shall make these deeds is a question I did not solve hastily. I needed no time to conclude, that, inasmuch as my home and the land are both in this State, it would be very suitable to select my beneficiaries from among the people of this State. But, for a long time, I was at a loss to decide, whether to take my beneficiaries from the meritorious poor generally, or from the meritorious colored poor only.

I could not put a bounty on color. I shrank from the least appearance of doing so: and if I know my heart, it was equally compassionate toward such white and black men as are equal sufferers. In the end, however, I concluded to confine my gifts to colored people. I had not come to this conclusion had the land I have to give away been several times as much as it is. I had not come to it, were not the colored people the poorest of the poor, and the most deeply wronged class of our citizens. That they are so, is evident, if only from the fact, that the cruel, killing, Heaven-defying prejudice of which they are the victims, has closed against them the avenues to riches and respectability—to happiness and usefulness. That they are so, is also evident from the fact, that, whilst white men in this State, however destitute of property, are allowed to vote for Civil Rulers, every colored man in it, who does not own landed estate to the value of two hundred and fifty dollars, is excluded from the exercise of this natural and indispensably protective right. I confess, that this mean and wicked exclusion has had no little effect in producing my preference, in this case. I confess, too, that I was influenced by the consideration, that there is great encouragement to improve the condition of our free colored brethren, because that every improvement in it contributes to loosen the bands of the enslaved portion of their outraged and afflicted race.

And, now, will you permit me to tax you with no little labor—the labor of making out a list of the colored men in certain counties, who shall receive a deed of land from me? My only restrictions upon you in making out this list, is,

1st. That upon it there be the name of no person younger than twenty-one and no person older than sixty.

2d. That there be upon it the name of no person who is in easy circumstance as to property; and no person, who is already the owner of land.

3d. That there be upon it the name of no drunkard—and I had almost added of no person who drinks intoxicating liquor—since to drink it, though ever so moderately, is to be in the way to drunkenness.

4th. That the total number of names in the list be one thousand nine hundred and eighty-five; that

127 thereof be the names of the persons residing in the county of

						Suffolk.
215	"	"	"	"	"	Queens.
197	"	"	"	"	"	Kings.
861	"	"	"	"	"	New York.
32	"	"	"	"	"	Richmond.
31	"	"	"	"	"	Rockland.
115	"	"	"	"	"	Westchester.
150	"	"	"	"	"	Dutchess.
5	"	"	"	"	"	Sullivan.
106	"	"	"	"	"	Ulster.
136	"	"	"	"	"	Orange.
10	"	"	"	"	"	Putnam.

I take the liberty to suggest, that the true course, in the case of each of the aforesaid counties, will be to have the names of the persons who are qualified to share in my lands, or rather to share in the chance of getting them, written on slips of paper—these slips put in a vessel—and as many drawn therefrom as there are persons in the county to receive deeds.

Could I receive this list by the first day of the next month (and I most earnestly hope that I can), I should be able to put a considerable share of the deeds into your hands by the first day of the following month; and, in that case, the grantees might be put in possession of them by the middle of October. It may be a year or more, ere I can supply all with deeds—and it is possible that some may be finally unsupplied. A part of the names— that is, an incomplete list, you might be able to send me in a week or two.

Do not fail to have the names and places of residence written very legibly. Should it be so, that, from the death of some of the grantees, or from other cause or causes, you cannot deliver all the deeds, you will, in that case, promptly return me such as are undelivered, and recommend other persons as worthy of the land described in them. The deeds will come to the grantees clear of all fees for drawing them, and taking the acknowledgement of their execution.

For all this service which I ask at your hands, I can make you no other compensation than that of thanking you for helping me promote a scheme of justice and benevolence.

There is still a balance of purchase money and interest due to the State of New York, on a large proportion of the parcels of land. The aggregate is a very large sum. But I propose to begin paying it within six months, and I hope to have it all paid within two years.

There is also a great amount of taxes due on them—for which they will be sold next year, or the year after, if not previously paid. I will pay the taxes so far as to prevent such sale—and this will be in full of all taxes up to 1844 or 1845 exclusive. I should be grieved, and have abundant reason to be, should any of the grantees suffer their parcels of land to be sold for the non-payment of taxes.

Among the parcels which I give away, will doubtless be found some that are unfit for cultivation. Most of these, however, will be more or less valuable for timber. I hope that the grantees will prize their lands sufficiently to guard them against trespassers.

I have a few large tracts of land, which, because they are either very remote from settlements, or very mountainous and sterile, I prefer selling for what they will bring, to giving them away to those who need lands for agriculture.

I write to gentlemen in other parts of the State, asking of them service in respect to other counties similar to those which I ask of you.

Very respectfully,

Your Friend

Gerrit Smith

Source: Octavius Brooks Frothingham, *Gerrit Smith: A Biography* (New York, 1878), 102–105.

S. Declaration of Sentiments, Seneca Falls, 1848

The year 1848 witnessed a series of momentous political events around the world that threatened to alter dramatically the balance of power between nations and among citizens. In Europe, revolutionary movements launched a series of ill-fated insurrections to overturn conservative hegemony. At Guadalupe Hidalgo, American and Mexican envoys agreed on a treaty that ended the war between the two nations and dramatically increased the size of the United States. Overnight, the nation gained over five hundred thousand square miles of formerly Mexican territory. And in upstate New York, in the village of Seneca Falls, over two hundred women and men met on July 19 and 20 at the first women's rights convention in American history.

Home to Elizabeth Cady Stanton, one of the organizers of the convention, Seneca Falls was one of several New York communities that were particularly affected by the reform movements of the antebellum era. Those who attended the July convention had traveled various paths in the preceding years and decades. Many had been swept up in the optimistic evangelical religiosity of the Second Great Awakening. Their new middle-class Christianity led some to advocate not only an equality of souls but also political equality between the sexes. Another vital influence for many at Seneca Falls in 1848 was the abolitionist movement, particularly the radical circles associated with the American Anti-Slavery Society. Women abolitionists had made bold new claims on the public arena in the 1840s, even as some of their male colleagues sought to silence female activists.

One hundred women and men signed on to the Declaration of Sentiments. Stanton and her co-organizer, Lucretia Mott, imagined various audiences for their founding statement. Certainly they sought to reach out to national and international public opinion; copies were sent out to other cities in North America and Western Europe. The Seneca Falls leadership also grasped the local dimensions of their movement and worked to build on their success across upstate New York. The Rochester Woman's Rights Convention gathered one month later.

Why did the authors of the Declaration of Sentiments make such explicit use of the 1776 Declaration of Independence? How did suffrage fit into the comprehensive set of resolutions offered at Seneca Falls? In what ways did Stanton and her colleagues borrow from some of the arguments made by black activists in the quarter century since 1821?

*   *   *

Declaration of Sentiments and Resolutions

When, in the course of human events, it becomes necessary for one portion of the family of man to assume among the people of the earth a position different from that which they have hitherto occupied, but one to which the laws of nature and of nature's God entitle them, a decent respect to the opinions of mankind requires that they should declare the causes that impel them to such a course.

We hold these truths to be self-evident: that all men and women are created equal; that they are endowed by their Creator with certain inalienable rights; that among these are life, liberty, and the pursuit of happiness; that to secure these rights governments are instituted, deriving their just powers from the consent of the governed. Whenever any form of government becomes destructive of these ends, it is the right of those who suffer from it to refuse allegiance to it, and to insist upon the institution of a new government, laying its foundation on such principles, and organizing its powers in such form, as to them shall seem most likely to effect their safety and happiness. Prudence, indeed, will dictate that governments long established should not be changed for light and transient causes; and, accordingly, all experience has shown that mankind are more disposed to suffer, while evils are sufferable, than to right themselves by abolishing the forms to which they were accustomed. But when a long train of abuses and usurpations, pursuing invariably the same object, evinces a design to reduce them under absolute despotism, it is their duty to throw off such government and to provide new guards for their future security. Such has been the patient sufferance of the women under this government, and such is now the necessity which constrains them to demand the equal station to which they are entitled.

The history of mankind is a history of repeated injuries and usurpations on the part of man toward woman, having in direct object the establishment of an absolute tyranny over her. To prove this, let facts be submitted to a candid world.

He has never permitted her to exercise her inalienable right to the elective franchise.

He has compelled her to submit to laws, in the formation of which she had no voice.

He has withheld from her rights which are given to the most ignorant and degraded men—both natives and foreigners.

Having deprived her of this first right of a citizen, the elective franchise, thereby leaving her without representation in the halls of legislation, he has oppressed her on all sides.

He has made her, if married, in the eye of the law, civilly dead.

He has taken from her all right in property, even to the wages she earns.

He has made her, morally, an irresponsible being, as she can commit many crimes with impunity, provided they be done in the presence of her husband. In the covenant of marriage, she is compelled to promise obedience to her husband, he becoming, to all intents and purposes, her master—the law giving him power to deprive her of her liberty and to administer chastisement.

He has so framed the laws of divorce, as to what shall be the proper causes and, in case of separation, to whom the guardianship of the children shall be given, as to be wholly regardless of the happiness of the women—the law, in all cases, going upon a false supposition of the supremacy of man and giving all power into his hands.

After depriving her of all rights as a married woman, if single and the owner of property, he has taxed her to support a government which recognizes her only when her property can be made profitable to it.

He has monopolized nearly all the profitable employments, and from those she is permitted to follow, she receives but a scanty remuneration. He closes against her all the avenues to wealth and distinction which he considers most honorable to himself. As a teacher of theology, medicine, or law, she is not known.

He has denied her the facilities for obtaining a thorough education, all colleges being closed against her.

He allows her in church, as well as state, but a subordinate position, claiming apostolic authority for her exclusion from the ministry, and, with some exceptions, from any public participation in the affairs of the church.

He has created a false public sentiment by giving to the world a different code of morals for men and women, by which moral delinquencies which exclude women from society are not only tolerated but deemed of little account in man.

He has usurped the prerogative of Jehovah himself, claiming it as his right to assign for her a sphere of action, when that belongs to her conscience and to her God.

He has endeavored, in every way that he could, to destroy her confidence in her own powers, to lessen her self-respect, and to make her willing to lead a dependent and abject life.

Now, in view of this entire disfranchisement of one-half the people of this country, their social and religious degradation, in view of the unjust laws above mentioned, and because women do feel themselves aggrieved, oppressed, and fraudulently deprived of their most sacred rights, we insist that they have immediate admission to all the rights and privileges which belong to them as citizens of the United States.

In entering upon the great work before us, we anticipate no small amount of misconception, misrepresentation, and ridicule; but we shall use every instrumentality within our power to effect our object. We shall employ agents, circulate tracts, petition the state and national legislatures, and endeavor to enlist the pulpit and the press in our behalf. We hope this Convention will be followed by a series of conventions embracing every part of the country.

Whereas, the great precept of nature is conceded to be that "man shall pursue his own true and substantial happiness." Blackstone in his Commentaries remarks that this law of nature, being coeval with mankind and dictated by God himself, is, of course, superior in obligation to any other. It is binding over all the globe, in all countries and at all times; no human laws are of any validity if contrary to this, and such of them as are valid derive all their force, and all their validity, and all their authority, mediately and immediately, from this original; therefore,

Resolved, That such laws as conflict, in any way, with the true and substantial happiness of woman, are contrary to the great precept of nature and of no validity, for this is "superior in obligation to any other."

Resolved, That all laws which prevent woman from occupying such a station in society as her conscience shall dictate, or which place her in a position inferior to that of man, are contrary to the great precept of nature and therefore of no force or authority.

Resolved, That woman is man's equal, was intended to be so by the Creator, and the highest good of the race demands that she should be recognized as such.

Resolved, That the women of this country ought to be enlightened in regard to the laws under which they live, that they may no longer publish their degradation by declaring themselves satisfied with their present position, nor their ignorance, by asserting that they have all the rights they want.

Resolved, That inasmuch as man, while claiming for himself intellectual superiority, does accord to woman moral superiority, it is preeminently his duty to encourage her to speak and teach, as she has an opportunity, in all religious assemblies.

Resolved, That the same amount of virtue, delicacy, and refinement of behavior that is required of woman in the social state also be required of man, and the same transgressions should be visited with equal severity on both man and woman.

Resolved, That the objection of indelicacy and impropriety, which is so often brought against woman when she addresses a public audience, comes with a very ill grace from those who encourage, by their attendance, her appearance on the stage, in the concert, or in feats of the circus.

Resolved, That woman has too long rested satisfied in the circumscribed limits which corrupt customs and a perverted application of the Scriptures have marked out for her, and that it is time she should move in the enlarged sphere which her great Creator has assigned her.

Resolved, That it is the duty of the women of this country to secure to themselves their sacred right to the elective franchise.

Resolved, That the equality of human rights results necessarily from the fact of the identity of the race in capabilities and responsibilities.

Resolved, That the speedy success of our cause depends upon the zealous and untiring efforts of both men and women for the overthrow of the

monopoly of the pulpit, and for the securing to woman an equal participation with men in the various trades, professions, and commerce.

Resolved, therefore, That, being invested by the Creator with the same
capabilities and same consciousness of responsibility for their exercise, it
is demonstrably the right and duty of woman, equally with man, to promote every righteous cause by every righteous means; and especially in regard to the great subjects of morals and religion, it is self-evidently her
right to participate with her brother in teaching them, both in private and
in public, by writing and by speaking, by any instrumentalities proper to
be used, and in any assemblies proper to be held; and this being a self-evident truth growing out of the divinely implanted principles of human nature, any custom or authority adverse to it, whether modern or wearing
the hoary sanction of antiquity, is to be regarded as a self-evident false-
hood, and at war with mankind.

Source: Elizabeth Cady Stanton, Susan B. Anthony, and Matilda Joslyn Gage,
eds., *History of Women's Suffrage,* vol. 1 (New York, 1887), 70.

T. Anti–Property Qualification Pamphlet, 1860

In the late 1850s, as the Republican Party emerged in New York and nationally, the political culture of the Empire State was significantly altered. Opposition to the extension of slavery lay at the heart of early Republican ideology across the nation. In New York, the new party's leaders viewed the issue of equal manhood suffrage as both a possible source of partisan strength and a potential trap. Republicans in the legislature worked to hold a statewide referendum on the property qualification; for several years, their efforts failed due to internal party divisions and Democratic opposition. The referendum act finally passed the legislature in early 1860, clearing the way for a statewide campaign over race and suffrage, even as the nation was descending into civil war.

In 1860, Democratic politicians were explicit in their denunciations of those who would grant black men the right to vote. Party leaders appealed for support by playing to fears of miscegenation and economic competition. In the campaign to maintain the property qualification, the first hints of the new white supremacist politics of the postbellum era were visible. Many Republican politicians remained wary of publicly embracing the fight against the property qualification. Some Republicans, in fact, campaigned by emphasizing their abhorrence of racial equality. In a campaign season where candidates from Abraham Lincoln on down had to distance themselves from the label "Black Republican," the fight for equal suffrage was often abandoned.

It fell to black writers, ministers, and activists to organize and lead the fight against the property qualification. Statewide and local conventions were held. William C. Nell, the black abolitionist and author of *Colored*

New York State Campaign Pamphlet for 1860.

PROPERTY QUALIFICATION

OR

NO PROPERTY QUALIFICATION:

A FEW FACTS

FROM THE RECORD OF PATRIOTIC SERVICES OF THE COLORED MEN OF NEW YORK,

DURING THE WARS OF 1776 AND 1812,

WITH A COMPENDIUM OF THEIR PRESENT BUSINESS, AND PROPERTY STATISTICS.

COMPILED BY

WILLIAM C. NELL,

AUTHOR OF "COLORED PATRIOTS OF THE AMERICAN REVOLUTION."

NEW YORK:

FOR SALE BY THOMAS HAMILTON, 48 BEEKMAN STREET,

AND WM. H. LEONARD, 5 BEEKMAN STREET.

1860.

Figure 9 Cover page of William C. Nell's *Property Qualification or No Property Qualification.*

[Cover page of William C. Nell, *Property Qualification or No Property Qualification* (New York, 1860).] *Reprinted by permission of the Houghton Library, Harvard University.*

Patriots of the American Revolution, composed one of the campaign's most significant pamphlets. *Property Qualification or No Property Qualification* advanced a wide range of arguments and marshaled various types of evidence to argue for the belated removal of the 1821 property qualification. As in his earlier works, Nell emphasized the heroic actions of various black veterans of the Revolutionary War and the War of 1812. He also cited a range of black and white New Yorkers who, in the 1850s, had struggled to sustain the black freedom struggle, even after the defeat of 1846 and the consequences of the compromise of 1850.

In November 1860, New Yorkers again rejected equal manhood suffrage, by a vote of 345,791 (63.6 percent) to 197,889. Though constituting a slightly smaller majority than in 1846, the electorate that voted to maintain the property qualification gave 54 percent of their votes to Abraham Lincoln for president.[32]

Why did Nell make use of such an array of arguments and sources? How did the terms of debate shifted in the four decades since 1821?

*   *   *

Property Qualification or No Property Qualification

The Property Qualification

At the Free Suffrage Convention held in New York city, May 17th, 1860, Wm. J. Watkins,[33] Chairman of the Committee on Resolutions, reported the following, which were adopted.:—

Resolved, That the colored people of the State of New York, in laboring for the abolition of the property qualification imposed upon us in the Constitution as a requisite for the exercise of the elective franchise, base our claim upon the principle of human freedom and equality set forth in the Declaration of Independence—that instrument of which Americans are justly proud.

Resolved, That, as descendants of the Revolutionary dead, as citizens of this State, as citizens of the United States, we appeal to every voter in the Empire State to give to the world a practical recognition of the principle upon which this government professes to be based, by voting at the November election to strike out from the State Constitution that unjust, anti-Christian and anti-Republican qualification clause which now disgraces it.

It is believed that the debate in the Convention of 1821, on the military services of colored men, had a powerful influence in securing to them the right of suffrage, but it must also be recorded, that colored citizens of the Empire State were ungenerously subjected to a property qualification of two hundred and fifty dollars. An opportunity is now presented to every voter to assist in removing this unjust restriction, by depositing his ballot in favor of "No Property Qualification."

Nell proceeded to spend several pages recounting the "Military Services of Colored Men of New York." He quoted at length from Dr. Robert Clarke's remarks at the 1821 convention before turning to the heroic deeds of Jack Peterson and Moses Sherwood in the Revolutionary War and the War of 1812, respectively.

Nell next pointed to the patriotic service of Peter Williams and his son, the Reverend Peter Williams. Here, he reprinted an 1835 oration by the younger Williams in New York City.

"We are NATIVES of this country; we ask only to be treated as well as FOREIGNERS. Not a few of our fathers suffered and bled to purchase its independence; we ask only to be treated as well as those who fought against it. We have toiled to cultivate it, and to raise it to its present prosperous condition; we ask only to share equal privileges with those who come from distant lands to enjoy the fruits of our labor."

Nell continued with brief biographical sketches of other African American military heroes. After citing an 1840 speech from the Reverend Henry Highland Garnet,[34] Nell reprinted portions of several recent talks by William J. Watkins.

"Is color a constitutional disqualification? If so, there are a great many so called *white* men, who are not citizens, for we know not a few who would be taken for colored men, if complexion were the standard."

"Now, it is an historic fact, that black men, in some instances, whole companies of these sable warriors, during the struggle for independence, fought side by side with their paler brethren. From the inception to the close, they fought bravely. This no one will attempt to deny, who knows any thing about the history of the Revolution. Now, if those who *vi et armis*,[35] defended the country, were recognized as citizens, and if black men, in common with white men, were its defenders, what does the Chief Justice mean by shamelessly insisting that colored men of that day were not so recognized? O the spotless purity of the Federal Judiciary!"[36]

"I hold that the enforcement of the property qualification against the black man, who has been guilty of no offence against the laws, and of whose fidelity and patriotism there can be no doubt, is unjust, unmagnanimous and unconstitutional. Native-born Americans should not be excluded from the right of suffrage because they have no property qualification, when foreign-born citizens are allowed to vote without any such qualification.

["]If men are black, still they are men. They have the same hopes, the same desires, the same passions, the same sympathies, the same fears that belong to their white brethren, who assume such superiority over them. Then why crush them under the iron heel of despotism, and make them a standing monument of your cruelty and inhumanity? Why not be just and righteous, lift them up from the dust, and welcome them to a position on a common platform with others of the race?"

Nell moved on to introduce excerpts of other notable recent speeches in New York State. The pamphlet concluded with this extended discussion of property holding among African Americans in New York.

Business and Property Relations of the Colored Citizens of New York

The following statistical sketch is condensed from various reports of Dr. J. M'Cune Smith[37] and others:—

Throughout the State of New York, colored men are occupied or employed as farmers, blacksmiths, engineers, inventors, carpenters, machinists, cabinet makers, engravers, masons, type founders, brass founders, merchant tailors, hair dressers, hatters, painters, coopers, tinsmiths, printers, shoemakers, silver platers, jewellers, musicians, watch makers, chemists, grocers, drug store keepers, professors, clergymen, editors, teachers, physicians, stock and land brokers, stone cutters, ship builders, lumber dealers, sail makers, wheelwrights, traders, &c., &c.

The cities of New York, Brooklyn, and Williamsburgh contain more than a third of the entire colored population of the State. A hurried investigation, in which many instances have been overlooked, and all the estimates rendered low, show that colored persons have invested in business, carried on by themselves—

In New York City,	$755,000
In the City of Brooklyn,	$76,200
In the City of Williamsburg,	$4,900
TOTAL	$836,100

As to the condition of the masses of our population in these cities, we adduce the respectable authority of the *New York Tribune* for the statement, that colored beggars are extremely scarce in New York, except such as come from "the South, asking for money wherewith to buy their own muscles, blood and bones."

The Colored Home and Orphan Asylum contained all the colored poor, dependent on public support, with a very few exceptions. In New York City, the colored population to the white, fairly estimated, is as one to 25; hence the colored population of that city are 27 per cent less burdensome than is the white population to the poor fund. And this happy state of things has arisen, in part, from the fact that the former class have mutual benefit societies, with a cash capital of $30,000 dollars, from which they take care of their sick and bury their dead.

Citing an October 1859 speech by the Reverend Henry Ward Beecher, Nell asserted that African Americans in Manhattan and Brooklyn owned property valued at "5 millions of dollars."

And are not these patriotic, industrious, provident, exemplary citizens deserving equal rights at the ballot box?

Years ago, (says Dr. J. M'Cune Smith,) when abroad, the only circumstance which could create a feeling of shame for our State, in my mind, was the charge, that in 1777, when it was perilous to life to be a citizen of New York, she made colored men citizens, and that afterwards, in 1821, when it was safe and honorable to be a citizen, she disfranchised her colored citizens. Let me entreat you, remove this reproach from the fair fame of our noble State!

Gratitude is one of the virtues which the veriest hater of the colored man has never denied him; and this sentiment will never be called into

Figure 10 Parade of African American Troops
Less than a year after the Draft Riots targeted New York City's black community, the African American Twentieth Infantry paraded in front of Manhattan's Union League Club on March 5, 1864. [From *Frank Leslie's Illustrated Newspaper*, March 26, 1864.] *Reprinted by permission of the President and Fellows of Harvard College.*

such full exercise, as when the last shackle, the last emblem of degradation, shall be removed from the man of color!

> Oh yield him back his privilege! No sea
> Swells like the bosom of a man set free![38]

Source: William C. Nell, *Property Qualification or No Property Qualification: A Few Facts from the Record of Patriotic Services of the Colored Men of New York during the Wars of 1776 and 1812, with a Compendium of Their Present Business and Property Statistics* (New York, 1860).

U. Report on Suffrage, New York State Constitutional Convention, 1867–1868

Though the Civil War ended in April 1865, the rest of the nation was about to discover what New Yorkers had known for a half-century: namely, the end of slavery in no way guaranteed freedpeople the full rights of citizenship. As Reconstruction became a national project, Americans embarked on a searching examination of their most cherished public values. Northern states held a number of constitutional conventions in the immediate aftermath of the war. New York's was one of the most influential.

Even before Appomattox, black New Yorkers had been calling for a state convention. In 1865 and 1866, Dr. William H. Johnson of Albany led a statewide drive to drum up support for holding a convention. The State Central Committee of Colored Citizens focused almost exclusively on the need for constitutional revision in the first two years after the Civil War. With the 1866 reelection of Republican governor Reuben Fenton, the path was cleared for a constitutional convention that would meet in the summer of 1867.

Quickly, the 1867–1868 convention returned to the debates of 1821; the Committee on the Right of Suffrage, under Chairman Horace Greeley's command, was by far the most controversial body in Albany. Greeley's committee received a flood of petitions from all over the Empire State, demanding black suffrage, women's suffrage, and numerous other reforms. Greeley made it clear from the outset that he was an advocate of "impartial suffrage," meaning the removal of the 1821 property qualification. While the committee's Republican majority quickly moved to abolish the racially discriminatory suffrage provisions in the state constitution, the Democratic minority succeeded in dragging out debate into the next year.

In the meantime, the state Republican Party was routed in the November elections around the state. New York's Democrats had managed to turn the debate over black political rights into a question of "negro supremacy" in the popular press and on the convention's floor. By early 1868, a demoralized Republican Party agreed to the Democrat insistence on separate submission. The new constitution would be put to a statewide referendum in November 1869, but the revised suffrage provisions would be voted on separately. Most delegates recognized that this spelled doom for "impartial suffrage" in New York.

How did the Greeley Report address the issue of equal manhood suffrage? In what ways had the debate changed from 1821 and 1846? (See documents L and Q.) How did Greeley's committee define the right of suffrage? How can we account for the committee's unprecedented concern for registration of voters?

*   *   *

Greeley Committee Report, June 28, 1867

Report of the Committee on the Right of Suffrage and Qualifications to Hold Office

Mr. Greeley, from the above standing committee, reports as follows:

Your committee, having given careful attention to the subject referred to them, have prepared as a substitute for Article II, of the present constitution, the following:

ARTICLE—.

SEC. 1. Every man of the age of twenty-one years who shall have been an inhabitant of this State for one year next preceding an election, and for the last thirty days a citizen of the United States, and a resident of the election district where he may offer his vote, shall be entitled to vote at such election, in said district, and not elsewhere, for all officers elected by the people.

Provided, That idiots, lunatics, persons under guardianship, felons and persons convicted of bribery, unless pardoned or otherwise restored to civil rights, shall not be entitled to vote. No person who shall at any time within thirty days next preceding, have been a public pauper, shall vote at any election. No person who shall receive, expect to receive, pay, or offer to pay any money or other valuable thing to influence or reward a vote to be given at an election, shall vote at such an election; and, upon challenge for such cause, the person so challenged shall, before the inspectors receive his vote, swear or affirm before such inspectors that he has not received, does not expect to receive, has not paid nor offered to pay, any money or other valuable thing to influence or reward a vote to be given at such election. Laws may be passed excluding from voting at an election every person who shall have made, or who shall be interested in, a bet or wager depending upon the result thereof.

SEC. 2. For the purpose of voting, no person shall be deemed to have gained or lost a residence by reason of his presence or absence while employed in the service of the United States, nor while engaged in the navigation of the waters of this State, of the United States, or of the high seas, nor while kept in any almshouse or other asylum, at the public expense, nor while confined in any public prison. And the Legislature shall prescribe the manner in which electors absent from their homes in time of war, in the actual military or naval service of the State, or of the United States, may vote, and shall provide for the canvass and return of their votes.

SEC. 3. Laws shall be made for ascertaining by proper proofs the citizens who shall be entitled to the right of suffrage hereby established. And the Legislature shall provide that a register of all citizens entitled to the right of suffrage in each election district shall be made and completed at least six days before any election; and no person shall vote at such election who shall not have been registered according to law; but such laws shall be uniform in their requirements throughout the State.

SEC. 4. All elections by the citizens shall be by ballot, except for such town officers as may by law be directed to be otherwise chosen.

SEC. 5. No person who is not, at the time of taking the oath of office, an elector, shall hold any office under this Constitution. All officers shall, before they enter on the duties of their respective offices, take and subscribe the following oath or affirmation:

"I do solemnly swear (or affirm) that I will support the Constitution of the United States, and the Constitution of the State of New York; and that I will faithfully discharge the duties of (the office he is to hold) according to the best of my ability."

It will be seen that the existing article has been retained by us in substance, and that the qualifications of a legal voter proposed by us be:

1. Adult rational manhood.
2. Citizenship of the United States of not less than thirty days' standing.
3. Residence in the State for the year preceding.
4. Residence in the election district for the last thirty days.
5. Freedom from crime.
6. Exemption from dependence on others, through pauperism or guardianship.

The material changes we recommend are these:

1st. Strike out all discriminations based on color. Slavery, the vital source and only plausible ground of such invidious discrimination, being dead, not only in this State, but throughout the Union, as it is soon to be, we trust, throughout this hemisphere, we can imagine no tolerable excuse for perpetuating the existing proscription. Whites and blacks are required to render like obedience to our laws, and are punished in like measure for their violation. Whites and blacks were indiscriminately drafted and held to service to fill our State's quotas in the war whereby the Republic was saved from disruption. We trust that we are henceforth to deal with men according to their conduct, without regard to their color. If so, the fact should be embodied in the Constitution.

We ask you to abolish the present requirement of four months' residence in a county as a pre-requisite to voting. This exaction bears hardly on such residents of cities as spend their summer mainly in the country, and cannot afford to maintain a double residence. Thousands of intelligent and patriotic young mechanics, employed as carpenters, bricklayers, painters, plumbers, gas-fitters, &c., by masters located in our great cities, are sent out to work in neighboring counties for periods over which they have no control, and in November find their right to vote anywhere questionable, if not invalid. Hundreds of Methodist and other clergymen who are assigned to new charges in summer, find themselves disfranchised when our State election comes around. Under circumstances which impel doubt as to the right of a citizen to vote, the conscientious refrain, while the unscrupulous insist. We hold it wise to abolish a requirement which debars thousands of capable and worthy citizens, while it is a constant incitement to distortion or suppression of truth, to dissimulation and perjury.

At present, a resident in any county for four months is allowed to vote at the poll of any district wherein he actually resides on the day of election, though he may be a total stranger in that district, and does not pretend to have resided in it two days, only he must vote to fill an office he could not have voted to fill before his change of residence. But how are inspectors to know the contents of his folded ballot? And how are frauds to be prevented in districts where the preponderance of one party is overwhelming? It seems advisable to your committee to require an absolute residence by the voter of thirty days in the district where he tenders his ballot. This will give time for proper scrutiny, and will, when accompanied by an efficient registry, afford a substantial barrier against fraud. And the cases must be few indeed where the requirement of a thirty days' residence before voting will work individual hardship or affect the result of an important election.

Our present Constitution requires that naturalization shall precede voting by at least ten days; a memorial referred to us asks that this interval be extended to sixty days. We have fixed on thirty days as the proper time. We would stop the hunting out and dragging up before courts of indifferent and often reluctant immigrants in order to crowd them into citizenship, in order to affect by their votes the result of a pending election. This is the object of the present requirement of ten days' interval, and it will be far more completely accomplished by extending the prescribed term to thirty days. It is well, moreover, that the terms of citizenship and residence in the election district should be identical, so as to avoid complexity and possible misapprehension. Should we extend the interval between naturalization and voting to sixty days, the change would be inveighed against as impelled by a spirit of hostility to adopted citizens, or by a desire to impede naturalization. We trust the Convention will assent to our proposition.

As to disfranchisement of criminals and law-breakers, what we propose is very nearly identical with what is now prescribed, partly by the Constitution, partly by statute. It has seemed to us advisable to make the qualifications of voters as specific and unambiguous as possible, and to fix them, so far as may be, in the Constitution.

We propose that public paupers shall not be voters. We hold that to allow the inmates of almshouses, subsisting upon the charity of the public, to vote, is to accord an excessive influence and power over the results of our elections to the keepers of those establishments, whose retention in office is often at stake, each of whom can appeal with effect to his boarders not to vote him out of house and home. The end is now awkwardly contemplated in the provision that no pauper shall gain or lose a residence by virtue of his stay in an almshouse; but it is evaded by sending the paupers, under watchful keepers, just prior to an important election, to the towns or wards whence they came, there to be registered and vote, when they are welcomed back to their old haunts as patriots who have been absent in their country's and their keeper's service. Specific disfranchisement will add to the wholesome horror of pauperism now cherished by most Americans, and there seems to be no good reason for allowing paupers to govern by their votes the policy of our country and State, and at the same time enabling them to supersede a keeper who may have been so cruel as to require the able-bodied among them to work. At all events, let this matter be dealt with frankly.

Having thus briefly set forth the considerations which seem to us decisive in favor of the few and moderate changes proposed above, we proceed to indicate our controlling reasons for declining to recommend other and, in some respects, more important innovations.

Your committee does not recommend an extension of the elective franchise to women. However defensible in theory, we are satisfied that public sentiment does not demand, and would not sustain, an innovation so revolutionary and sweeping, so openly at war with a distribution of duties and functions between the sexes as venerable and pervading as government itself, and involving transformations so radical in society and domestic life. Should we prove to be in error on this head, the Convention may overrule us by changing a few words in the first section of the proposed article.

Nor have we seen fit to propose the enfranchisement of boys above the age of eighteen years. The current of ideas and usages in our day, but especially in this country, seems already to set quite too strongly in favor of the relaxation, if not total overthrow of parental authority, especially over half grown boys. With the sincerest good-will for the class in question, we submit that they spend the hours which they can spare from their labors and their lessons more usefully and profitably in mastering the wisdom of the sages and philosophers who have elucidated the science of government, than in attendance on midnight caucuses or in wrangling around the polls.

The proposition that a tax should be assessed on and collected from voters, is commended, like some others by plausible analogies. The rightful and intimate connection between taxation and representation was a potent watchword of our Revolutionary fathers; yet we cannot ignore the fact that the Constitution of 1821 having, like its predecessors, embodied this principle, an amendment striking out this qualification, and thus establishing manhood suffrage, was adopted by the Legislature of 1825, and ratified by an overwhelming popular vote in 1826; yeas, 127,077, nays, 3,215. We do not feel called upon to appeal from their judgment.

Nor have we chosen to adopt any of the schemes of disfranchising illiterate persons which have been referred to us. We freely admit that ignorance is a public evil and peril, as well as a personal misfortune, and we are ready to march abreast with the foremost in limiting its baleful influence. But men's relative capacity is not absolutely measured by their literacy acquirements; and the State requires the illiterate, equally with others, to be taxed for their support, and to shed their blood in her defense. We prefer that she shall persist in her noble efforts to instruct and enlighten all her sons by means less invidious and more genial than disfranchisement. Were there no other consideration impelling to this decision, we should rest on and defer to the forcible truths, that ability to read and write is not absolute, but comparative; that inspectors of election are fallible and swayed by like passions with other men—and that they might be tempted, in an exciting and closely contested election, to regard with a partial fondness, almost parental, the literary acquirements of those claimants of the franchise who were notoriously desirous of voting the ticket of those inspectors' own party, while applying a far sterner and more critical rule to those who should proffer the opposite ballots.

Our present Constitution authorizes the Legislature to pass laws designed to ascertain, by proper proofs, the persons entitled to exercise the right of suffrage. We recommend that those laws shall provide for a registration of all the legal voters, to be completed at least six days before each State election, and that none other than registered electors shall vote. Your committee are confident that the experiences of our State and of the civilized world, fully justifies these requirements. Unless the ballot-box is to be regarded and treated as a spittoon, no person should be allowed to vote whose right to do so is not fully ascertained and unquestionable. In a rural neighborhood where every one who approaches the ballot-box is known to dozens of either party, the frauds of unregistered voting may be mainly confined to those districts where the ascendancy of one party is practically unchecked; but in any densely peopled district where hundreds offer to vote who are known only to their few cronies, the case is totally different. Not to register the names of the voters, so as to give time for deliberate and general scrutiny, not merely by the few who may chance to be present when a particular vote is tendered is to stimulate knavery and offer a premium on fraud. It is to proclaim the right of suffrage worthless and proffer to each vagrant or felon half a dozen votes at every election which he may condescend to patronize. To uphold a registration of deeds, yet oppose a registration of voters, is virtually to assert a higher value, a more precious importance in our lands than in our liberties. Doubtless, some frauds will be committed where suffrage is so nearly universal, no matter what safeguards may be thrown around the elective franchise; but to maintain that registration, while it does afford protection to the titles whereby we hold our lands, will give none to our right of suffrage is to defy reason and insult our common sense. Your committee would urge that this precious right, so fundamental to all others, be carefully shielded from corruption, and that the main safeguards against its abuse should not be left to unstable and fluctuating statutes, but should be firmly imbedded in the Constitution.

Your committee, having thus fulfilled the duty imposed on them, ask to be discharged from the further consideration of the memorials referred to them, and that these, with this report, be committed to a Committee of the Whole.

HORACE GREELEY,

Chairman,

LESLIE W. RUSSELL,

WM. H. MERRILL,

GEO. WILLIAMS.

Albany, *June 28th*, 1867

Source: *Documents of the Convention of the State of New York, 1867–68*, vol. 1 (Albany, 1868); Edward F. Underhill, *Proceedings and Debates of the Constitutional Convention of the State of New York* (Albany, 1868).

V. Letter to the Editor: Elizabeth Cady Stanton on Sojourner Truth, 1867

Antebellum combatants over racialized citizenship continued during Reconstruction to battle one another over the property qualification. But the pre–Civil War coalition of black abolitionists and white reformers who had challenged not only slavery but also political and social inequality had begun to fray. Veteran African American activists, including the abolitionist icon Sojourner Truth, remained committed to achieving full equality, even as the steadfastness of white Republican and white feminist support for black suffrage wavered.

By contrast, as New Yorkers once again revisited the property restriction of 1821, Democrats rallied around long-held racist positions. For a white supremacist such as Samuel J. Tilden, the Wall Street lawyer, future governor, and leader of the state Democratic Party, the political lessons of past suffrage debates were clear. As the architect of the reconstructed Democratic Party—both in New York State and nationally—Tilden embraced the politics of disfranchisement. For Tilden, the property qualification held open the possibility of reviving the Democratic Party; in 1868, he advised party leaders that "our policy must be *condemnation and reversal of negro supremacy.*" Tilden went on to recount his long experience with the politics of racial exclusion:

> On no other issue can we be so unanimous among ourselves. On no other question can we draw so much from the other side and from the doubtful. It appeals . . . to the adopted citizens—whether Irish, or Germans; to all the working men; to the young men just becoming voters.[39]

Figure 11 Portrait of Sojourner Truth
Portrait of abolitionist crusader Sojourner Truth, 1864. Pictured here in her sixties, the former Ulster County, New York, slave continued to advocate for African American and women's rights.
Reprinted by permission of the Photographs and Prints Division, Schomburg Center for Research in Black Culture, the New York Public Library, Astor, Lenox and Tilden Foundations.

New York democracy took Tilden's advice to heart and mounted a campaign against equal manhood suffrage for the remainder of the 1860s.

Amid resurgent postbellum white supremacist politics in New York, anti-property-qualification forces asserted a very different vision of American politics after the Civil War. State and national conventions of African Americans called for a redefinition of American citizenship and an extension of suffrage to all men. In New York, black organizations lobbied the Greeley committee and the constitutional convention as a whole to remove the property qualification.

On a visit to her one-time home state—New York—for an equal rights convention in 1867, Sojourner Truth voiced her personal frustration with the legacies of 1821, the failures of Greeley and the Republicans, and the mounting opposition to racial equality. Truth, born a slave in late eighteenth-century New York, worked for black freedom and women's rights until her death in 1883. In this letter to the editor of the *New York World*, Elizabeth Cady Stanton relays her sense of Truth's ideas about suffrage, ideas that placed Truth in opposition to Stanton.[40]

What did Truth think about educational or property requirements for suffrage? What were Truth's primary frustrations with the political culture of the late 1860s? How did Stanton portray Truth in this letter to the editor?

*   *   *

Elizabeth Cady Stanton to the New York World

To the Editor of the *World*:
—We have had the pleasure of entertaining Mrs. Stowe's "Lybian Sybil"[41] at our home for the last week, and can bear testimony to the marvelous wisdom and goodness of this remarkable woman. She was a slave in this State for forty years, and has devoted forty years of freedom to the best interests of her race. Though eighty years of age, she is as active and clearsighted as ever, and "understands the whole question of reconstruction, all its 'quagmires and pitfalls,' as she says, as well as any man does."

The morning after the Equal Rights Convention, as the daily journals one by one made their appearance, turning to the youngsters of the household, she said: "Children, as there is no school to-day, will you read Sojourner the reports of the Convention? I want to see whether these young sprigs of the press do me justice. You know, children, I don't read such small stuff as letters, I read men and nations. I can see through a millstone, though I can't see through a spelling-book. What a narrow idea a reading qualification is for a voter! I know and do what is right better than many big men who read. And there's that property qualification! just as bad. As if men and women themselves, who made money, were not of more value than the thing they made. If I were a delegate to the Constitutional Convention I could make suffrage as clear as daylight; but I am afraid these Republicans will 'purty, purty' about all manner of small things week out and week in, and never settle this foundation question after all." Sojourner then gathered up her bag and shawl, and walked into the parlor in a stately manner, and there, surrounded by the children, the papers were duly read and considered. The *Express*, the *Post*, the *Commercial Advertiser*, the *World*, the *Times*, the *Herald*, the *Tribune*, and the *Sun*, all passed in review. The *World* seemed to please Sojourner more than any other journal. She said she liked the wit of the *World*'s reporter; all the little texts running through the speeches, such as "Sojourner on Popping Up," "No Grumbling," "Digging Stamps," "Biz," to show what is coming, so that one can get ready to cry or laugh, as the case may be— a kind of sign-board, a milestone, to tell where we are going, and how fast we go. The readers then call her attention to the solid columns of the other papers, and the versification of the *World*. She said she did not like the dead calm. She liked the breaking up into verses, like her songs. That is a good thing; it gives the reporter time to take breath and sharpen his pen, and think of some witty thing to say; for life is a hard battle anyway, and if we can laugh and sing a little as we fight the good fight of freedom, it makes it all go easier. "But, children, why did you not send for some of those wicked Democratic papers that abuse all good people and good things." "They are all here," said the readers in a chorus. "We have read you all the Republicans and the Democrats say." "Why, children, I can't tell one from the other. The millennium must be here, when one can't tell saints from sinners, Republicans from Democrats. Is the *World* Horace Greeley's paper?" "Oh, no; the *World* is Democratic!" "Democratic! Why, children, the *World* does move! But there is one thing I don't exactly see; if the Democrats are all ready to give equal rights to all, what are the Republicans making such a fuss about? Mr. Greeley was ready for this twenty years ago; if he had gone on as fast as the Democrats he should have been on the platform, at the conventions, making speeches, and writing resolutions, long ago." "Oh," said some one of larger growth,

"Mr. Greeley is busy with tariffs and protective duties. What do you think, Sojourner, of free trade? Do you think if England and France have more dry-goods than they want that they had better send them to us, and we in turn send them our fruits and flowers and grains; our timber, iron, fish, and ice?" "Yes, I go for everything free. Let nature, like individuals, make the most of what God has given them, have their neighbors to do the same, and then do all they can to serve each other. There is no use in one man, or one nation, to try to do or be everything. It is a good thing to be dependent on each other for something, it makes us civil and peaceable. But," said Sojourner, "where is Theodore Tilton's paper?" "Oh, the *Independent* is a weekly, it came out before the Convention." "But Theodore is not a weekly; why did he not come to the Convention and tell us what he thought?" "Well, here is his last paper, with a grand editorial," and Sojourner listened to the end with interest. "That's good," said she, "but he don't say woman." "oh, he is talking about sectarianism, not suffrage; the Church, not the State." "No matter; the Church wrongs woman as much as the State. 'Wives, obey your husbands,' is as bad as the common law. 'The husband and wife are one, and that one the husband.' I am afraid Theodore and Horace are playing bo-peep with their shadows. Did you tell me that Mr. Greeley is a delegate to the Constitutional Convention?" Yes, and I hope that he will soon wake up to the fact that the Democrats are going ahead of him, and instead of writing articles on "Democracy run mad," on tariffs and mining interests, it behooves him to be studying what genuine republicanism is, and whether we are to realize it in the Empire State this very year or not. "Speaking of shadows," said Sojourner, "I wish the *World* to know that when I go among fashionable people in the Church of the Puritans, I do not carry 'rations' in my bag; I keep my shadow there. I have good friends enough to give me clothes and rations. I stand on principle, always in one place, so everybody knows where to find Sojourner, and I don't want my shadow even to be dogging about here and there and everywhere, so I keep it in this bag." "I think," said one of the group, "the press should hereafter speak of you as Mrs. Stowe's Libian Sybil, and not as 'old church woman.'" "Oh, child, that's good enough. The *Herald* used to call me 'old black nigger,' so this sounds respectable. Have you read the *Herald* too, children? Is that born again? Well, we are all walking the right way together. I'll tell you what I'm thinking. My speeches in the Convention read well. I should like to have the substance put together, improved a little, and published in tract form, headed 'Sojourner Truth on Suffrage;' for if these timid men, like Greeley, knew that Sojourner was out for 'universal suffrage,' they would not be so afraid to handle the question. Yes, children, I am going to rouse the people on equality. I must sojourn once to the ballot-box before I die. I hear the ballot-box is a beautiful glass globe, so you can see all the votes as they go in. Now, the first time I vote I'll see if a woman's vote looks any different from the rest—if it makes any stir or commotion. If it don't inside, it need not outside. That good speech of Henry Ward Beecher's made my heart leap for joy; he just hit the nail right on the head when he said you never lost anything by asking everything; if you bait the suffrage-hook with a woman you will certainly catch a black man. There is a great deal in that philosophy, children. Now I must go and take a smoke!" I tell you in confidence, Mr. Editor, Sojourner smokes!

Yours respectfully,   E. C. S.

P.S.—She says she has been sent into the smoking-car so often she smoked in self-defense—she would rather swallow her own smoke than another's.

Source: Elizabeth Cady Stanton, Susan B. Anthony, and Matilda Joslyn Gage, *History of Women Suffrage*, vol. 2: 1861–1876. (New York: Fowler & Wells, 1882), 926–928.

W. "Appeal to Christians," 1869

In 1869, African American New Yorkers recommitted themselves to the work of eliminating the property qualification. A year after the constitutional convention disbanded, the state's voters once again were slated to vote on New York's racially discriminatory suffrage law. The state legislature in Albany had already ratified the Fifteenth Amendment to the U.S. Constitution; it was a near-certainty that, by early 1870, the required three-fourths of the states would have done likewise, and equal manhood suffrage would be federal law. In spite of this national success, New York blacks argued that the state needed to take action independently to disown the legacies of 1821.

That fall, the leadership of the campaign against the property qualifications was composed largely of black ministers. Led by the Reverend William F. Butler, African American religious leaders organized from the pulpit, appealing to both their black congregations and their white co-religionists. This document—"An Appeal to Christians"—was the culmination of such efforts. All congregations in New York were asked to reserve Sunday, October 31, for sermons on the meanings and necessity of equal citizenship. In this fusion of the religious and the political, black ministers sought to place morality at the center of the political realm so as to advance the cause of civil equality.

Not all African American organizing in late 1869 centered on the church. In September and October, black workers and reformers combined to establish the New York City Labor Council. Meeting throughout the campaign season, the organization was made up of wage laborers—both men and women—and a few physicians and clergymen. Alongside the organization's emphasis on economic issues, the short-term goal of the new council was immediate suffrage reform. The struggle for the franchise was joined to the struggle for economic justice, as the council demanded jobs, land reform, cooperative workshops, and a wide range of other reforms.

As the 1869 election neared, tempers flared across the city. Democratic rallies were brimmed with rabidly antiblack speeches. On the night of October 29, just four days before the election, two African American ministers—William Butler and Jacob Thomson—were savagely stoned and beaten on Hudson Street. The two leaders of the struggle against the property qualification narrowly escaped death. On November 2, New York State voters for a third time upheld the property qualification of 1821. The result was far closer than in 1846 or 1840; yet, by a vote of 282,403 to 249,802, New Yorkers maintained the property qualification.

How did New York's black ministers advance the cause of equal manhood suffrage, given the changed context of the late 1860s? How did this call for the removal of the property qualification differ from earlier such demands? (See documents P and T.) How did postbellum ministers compare to their antebellum forebears in their blending of politics and faith? (See document O.)

*   *   *

Appeal to Christians, From the Detroit Post

Five colored clergymen and four colored laymen, belonging to different denominations in the State of New York, appeal to their fellow Christians there to vote for the abolition of the constitutional clause which denies a colored man the franchise, unless he owns two hundred and fifty dollars more than he owes. This odious distinction is a disgrace to the statute book of a Christian State. It would dishonor a pagan community. For it not only discriminates against color, but it declares that the idleness and unthrift which are unpardonable in a black man shall work no forfeiture of rights in a white one. It declares that industry and economy are virtues to be encouraged, and their absence to be punished; but it punishes their absence in one class of men and ignores them in another. It acknowledges that there are other tests for the suffrage than that of color, and then ridicules and degrades those tests by making them apply to color. It is an illogical, conceited, barbarous wrong; worse in its spirit, if not in its results, than a wholesale disfranchisement because "a man's an ignorant nigger" whatever he may be worth. The colored gentlemen alluded to have asked every clergymen in the State to say something in his pulpit, Sunday, in behalf of their cause. They ask for the prayers of all men, and the aid of the religious press. They appeal in words that ought to touch every heart that has the faintest conception of the spirit of Christianity, and the mission of its founded. They say:

"We are few, poor, and despised. You are relatively many, rich, and powerful; and you make us realize the gulf that separates us. We are shut out of schools and seminaries, then taunted with our ignorance; we are excluded from workshops, and flouted as idle and beggarly; every avenue to political or social eminence is sternly closed against us, and men wonder that we lack energy, thrift, and aspiration. God grant that you may never feel, as we do, the agony of seeing your children insulted and tortured, for no pretence or cause or reason but the color which they inherit, and which it is beyond their power to change."

Yet there are hundreds of thousands of men and women in this land, who utter the shibboleths of Christianity, and partake of its sacraments, and perform its ceremonies, to whom such an appeal falls upon deaf ears; and who, while claiming a monopoly of the religion of Christ, are such infidels to its true spirit and such deniers of its magnificent creed wide as humanity itself, that the words we have quoted above will evoke only sneers or anger. This is not true of the great body of the Protestant Church in the North, but it is true of many in that Church, and of the masses in the Catholic Church.

[Our readers are already aware the "Appeal to Christians" did not suffice to accomplish the abolition of the odious and unjust "property qualification" for colored voters in the Empire State. The State is therefore still disgraced, and colored men, without property, are not yet politically free. Christians, in the true sense, are evidently in the minority.—Ed. Standard.]

Source: "An Appeal to Christians," *National Anti-Slavery Standard*, November 13, 1869.

X. Fifteenth Amendment to the U.S. Constitution, 1870

In 1870, the long reconstruction of New York became linked to a broader, national process. The 1821 property qualification ultimately was removed, but only after the enactment of the third of the Reconstruction amendments to the U.S. Constitution.

The contradictions between the state and the federal constitutions caused a peculiar state of affairs in New York in early 1870. The required three-fourths of the states had ratified the Fifteenth Amendment by the late winter; equal manhood suffrage was now the law of the land. Yet the New York City Democratic Party began the new year with an attempt to rescind the state's ratification. Tammany legislators in Albany campaigned throughout January 1870 against the soon-to-be-enacted Fifteenth Amendment. The Democratic-controlled legislature even voted to rescind the state's ratification, an action that was never recognized by the U.S. Congress and the secretary of state in Washington. Party leaders such as New York City comptroller Peter B. Sweeny regularly celebrated "the end of the negro agitation" and claimed that the coming struggle was over federal control of suffrage.[42]

Manhattan's black community organized around the achievement of equal manhood suffrage in the early months of 1870. To celebrate enfranchisement, African American New Yorkers prepared a mass celebration of the amendment's ratification for April 8. In the weeks leading up to the celebration, there were numerous political gatherings in the metropolitan black community; most were held at local houses of worship. A reporter at the late March planning meeting at Rev. Turpin's Bethel Church remarked: "I have never seen an assemblage more full of joy—exuberant joy." Less than six months after New Yorkers had rejected a state

Figure 12 Fifteenth Amendment Celebration
New York City's African American community took to the streets to celebrate the
passage of the Fifteenth Amendment and its promise of voting rights to adult
male citizens regardless of color. *From Frank Leslie's Illustrated Newspaper, April 30,
1870. Reprinted by permission of the President and Fellows of Harvard College.*

constitutional amendment guaranteeing equal manhood suffrage, black
New Yorkers understood that it was the federal government that was
guaranteeing their suffrage.[43]

On April 8, black Manhattanites commemorated the adoption of the
Fifteenth Amendment with a mass parade down Broadway, from Thirty-
fourth Street to Union Square. More than fifteen thousand onlookers—
men and women, mostly black—lined the parade route. The seven thousand marchers were all African American men. Marching behind a banner that read "We Ask Nothing but a Fair Race in Life," the assembled
veterans groups, military clubs, and benevolent associations celebrated
the elevation of black men to equal citizenship.[44]

To what extent was this last of the Reconstruction amendments targeted as much at the North as at the South? What were the implications
of federal action for the future of "jim crow New York"?

* * *

The amendment's text is followed by New York's belatedly revised suf-frage clause of 1874, which implicitly recognized the meaning of the Fif-teenth Amendment for citizenship in New York.

Fifteenth Amendment to the U.S. Constitution, 1870

Section 1. The right of citizens of the United States to vote shall not be denied or abridged by the United States or by any State on account of race, color, or previous condition of servitude.

Section 2. The Congress shall have power to enforce this article by appropriate legislation.

New York's Revised Suffrage Clause, 1874

SECTION 1. Every male citizen of the age of twenty-one years who shall have been a citizen for ten days and an inhabitant of this State one year next preceding an election, and for the last four months a resident of the county and for the last thirty days a resident of the election district in which he may offer his vote, shall be entitled to vote at such election in the election district of which he shall at the time be a resident, and not elsewhere, for all officers that now are or hereafter may be elective by the people, and upon all questions which may be submitted to the vote of the people, provided that in time of war no elector in the actual military service of the State, or of the United States, in the army or navy thereof, shall be deprived of his vote by reason of his absence from such election district; and the Legislature shall have power to provide the manner in which and the time and place at which such absent electors may vote, and for the return and canvass of their vote in the election district in which they respectively reside.

S[ECTION] 2. No person who shall receive, expect or offer to receive, or pay, offer or promise to pay, contribute, offer or promise to contribute to another, to be paid or used, any money or other valuable thing as a compensation or reward for the giving or withholding a vote at an election, or who shall make any promise to influence the giving or withholding any such vote, or who shall make or become directly or indirectly interested in any bet or wager depending upon the result of any election, shall vote at such election; and upon challenge for such cause, the person so challenged, before the officers authorized for that purpose shall receive his vote, shall swear or affirm before such officers that he has not received or offered, does not expect to receive, has not paid, offered or promised to pay, contributed, offered or promised to contribute to another, to be paid or used, any money or other valuable thing as a compensation or reward for the giving or withholding a vote at such election, and has not made any promise to influence the giving or withholding of any such vote, nor made or become directly or indirectly interested in any bet or wager depending upon the result of such election. The Legislature, at the session thereof next after the adoption of this section, shall and from time to time thereafter may, enact laws excluding from the right of suffrage all persons convicted of bribery or of any infamous crime.

AND WHEREAS, The said proposed amendment was agreed to by a majority of the Members elected to each of the two houses of the said Legislature, entered on their journals, with the yeas and nays taken thereon, and referred to the Legislature to be chosen at the then next general election of Senators;

AND WHEREAS, Such election has taken place, and said proposed amendment was duly published for three months previous to the time of making such choice, in pursuance of the provisions of section one of article thirteen of the constitution; therefore,

Resolved (if the Senate concur), That the Assembly do agree to the proposed amendment,

State of New York

In Assembly, January 23, 1874

The foregoing resolutions were duly passed.

By order of the Assembly.

John O'Donnell, Clerk.

State of New York,

In Senate, April 10, 1874

The foregoing resolutions were duly passed.

By order of the Senate.

Henry A. Glidden, *Clerk.*

Source: Fifteenth Amendment to the U.S. Constitution, ratified on February 3, 1870; New York State Assembly, *Journal*, 97th sess., 1874, 925–926.

Y. Newspaper Coverage of First
Equal Manhood Suffrage Election, 1870

On November 8, 1870, African American men for the first time since the early nineteenth century, when slavery still was practiced in the state, voted on equal terms with white men in New York. Nearly fifty years after the fateful 1821 convention, property qualifications no longer disfranchised black citizens. Equal manhood suffrage did not come about in New York simply as the result of constitutional amendment. Congress passed a series of Enforcement Acts in 1870 and 1871, designed to protect black voting rights both in the South and in the urban North.

In 1870, federal officials empowered local blacks to serve as armed federal marshals in and around polling places in lower Manhattan on Election Day. The swearing in of African American federal marshals coincided with the widespread political mobilization of black Manhattan that fall. Local activists had been organizing since the spring's celebrations of the Fifteenth Amendment's ratification. Urban delegates dominated the State Convention of Colored Voters in Syracuse. In the midst of this resurgent black community, black deputy marshals exerted power—real and symbolic—on the streets of Manhattan as Election Day neared in late October and early November of 1870. Friend and foe alike invested great importance in these symbols of Reconstruction's revolutionary consequences in Manhattan.

Several incidents of police intimidation and harassment of black citizens took place in the weeks leading up to the election. The Tammany-controlled police department directed its forces against the black neighborhoods of lower Manhattan and particularly against the agents of the federal government. A wave of police-initiated arrests and violence in late

Figure 13 Swearing-in of U.S. Marshals
Swearing-in of federal deputy marshals—white and black—on October 28, 1870. Eleven days later, these officials would help oversee the first equal manhood suffrage election in New York's history. *From Frank Leslie's Illustrated Newspaper, November 19, 1870. Reprinted by permission of the President and Fellows of Harvard College.*

October was centered in Manhattan's Eighth Ward, the center of the metropolitan black community. The number of arrests made in the downtown black community on October 31 coincided with a meeting of "the colored citizens of the Sixth District" on lower Sixth Avenue that night. Police actions regularly followed such African American public meetings in the Eighth Ward.

New Yorkers couldn't help but recognize the increased military presence in the city. The sloop-of-war *Guerriere* was docked in the East River to receive those accused of illegal voting. General Irvin McDowell placed the soldiers in the Department of the East under local Republican command. George Templeton Strong, the Republican lawyer, was positively ecstatic at the imposing display of federal might. As November 8 neared, he noted in his diary that "an outbreak on a large scale, thoroughly repressed and followed by a month of martial law judiciously administered might do New York much good."[45]

In the buildup to Election Day, all sides worried over the possibilities of mass violence. The *Journal of Commerce* warned of a "federal invasion of New York," claiming that the president had "ordered to New York all the available soldiers and marines east of the Mississippi." The city police ordered all officers to be on duty for the entire polling day on November 8. Local authorities and federal official brokered an uneasy truce late in the afternoon on November 7. U.S. marshals were to be stationed inside polling places, while at least two New York City police officers would stand guard outside.[46]

On Election Day itself, six thousand deputy marshals and twenty-five hundred police oversaw the ballot boxes. The election's most noteworthy feature was the presence of African Americans at the polls. One journalist noted that "the most popular man was the new-made citizen—the colored man. . . . An unusual number of negroes were on the street: and in one or two districts they distributed the tickets."[47]

How did New Yorkers react to the belated achievement of equal manhood suffrage? How, in particular, did black New Yorkers mark this historic occasion? How do you account for the violence that took place on Election Day around the city?

*   *   *

The Day Here

Scenes and Incidents

The election passed very quietly in this City, although as appears elsewhere a very large number of arrests (mostly for political reasons) were made. The faces of passers-by who halted at the polling places, bore an inquiring look, and everybody seemed to be interested in the result.

Policemen guarded the doors of the polls, and the United States marshals stood inside watching the ballot-boxes and the voters as they stepped up to deposit their votes. Behind the boxes sat the State inspectors and the United State supervisors of election, who were seemingly possessed with but one idea, which was that of a strict attention to their special duties. Outside crowds of the usual class of people brought out by an election, pressed round the doors. There were to be seen rough and respectable citizens, colored men and men of all nationalities, sober looking men and men with red noses and other signs of bibulous tendencies. Many of the latter class were plentifully supplied with liquor during the day. Carriages and light wagons were recklessly driven about the streets by politicians, to the imminent danger of pedestrians. Many "gin-mills," whose doors were closed in front, kept an opening in the rear. J. K. MURPHY, keeper of a corner liquor-store uptown, and reported to be in the pay of LAWRENCE O'BRIEN, kept open all day, and must have rendered invaluable service. A drunken man in the saloon stated that he had received $100 from LARRY O'BRIEN to work for him, and that he was to meet him at 4 o'clock in the evening. From the appearance of a half dozen intoxicated men in his company, it is probable that he had been laboring to get others drunk, to influence their votes, and had finally succumbed to King Alcohol himself. Votes were bought openly in the Twentieth Ward, the price paid for them being from $1 to $5 per vote. . . .

Respectable colored men of the Twentieth Ward were much outraged and felt great indignation against some of their people who had been tampered with by men working for O'BRIEN, and who substituted O'BRIEN's name for GRIDLEY's, for a few dollars paid to them. Their number, however, was small. At the corner of Thirty-eighth-street and Seventh-avenue, a "shindy"[48] was indulged in by some of the enthusiastic supporters of LEDWITH and the Tammany men. A few bloody noses and cut lips were the result of the affray. It was speedily quelled by the Police, who were somewhat impeded in their movements by the "municipal specials," who were a "rum-looking" set, armed with clubs, and many of them drunk the greater part of the day. . . .

In the Seventh Ward, in the afternoon, WILLIAM CRAVEN, of No. 82 Madison-street, was arrested, after voting, by Deputy United States Marshal P. J. O'BRIEN. A warrant had been issued in this case two days ago, charging accused with false registry. The affair occurred at the corner of East Broadway and Market-street. CRAVEN had just come out from voting when the marshal tapped him on the shoulder and informed him that he was a prisoner. At once friends pressed around and attempted a rescue. A revolver was thrust into the marshal's mouth, and he was otherwise threatened. Revolvers were drawn, and clubs freely used. For a time there was great excitement—the crowd surging to and fro and uttering shouts and cries. Reinforcements under Marshal BRACKET and the Police arrived, and the prisoner was conveyed to the Madison-street Station-house. JAMES CAIN, of 21 Hamilton-street, was also arrested for illegal voting and lodged in Ludlow-street Jail.

The Eighth and Ninth Wards are the strongest of the negro vote, and as might naturally be expected that vote was cast in favor of the Republican candidates. The vast majority of the negro vote in the City is located in that section bounded by Canal, Sullivan, Houston-street and the North River.[49] . . . The Ward was quiet during the whole day, all reports in the evening papers of yesterday to the contrary notwithstanding. The negroes affiliated in most pleasant terms with the voters of both parties, and discussion of men and measures was carried on with spirit on both sides. The only thing of note which occurred during the day was about 2 ½ P.M., when two drunken men stood on the sidewalk opposite the United States Army headquarters, and began to blackguard the United States soldiery who were quartered in that building. A crowd having collected at this point the two men were taken into custody by the Police and locked up in the Eighth Precinct Station-house. Yesterday, a colored man residing in the Fourteenth Ward was seen distributing the through [sic] Democratic ticket to others of his race. He was stationed on the corner of Hester-street and Baxter. The voting in the Eighth Ward was done very quietly, excepting a little excitement in the morning on the part of the colored voters of that Ward. It originated from the voting of the Democratic ticket by one of their own color, and his attempt at repeating on the same ticket. His arrest was ordered by one of the colored deputy marshals, and he was taken to the Wooster-street Police Station. In the Fourteenth Ward several rows occurred at the closing of the polls. . . .

At 4 ½ o'clock a general melee between a number of special policemen and deputy marshals took place on the corner of Seventeenth-street and Ninth-avenue. For some few moments affairs seemed serious, but a mutual withdrawal of the forces produced a calm. There were no arrests. . . .

The United States Officials—

Measures for the Enforcement of Congressional Law—

Troops Held in Readiness—

Conference of National and Local Authorities—

Protection Extended to the Deputy Marshals

The old Federal building in Chambers-street, in which are located the offices of the United States Commissioners, the Marshal and the District-Attorney, was the scene of unusual excitement yesterday. The corridors constantly echoed with the tramp of prisoners arrested for violating the Congressional Election law. Numerous carriages were kept in readiness in front of the building for the purpose of conveying the prisoners to jail. At daylight the Marshal's office was placed in telegraphic communication with the various sections of the City, including GEN. MCDOWELL's head-quarters, by a special wire attached to the Western Union line, and an operator was detailed to receive messages from the chief deputy marshals and supervisors of the different districts, and to forward orders for the guidance of the latter officials in cases of emergency. . . .

The Federal Troops and the Militia

During yesterday forenoon members of the First Division National Guard were somewhat nervous, as many of them expected that the alarm would be sounded for their services. But as the day wore on and no alarm came, our citizen soldiers became easy in their minds and forgot to listen for the fire-bells. . . .

The movements of United States troops on Monday night were singularly successful, so far as secrecy went. Citizens happening to be in Broadway, near Reade-street, about 9 o'clock, were surprised by the silent progress of five or six companies of the First Regiment Artillery. The men wore their overcoats, and had their blankets slung over their shoulders in true campaign style. These troops were under command of GEN. HUNT, and crossed Broadway in a few seconds, and suddenly disappeared from view. They were safely quartered in the upper portion of a building in Reade-street, and remained there all day in readiness for any movement calculated to disturb the peace of the City. There were other bodies of troops quartered in the City, a portion being located in the Army building in Houston-street. The men were kept rigidly indoors, and their presence was scarcely suspected by the public. Very few of the policemen on post seemed to recognize the troops as they passed, and it was not until after daylight yesterday that the fact of their presence became generally known or was credited by those who sought to prevent their entrance into the City. These troops were intended for the protection of the Government offices and buildings in case of any extended disturbance, which happily did not occur. The frigate *Narraganset* was stationed in the East River near the foot of Wall-street, and it was understood that she would be used to sweep the street to protect the United States Treasury. The iron-clad *Guerriere* lay in the North River, near Chamber-street, for any service that might be required. Both vessels were the objects of much attention from those who were in the vicinity of their anchorage, but no especial signs of life on board were noticeable. The marines from the frigates were consolidated with those in barracks at the navy-yard, and the other troops were kept in garrison, in the harbor, in readiness for instant advice, which was not called for.

Source: "The Day Here," *New York Times*, November 9, 1870.

Z. Excerpts from Tilden Commission Report, 1877

The year 1877 marked the end of Reconstruction for the nation. Republican Rutherford B. Hayes entered the White House, having defeated New York governor Samuel J. Tilden in one of the most contested elections in the nation's history. Thousands of federal troops were removed from the South, leaving "Redeemer" white supremacist governments across the former Confederacy. An era of national commitment to enforcing equal political rights for all citizens drew to a tragic close. In the Empire State, 1877 culminated a full century of debate on suffrage and citizenship. In the hundred years since the Kingston Convention of 1777, New Yorkers had long struggled to give substance to citizenship. In this final drama of the first century of New York's—and the nation's—ongoing reconstruction, the Tilden Commission, a ten-man panel appointed in 1875 by then-governor Tilden, and which included the leading editor E. L. Godkin among its members, took a leading role. The commissioners abandoned racial restrictions and instead advanced the idea of property qualifications for all urban voters in certain municipal elections.

After fifteen months of deliberations, the Tilden Commission issued its report to the state legislature in March 1877. The proposal to amend the state constitution with new property qualifications sparked a statewide debate that spring; in May, the legislature passed legislation that would have enacted the commission's recommendations. In nineteenth-century New York, however, two consecutive legislatures needed to pass such amendments before they could be submitted to the state's voters. Thus, the November 1877 election became a referendum on suffrage and citizenship in the Empire State. Opponents of property qualifications—a coalition that brought together urban and rural voters—managed to elect an anti–Tilden Commission legislature. Although the plan for amending the state constitution would eventually go down to defeat, the Tilden commissioners ushered in an age of policy making by unelected commissions and articulated a growing dissatisfaction with democratic government on the part of Empire State elites.

How did the Tilden commissioners justify their attempt once more to limit the suffrage in New York's cities? Were there any echoes of the arguments put forth by earlier disfranchisers, especially those at the 1821 Constitutional Convention (see document L)?

Tilden Commission Report, 1877

Report of the Commission to Devise a Plan for the Government of Cities in the State of New York

To the Senate and Assembly of the State of New York:
The undersigned, commissioners appointed by the Governor of this State, pursuant to a concurrent resolution of the Senate and Assembly, passed May 22d, 1875, to devise a plan for the government of cities, and to report the same to the Legislature, respectfully present the following report:

ORIGIN OF THE COMMISSION

The Governor, in a special message, communicated to the Legislature, May 22d, 1875, called attention to the evils of our municipal systems, and the necessity of adopting a permanent and uniform plan for the government of the cities of the State, and recommended the appointment of a commission to consider the subject.

On the same day a concurrent resolution was introduced in the Senate and adopted by the Senate and Assembly, which was in these words:

"*Whereas*, the Governor, in his special message of May eleventh, eighteen hundred and seventy-five, called the attention of the Legislature to the evils arising from our unstable municipal systems, and the necessity of adopting a permanent and uniform plan for the government of the cities of the State, therefore

Resolved, (if the Assembly concur), That the governor be, and hereby is, authorized to appoint a commission of not more than twelve persons, whose duty it shall be to consider the subject referred to in said message, to devise a plan for the government of cities, and to report the same to the next Legislature.

Resolved, That the Committee on Ways and Means report a suitable appropriation to defray the actual expenses of the commission, to be audited by the comptroller, provided, that the commission shall receive no compensation for their services.

Twelve persons were appointed by the Governor under the above resolution, all of whom, except President Martin B. Anderson, of Rochester, accepted the duty thus devolved upon them.

The commission organized immediately after their appointment, and the first meeting was held on the fifteenth day of December, 1875. Mr. William M. Evarts[50] was chosen president of the commission. It seemed necessary to have the aid of some suitable person, not a member of the commission, to keep the minutes of the proceedings, conduct the correspondence, and have charge of the documents of the body, and for this purpose, Mr. Sidney De Kay, of New York, was selected.

Its Work

The commission proceeded at once with the performance of their task by assigning to the several members the duty of making investigations and reports upon particular branches of the general subject of municipal government. They hoped to be able to bring their labors to a conclusion in season to present their report to the Legislature of 1876; but they were of the opinion that but little value could be attached to the recommendations of any such body unless preceded by the most deliberate consideration; and such was the magnitude of the subject with which they had to deal, the difficulties with which it was at every turn beset, and the earlier diversity of opinion among themselves, that they found it impossible to accomplish their work before the adjournment of 1876, and the Legislature of that year extended the time for the making of their report to the present session.

Notwithstanding the devotion, since that period, of more time than before to their task, it has been necessarily protracted to the present moment. It is now completed, and it becomes the present duty of the Commission to submit to your honorable bodies the results of their labors, together with an explanation of their recommendations, and a statement of the grounds and reasons upon which they are founded.

The message of Governor Tilden, of May 11th 1875, which led to the creation of this Commission, treats, at length, of the history and present condition of the governments of our cities, especially that of the city of New York; of the mischiefs and public burdens, both of debt and taxation, under which these communities now labor; and of the wide departures from sound principles of local government which have marked the recent administration of the affairs of the Metropolis. The concurrent resolution makes it the duty of this Commission "to consider the subject referred to in said message, to devise a plan for the government of cities, and to report the same."

The purpose, therefore, of the Legislature in passing the resolution seems plainly to have been to submit the whole subject of the local government of cities to that deliberate review which can, it may be supposed, be best given to it by a small number of persons specially delegated for that purpose, to the end that some plan of administration may be devised which may commend itself as furnishing the promise of a permanent improvement.

THE EVILS EXISTING IN THE GOVERNMENTS OF CITIES

The first step to be taken is a consideration of the evils which infest the administration of our city governments. No statement or illustration of these is requisite to a conviction of their existence. A clear perception, however, of these evils, and of their origin, causes, connections and results, is indispensable to any useful contrivance for their redress. It will tend to distinctness, in this respect, to begin the statement with, the last results of bad administration as they reach and become burdens upon the citizen; and afterwards point out the causes which produce them.

FIRST.—*The accumulation of permanent municipal debt.* . . .

SECOND.—*The excessive increase of the annual expenditure for ordinary purposes.* . . .

But the deplorable financial condition of our principal cities, to which we have given such prominence, has causes, a clear perception of which must precede any intelligent action in contriving remedies. We desire to avoid in this division of our subject, so far as possible, all matters upon which differences of opinion are likely to arise, and shall therefore refer, not to the more remote, and, perhaps, fundamental causes, but to those which are direct, immediate and palpable, the operation of which can be clearly pointed out.

CAUSES OF THE EXISTING EVILS

FIRST.—*Incompetent and unfaithful governing boards and officers.* . . .

SECOND.—*The introduction of State and National Politics into municipal affairs.* . . .

The Report next advanced an extensive interpretation of the problems in contemporary politics.

The motives which lead to a pushing of these general political divisions to their present mischievous extremes should be clearly comprehended. They are exceedingly powerful, and will not yield to ordinary resistance:

1. The great prizes, in the shape of place and power, which are offered on the broad fields of state and national politics, offer the strongest incentives to ambition. Personal advancement is in these fields naturally associated with the achievement of great public objects, and neither end can be secured except through the success of a political party to which they are attached. The strife thus engendered develops into a general battle in which each side feels that it cannot afford to allow any odds to the other. If one seeks to turn to its advantage the patronage of municipal office, the other must carry the contest into the same sphere. It is certain that the temptation will be withstood by neither. It thus becomes the direct interest of the foremost men of the nation to constantly keep their forces in hostile array, and these must be fed by, among other ways, the patronage to be secured by the control of local affairs. The concerns which fill the imaginations of ambitious men are deemed supreme; and sufficient to justify the partial sacrifice of subordinate and local interests. This is a grave error, engendered by the existing political conditions of city government arrangements.

2. Next to this small number of leading men, there is a large class, who though not dishonest or devoid of public spirit, are led by habit and temperament to take a wholly partisan view of city affairs. Their enjoyment of party struggles, their devotion to those who share with them triumphs and defeats of the political game are so intense, that they gradually lose

sight of the object for which parties exist, or ought to exist; and considerable proportions of them, in their devotion to politics, suffer themselves to be driven from the walks of regular industry, and at last become dependent for their livelihood on the patronage in the hands of their chiefs. Mingled with them is nearly as large a number to whom politics is simply a mode of making a livelihood, or a fortune, and who take part in political contests without enthusiasm, and often without the pretence of interest in the public welfare, and devote themselves openly to the organization of the vicious elements of society, in combinations strong enough to hold the balance in a closely contested election, overawe the political leaders, and secure a fair share of the municipal patronage, or else extort immunity from the officers of the law.

3. The rest of the community, embracing the large majority of the more thrifty classes, averse to engaging in what they deem the "low business" of politics, or hopeless of accomplishing any substantial good in the face of such powerful opposing interests, for the most part content themselves with acting in accordance with their respective parties. When a municipal election occurs, most of them easily persuade themselves that, as the only question is which of the two parties is to have the control of local affairs, it is, of course, best that such control should be lodged with their own; and it is some satisfaction to them, when no other good can be achieved, to gain a small political triumph. Others, troubled with the sense that a duty is imposed upon them to vote for meritorious candidates feebly and vainly labor on the morning of the election to discriminate between the respective merits of obscure contestants. Some few rise to the virtue of seasonable inquiry, and congratulate themselves upon the performance of the solemn duty of replacing a notoriously unworthy name, by some selection of their own.—The usually meagre return of scattering votes is the measure of the efficiency of this class of citizens.

It is through the agency of the great political parties organized and operating as above described, that our municipal officers are, and long have been selected. It can scarcely be matter of wonder, then, that the present condition of municipal affairs should present an aspect so desperate.

THIRD.—*The assumption by the Legislature of the direct control of local affairs. . . .*

PLAN OF THE COMMISSION

In dealing with the general subject committed to them, the commission was necessarily led into an extended survey and examination of the ori-

gin and nature of our existing municipal corporations; the relations
which they sustain to the sovereign power of the State; the character and
extent of the powers conferred upon them; and the mode in which those
powers have been exercised and regulated, both in reference to the general functions of government, and to those specially relating to the vital
question of municipal expenditure, debt and taxation. This survey and
examination led, at an early period, to the fundamental question, whether
the general application of universal suffrage in the election of the local
guardians and trustees of the financial interests of these public corporations, was in accordance with sound principles, or suitable to our present
condition. Entertaining however, a natural jealousy of any suggestion
which might wear the appearance of a departure from the principles of
American polity, they preferred to direct their first efforts towards the dis-
covery of some mode of rearranging the local administration, which,
without disturbing the elective system, should give promise of a reform of
existing abuses. As already shown, all such efforts appeared to them, after
the fullest consideration, to be misdirected; and the question remained
whether the election by universal suffrage of the local guardians of the financial concerns of cities can be safely retained. This report has thus far
been largely devoted to a recapitulation of the discussions and conclusions through which they were led, or rather forced, to a consideration of
the principal question above stated. We have pursued this method because we recognize and appreciate the natural disinclination of our citizens to attribute the disorders of our political system to the operation of
general suffrage. After the most careful deliberation, our conclusion is
that the choice of the local guardians and trustees of the financial concerns of cities should be lodged with the taxpayers. To admit to a participation in such choice, those who make no contribution to the funds to
be administered is not in conformity with the principles on which human
affairs are conducted, and is a departure from the general policy of this
State, as frequently declared by the Legislature.

THE PRINCIPLE ON WHICH IT RESTS

The distinctions between the general government of the State and the
government of its local divisions—very important to be observed—are
often overlooked. We have heretofore, in general terms, adverted to them.
They need a more pointed statement. The province of the State government consists in laying down the general principles and determining the
civil polity of the State in establishing the rights of persons, determining

the conditions upon which property may be acquired, held and enjoyed, and framing the governmental agencies through which all rights may be secured. All these matters are of *general*, and not merely *local*, interest. They concern all citizens throughout the State in a similar manner, although some may not concern them in an equal degree.

For the purpose of carrying out the general systems thus established, certain powers are entrusted by the State to local officials for special, administrative, and local purposes. Those powers (to borrow the precise language of Governor Tilden in the message already referred to), "in the most completely developed municipality, embrace the care of police, health, schools, street cleaning, prevention of fires, supplying water and gas, and similar matters, most conveniently attended to in partnership by persons living together in a dense community, and the expenditure and taxation necessary for those objects. The rights of persons, property, and the judicial systems instituted for their preservation—general legislation—government, in its proper sense; these are vast domains which the functions of municipal corporations and municipal officers do not touch."

It is next to be observed that much the larger part of this administration of the affairs of municipalities consists in the raising by taxation, from the owners of property therein, a common fund for carrying out the local purposes above referred to, and the due application of that fund.

It is this domain of government proper which constitutes the true field for the operation of the principles and methods of universal suffrage. It is here that all actually possess, and feel that they possess, both a common and an individual interest, and an interest which will not, in general, be either bartered, betrayed or neglected, and which cannot be measured by any pecuniary standard. The rights of persons must be equal, and though all persons have not equal rights to property, they have equal rights to equal rules respecting property. This equality can be secured only through a legislative body in which all are represented, and can be maintained only when the general executive and judicial officers are subject to responsibility to all alike. In the election of the central Legislature, and of the general executive and judicial officers, all citizens should therefore participate.

The case, in respect to the choice of the local guardians of municipal funds is very different. In all our cities there are many who make no direct contribution whatever to these funds, and have no just title to say how much shall be exacted from other people, and to what purposes the contributions should be applied. It may be said that the burden of supporting government falls in some manner upon all. In a remote and indirect way a small part of the burden of local taxation falls upon those who do not directly contribute. But this is so inappreciable, and by them so little understood, as to be wholly immaterial to the present discussion.

The main object of local government, in this respect, is to secure faithful administration of financial trusts—to place the control of enormous sums of money in the hands of those who will see that they are applied to their proper uses. Knowing, as we do, that this control is, and must necessarily be, sought for by those whose object is to pervert it, and who will devote themselves, with restless effort, to the formation of powerful combinations to gain it, we deliberately, under our present system, throw these enormous prizes into the arena occupied by the contending factions. It would indeed be strange if the results of such a system were other than we find them. Our object is, or should be, to select from the community such guardians as prudent stockholders would choose to manage the concerns of a great corporation. The plan adopted hitherto seems no better adapted to secure a good administration than a mode of election in a railway corporation, by which conductors, brakemen, truckmen, engineers and passengers, should have an equal right with stockholders to vote for directors. Indeed, when our present system is fairly subjected to the test of principle, there seems to be little room for argument. It stands self-condemned. . . .

The measure we recommend is not in opposition to the principle of general suffrage, but in support of it—as much so as if the sole duty of this commission had been to consider how that principle could be best preserved and perpetuated. No surer method could be devised to bring the principle of universal suffrage into discredit, and prepare the way for its overthrow, than to pervert it to a use for which it was never intended, and subject it to a service which it is incapable of performing.

Even now sarcasm and ridicule are frequently levelled against the system of universal suffrage, as if it were a contrivance unsuited to any department of human affairs. Such criticism seems wholly misdirected. This principle, justly applied, is the true foundation of our government, and a leading source of our strength and prosperity as a nation. It is not the use, but the abuse of the principle that can ever bring it into contempt or endanger its preservation. To expect frugality and economy in financial concerns from its operation in great cities, where perhaps half of the inhabitants feel no interest in these duties, is to subject the principle to a strain for which it is not designed, and which it cannot bear. All true friends of the system should unite in rescuing it from such perils.

Enough has been said to vindicate the conclusion of this commission that a body, representative of the taxpayers, is necessary as an integral part of the local government of cities. Inasmuch as this conclusion enters into the plan to be proposed by them as a fundamental element, it has seemed to us best that a vindication of it should precede the statement of that scheme.

The Committee then called for a constitutional amendment to implement its principles and objectives. Each city was to have a Board of Finance. Only taxpayers owning property valued at no less than $500 or those who rented for no less than $250 per annum were to vote for members of such boards.

CONCLUDING REMARKS

The submission of this report completes the task assigned to the Commission. The amount of time, labor and thought bestowed upon the work are not to be measured by the mere text of the amendments to the Constitution which are proposed, or by the summary of views and conclusions therewith presented. The whole system of municipal establishments, its nature, its objects, its defects, the experiments to which it has been subjected, the present condition which it exhibits, and the means of its improvements, have been the subject of continuous and earnest investigation, and have been discussed at length, in written papers and orally at the regular meetings of the Commission. Many subjects which have received a large degree of attention are omitted as not necessary, in view of the results arrived at; no small part of the labor has consisted in reducing the text of the proposed amendments to the smallest possible compass, while embracing within it all the elements essential to completeness. The force and meaning of the particular terms employed, as well as the scope and purport of every general provision, have been carefully considered; and while it is impossible to present by reports of the debates and deliberations, the course of the arguments and decisions of the Commission, in the same manner as those of more popular bodies, it is none the less true that they have covered the wide range which it was necessary to explore in order to arrive at the results embodied in this report. In these results the undersigned members of the Commission concur, and they may be permitted to close their labors with the expression of the hope that the plan which they propose, if it shall be approved by the Legislature and adopted by the people, may secure those public benefits which have been the sole aim of the Commission.

ALL OF WHICH IS RESPECTFULLY SUBMITTED.
Dated New York, 24th February, 1877.
WM. M. EVARTS,
SAML. HAND,
E. L. GODKIN,
JOHN A. LOTT,
JOSHUA M. VAN COTT,
JAS. C. CARTER,
OSWALD OTTENDORFER,
WM. ALLEN BUTLER,
SIMON STERNE,
HENRY F. DIMOCK.

Nota Bene.—I Concur in the results of the foregoing report, except as to qualifications of voters for the Board of Finance, and the powers of that Board to appoint the law and financial officers. I think the qualifications of voters for the large cities should be the same as those prescribed for the smaller cities, and that the Board of Finance should have no appointing power.
SAMUEL HAND

Source: New York (State) Commission to Devise a Plan for the Government of Cities in the State of New York, "Report of the Commission to Devise a Plan for the Government of Cities in the State of New York," in *Documents of the Assembly of the State of New York, 100 Session—1877* (Albany, 1877).

Bibliographic Essay

This collection is by its nature interdisciplinary and taps into numerous historical subfields. Topics range from slavery to emancipation, from electoral politics to popular culture, from political theory to social history. This essay has two purposes: first, to direct readers to the scholarly resources upon which the authors drew in writing introductory essays, headnotes, and editorial notes; second, to assist students and scholars with their own investigations into race, citizenship, and the political culture of New York between the American Revolution and the end of Reconstruction. This essay is not meant to be an exhaustive survey of this vast scholarly landscape. Rather, the essay highlights crucial recent scholarship, classic works on the subject, as well as lesser-known works and older scholarly contributions that researchers might otherwise overlook. For additional information on sources, readers should consult the citations in the text itself.

General Works

Broad theoretical and synthetic approaches to American citizenship have deeply informed this study of African American citizenship in a particular time and place. For two studies by political scientists who have studied citizenship's contested nature and have articulated elegant definitions of citizenship upon which the present study directly draws, see Judith N. Shklar, *American Citizenship: The Quest for Inclusion* (Cambridge, Mass., 1991); and Rogers M. Smith, *Civic Ideals: Conflicting Visions of Citizenship in U.S. History* (New Haven, 1997).

In recent years, historians also have made valuable contributions to the study of citizenship's contested terrain. Alexander Keyssar, *The Right to*

Vote: The Contested History of Democracy in the United States (New York, 2000), stands as the definitive historical work on American suffrage; moreover, for information on states other than New York, we have relied on the appendix to Keyssar's study, in which he has organized information on the suffrage laws of each state into remarkably clear tables. For a stimulating study that emphasizes the obligations, rather than the rights, associated with American citizenship, see Linda K. Kerber, *No Constitutional Right to Be Ladies: Women and the Obligations of Citizenship* (New York, 1998). Two recent works that synthesize the broad history of American freedom and democracy from different perspectives are Eric Foner, *The Story of American Freedom* (New York, 1998); and Robert H. Wiebe, *Self-Rule: A Cultural History of American Democracy* (Chicago, 1995).

A somewhat older set of works helped set the stage for these newer studies of race and citizenship, as well as the raft of more focused studies discussed later in this bibliographic essay. Leon Litwack, *North of Slavery: The Negro in the Free States, 1790–1860* (Chicago, 1961), laid the groundwork for all subsequent studies of African American life in the antebellum North. Chilton Williamson, *American Suffrage: From Property to Democracy, 1760–1860* (Princeton, 1960), still offers a valuable overview of voting rights from colonial times to the eve of the Civil War; for the present study, Williamson's analysis of the intricacies of suffrage politics in Connecticut was particularly useful.

As the chronologies and the introduction to this work indicate, New York's struggles over race, slavery, and citizenship occurred in a trans-Atlantic context. David Brion Davis, *The Problem of Slavery in the Age of Revolution, 1770–1823* (Ithaca, N.Y., 1975) and *Slavery and Human Progress* (New York, 1984), brilliantly integrates the history of slavery and emancipation into the broader currents of American and, indeed, world history. In preparing our timelines, the following works were especially important: Davis, *Problem of Slavery*; Seymour Drescher, *Capitalism and Antislavery: British Mobilization in Comparative Perspective* (New York, 1987); and Paul Finkelman and Joseph C. Miller, eds., *Macmillan Encyclopedia of World Slavery* (New York, 1998).

African American history in New York has received increasing scholarly attention in recent years. Graham Russell Hodges, *Root and Branch: African Americans in New York and East Jersey* (Chapel Hill, 1999), a sweeping and penetrating overview, has been an invaluable source on a variety subjects discussed in this book. The study of New York history and life in general will never be the same after the publication of the massive and brilliant *Gotham: A History of New York City to 1898*, by Edwin G. Burrows and Mike Wallace (New York, 1999). *Gotham* provided particular insight on the origins of "Jim Crow" minstrelsy, black life in New York City, and the history of *Freedom's Journal*, America's and New York City's first black newspaper.

Charles Z. Lincoln, *The Constitutional History of New York, from the Beginning of the Colonial Period to the Year 1905, Showing the Origin, Development, and Judicial Construction of the Constitution* vols. 1–2 (Rochester, 1906), offers useful documents and commentary on the entire period covered by *Jim Crow New York*.

Slavery, Abolition, and Citizenship, 1777–1817

A rich literature has grown up around the history of slavery in New York, focusing on a range of locations and time periods. Edgar J. McManus, *A History of Negro Slavery in New York* (Syracuse, 1966), provides the broadest overview. For more focused recent studies, see Michael Edward Groth, "Forging Freedom in the Mid-Hudson Valley: The End of Slavery and the Formation of a Free African American Community in Dutchess County, New York, 1770–1850" (Ph.D. diss., SUNY-Binghamton, 1994); Richard Shannon Moss, *Slavery on Long Island: A Study in Local Institutional and Early African American Communal Life* (New York, 1993); Thelma Wills Foote, "Black Life in Colonial Manhattan" (Ph.D. diss., Harvard University, 1991); A. J. Williams-Myers, "The African Presence in the Hudson River Valley: The Defining Relationships between Masters and Slaves," *Afro-Americans in New York Life and History* 12 (January 1988), 81–98; and Carl Nordstrom, "The New York Slave Code," *Afro-Americans in New York Life and History* 4 (January 1980), 7–26. For key demographic data on slavery in New York, see Thomas J. Davis, "New York's Long Black Line: A Note on the Growing Slave Population, 1626–1790," *Afro-Americans in New York Life and History* 2 (January 1978), 41–60. Placing black resistance during the Revolutionary War in its larger context is James W. S. G. Walker, "Blacks as American Loyalists: The Slaves' War for Independence," *Historical Reflections/Reflections Historiques* 2 (1975), 51–67.

Shane White, *Somewhat More Independent: The End of Slavery in New York City, 1770–1810* (Athens, Ga., 1991), offers a richly textured social history of African American life in New York City during the period that marked the transition from slavery to freedom. White provides valuable demographic data on slaveholding and runaway slaves during the Revolutionary and early national period in New York, as well as a fascinating analysis of the Pinkster holiday. Vivienne L. Kruger, "Born to Run: The Slave Family in Early New York, 1626–1827" (Ph.D. diss., Columbia University, 1985), contains a stunning amount of data on black life, including life in rural areas, during the transition from slavery to freedom. For two recent syntheses of early African American social history that help situate New York in its broader regional and national contexts, see James Oliver Horton and Lois E. Horton, *In Hope of Liberty: Culture, Community and Protest among Northern Free Blacks, 1700–1860* (New York, 1997); and Ira Berlin, *Many Thousands Gone: The First Two Centuries of Slavery in North America* (Cambridge, Mass., 1998).

The abolition of slavery in the states north of Maryland, including New York, has received uneven attention. The best overview of the subject remains Arthur Zilversmit, *The First Emancipation: The Abolition of Slavery in the North* (Chicago, 1967). Joanne Pope Melish, *Disowning Slavery: Gradual Emancipation and "Race" in New England, 1780–1860* (Ithaca, N.Y., 1998), is a stimulating study of the cultural implications of emancipation in the regions to the north and east of New York. On Pennsylvania, which initiated gradual abolition almost a generation before New York, see Gary B. Nash and Jean R. Soderlund, *Freedom by Degrees: Emancipation in Pennsylvania and Its Aftermath* (New York, 1991). For provocative interpretations of Northern emancipation from the perspective of economic historians, see Robert William Fogel and Stanley L. Engerman, "Philanthropy at Bargain Prices: Notes on the Economics of Gradual Emancipation," *Journal of Legal Studies* 3 (June 1974), 377–399; and Claudia Dale Goldin, "The Economics of Emancipation," *Journal of Economic History* 33 (March 1973), 66–85. Works by Groth, Kruger, Berlin, the Hortons, and White listed in the previous paragraphs offer insight into the subject of abolition in New York.

The most comprehensive study focused on the debate over gradual abolition is David N. Gellman, "Inescapable Discourse: The Rhetoric of Slavery and the Politics of Abolition in Early National New York" (Ph.D. diss., Northwestern University, 1997). The Papers of the Society for Promoting the Manumission of Slaves in New York City, more commonly referred to as the New-York Manumission Society, are housed at the New-York Historical Society in New York City. Newspapers published throughout the state during the late eighteenth century provide ample primary material on slavery and abolition during the early national period.

Shane White and Graham Russell Hodges, discussed above, provide excellent studies of free black life in early national New York, as does Leslie Marie Harris, "Creating the African American Working Class: Black and White Workers, Abolitionists and Reformers in New York City, 1785–1863" (Ph.D. diss., Stanford University, 1995), which includes valuable insights into African American community organizations. See also Robert J. Swan, "John Teasman: African American Educator, and the Emergence of Community in Early Black New York City, 1787–1815," *Journal of the Early Republic* 12 (Fall 1992), 331–356; Marvin Edward McAllister, "'White People Do Not Know How to Behave at Entertainments Designed for Ladies and Gentlemen of Colour': A History of New York's African Grove/American Theatre" (Ph.D. diss., Northwestern University, 1997); Paul A. Gilje and Howard B. Rock, "'Sweep O! Sweep O!': The African American Chimney Sweeps and Citizenship in the New Nation," *William and Mary Quarterly* 51, 3d. ser. (July 1994), 507–538; and Gary B. Nash, "Forging Freedom: The Emancipation Experience in Northern Seaport Cities, 1775–1820," in *Slavery and Freedom in the Age of the American Revolution*, ed. Ira Berlin and Ronald Hoffman (Charlottesville, Va., 1983), 3–48. For a biography that sheds important light on the struggles of free blacks in rural New York, see Nell Irvin Painter, *Sojourner Truth: A Life, a Symbol* (New York, 1996).

On black voting during the era, see Charles W. Wesley, "Negro Suffrage in the Period of Constitution-Making, 1787–1865," *Journal of Negro History* 32 (April 1947), 143–168; and Dixon Ryan Fox, "The Negro Vote in Old New York," *Political Science Quarterly* 32 (June 1917), 252–275. Shane White, "'It Was a Proud Day': African American Festivals and Parades in the North, 1741–1834," *Journal of American History* 81 (June 1994), 13–50; and David Waldstreicher, *In the Midst of Perpetual Fetes: The Making of American Nationalism, 1776–1820* (Chapel Hill, 1997), provide insight into the cultural and racial politics of public celebration during the early national period.

The early political and constitutional history of New York has, over the years, attracted the attention of a variety of talented historians. Alfred F. Young, *The Democratic Republicans of New York: The Origins, 1763–1797* (Chapel Hill, 1967); and Richard Morris, ed., *John Jay: The Making of a Revolutionary, Unpublished Papers, 1745–1780* (New York,

1975), were particularly helpful in preparing this volume. See also Edward Countryman, *A People in Revolution: The American Revolution and Political Society in New York, 1760–1790* (Baltimore, 1981); and John P. Kaminski, *George Clinton: Yeoman Politician of the New Republic* (Madison, Wis., 1993).

Two excellent articles on the competitive, not to mention corrupt, nature of campaigns and elections in early New York State are Harvey Strum, "Property Qualifications and Voting Behavior in New York, 1807–1816," *Journal of the Early Republic* 1 (Winter 1981), 347–371; and Alan Taylor, "'The Art of Hook and Snivey': Political Culture in Upstate New York during the 1790s," *Journal of American History* 79 (March 1993), 1371–1396. Essays in Manfred Jones and Robert V. Wells, eds., *New Opportunities in a New Nation: The Development of New York after the Revolution* (Schenectady, N.Y., 1982), highlight the state's rapid post-Revolution growth and expansion.

For treatments of freemanship laws and practices in New York City, see Robert Francis Seybolt, *The Colonial Citizen of New York City* (Madison, Wis., 1918); and Michael Kammen, *Colonial New York: A History* (New York, 1975). Helpful in contextualizing local New York debates over citizenship is James H. Kettner, *The Development of American Citizenship, 1608–1870* (Chapel Hill, 1978).

The Convention of 1821 and the Politics of Disfranchisement

In addition to the works by Litwack, Williamson, and Wesley cited above, a brief review of the complex details of black disfranchisement in the North can be found in James Truslow Adams, "Disfranchisement of Negroes in New England," *American Historical Review* 30 (April 1925): 543–547.

For a classic overview of the emergence of nineteenth-century racism, see George M. Fredrickson, *The Black Image in the White Mind: The Debate on Afro-American Character and Destiny, 1817–1914* (New York, 1971). For a penetrating analysis of popular antebellum racism, particularly as it relates to the "Jim Crow" character and the rise of the New York City minstrel theater, see Eric Lott, *Love and Theft: Blackface Minstrelsy and the American Working Class* (New York, 1993). For additional insight into black minstrelsy and cultural racism, see Sam Denison,

Scandalize My Name: Black Imagery in Popular Music (New York, 1982); and Robert C. Toll, *Blacking Up: The Minstrel Show in Nineteenth-Century America* (New York, 1974). David R. Roediger, *The Wages of Whiteness: Race and the Making of the American Working Class*, rev. ed. (New York, 1999), has cast the issues of race, including the New York minstrel stage, in terms that have stimulated much new research and debate.

On connections between national and New York politics, particularly the Missouri crisis and Martin Van Buren's role in the emergence of the second-party system, see Richard H. Brown, "The Missouri Crisis, Slavery, and the Politics of Jacksonianism," *South Atlantic Quarterly* 65 (Winter 1966), 55–72. See also Joseph L. Arbena, "Politics or Principle? Rufus King and the Opposition to Slavery, 1785–1825," *Essex Institute Historical Collections* (January 1965), 56–77; Don E. Fehrenbacher, *The South in Three Sectional Crises* (Baton Rouge, 1980); and Donald L. Robinson, *Slavery in the Structure of American Politics, 1765–1820* (New York, 1971). As on many other aspects of Jacksonian America, Charles Seller, *The Market Revolution: Jacksonian America, 1815–1846* (New York, 1991), offers a stimulating overview of the Missouri crisis and national politics in general.

The best source for studying the 1821 New York Constitutional Convention directly is Nathaniel H. Carter and William L. Stone, *Reports of the Proceedings and Debates of the Convention of 1821, Assembled for the Purpose of Amending the Constitution of the State of New York* (Albany, 1821). For documents and commentary comparing constitutional revision in New York to the same process in Massachusetts and Virginia, see Merrill D. Peterson, ed., *Democracy, Liberty, and Property: The State Constitutional Conventions of the 1820s* (Indianapolis, 1966).

On partisan politics in New York leading up to and including New York's 1821 Constitutional Convention, see John Anthony Casais, "The New York State Constitutional Convention of 1821 and Its Aftermath" (Ph.D. diss., Columbia University, 1967). Casais's description of the origins of the convention and his compilation of partisan affiliations and voting tendencies of the convention delegates has proved particularly valuable for the present study. See also Anthony Gronowicz, *Race and Class Politics in New York City before the Civil War* (Boston, 1998), for a study that integrates race into a reinterpretation of antebellum New York City politics. Evan Cornog, *The Birth of Empire: DeWitt Clinton and the American Experience, 1769–1828* (New York, 1998), has written an important biography of the leading figure in both New York politics and New York's geographical and economic development during this period. For a useful study of Martin Van Buren, see Donald B. Cole, *Martin Van Buren and the American Political System* (Princeton, 1984). Judith Wellman, "Women's Rights, Republicanism, and Revolutionary Rhetoric in Antebellum New York State," *New York History* 69 (July 1988), 352–384, offers a valuable analysis of the relationship between the rhetoric of gendered and racial exclusion at the convention. Jabez D. Hammond, *The History of Political Parties in the State of New-York, from the Ratification of the Federal Constitution to December, 1840,* 4th ed. (Syracuse, 1852), provides a nineteenth-century political insider's account of New York politics.

The Long Reconstruction, 1821–1877

The half-century after 1821, as New York and the nation moved toward Civil War and on to Reconstruction, has been the subject of a rich and varied historiography. For the best study of the struggle against the 1821 property qualification in mid-nineteenth-century New York, see Phyllis F. Field, *The Politics of Race in New York: The Struggle for Black Suffrage in the Civil War Era* (Ithaca, N.Y., 1982). Though colored by the author's staunchly nativist views, Joel Tyler Headley, *The Great Riots of New York, 1712–1873* (New York, 1873), is a useful guide to the urban uprisings of the period. Studying New York City alongside New Orleans and San Francisco makes Mary P. Ryan, *Civic Wars: Democracy and Public Life in the American City during the Nineteenth Century* (Berkeley, 1997), a particularly illuminating study of the transformations in urban political culture between the 1820s and the 1870s. Two recent works have offered original reinterpretations of the public culture of early nineteenth-century New York: Carol Sheriff, *The Artificial River: The Erie Canal and the Paradox of Progress, 1817–1862* (New York, 1996); and Alan Taylor, *William Cooper's Town: Power and Persuasion on the Frontier of the Early American Republic* (New York, 1995).

In the 1820s and 1830s, the Empire State was the site of important political, social, and cultural transformations. The studies of Lee Benson, *The Concept of Jacksonian Democracy: New York as a Test Case* (Princeton, 1961); and Anthony Gronowicz, already cited, illuminate important dimensions of the political culture of Jacksonian democracy. Linda K.

Kerber, "Abolitionists and Amalgamators: The New York City Race Riots of 1834," *New York History* 48 (1967), 28–39, usefully places race at the center of her study of antebellum urban disorder. Jonathan D. Sarna, *Jacksonian Jew: The Two Worlds of Mordecai Noah* (New York, 1981), explores the complex public life of the editor of the *National Advocate*.

James Brewer Stewart has recently argued that the antebellum North gave rise to a culture of "racial modernity"; see James Brewer Stewart, "Modernizing 'Difference': The Political Meanings of Color in the Free States, 1776–1840," *Journal of the Early Republic* 19 (Winter 1999), 691–712. The antebellum history of race and public life in New York is documented in the previously cited Harris, "Creating the African American Working Class"; Rhoda G. Freeman, "The Free Negro in New York before the Civil War" (Ph.D. diss., Columbia University, 1966); and George E. Walker, *The Afro-American in New York City, 1827–1860* (New York, 1993).

Antebellum New York City has been the subject of some of the most important works of social history in recent decades. Particularly useful studies include Christine Stansell, *City of Women: Sex and Class in New York, 1789–1860* (New York, 1986); Sean Wilentz, *Chants Democratic: New York City and the Rise of the American Working Class, 1788–1850* (New York, 1984); and Richard B. Stott, *Workers in the Metropolis: Class, Ethnicity, and Youth in Antebellum New York City* (New York, 1990). Tyler Anbinder, *Five Points: The Nineteenth-Century New York City Neighborhood That Invented Tap Dance, Stole Elections and Became the World's Most Notorious Slum* (New York, 2001), is a lively and thoroughly researched depiction of nineteenth-century New York's most notorious community. For cultural battles in 1840s New York, featuring Walt Whitman, Herman Melville, and John L. O'Sullivan, among others, see Edward L. Widmer, *Young America: The Flowering of Democracy in New York City* (New York, 1998). A particularly original reinterpretation of urban politics is offered in Amy Bridges, *A City in the Republic: Antebellum New York and the Origins of Machine Politics* (New York, 1984).

For race and the anteblleum North more generally, see Horton and Horton, *In Hope of Liberty*, previously cited; Leonard P. Curry, *The Free Black in Urban America, 1800–1850: The Shadow of the Dream* (Chicago, 1981); and Patrick Rael, *Black Identity and Black Protest in the Antebellum North* (Chapel Hill, 2002).

On the 1846 New York Constitutional Convention, see John Langley Stanley, "Majority Tyranny in Tocqueville's America: The Failure of Negro Suffrage in New York State in 1846" (Ph.D. diss., Cornell University, 1966). The 1846 convention took place against the backdrop of the antirent wars in the Empire State; see Reeve Huston, *Land and Freedom: Rural Society, Popular Protest, and Party Politics in Antebellum New York* (New York, 2000); and Charles W. McCurdy, *The Anti-Rent Era in New York Law and Politics, 1839–1865* (New York, 2001).

While historians have tended to focus on the New England origins of American abolitionism, the Empire State was a central site for antislavery activism in the mid–nineteenth century. On Gerrit Smith, see John Stauffer, *The Black Hearts of Men: Radical Abolitionism and the Transformation of Race* (Cambridge, Mass., 2002). A useful nineteenth-century biography of Smith is Octavius Brooks Frothingham, *Gerrit Smith: A Biography* (New York, 1878). Benjamin Quarles, "Letters from Negro Leaders to Gerrit Smith," *Journal of Negro History* 27 (October 1942), 432–453, reveals some reactions to Smith's land reform plans. For additional insights into the interracial dimensions of abolition in New York, see John R. McKivigan, "The Frederick Douglass–Gerrit Smith Friendship and Political Abolitionism in the 1850s," in *Frederick Douglass: New Literary and Historical Essays*, ed. Eric J. Sundquist (Cambridge, Mass., 1990). On James McCune Smith, see David W. Blight, "In Search of Learning, Liberty and Self Definition: James McCune Smith and the Ordeal of the Antebellum Black Intellectual," *Afro-Americans in New York Life and History* 9 (July 1985), 7–25. For Henry Highland Garnet, see Joel Schor, *Henry Highland Garnet: A Voice of Black Radicalism in the Nineteenth Century* (Westport, Conn., 1977); and Earl Ofari, *Let Your Motto Be Resistance: The Life and Thought of Henry Highland Garnet* (Boston, 1972).

The Seneca Falls Convention of 1848 and the history of women's rights activism across New York State are explored in a number of works: Nell Painter's biography of *Sojourner Truth*, already cited; Ellen Carol DuBois, *Feminism and Suffrage: The Emergence of an Independent Women's Movement in America* (Ithaca, N.Y., 1978); Nancy A. Hewitt, *Women's Activism and Social Change: Rochester, New York, 1822–1872* (Ithaca, N.Y., 1984); Judith Wellman, already cited; and Elizabeth Cady Stanton, Susan B. Anthony, and Matilda Joslyn Gage, *A History of Woman Suffrage*, vols. 1 and 2 (Rochester, 1881, 1882).

The single best study of New York politics in the era of the Civil War is Iver Bernstein, *The New York City Draft Riots: Their Significance for American Society and Politics in the Age of the Civil War* (New York, 1990). Eric Foner, *Reconstruction: America's Unfinished Revolution, 1863–1877* (New York, 1988), describes the ongoing "Reconstruction of the North." New York City's place in national politics in the era of the Civil War and Reconstruction is covered in David Quigley, *Second Founding: New York City and the Reconstruction of American Democracy* (New York, 2003). See also Heather Cox Richardson, *The Death of Reconstruction: Race, Labor, and Politics in the Post–Civil War North, 1865–1901* (Cambridge, Mass., 2001). William Gillette offers an insightful examination of black enfranchisement and white resistance in two works: *Retreat from Reconstruction, 1869–1879* (Baton Rouge, 1979) and *The Right to Vote: Politics and the Passage of the Fifteenth Amendment* (Baltimore, 1965). Ena Farley, *The Underside of Reconstruction New York: The Struggle for Black Equality* (New York, 1993), is a suggestive study of the white supremacist dimensions of New York life after the Civil War. Other studies of postbellum New York society and politics include James C. Mohr, *The Radical Republicans and Reform in New York during Reconstruction* (Ithaca, N.Y., 1973); and Jerome Mushkat, *The Reconstruction of the New York Democracy, 1861–1874* (Rutherford, N.J., 1981). On the Tilden Commission, see Alexander Keyssar, already cited; and Sven Beckert, *The Monied Metropolis: New York City and the Consolidation of the American Bourgeoisie, 1850–1896* (New York, 2001).

Notes

NOTES TO PART I

1. Graham Russell Hodges, "Black Revolt in New York and the Neutral Zone," in *New York in the Age of the Constitution, 1775–1780*, ed. Paul A. Gilje and William Pencak (Rutherford, N.J., 1993), 21–40.

2. Edgar J. McManus, *A History of Negro Slavery in New York* (Syracuse, 1966), 172, 199.

3. Graham Russell Hodges, ed., *The Black Loyalist Directory: African Americans in Exile after the American Revolution* (New York, 1996), xi, 217–223.

4. Richard Morris, ed., *John Jay: The Making of a Revolutionary, Unpublished Papers, 1745–1780* (New York, 1975), 402; Henry P. Johnston, ed., *The Correspondence and Public Papers of John Jay* (New York, 1890), 1:136.

5. Voice vote.

6. Pounds were a standard British monetary unit; the New York constitution used the British measure for its property-holding requirement, which was later converted to $50. Forty shillings was the equivalent of two English pounds and was later converted to $5. Based on an examination of census data from 1790, one historian estimates that this standard qualified approximately 58 percent of white males to vote, with a 70 percent rate of qualification if only heads of households are counted; see Alfred F. Young, *The Democratic Republicans of New York: The Origins, 1763–1797* (Chapel Hill, 1967), 84–85.

7. With its 1775 cutoff date, this provision forestalled the extension of the franchise to urban residents with insufficient property to qualify as voters in state elections. Freemanship was a status conferred on men born in the city or granted by municipal authorities to city residents deemed worthy. Freemanship guaranteed the full rights and privileges of the city, including the right to vote in municipal elections. In colonial times, New York City restricted free black access to freemanship. In the postindependence period, exclusion of free blacks from many crafts and trades also prevented them from achieving this status. An 1804

state law made the state's property-holding requirements for voting a prerequisite for freemanship, which at least in theory lessened the impact of voting rights discrimination for municipal elections. See Graham R. Hodges, "Legal Bonds of Attachment: The Freemanship Law of New York City, 1648–1801," in *Authority and Resistance in Early New York*, ed. William Pencak and Conrad Edick Wright (New York, 1988), 226–244; and Edwin G. Burrows and Mike Wallace, *Gotham: A History of New York City to 1898* (New York, 1999), 140, 330.

8. Quakers, members of the religious society also known as the Friends, banned the taking of oaths, which, taken literally, call on God as a witness to the veracity of the oath taker.

9. One hundred pounds was subsequently converted to $250, a freehold requirement large enough to exclude more than two-thirds of adult males from voting in senatorial and gubernatorial elections in the late eighteenth century; Young, *Democratic Republicans*, 83–85.

10. A person of mixed African and Native American descent.

11. The 1777 constitution provided that, instead of merely going to the governor—the state's executive—for approval, all legislation approved by both houses of the legislature be considered by a body known as the Council of Revision. This council included the governor, the chancellor of the state court system, and members of the state supreme court.

12. The legislative history of the failed gradual emancipation bill of 1785 can be followed in *Journal of the Assembly of the State of New-York, at Their Second Meeting of the Eighth Session* (New York, 1785), 48, 49, 53–56, 62–64, 76–77, 86, 119–120; and *Journal of the Senate, of the State of New-York, at Their Second Meeting of the Eighth Session* (New York, 1785), 8, 15, 20–23, 39, 42, 45, 55–56.

13. Quacco and Mingo are meant to be African-sounding names. The name Quacco is of West African origin. Such names appeared in New York newspapers to denote, often derisively, African American characters.

14. Isaac Bickerstaff, *The Padlock: A Comic Opera* (London, 1768); *The Oxford Companion to English Literature*, 4th ed. (New York, 1967), 607; Sylvia Wynter, "The Eye of the Other: Images of the Black in Spanish Literature," and Carter G. Woodson, "Attitudes of the Iberian Peninsula (in Literature)," in *Blacks in Hispanic Literature: Critical Essays*, ed. Miriam DeCosta (Port Washington, N.Y., 1977), 18, 37–38.

15. Quoted from the second paragraph of the Declaration of Independence.

16. A reference to American sailors seized by pirates and held in captivity on the Mediterranean coast of North Africa.

17. This biblical quotation is from Acts 18:26.

18. Miller followed his statement of the religious imperative to oppose slavery with several paragraphs criticizing attempts to justify slavery on biblical grounds.

19. Miller refers to the entire United States, not New York specifically, in this section of his speech.

20. In February 1785, Aaron Burr, representing New York City in the state assembly, proposed immediate abolition. His proposal was voted down thirty-three to thirteen (see *Journal of the Assembly* 8, 53). Although Burr also supported gradual abolition, most of the supporters of Burr's amendment were actually opponents of any form of abolition, who apparently voted for Burr's bill as a political ploy.

21. Town officials responsible for dispensing local poor relief and indenturing to local households children not supported by their parents.

22. The state legislature reduced this subsidy in 1802 and entirely repealed this portion of the emancipation law in 1804, finding that slave owners were taking advantage of this provision to officially abandon their slaves' children, only to be appointed the masters of the same children by the overseers of the poor. This allowed slaveholders and former slaveholders to receive state funds to support children who otherwise would have been bound to their households until well into adulthood. Concerned about the cost of this provision to the state, legislators repealed the state subsidy but not gradual abolition itself. See *Laws of the State of New-York, Passed at the Twenty-Fifth Session* (Albany, 1802), 82–83; and *Laws of the State of New-York* (Albany, 1804), 479–480.

23. Shane White, *Somewhat More Independent: The End of Slavery in New York City, 1770–1810* (Athens, Ga., 1991), 26.

24. The Federalist Party.

25. John Adams (1735–1826) of Massachusetts was the second president of the United States. Charles Cotesworth Pinckney (1746–1825) of South Carolina represented his state at the U.S. Constitutional Convention in 1787 and was Federalist candidate for vice president in 1800 and president in 1804 and 1808. Rufus King (1755–1827) served as a delegate from Massachusetts to the U.S. Constitutional Convention. Shortly thereafter he moved to New York, representing his adopted state as U.S. senator from 1789 to 1796 and again from 1813 to 1825. King also was the Federalist candidate for vice president in 1804 and 1808, Federalist nominee for president in 1816, and two-time ambassador to Great Britain. In addition, King served as a delegate to the 1821 New York State Constitutional Convention. Timothy Pickering (1745–1829), of Massachusetts and Pennsylvania, served Washington and Adams as secretary of state and later represented Massachusetts in the U.S. Senate from 1803 to 1811.

26. Responding to the harassment of U.S. shipping by the British navy in its quest to cut off food supplies to Napoleonic France, President Jefferson prompted the U.S. Congress to pass an Embargo Act in 1807. This secession of foreign trade was an unsuccessful attempt to pressure warring European powers to respect the United States as a neutral country with the right to trade freely. The policy imposed great hardships on the domestic U.S. economy.

27. In other words, the Democratic-Republican, or Jeffersonian, Party.

28. Sydney refers here to Thomas Jefferson.

29. A reference to the fact that by the terms of his will, Washington, upon his death, freed his slaves and made provisions for their future working and living conditions.

30. Alexander Hamilton died of gunshot wounds sustained in a duel with his political archenemy Aaron Burr in 1804.

31. Harvey Strum, "Property Qualifications and Voting Behavior in New York, 1807–1816," *Journal of the Early Republic* 1 (Winter 1981), 348.

32. According to the Oxford English Dictionary, "the action of making oneself legally responsible for the fulfillment of a contract."

33. New Jersey was last, enacting gradual abolition in 1804.

34. *Freedom's Journal*, July 13, 1827, published Tompkin's 1817 remarks. On this pioneering African American newspaper, see document N.

NOTES TO PART II

1. The delegates debating and voting on the future of African American citizenship were all males. Ninety of the 126 delegates were between the ages of forty and sixty years old, with the median age falling in the forty to fifty-year-old range. More than half the delegates reported their profession or occupation as agricultural. The "farmer" category in the still mostly rural state, however, was quite broad and included members of the state's great landholding families. Thirty-seven delegates listed were lawyers, several of whom were prominent contributors to convention debates. Nine delegates identified themselves as merchants, seven as "mechanics," and five as medical doctors. All but one of the delegates stated America as their place of birth, over half from New York itself, about a quarter from Connecticut, and much smaller numbers from eight other states. While delegates were not surveyed for racial identity, almost certainly they all would have been classified as white. Over half listed their father's ancestry as English, with much smaller numbers listing Dutch, Scottish, or other northern European origins; one delegate recorded Italian descent, while four others provided no ethnic information.

2. John Langley Stanley, "Majority Rule in Tocqueville's America: The Failure of Negro Suffrage in New York State in 1846" (Ph.D. diss., Cornell University, 1966), 11.

3. Chilton Williamson, *American Suffrage: From Property to Democracy, 1760–1860* (Princeton, 1960), 195.

4. Connecticut had begun gradual abolition in 1784, granting freedom to the children of the state's small slave population at age twenty-five. The state did not enact a full, formal abolition of slavery until 1848.

5. Williamson, *American Suffrage*, 164–172, 182–190, 195; James Truslow Adams, "Disfranchisement of Negroes in New England," *American Historical Review* 30 (April 1925), 543–547.

6. In 1803, President Thomas Jefferson authorized the purchase for $15 million of a vast tract of French-owned land west of the Mississippi River. The purchase not only included the present-day state of Louisiana but also land that would become all or part of thirteen other states.

7. This began as a resolution in the assembly, the lower house of the New York state legislature.

8. See Jonathan D. Sarna, *Jacksonian Jew: The Two Worlds of Mordecai Noah* (New York, 1981).

9. Samuel A. Hay, *African American Theatre: An Historical and Critical Analysis* (Cambridge, Eng., 1994), 13.

10. *National Advocate*, September 24, 1821.

11. The theater was located at 38 Thomas Street, between Chapel and Hudson. Edwin G. Burrows and Mike Wallace, *Gotham: A History of New York City to 1898* (New York, 1999), 487.

12. James Tallmadge Jr. (1778–1853), a Bucktail delegate from Dutchess County, was a prominent lawyer who achieved lasting fame as the New York congressman who proposed the 1819 antislavery amendment that touched off the Missouri crisis (see document K).

13. Nathan Sanford (1777–1838) of New York City was affiliated with the Tammany wing of the Republican Party. A prominent politician, Sanford served at various times as speaker of the assembly, state senator, and, from 1815 to 1821 and 1826 to 1831, U.S. senator. A lawyer, he also served as chancellor of the state's equity courts during 1823–1826.

14. In the English political system, the monarch, the House of Lords, and the House of Commons, the three recognized independent branches of government, theoretically represented three distinct social groupings—or estates—in society; respectively, the royalty, the nobility, and the common people. Different rules governed the selection of representatives of each estate.

15. There were not property-holding requirements limiting the right of adult men to vote in Pennsylvania and adult white men to vote in Ohio.

16. A patronizing reference to women.

17. American Indians.

18. As of 1820, fourteen of twenty-three states had some form of racial barrier to voting rights.

19. Garments.

20. Van Rensselaer, as a major general in the militia during the War of 1812, led an unsuccessful campaign against the British along the U.S.-Canadian frontier in the Great Lakes region bordering western New York. Van Rensselaer resigned his command as a result.

21. Under Jacob J. Brown (1775–1828), U.S. troops successfully resisted the British siege of Fort Erie, located across the Canadian border, in September 1814. Peter Buell Porter (1773–1844), Republican politician turned militia commander, led the assault that lifted the British siege.

22. Battle of New Orleans, January 8, 1815, in which American soldiers, militiamen, and others routed British forces.

23. Stephen Van Rensselaer (1764–1839) inherited the vast landholdings of the Rensselaer patroonship. A Federalist, he served in the state assembly and state senate and as lieutenant governor from 1795 to 1801. He also ran unsuccessfully for governor of New York on two occasions and later served in the U.S. Congress. In addition, Van Rensselaer participated in economic development initiatives such as the Erie Canal.

24. Peter Augustus Jay (1776–1843), the eldest child of Founding Father and former governor of New York John Jay, represented Westchester County at the 1821 convention. An attorney, a Federalist, and a former member of the state assembly, Peter A. Jay was appointed by Governor DeWitt Clinton as a New York City criminal court judge in 1820, a post Jay held briefly.

25. North Carolina did not constitutionally bar free blacks from voting until 1835, Virginia until 1830, and Pennsylvania until 1838. The Connecticut constitution was more ambiguous than Jay suggested, as, prior to that state's 1818 constitution, Connecticut had begun to disfranchise blacks by law. See document J.

26. Jay quoted from article 4, section 2 of the U.S. Constitution, as did subsequent delegates speaking against disfranchisement.

27. By a 1792 act of the U.S. Congress, "each and every free able-bodied white male citizen of the respective states" between the ages of eighteen and forty-five was to enroll in the state militia. See "An Act more effectually to provide for the National Defence by establishing an Uniform Militia through the United States," in *The Public Statutes at Large of the United States of America from the Organization of the Government in 1789, to March 3, 1845.* 1 (Boston, 1845), 271.

28. Erastus Root (1773–1846), of Delaware County, enjoyed a long career in New York politics. A lawyer by training, Root served three terms in the U.S. Congress prior to the 1821 convention. In the years after the convention, Root served as lieutenant governor, as speaker of the New York Assembly, and another term in the U.S. Congress. A Bucktail Republican, Root later joined the Whig Party.

29. The total population of New York City in 1820 was 123,706. Free African Americans comprised 10,886 of that total, while 518 blacks remained in slavery; see Ira Rosenwaike, *Population History of New York City* (Syracuse, 1972), 18.

30. A reference to the fact that even though in several places the U.S. Constitution accounts for the existence and the perpetuation of slavery, the drafters of that document excluded any explicit reference to slaves and slavery.

31. A paraphrase of article 1, section 2 of the U.S. Constitution. The actual text reads: "Representatives and direct Taxes shall be apportioned among the several States which may be included within this Union, according to their respective Numbers, which shall be determined by adding to the whole Number of free Persons, including those bound to Service for a Term of Years, and excluding Indians not taxed, three fifths of all other Persons." This last phrase is a reference to slaves.

32. A biblical reference to Exodus 20:5, echoed later in the convention by Peter Jay. In Exodus, shortly before delivering the Ten Commandments, God warns the Israelites that the descendants of those who shun divine instructions shall be made to suffer.

33. See "An Act to authorize the Raising of two Regiments of Men of Colour," in *Laws of the State of New-York, Passed at the Thirty-Sixth, Thirty-Seventh and Thirty-Eighth Sessions of the Legislature, Commencing November 1812, and Ending April 1815, vol. III* (Albany, 1815), 22–23.

34. This sentence is a close paraphrase of the opening line of Thomas Paine's famous American Revolutionary pamphlet *The Crisis*, no. 1, published in December 1776.

35. The phrase can be translated as "The utterance of one person is the exclusion of another." In essence, Young is saying that the state's reliance on the federal government's rules for service in the militia automatically precluded black militia service.

36. Native Americans.

37. James Kent (1763–1847) was chancellor of the New York equity courts at the time of the convention, having previously served as chief judge on the New York State Supreme Court. After his retirement from the state courts in 1823, Kent authored his four-volume *Commentaries on American Law*, a major and often-reprinted work of legal scholarship.

38. Abraham Van Vechten (1762–1837) was the New York state attorney general from 1809 to 1811 and from 1813 to 1815, having previously served in both the state senate and the state assembly.

39. Ambrose Spencer (1765–1848), a Clintonian delegate from Albany, was a forceful presence in New York state politics during the first two decades of the nineteenth century. He began his political career as a Federalist but became a Republican in 1798. He worked closely with DeWitt Clinton to control patronage in the state through the Council of Appointments. Spencer served on the state supreme court from 1804 to 1823, and for the last four years of that term as chief justice. He later served in the U.S. Congress.

40. Jacob Radcliff (1764–1844), a Federalist representing New York City, served in a variety of public offices prior to the convention, including on the state supreme court and as mayor of New York City.

41. Prisons.

42. Literally translatable as "foolish fire," this Latin expression indicates a person who speaks without having worked out the logic of his or her stated position.

43. Kent's use of the term *minorities* does not correspond with our own contemporary usage of the term to describe racial and ethnic groups such as African Americans, Asian Americans, and Hispanic Americans. In the parlance of the eighteenth and nineteenth centuries, "minorities" meant a less-numerous class of people—usually those with significant wealth or property or holding an unpopular set of beliefs—who, in an unrestricted democracy, would find their rights and interests at risk.

44. A reference to William Shakespeare's play *The Merchant of Venice*. Shylock was the name of a Jewish moneylender cast as a villain, often with anti-Semitic overtones. Here Livingston invokes the negative image of Shylock not for anti-Semitic purposes but rather as a term of contempt for wealthy merchants and bankers, whose interests and virtues he contrasts with those of ordinary citizens.

45. Literally, Holy of Holies, or the inner sanctum of the ancient Jewish temple in Jerusalem.

46. All military engagements against the British during the War of 1812.

47. "Virtual representation" was the British idea that the colonies did not need to elect and dispatch actual representatives to Parliament because, as British subjects, Americans' interests were already taken into consideration.

48. John Duer (1782–1858), a Federalist, represented Orange County at the convention. Duer, a lawyer who once studied under Alexander Hamilton, in the years after the convention served as a U.S. district attorney and superior court judge, as well as producing works of legal scholarship.

49. Although it is very difficult to make precise comparisons between dollar values in the early nineteenth century and the early twenty-first century, in 1821, $250 was a substantial sum. A farm laborer with steady employment would likely have earned far less than that sum in a year. For African Americans emerging from slavery with few assets and little or no inherited property, acquiring a $250 freehold unencumbered by a mortgage would have been extremely difficult—indeed, even more so given the job discrimination that blacks often faced.

50. The phrase "visiting the sins of the fathers upon the children" derives from the biblical book of Exodus 20:5. See note 32 above.

51. Though the editors claim thirty-one votes against, only thirty names appear in the roll-call tally.

52. John Scott Eldon (1751–1838) served as England's lord chancellor, a high judicial post, during the first three decades of the nineteenth century; Sir William Scott, Lord Stowell (1745–1827), served as judge of the High Court of Admiralty, 1798–1827.

53. The 1772 Somerset case was a landmark in British legal history; Lord Mansfield ruled that James Somerset, a slave, was free as English law neither "al-

lowed [nor] approved" of slavery. England's highest court invalidated slavery on English soil but did not address the question of abolition in the British Empire.

54. Charles Z. Lincoln, *The Constitutional History of New York* (Rochester, N.Y., 1906), 1:754; 2:3–5.

NOTES TO PART III

1. "Address of the New York State Convention of Colored Citizens, to the People of the State," *Colored American*, December 19, 1840.

2. Dixon Denham (1786–1828) and Hugh Clapperton (1788–1827) were the first Europeans to travel to what is now northern Nigeria, returning to London in 1825.

3. The 1820 U.S. census indicates approximately ten thousand slaves in New York. One historian estimates that in the southern six counties of the state (Kings, New York, Queens, Richmond, Suffolk, Westchester), 2,866 received their freedom when the abolition law went into effect in 1827; see Vivienne Kruger, "Born to Run: The Slave Family in Early New York, 1626–1827" (Ph.D. diss., Columbia University, 1985), 780–783.

4. The great black abolitionist, newspaper editor, and former slave Frederick Douglass offered the most famous expression of nineteenth-century black ambivalence about the Fourth of July in his speech "What to the Slave Is the Fourth of July?," delivered on July 5, 1852, in Rochester, New York.

5. In 1741, thirty black New Yorkers were put to death after authorities uncovered an alleged plot to burn down New York City. Hamilton likens the 1741 prosecutions to the infamous Salem, Massachusetts, witchcraft trials of 1692 because so much of the testimony implicating alleged New York plotters was of dubious veracity and was coercively extracted amid public hysteria. Some modern historians give much more credence to the actual existence of a conspiracy than Hamilton did in this speech.

6. A biblical reference to Isaiah 57:20.

7. Hamilton's remarks here were aimed specifically at Thomas Jefferson by quoting the Declaration of Independence and paraphrasing beliefs expressed in Jefferson's widely read *Notes on the State of Virginia* (1785).

8. Paraphrased from the Fifth Amendment to the U.S. Constitution.

9. Thomas Clarkson (1760–1846), one of the leading English abolitionists, campaigned tirelessly against the British slave trade and later advocated the abolition of slavery in the British West Indies. He started his long abolitionist career with *An Essay on the Slavery and Commerce of the Human Species* (1786), originally composed for an essay competition at Cambridge University.

10. Thomas Eddy (1758–1827) was a New York City Quaker whose business successes propelled him into a variety of reform causes, especially prison

reform, as well as into the antislavery movement. John Murray Jr. (1737–1808) was a founding member and active figure in the New-York Manumission Society, serving that organization as treasurer for many years. A wealthy Quaker merchant, Murray also participated in a variety of other reform causes and business enterprises. See prior documents for biographical information on John Jay and Daniel Tompkins.

11. Thomas Clarkson, William Wilberforce, William Pitt, Charles James Fox, William Wyndham Grenville, George Washington, John Adams, Thomas Jefferson, John Hancock, and Benjamin Franklin. Grenville (1759–1834) was briefly British prime minister and a moving force behind the abolition of the British slave trade. Pitt (1759–1806) served as prime minister of Britain during 1783–1801 and 1804–1806. Pitt's career coincided with intense periods of agitation against the British slave trade, and Pitt himself identified openly with the abolitionist cause. Fox (1749–1806), was a leading Whig politician who briefly served on three occasions as British foreign secretary. His political rivalry with Pitt notwithstanding, Fox, too, embraced antislavery beliefs, working for the passage in 1806 of a parliamentary resolution supporting in principle the abolition of the slave trade. John Hancock (1737–1793) was president of the Continental Congress at the signing of the Declaration of Independence and served several terms as governor of Massachusetts during the period when the state's courts invalidated slavery there. Paul claims all of these men for the antislavery cause, even though the depth and sincerity of the commitment to abolition among them varied widely. As the inclusion of Jefferson suggests, Paul interpreted opposition to slavery and commitment to human equality in the broadest possible terms.

12. A reference to the system of channels that provided water to ancient Jerusalem.

13. Paul then provided a list of New York state senators and representatives to the state assembly who voted for the law that ended New York slavery in 1827.

14. New York State Assembly, *Journal*, 49th sess., 1826, appendix C, table X, cited in Phyllis F. Field, *The Politics of Race in New York* (Ithaca, N.Y., 1982), 37.

15. Carl D. Arfwedson, *The United States and Canada, in 1832, 1833, and 1834*, quoted in Leon Litwack, *North of Slavery* (Chicago, 1961), 83–84.

16. Leonard P. Curry, *The Free Black in Urban America, 1800–1850* (Chicago, 1981), 73. Linda K. Kerber overstates the case, but not by much, when she portrays "a New York as firmly Jim Crow [in the 1830s] as if the term had already been invented." Linda K. Kerber, "Abolitionists and Amalgamators: The New York City Race Riots of 1834," *New York History* 48 (1967), 28. Richard B. Stott, *Workers in the Metropolis* (New York, 1990), 145.

17. Even before 1840, opponents of black suffrage often invoked the specter of black criminality; in response, black activists argued for an environmentalist understanding of criminal behavior.

18. Various battles and engagements in the War of 1812. Commodore Oliver Hazard Perry commanded the American fleet in the Battle of Lake Erie.

19. A shield or defensive armor.

20. The legislation calling for the 1821 Convention removed the property qualification for all men in New York State—black and white.

21. "The morning stars sang together, and all the sons of God shouted for joy"—Job 38:7.

22. Revelation 22:16.

23. "For He hath made of one blood all the nations of the world to dwell on the face of the earth together"—Acts 17:26.

24. Former governor William Bouck, who served as chairman of the Committee on the Elective Franchise at the convention.

25. Russell is referring to continued disfranchisement of African American men in New Jersey, Pennsylvania, and Ohio.

26. On continued discrimination against African Americans in New York City, see Graham Hodges, *The New York City Cartmen, 1667–1850* (New York, 1986), 158–159.

27. Referring to John Kennedy's extensive use of crime statistics to make the case for disfranchisement.

28. By far the best treatment of Gerrit Smith is John Stauffer, *The Black Hearts of Men: Radical Abolitionists and the Transformation of Race* (Cambridge, Mass., 2002).

29. A secret group of radical abolitionists in New England and New York who funded John Brown as he raised small army to launch a slave insurrection in Virginia. The other five men were Thomas Wentworth Higginson, Samuel Gridley Howe, Theodore Parker, Franklin Sanborn, and George Luther Stearns.

30. Smith is referring to the recent and ongoing antirent protests in rural New York. See Reeve Huston, *Land and Freedom: Rural Society, Popular Protest, and Party Politics in Antebellum New York* (New York, 2000).

31. "O my soul, come not thou into their secret; unto their assembly, mine honor, be not thou united: for in their anger they slew a man, and in their self-will they digged down a wal."—Gen. 34:25.

32. Field, *Politics of Race*, 127.

33. Watkins was a general agent of the New York State Suffrage Association. In 1859, he spoke before the New York State Assembly in support of a statewide referendum. See Field, *Politics of Race*, 94.

34. Garnet was one of the leading black ministers in New York State; he was also quite controversial, due to his long association with colonization supporters.

35. By force and arms.

36. Here Watkins alluded to Chief Justice Roger Brooke Taney's 1857 decision in *Scott v. Sanford*.

37. James McCune Smith (1811–1865) was a preeminent African American

social critic and physician in the nineteenth century. See Stauffer, *Black Hearts of Men*.

38. From William Wordsworth's 1829 poem "Liberty."

39. Samuel J. Tilden letter of February 28, 1868, Box 6, Tilden Papers, New York Public Library.

40. Nell Irvin Painter, *Sojourner Truth: A Life, a Symbol* (New York, 1996), 229–230.

41. Referring to Harriet Beecher Stowe's exoticizing profile of Truth in the April 1863 *Atlantic Monthly*.

42. William Gillette, *The Right to Vote* (Baltimore, 1965), 115; interview with Peter B. Sweeny, *New York Herald*, November 26, 1869.

43. "Rejoicings in New York," *New Era*, April 14, 1870, 2.

44. "The Enfranchised Rejoicing," *New York Herald*, April 9, 1870; *New York Times*, April 9, 1870.

45. "Federal Preparations," *New York Times*, November 8, 1870, 1. *The Diary of George Templeton Strong*, edited by Allan Nevins and Milton Halsey Thomas (New York, 1952), October 27, 1870.

46. "The Federal Invasion of New York," *Journal of Commerce*, October 26, 1870, 2; "The Election," *New York Evening Post*, November 7, 1870, 4; *Journal of Commerce*, November 8, 1870; *New York Times*, November 9, 1870, 1.

47. "The Election," *New York Evening Post*, November 8, 1870, 2, 3.

48. A row or a commotion.

49. Hudson River.

50. William Maxwell Evarts (1818–1901), a leading New York Republican lawyer, defended President Andrew Johnson against impeachment charges, then served as Johnson's attorney general, was chief counsel for Rutherford B. Hayes before the Electoral Commission in 1877, and went on to serve as secretary of state and as U.S. senator from New York.

Index

Abolition: Canada, 22; and the 1821
  constitutional convention, 94–95,
  100, 108, 188, 194–197; New
  York (1827), 18, 23, 67–72, 74,
  121, 197, 218–235; North, 15, 20;
  South, 6; United States, 209. *See
  also* Gradual Abolition
Abolitionists, 203–204, 249, 260,
  286. *See also* American Anti-Slavery Society; Antislavery; New-York
  Manumission Society
Adams, John, 22, 231
Africa, 11, 21, 37–38, 41, 57, 209,
  215, 216, 228, 229, 234, 257. *See
  also* Colonization
African Americans: activists, conventions, and political organizations,
  202–203, 206, 219, 236–248,
  273–274, 278, 288, 300; appear-
  ing before 1846 convention, 254;
  capacity for citizenship debated,
  10, 42, 44, 50, 51, 58, 62, 88–89,
  107, 111–113, 121, 125, 127, 133,
  136–137,156,169,179, 184, 186,
  225, 238, 240, 243, 256; celebrating emancipation, 218–219; celebrating enfranchisement, 295–296;
  demography for New York discussed, 14, 32, 56, 67, 75, 76–77,
  113–114, 116, 132, 146, 182, 247;
  employment and property holding
  of, 17, 50, 212, 275–276; free, 1,
  191–192; petition to the 1821 convention, 107; rural, 4, 17; soldiers
  in Civil War, 209; southern, 253;
  women, 88, 126, 226. *See also*

Community formation amongst
  free African Americans
African Free School, 17, 20, 39, 40
African Grove Theatre, 87–89, 212
Africans, 14, 50, 58
African Zion Church, 218, 219
Alabama, and African American suf-
  frage, 135
Albany, 1, 18, 36, 203
Algerian captivity, 43, 89
Aliens (immigrants), 107, 115, 124,
  126, 139–140, 162, 163, 191, 192,
  239, 255–256, 267, 274. *See also*
  Immigration
American Anti-Slavery Society, 207,
  265
American Colonization Society, 18, 23
American Convention for Promoting
  the Abolition Slavery and Improv-
  ing the Condition of the African
  Race, 22
American Revolution, 2, 8, 13, 14,
  15, 19, 33, 128, 154, 166,
  179–180, 222, 243, 273, 274, 284
Anderson, Martin B., 309
Anthony, Susan B., 204
Antietam, 6
Antirent politics, 249
Antislavery, 9, 15; organizations, 2,
  34. *See also* Abolition; American
  Anti-Slavery Society; American
  Convention for Promoting the
  Abolition Slavery and Improving
  the Condition of the African Race;
  Ladies Anti-Slavery Society; New-
  York Manumission Society.

Aristocracy, 133, 155
Arizona, 208
Army, U.S., involvement in first equal manhood suffrage election, 304–306
Articles of Confederation, 19
Atlanta, Georgia, 6
Austrian Empire, 208

Bacon, Ezekiel, speaks at 1821 convention, 181–182
Ballots, 27, 81, 143, 280, 282
Bearing arms, 5
Beecher, Henry Ward, 276, 291
Bethel Church, 295
Bible, quoted or invoked, 43, 118, 223, 230, 231, 232, 234, 250, 251, 256, 258, 261, 269
Bickerstaff, Isaac, 36
Black Codes, 209
Bowdoin College, 212
Briggs, Olney, speaks at 1821 convention, 177–178, 180–181, 195, 199
Britain, 14, 22, 37–38; antislavery activities in, 20, 56, 185, 207, 231; as cautionary example of urban growth, 151; evacuation of New York City, 15, 20, 222; promise of freedom to African Americans during American Revolution, 33; slavery and abolition, 23, 56, 185, 198, 207, 208, 229, 231, 251; social mobility in, 185; social order in, 258; suffrage and, 103, 210
Brooklyn, 276
Brown, Jacob J., 109
Brown, John, 209, 260
Bruce, Benjamin, speaks at 1846 convention, 250–252
Bucktail Republicans, 74–75; at 1821 convention, 95, 100, 183
Buel, David Jr., speaks at 1821 convention, 160–161, 195
Bull Run, 6
Burr, Aaron, 333, 334
Butler, Rev. William F., 292–293
Butler, William Allen, 317

Cain, James, 304
California, 208

Canada, 14, 20, 22
Capitalism, 1
Carter, James, 317
Carter, Nathaniel H., 94
Central America, 207
Cervantes, Miguel de, 36–37
Children, and right of suffrage, 107, 126, 255
Christ, 231, 234, 240, 294
Citizens, 1, 46, 111, 307; African Americans as, 7, 31–32, 45, 128, 239, 251, 273; and Missouri Crisis, 86
Citizenship, 7, 13, 257, 276, 288, 292; African American, 2, 9, 16, 56, 76, 78, 95, 102, 126, 127, 128, 138, 142, 183, 209, 218, 239, 242, 296; defined, 4–5, 91; full, 5, 15, 81, 175, 183, 204, 219, 278; racialized, 2, 6, 189, 276, 286; and suffrage, 5, 241–242, 282; and U.S. Constitution, 210; women, 5, 77–78, 189, 267
Civil Rights movement, 3
Civil War, U.S., 1, 6, 8, 10, 204–205, 209, 278
Clapperton, Hugh, 216
Clarke, Robert, 180, 274; speaks at the 1821 convention, 117–122
Clarkson, Thomas, 20, 229, 231
Clergy barred from officeholding, 138–139
Clinton, DeWitt, 23, 73, 74, 94, 337
Clinton, George, 22
Clinton, Sir Henry, 14
Clintonians, 75, 76
Colonial New York, 4, 13, 14, 18, 26, 179, 186–187, 243, 331
Colonies, English, 14
Colonization, 18, 21, 23, 57, 212–213, 219. *See also* American Colonization Society
Colorado, 208
Colored American, 236
Colored Orphans' Asylum, 205, 276
Commercial Advertiser, 94
Community, formation amongst free African Americans, 16, 17, 56, 113, 186, 212, 219, 240, 275–276, 300

Compromise of 1850, 208
Compromise of 1877, 307, 342
Confiscation Act, 209
Congress, United States, 6, 84–86, 207, 210, 230, 295
Connecticut, 20, 21; right of suffrage in, 74, 79, 81–83, 107, 112, 122, 124, 125, 129–130
Conscription Act of 1863, 205
Constitution, New York (1777), 10, 13, 19, 25–29, 75, 78, 135, 139, 237–238, 246
Constitution, New York (1821): amended, 200; legacy, 201–203, 206, 236–237, 278; second article defining suffrage requirements, 199–200
Constitution, United States, 228, 245–246; absence of the words "slave" or "slavery" in, 117; Bill of Rights, 21; compromises over slavery, 15–16, 21; "emancipating spirit of," 45; Fifteenth Amendment, 6, 201, 204, 205, 210, 292, 295–297; Fifth Amendment, 339; Fourteenth Amendment, 5, 6, 210; "Privileges and Immunities" clause (article 4, section 2), 112, 118, 124–125, 126, 129–130, 131–132, 138; ratification, 21; representation apportioned (article 1, section 2), 118; Thirteenth Amendment, 6, 209
Constitutional Convention, New York (1821), 1, 2, 8, 9, 10, 11, 90–96, 127, 218, 246; characteristics of delegates attending, 334; excerpts, 99–200; law authorizing, 96–99; partisan divisions at, 75
Constitutional Convention, New York (1846), 203, 208; excerpts, 249–259
Constitutional Convention, New York (1867–1868), 205, 210, 278–285, 288–289; petitions to, 278
Convention of the Free People of Colour, 219
Cooper Union, 204
Cornish, Samuel, 212–213

Council of Revision, 31–32, 33, 78
Cramer, John, speaks at the 1821 convention, 100, 158–160
Craven, William, 303
Cuba, 67
Culture, 8, 9

Declaration of Independence, 14, 25, 26, 122, 158, 218, 228, 237, 243, 245–246, 266, 273; quoted, 42, 117–118, 123, 157, 184, 221–222, 224, 247, 251–252
DeKay, Sidney, 309
Democracy, 1, 2, 6, 7, 10, 13, 16, 64, 74, 78, 81, 90; dangers of, 149–150, 171, 179, 201, 257; interracial, 203
Democratic Party, 203, 205, 210, 236, 249, 271, 279, 286, 289, 293, 295, 304. *See also* Republican Party (Democratic-Republican, Jeffersonian), Tammany Hall political organization
Denham, Dixon, 339
Denmark, 208
Dimock, Henry F., 317
Disfranchisement, 28; 34; of African American New Yorkers, 9, 10, 32, 202, 236–237, 241–245, 257; of clergy, 281; and the convention of 1821, 76, 102–142, 174–188, 189, 194, 198–199, 276; and paupers, 282–283; total black disfranchisement proposed, 203; and women, 268
Douglass, Frederick, 208; "What to the Slave Is the Fourth of July," 204, 208
Draft Riots, New York City (1863), 205, 209
Dred Scott decision, 209, 275
Dueling, 144
Durer, John, speaks at 1821 convention, 168–169
Dutch, 4, 14, 17, 18. *See also* New Netherland

Eastwood, Asa, speaks at 1821 convention, 182
Eddy, Thomas, 230

Education, 17, 113, 214, 225–226, 233, 239–240, 268. *See also* African Free School

Edwards, Ogden, speaks at the 1821 convention, 173, 189–191

Elden, John Scott, 185

Elections, 13, 27

Emancipation: immediate, 45, 58, 113, 122, 140–141, 196, 197; merits debated, 34–35, 42, 46. *See also* Abolition; Gradual abolition (New York)

Emancipation Proclamation, 6, 209

Embargo Act, 333

Employment, African Americans in New York, 17, 50, 212

Enforcement Acts, 206, 210, 300, 305

Environmentalism, 50, 340–341

Equality, 6, 9, 10, 16, 43, 47, 57, 77, 106, 158, 184, 185, 219, 225, 228, 231, 245–246, 265, 269, 291

Equal manhood suffrage, 271, 300; first election conducted under the principle of, 205–206, 210, 300–306; guaranteed by the Fifteenth amendment, 205, 295; rejected in statewide referendums, 201, 203, 208, 209, 210, 259, 273, 279, 293

Equiano, Olaudah, 21

Erie Canal, 73, 207

Europe, 11, 265

Evarts, William M., 309, 317

Fairlie, James, 100; speaks at the 1821 convention, 111, 177, 198

Federalist Party, 60, 73, 74, 81; African-American support for, 16–17, 57, 61–62, 64, 76, 145; at constitutional convention of 1821, 75

Fenton, Reuben, 278

Feminism, 204, 265–270, 286. *See also* Seneca Falls Convention; Women

First Colored Presbyterian Church, 212

Ford's Theater, 6

Fort Sumter, 6

Fourth of July, 204, 208, 218, 227, 230

Fox, Charles James, 231

France, 21, 22, 23, 151, 208, 210

Franchise, rules in New York, 25–29. *See also* Freehold requirement for voter eligibility; Suffrage; Voting

Franklin, Benjamin, 214, 231

Freedom, 2, 6, 7, 37–38, 59. *See also* Liberty

Freedom's Journal, 207, 212–217, 218, 219

Freehold requirement for voter eligibility, 26–27, 64, 73, 76, 81–83, 90–91, 136, 165, 170–171, 190, 238, 246, 286, 289; "Appeal to Christians" against, 292–294; conservative defense of at 1821 convention, 146–153, 156, 164, 169; eligibility for voting on the Convention Act, 96, 104, 109, 126; elimination proposed at 1867 convention, 281; Fifteenth Amendment supercedes, 295; imposed exclusively on African Americans, 184–185, 198–199, 201, 236, 238–239, 242, 252–259; pamphlet critiquing, 271–277; plan to circumvent, 260–264; Republican opposition in 1850s, 271; resolution against, 273–274

Freemanship, 331–332

Free Soil Party, 208, 209

Free Suffrage Convention, 273–274

Free trade, 290

French Revolution, 154

Friends, Society of. *See* Quakers

Fugitive Slave Act (1850), 6

Gabriel's Rebellion, 22

Garnet, Henry Highland, 248, 274

Garrison, William Lloyd, 207

Georgia, 140

Gettysburg, 6

Godkin, E. L., 307, 317

Gradual abolition (New York), 8, 26, 33, 39, 132, 186; advocated, 45, 47, 58; defeat of (1785), 30–32; law (1799), 10, 16, 22, 52–55, 57, 67, 127

Grant, Ulysses S., 210
Great Awakening: First, 15; Second, 17, 204, 265
"Great Negro Plot" of 1741, 222
Greece, 242
Greeley, Horace, 278, 285, 288, 289–291
Grenville, William Wyndham, 231

Haiti, 57, 216, 231, 257. *See also* Saint Domingue
Hamilton, Alexander, 39, 57, 60, 62
Hamilton, William, 218–219; speech by, 221–226
Hammon, Jupiter, 20
Hancock, John, 231
Hand, Samuel, 317
Harper's Ferry, 6
Hayes, Rutherford B., 307, 342
Higginson, Thomas Wentworth, 341
Highway service as qualification for franchise, 91, 103, 104, 108, 133, 152, 168, 169, 176, 181, 190, 193
Howe, Samuel Gridley, 341
How the Other Half Lives (Riis), 7
Hudson Valley, 14, 30, 52
Hunt, John, speaks at 1846 convention, 255–257

Illinois, 21; and African American suffrage, 135
Immigration, 3, 7, 61, 65, 252; and naturalization, 29, 282. *See also* Aliens
Independence, United States, 13, 20, 25, 31, 33
India, 233, 242
Indiana, 21; and African American suffrage, 135
Indians, American, 107, 124, 126, 137–138, 139, 157, 242, 243, 252
Ireland, 242
Islam, 258

Jackson, Andrew, 1
Jacksonian democracy, 1, 8
Jamaica, 207
Jay, John, 22, 23, 39, 52, 57, 60, 230, 246

Jay, Peter Augustus, 110, 124, 168, 197, 236; speaks at the 1821 convention, 111–114, 138–142, 179, 196
Jay Treaty, 22
Jefferson, Thomas, 22, 23, 57, 60, 62, 74, 76, 77, 164, 224, 231, 232
Jews, 87, 256, 258, 338
Jim Crow, defined, 3–4. *See also* Segregation
Johnson, Andrew, 342
Johnson, William H., 278
Journal of Commerce, 302
Jury service, 29, 123, 125, 128, 129, 178, 182

Kansas, 6
Kansas-Nebraska Act, 209
Kennedy, John A., 250; speaks at 1846 convention, 253–255
Kent, James, 126; speaks at the 1821 convention, 124–125, 149–153, 178, 188, 189, 196
Kentucky, 22; and African American suffrage, 135
Kidnapping, 17, 67–68, 71
King, Rufus, 60, 168; and Missouri Crisis, 85; speaks at 1821 convention, 99, 126–127, 169–170, 192, 197–198
King George III, 13
Kingston Constitution. *See* Constitution, New York (1777)
Know-Nothings, 209

Ladies Anti-Slavery Society, 204
Land reform, 260–264
Latin America, 23
Liberia, 213
Liberty, 14, 35, 41, 46, 231, 228, 229, 232, 243
Liberty Party, 208
Lincoln, Abraham, 6, 204–205, 209, 249, 271, 273
Literacy: and citizenship, 257; as qualification for voting, 284, 289
Livingston, Peter R., 100, 168; speaks at 1821 convention, 101, 135–138, 154–155, 170

Long Island, New York, 14, 20, 30, 52
Lott, John A., 317
Louisiana, 23; and African American suffrage, 135
Louisiana Purchase, 23, 84
L'ouverture, Toussaint, 22
Loyalism, 33, 34–35

Madison, James, 57
Maine, 81
Manhattan, 13, 14, 73, 77, 87, 205, 206, 256, 295–296, 300; eighth ward, 301, 304; fourteenth ward, 304; ninth ward, 304; twentieth ward, 303. *See also* New York City
Manifest Destiny, 249
Manumission, 16, 20, 39, 42, 68, 180
Marshals, U.S., 300, 302–305
Maryland, 20
Massachusetts, 14, 20, 21, 74, 81, 82, 84, 249
Merrill, William H., 285
Methodists, 281
Mexican-American War, 208, 249, 265
Mexico, 6, 207, 258
Michigan, 21
Military service, 116, 177, 284; absentee balloting for those in service, 297; African American, 19, 33, 108, 114, 115, 119–120, 156, 180, 209, 238, 243–244, 273–274, 281; aliens, 124; and War of 1812, 109, 159, 244, 274
Militia: African Americans excluded from service in, 123, 128, 129, 178, 182; federal law of 1791, 21–22, 108, 114, 116–117; possibility of federal government manipulation of laws regarding, 144–146; New York law governing, 29; service as qualification for voting, 82, 91, 96–97, 103, 104, 106, 109, 110, 132–133, 144, 145, 152, 155, 169, 170, 174, 190; strength of, 157
Miller, Samuel, 40–46
Minstrelsy, 3, 87. *See also* Jim Crow

Miscegenation, 224–225, 257, 258, 271
Mississippi, 23; and suffrage, 104, 135
Missouri, and African American suffrage, 135
Missouri Crisis, 6, 73, 76, 79, 84–86, 89; discussed at the 1821 convention, 100–102, 112, 113, 114, 116, 121, 126, 135
Mob violence, 4
Monroe, James, 18, 23, 156
Moral improvement and reform of African Americans, 225–226, 232, 233, 262
Moral reform, antebellum, 265
Morris, Gouverneur, 26
Mott, Lucretia, 265
Municipal suffrage and governance, 308–317
Murphy, J. K., 303
Murray, John Jr., 230

National Advocate, 87–89
Native Americans. *See* Indians, American
Natural rights, 162, 237, 244, 245, 250, 254–255, 268. *See also* Equality
Nell, William C., 271
"Neutral zone," 14
Nevada, 208
New England, 15, 59, 81, 230. *See also* Connecticut; Maine; Massachusetts; New Hampshire; Rhode Island; Vermont
New Hampshire, 81
New Jersey, 23, 125, 334; and African American suffrage, 252
New Mexico, 208
New Netherland, 4, 14, 18
New Orleans, 67
Newspapers, 16, 33, 36, 87, 94, 289–290; African American, 203, 212–217, 236; and coverage of first equal manhood suffrage election, 300–306
New York Association for the Political Elevation and Improvement of the People of Color, 203

New York City, 4, 14, 20, 21, 39, 52, 74; African Americans in, 17, 56, 114, 116, 135, 212, 257, 258, 275–276; British occupation, 33; celebration of emancipation, 218; fear regarding political influence of, 75, 76, 91, 116, 135, 136–137, 143, 149, 152, 164, 177, 193; first equal manhood election, 300–306; terms of representation under 1821 constitution debated, 188–193; and Tilden Commission, 310; violence against African American ministers, 293. *See also* Draft Riots of New York City (1863); Manhattan
New York City Labor Council, 292
New York City Society for Mutual Relief, 219
New-York Manumission Society, 15, 16, 18, 20, 39–40, 57, 62–63, 68, 223; speeches before, 40–51
New York Tribune, 276
New York World, 288
Noah, Mordecai, 87–89
North Carolina, right of suffrage in, 112
North Elba, New York, 261
Northwest Ordinance, 16, 20
Nullification Crisis, 207

O'Brien, Lawrence, 303
O'Brien, P. J., 303
Ohio, 21, 101; right of suffrage in 105, 135, 252
"Oh! Susannah," 3
"Old Folks at Home [Swanee River]," 3
Ottendorfer, Oswald, 317

Padlock, The (Bickerstaff), 36–37
Paine, Thomas, 337
Pan-Africanism, 233, 234
Panic of 1837, 207
Panic of 1873, 210
Paris Commune, 210
Parker, Theodore, 341
Partisanship: Federalist vs. Republican, 60–62, 64–65, 73–74, 81, 88; Bucktail vs. Clintonian, 74–76; in urban politics, 311

Patronage, 311–312
Patterson, Jack, 274
Paul, Nathaniel, 219–220; speech by, 226–235
Pennsylvania, 15, 19, 20, 21, 30, 34, 52; right of suffrage, 105, 112, 252
Perkins, Bishop, speaks at 1846 convention, 258–259
Personal liberty laws, 6
Peterson, Merrill D., 8
Pickering, Timothy, 60
Pickney, Charles Cotesworth, 60
Pinkster, 17, 18
Pitt, William, 231
Platt, Jonas, 144; speaks at 1821 convention, 145–146, 183–187
Police, 304; guarding the polls, 303; harassment of African American community, 300–301
Polk, James, 249
Popular sovereignty, 137, 140, 154, 162–163
Porter, Peter Buell, 109
Portugal, 209
Poverty, 7, 17, 195, 280
Property, rights and interests of, 42, 105, 109, 115, 155–156, 164, 171, 176–177, 314
Property holding requirement. *See* Freehold requirement for voter eligibility
Public opinion, 171

Quakers: antislavery, 15, 19, 20, 34, 39, 222; eligibility for franchise, 27; fee as alternative to militia service to qualify for franchise, 144; and military service, 29; patriotism questioned, 34–35; persecution of in colonial New England, 186–187

Race, 1, 9, 107; as qualification for citizenship, 75
Racism, 78, 89, 138, 223, 258; criticized, 41, 120, 125, 140–142, 214, 257; cultural, 2; Jefferson and, 57, 224, 244–245; legal, 3; political, 4, 286; popular prejudices, 77, 123, 125, 128, 129, 141–142, 182; "scientific," 77, 255, 256.

Racism, (*Continued*) *See also* African
    Americans, capacity for citizenship
    debated
Radcliff, Jacob, 126, 134, 154;
    speaks at 1821 convention, 135,
    155–156, 172, 193, 195
Ray, Charles, 260–261
Reason, C. L., 248
Reconstruction, 2, 10, 205–206, 210,
    286, 295–296, 307
Referendums on black freehold re-
    quirement, 201, 203, 208, 209,
    210, 259, 273, 279
Registration of voters, 106, 143,
    183, 279–280, 283–285
Religion, 17, 38, 56, 74, 294;
    African American, 113, 186,
    240–242, 292; and equality, 129.
    See also Bible
Religious freedom, 28, 163
Representation: apportionment of
    under the 1821 constitution,
    189–194; virtual, 191
Republicanism, 246–247
Republican Party, 204–205, 209,
    271, 279, 286, 289, 304
Republican Party (Democratic-Re-
    publican, Jeffersonian), 17, 18,
    57, 73, 74, 76, 81, 85; de-
    nounced, 60, 61, 64–65. *See also*
    Bucktail Republicans; Democratic
    Party
Residency requirement for voter eligi-
    bility, 27, 104, 110, 124, 132,
    144, 170, 174, 176, 181, 257,
    279, 281–282, 297
Revolutions of 1848, 265
Rhoades, Elijah, speaks at 1846 con-
    vention, 257
Rhode Island, 19, 20, 21, 81
Richmond, Virginia, 6
Riis, Jacob, 7
Rochester, New York, 204
Rochester Womanís Rights Conven-
    tion, 266
Root, Erastus, 142, 183, 236; speaks
    at the 1821 convention, 114–117,
    144, 153–154, 181, 195
Ross, John Z., 100, 161, 180; speaks
    at the 1821 convention, 105–110

Russell, John L., speaks at conven-
    tion of 1846, 252–253
Russell, Leslie W., 285
Russell, Samuel, 197
Russia, 209, 241
Russworm, John, 212–213

Saint Domingue, 16, 22, 23. *See also*
    Haiti; West Indies
Sanborn, Franklin, 341
Sanford, Nathan, 100; speaks at the
    1821 convention, 103–105
Science, 234
Scott, Sir William, 185
Secret Six, 260
Segregation, 1, 10, 74, 201–203,
    240, 242, 294; in employment, 4,
    212, 236, 257; residential, 236
Seneca Falls Convention, 204, 208,
    265–270
Serfdom, 208, 209, 241
Seymour, Horatio, 210
Shakespeare, William, 155
Sharpe, Peter, 86; speaks at 1821
    convention, 178, 196
Sherwood, Moses, 274
Shklar, Judith, 5
Sidney, Joseph, 57–63
Sierra Leone, 21
Sipkins, Henry, 203
Slaveholders, 47, 49
Slave insurrections, threat of, 251
Slavery, 11, 46, 107, 228, 230, 233,
    281; American, 40–41; and
    Britain, 37; Dutch, 4, 18; effect
    on slaveholders, 44; effects on
    slaves, 44–45; expansion west-
    ward, 271; New York, 4, 14, 16,
    19, 21, 33, 44–45, 67–72, 95,
    136, 179–180, 186, 194–195,
    202, 222; resistance, 14, 33, 222;
    southern, 10, 16, 58, 76, 184,
    203, 209, 215. *See also* Slaves;
    Slave Trade
Slaves, 6; New York, 1, 14, 30, 43,
    49; as property, 48; runaways, 2,
    16, 33, 56, 71. *See also* Slavery;
    Slave Trade
Slave Trade, 14, 15, 16, 17, 20, 21,
    23, 36, 40, 43, 56, 68, 70, 187,

210, 228, 229; end of U.S. participation in international slave trade (1808), 57–58. *See also* Slavery; Slaves

Smith, Elihu Hubbard, 40; speech before the Manumission Society, 46–51

Smith, Gerrit, 260–264

Smith, James McCune, 260–261, 275–276

Smith, Richard, speaks at the 1821 convention, 198

Somerset case, 185

South, 2, 3, 7, 42, 57, 61, 67, 107, 113, 141, 223, 251, 252; and the end of Reconstruction, 307

South Carolina, 140, 207, 209; suffrage in, 145. *See also*, Vesey, Denmark

Spencer, Ambrose, 130; speaks at the 1821 convention, 131–134, 146–148, 187, 198

Stanton, Elizabeth Cady, 204, 265, 286–291

State Central Committee of Colored Citizens, 278

State Convention of Colored Voters, 300

Staten Island, 30

Statutes, 52–55, 64–66, 67–72, 96–99

Stearns, George Luther, 341

Sterne, Simon, 317

Steward, Austin, 248

Stone, William L., 94

Stowe, Harriet Beecher, 288, 290

Strong, George Templeton, 302

Suffrage, 76, 219; revised suffrage clause (1874), 297–298; proposed institution of property requirements for voting on municipal governance, 307, 317. *See also* Freehold requirement for voter eligibility; Voting; Women

Suffrage Convention, 203

Supreme Court, United States, 6, 208, 209, 275

Sutherland, Jacob, 197; speaks at 1821 convention, 170–172, 196

Sweeny, Peter B., 295

Tallmadge, James Jr.: and Missouri Crisis, 84–85; speaks at the 1821 convention, 100–102, 134, 178, 194–195, 196

Tammany Hall political organization, 87, 210, 295, 300, 303

Taxes, 5, 27, 82, 91, 96–97, 103, 104, 106, 110, 129, 159, 170, 175, 176, 178, 181, 267, 283–284, 313, 316

Tayler, John, 86

Teasman, John, 17

Tennessee, 22

Texas, 6

Thomson, Jacob, 293

Tilden, Samuel J., 286, 288, 309, 314

Tilden Commission, 210, 307–317

Tilton, Theodore, 290

Tompkins, Daniel, 18, 23, 68, 75, 110, 230; at 1821 convention, 100, 156; speaks at the 1821 convention, 101, 156–158, 172, 191–192

Topp, William H., 248

Truth, Sojourner, 286–291

Turner, Nat, 207

Ulster County, 30

Universal (male) suffrage, 91–92, 134, 143, 149, 151–153, 163, 168, 169, 170, 172, 173, 175, 176, 185, 203, 285, 288, 291; discussed in Tilden Commission report, 313–315

Utah, 208

Van Buren, Martin, 10, 74, 75, 76, 85, 168, 170, 181, 236; elected president, 207, 236; Free Soil Party presidential nominee, 20; speaks at the 1821 convention, 101, 165–168, 172, 178, 187

Van Cott, Joshua M., 317

Van Ness, William, 168; speaks at the 1821 convention, 192

Van Rensselaer, J. Rutsen, speaks at the 1821 convention, 176–177

Van Rensselaer, Stephen, 108; speaks at the 1821 convention, 110–111

Van Vechten, Abraham, 154; speaks
    at the 1821 convention, 127–130,
    192–193
Vermont, 15, 19, 81, 124, 132
Vesey, Denmark, 207
Vicksburg, 6
Virginia, 23, 59, 61, 184; right of suf-
    frage in, 112, 145. *See also* Turner,
    Nat
Vogelsang, Peter, 203
Voting: African American, 7, 15, 16,
    18, 30, 57, 59, 64–66, 137, 141,
    145, 166, 213, 214, 236, 256,
    302–306; fear of manipulation by
    wealthy, 133, 153; fraud, 64–65,
    74, 81, 172, 176, 198, 258,
    282–285, 297–298, 303; immi-
    grants, 65, 74, 282; poor,
    159–160, 162, 167, 172, 252, 257,
    280, 282–283; and women, 77–78,
    107, 125–126, 161–162, 182, 255,
    267, 283, 290–291

Walker, Quok, 20
War of 1812, 18, 23, 73, 74, 81, 109,
    114, 117, 119–120, 156, 157, 159,
    244, 273
Washington, George, 19, 21, 39, 60,
    61, 62, 157, 231
Watkins, William J., 273; talks ex-
    cerpted, 274–275
West Indian Emancipation Day, 260

West Indies, 14, 36; abolition in
    British West Indies, 207, 208, 231.
    See also Haiti; Jamaica; Saint
    Domingue
Wheeler, Melancton, 170
Whigs, 209
Whitney, Eli, 22
Wilberforce, William, 56, 231
Wilberforce Philanthropic Associa-
    tion, 56
Williams, Elisha, speaks at the 1821
    convention, 161–165, 195, 196
Williams, George, 285
Williams, Peter, 274
Williams, Rev. Peter, quoted, 274
Wilmot Proviso, 208
Wisconsin, 21
Women, 5, 163; and abolitionism,
    204; African American, 88, 126,
    226; and property, 146; and suf-
    frage, 77–78, 107, 125–126,
    161–162, 182, 255, 267, 278, 283,
    290–291. *See also* Feminism;
    Seneca Falls Convention
Wordsworth, William, 277
Working class, 3, 4, 17, 170, 210, 292
Wright, Theodore, 260–261

Young, Samuel, 100, 117, 173; speaks
    at the 1821 convention, 111,
    122–124, 125–126, 174, 178, 180,
    187, 192, 199

About the Editors

David N. Gellman is assistant professor of history at DePauw University. He is the author of a forthcoming book on the abolition of slavery in New York.

David Quigley is assistant professor of history at Boston College. He is the author of the forthcoming *Second Founding: New York City and the Reconstruction of American Democracy.*

DATE DUE

MAY 0 3 2008			

#47-0108 Peel Off Pressure Sensitive